Andrew P. Davidson

IN THE SHADOW OF HISTORY

The Passing of Lineage Society

TRANSACTION PUBLISHERS
New Brunswick (U.S.A.) and London (U.K.)

Library of Congress Catalog Number: 95-25160
ISBN: 1-56000-230-1
Printed in the United States of America

Library of Congress Cataloging-in-Publication Data

Davidson, Andrew Parks
   In the shadow of history : the passing of lineage society / Andrew P. Davidson.
       p. cm.
   Includes bibliographical references and index.
   ISBN 1-56000-230-1 (alk. paper)
   1. Nuba Mountains (Sudan)—Economic conditions—Case studies. 2. Households—Sudan—Nuba Mountains—Case studies. 3. Kinship—Nuba Mountains—Case studies.   4. Economic anthropology—Sudan—Nuba Mountains—Case studies. I. Title.
HC835.D38 ~~1995~~ 1996
306'.09628—dc20   95-25160
                                                                         CIP

This book is dedicated to my parents, Helm and Frances, and to my children, Swati and Malcolm. They all hold a special place in my heart, no matter where our paths may lead.

Contents

List of Tables and Figures

Tables

Preface

This book attempts to explain some of the reasons for the unevenness of development processes and to document some of the consequences on people's lives resulting from their different integration into the modern world. While it is true that people make their own lives, they do so in a world not necessarily of their own choosing. Some benefit; others do not. Wider pressures—in this case modernization—bring about different structures of opportunities and constraints that routinely influence and shape individual decisions and actions. Our starting point, however, is with households and the communities in which they are embedded.

The household, as a basic unit of human social organization, represents, in large measure, a focal point in everyday life. Of course, the ways by which households are organized, the livelihood strategies formulated, and the activities its members carry out vary considerably. But households are not discrete entities; together with other households they form communities which, in turn, are connected to the wider society. In particular, this book reveals how those connections lead to the passing of lineage society and examines the different trajectories taken by three villages in the Nuba Mountains region of the Sudan into the modern world.

This book represents the outcome of an ambitious program of research that began in the mid-1980s and led to nearly two years of fieldwork in a rather remote area of the western Sudan. The initial intent, which changed little over the subsequent years, reflects a long-term interest in the transformation of rural economy and social organization. In the course of these years I have come to dismiss the notions of either disconnected "westernized" and "traditional" societies, or of a monolithic world-system that reduces everything everywhere to so many variations of the West. We must come to realize that there is no absolute logic of development, no "iron law" providing for neat unilinear outcomes in nice unambiguous forms. I hope that this book reconceptualizes development in such a way that the dynamics of historical transformation are made clear.

I first became curious about the Sudan while a student of South Asia—British India, to be exact. In attempts to understand the historical processes of British imperialism on the subcontinent, I became increasingly aware of furtive references to the Sudan, especially after the rise in the demand for cotton and Britain's growing uncertainty of maintaining global hegemony over world trade. Names such as Gordon, Gladstone, and Kitchener were the stuff of legends, but for me they increased my sensitivity to the growing interconnections in the burgeoning world economy. Later, I endeavored to understand just why the processes called modernity and capitalism were so successful in transforming the globe. This led me to begin reading about the Nuba Mountains as an area whose unique landscape and relative remoteness appeared to have suspended it in history. I was wrong.

The Nuba Mountains region was never isolated from the forces shaping the world. For one thing, it comprised a place to which peoples fled in times of turmoil or journeyed to in search of profit. The rugged mountains gave solace because they offered refuge, a haven of safety. It gave profit because historic trading lanes dissected the region and because many individuals calling it home eventually found themselves bonded in slavery. Nevertheless, even in the face of British imperial suzerainty, little progress was made in rationalizing social life and all that ensues. It has only been in recent years that we can begin to talk of the spread of modernity and the creation of a specifically capitalist market, both of which have led to the breakdown in longstanding social relations.

The Nuba Mountains thus presented me with an opportunity to glimpse firsthand the "logic" of modernization—the heavy-handed side as well as its seductive face. As with all social phenomena, it is not possible to accurately pinpoint the exact moment of its inception in the region, but it is a relatively recent arrival. One of the central development issues that this book addresses concerns transition and the absence of a firm division between "modern" and "traditional" societies, capitalist and noncapitalist societies. These ideal-typical situations rarely exist—if at all—in most countries. In light of this, the principle theoretical aims of this study are: to delineate a conceptual framework for household analysis; to discern the nature of the Nuba Mountain's society; and to reformulate the peasant debate with an eye towards recognizing the social complexities of small-scale household-based production.

As with any book, its writing is a rather long, frequently tedious, and always painful process. Now that it is finished, I can look back on the experience and smile, with tremendous gratitude to the many people who made this book possible. Needless to say, many people contributed to this study. My deepest appreciation goes to the people of the Nuba Mountains, especially the villagers of Somasem, Shair Tomat, and Shatt Damam, as well as the people of the provincial capital of Kadugli. Mahdi, Juma'a, Kuku Kaki, Tio, Osman, Umkom, Bakhit, Kubiya, and Faiza are just a few of the people who helped me along the way. They kindly made my concerns and efforts their own. To the degree that this study is a good one, it is due to their infinite patience, insights, and understanding. And now, with reports of genocide in the Nuba Mountains and the forced relocation of women and children to the north—committed by Sudanese troops and paramilitary organizations—I fear for their safety, and I mourn.

My first few months were spent in Khartoum, with Khider Kadaki and his family. Whenever I tired of rural life, I returned to Khider's home where I was always welcomed. Angelo Wani and his family also extended their hospitality to me while I was in Khartoum. Ahmed Al-Dirdiri of the Sudan Agricultural Extension in Shambatt, Mohammed Abu Sabah of the Western Sudan Agricultural Research Project station in Kadugli, Abdul Rahman Al Tilib of the Gezira Board, and Juma'a Silma of the Nuba Mountains Rural Development Project station in Kadugli also deserve special thanks. I also thank the faculty of the University of Khartoum, especially Paul Wani Gore and El Wathiq Kameir, who arranged affiliation for me with the sociology department. Mohammed Salih, a rural sociologist, was also extremely helpful in giving me his insights into the Nuba Mountains.

Special appreciation goes to David Mayo and Abannik Hino, whose understandings of rural Sudanese life provided great insight, and to Ellen Perry, David French, David McPheat, Tin Hta Nu, and Bligh Grant, who gave me immeasurable encouragement. I would also like to thank Christina Groters, who somehow knew that I would eventually finish this project.

But, most of all, I want to thank two people. First, heartfelt thanks goes to Johnson Gom, who traveled with me the first few months in the Nuba Mountains. Without his assistance my life would have been infinitely more difficult. Johnson had a knack with people and provided keen sociological insights, despite having only three years of formal education. In many respects, Johnson represents the hope and potential of the Sudan. Second, I reserve special gratitude for my former doctoral advisor and now colleague, Dr. Harry Schwarzweller, whose intellectual stimulation, arguments, and prodding helped me produce some of my best work. Throughout the years, Harry has also been a friend.

The funds for the fieldwork portion of this study were provided by the National Science Foundation's Divisions of Anthropology and Sociology, and by the Fulbright-Hayes Dissertation Abroad Program. I am grateful for their support.

1

Introduction

The human development experience has been and continues to be uneven, a phenomenon particularly evident in the modernization and restructuring of village life in less developed countries. This book is about such processes of change in the Nuba Mountains region of the Sudan. In particular, this book is concerned with the transformation in the organization and operation of households and about how opportunities and constraints associated with modernization supplant older forms of social relations that are engendered within different systems and within distinctly different contexts. In pace with those changes, the very meanings of older social relations are rapidly being relegated to a distant and often murky past, especially by the youth. And, more importantly, this book is about how individuals, as members of households, struggle to maintain or expand their welfare in the face of continuous uncertainty, when control over their destinies is increasingly slipping out of the comforting confines of the village. In short, I have a story to tell about the unfolding and variegated impact of the spread of modernity and its effects on the everyday lives of people. Like many stories, it is often a sad tale told again and again by those whom history frequently forgets—the stragglers and the dispossessed.

Overview

The Nuba Mountains, along with many other regions in the world, is undergoing enormously complex socioeconomic changes with far-reaching consequences to the well-being of its people. Stimulated by a wide variety of forces, the processes of development are dramatically reshaping village life and connecting, in ever more direct ways, the life chances of villagers to the burgeoning modern world. Of course, the

1

Nuba Mountains have never been immune from external forces that have intruded into the Sudan and northeast Africa. The region's turbulent past is convincing enough evidence.

Historically, the Nuba Mountains offered refuge to those displaced by episodic upheavals along the Nile River and elsewhere—this accounting in part for the diverse ethnic composition of its inhabitants. Interspersed on vast plains, the rugged mountain chains provided a natural haven from this or that empire or world-system. Despite the promise of sanctuary, the Nuba Mountains became a source of slaves and goods of local provenance as the strong preyed upon the weak, further unsettling the area. Later, Anglo-Egyptian rule, bringing a halt to the internecine warfare, introduced cotton production to the fertile plains by relocating whole villages, frequently by force of arms, to the fertile plains below the mountain aeries. And now, the modernization of agriculture and the expansion of product and labor markets appears to press people either to intensify the production of commodities or find other economic alternatives outside of their villages.

The casual visitor to the Nuba Mountains is immediately struck by the rather sharp cultural contrasts that set villages apart, differences that are readily apparent in settlement patterns, expressions of kinship, religious orientations, ties to secular urban centers, types of economic activities, and the organization of work. This impression is reinforced as the visitor traverses the region and as the grip of Arab culture in the north subtly gives way to the Africanized south. Without question, Islam is an important ethnographic fact in most areas of the Nuba Mountains, yet various indigenous belief systems still punctuate the rhythm of life in most villages, and a number of Nuba communities profess Christianity. Also, the location of a village itself attests as much to geographic terrain as it does to its relation with the world outside. Access to resources also varies markedly, as does the utilization of what is produced. Still, this impression, in many ways, rests on the surface. Despite initial conceptions, it soon becomes obvious that villages, in one way or another, are effectively tied into the national state and beyond through labor migration and remittances, cash-cropping and trade, schools and health dispensaries, and water pumps and flour mills. And, of course, the many government agricultural schemes provide a ready source of cash income. Clearly, the Nuba Mountains as a social entity is as much an artifact of its variant cultures as it is a creation of the modern world.

In the course of investigation, questions arise over how to effectively conceptualize and comprehend the variable effects of development presented by the disparate character of the region's villages. Furthermore, within such diverse settings, villagers formulate livelihood strategies to maintain or enhance their welfare. Of course, these strategies reveal the rich mosaic of human needs and perceptions; nevertheless, the consistent patterning of outcomes, when taken together, can disclose the structural characteristics that condition human action. What this implies is that human activity is not random; it necessarily reflects and is limited by context realized by people in the form of constraints. More importantly, constraints are imposed more by circumstances than by intention. But, constraints are not rigid manifestations of "iron laws" because the conditions they create are shaped and reshaped through the course of purposive human action. Put another way, in the quest to locate systematic and meaningful commonalities of behavior, a central concern becomes how to effectively draw together macro- (structured process) and micro- (individual agency) levels of analyses. Household, as an intermediate construct, provides one means to integrate the two levels.

By way of introduction, let us note that a household as a primary corporate social unit may be defined as a group of individuals (seldom one) associated with a particular domicile whose livelihood efforts, in the broadest sense, are directed towards mutual survival. The universal necessity of organizing domestic activities, however, merely magnifies the multiplicity of ways that these activities may be accomplished. Thus, we cannot expect households to necessarily exhibit similar organizational forms nor to carry out the same activities to reproduce themselves over time.

The purpose of this book, then, is to recount the livelihood strategies advanced by individuals as members of households in this particular locality and to better comprehend these strategies through the utilization of appropriate theoretical guidelines. This requires that we take into account the larger context and the forces that are shaping the Nuba Mountains region, and that we trace variant development processes through time and space. Three relatively specific tasks are at hand: (1) categorizing households in ways that are appropriate to the range of domestic collectivities; (2) abstracting from observed behaviors the principle foci of social life and political economy; and (3) furthering our understanding of the nature of rural transformation, particularly the modernization of agriculture and the reorganization of village life. A central analytical challenge, therefore, is to identify the relevant social and economic relations—including their underlying structural "logic"—not only within households, but those relations that link households within the village and to the wider socioeconomic environment. Further, given our concern with household livelihood strategies, additional concerns become the consequences of: (1) commodity and non-commodity production; (2) formal and informal market activities; and (3) wage and nonwage labor.

Optimally, of course, longitudinal data best coincide with this type of pursuit. Unfortunately, practicalities demanded a different course of action, namely cross-sectional research. In order to minimize the risks involved in drawing generalizations from this type of undertaking, sensitivity to variations in household livelihood strategies can be achieved through detailed comparative analysis. For this reason, three villages were selected for detailed study—Somasem, Shair Tomat, and Shatt Damam (see figure 1.1, of the Sudan and Nuba Mountains)—in order to better understand the broad range of opportunities and constraints, which ultimately condition what people ultimately can and cannot do. These villages, more or less, represent the variabilities of social life and economic activities in this diverse Nuba Mountain region.

The Problematic

Fieldwork is invariably preceded by the researcher's interest in specific theoretical and substantive issues. This account is no different; it reflects my own broad interests in the transformation of rural populations or, within the context of the Nuba Mountains, the transition from a lineage-based society to an increasingly modern one. Here, modernization signifies "the increase in the capacity for social transformation" and "is clearly linked with the process of structural differentiation and an increase in the formal rationality of social action" (Roxborough, 1988:756; also see Moore, 1979).[1] In this respect, important concerns include the effects of increased commercial activities and a cash economy on village life, as well as the ways in which economic rationalism and market mechanisms influence village relations. Still, the very rapid pace of modernization in the Nuba Mountains in recent years is different than that which occurred in Europe over a significantly longer period of time,

FIGURE 1.1
Map of the Nuba Mountains, Sudan

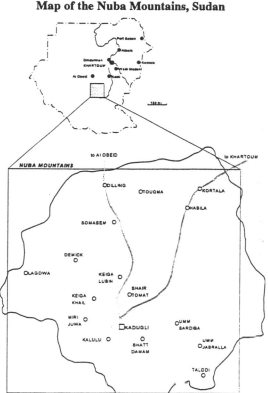

and thus the Nuba Mountains can serve to illustrate how some people contend with such rapidly changing and uncertain situations.

A central aim is to analyze these types of changes through detailing variations in household livelihood strategies and by examination of the social and economic factors affecting the form and function of households. Of course, a crucial element in understanding household livelihood strategies is the distribution and organization of material and nonmaterial resources. A guiding assumption is that a household's access to and utilization of land, labor, technology, and other resources, such as off-farm employment and social networks, engenders specific sets of relations upon which the maintenance and reproduction of the household depends. This, in turn, affords the basis or normative framework crucial to the formation of livelihood strategies and, in effect, determines their subsequent range of possibilities.

This study explores the various strategies set in motion by households in the Nuba Mountains to ensure their livelihoods in a rapidly changing socioeconomic environment. It would be a gross error, however, to assume that a household can and does make livelihood decisions, that a household is a conscious actor in its own right. After all, as Wolf (1991: 32) reminds us, "the household can neither decide or think, since analytic constructs are not so empowered." Too, the reification of household implies that it is a "thing" and removes it from what it is—a particular set of structured social relationships that bind people. However, as soon as we mention individual in relation to household, we have forced a dichotomy. My sense of household precludes this because I am advancing household as a concept that joins individuals within a household unit such that the two are inextricably combined. Within this framework, individuals form livelihood strategies and, as they are members of households, the strategies entail outcomes, favorable and otherwise, for household members and for the household as a whole.

The conceptualization of household is not without inherent difficulty, especially with regard to specifying membership, boundaries, and temporal development. How these issues are ultimately resolved holds great import for social analysis. The use of household as an organizing concept can provide a means to draw together two seemingly disparate levels of analysis: society and the individual or, more reasonably, structure and actor. In other words, the actions of individuals are integrated into the broader underlying structural dynamics through the analysis of household as an important structural unit that mediates the two (Davidson, 1991). As Sorokin (1947:40) so aptly wrote: "The most generic model of any sociocultural phenomenon is the meaningful interaction of two or more human individuals." The household, however, is but one sort of patterned relationship formed under the impress of the ongoing processes of wider social realities; other such structures include economic classes, political entities, ethnic groups, kinship collectivities, religious sects, age grades, and so on.

In order to understand why households follow particular livelihood strategies, households need to be considered according to how they organize activities to ensure their reproduction. Of course, this assumes that each household, through the class locations of its members, dictates of gender, possibilities of age, religious orientations, and responsibilities of kinship, has a certain set of material resources and, within these parameters, formulates livelihood strategies. The household filters the opportunities and constraints presented by the wider society, but always in conjunction with the needs, aspirations, and power of its respective members. Though households are capable of collective action, they are not necessarily democratic institutions, and consequently household strategies embody relations of superordination and subordination (Todd, 1985; Netting, 1993). Consequently, a household should not be thought of simply as an aggregate of individuals, as the sum of its constituent members. Furthermore, while specified social relations are delineated as a condition of household membership (e.g., husband/father, wife/mother, daughter, son, etc.), members are also bound up in social relationships outside of household affiliation, relations that may take precedence over those of the household. Household, as noted, represents but one structural parameter. How a household (through its members) relates to that larger socioeconomic environment will affect the strategies its members can and do adopt. The strategies adopted will, in turn, equally affect the form and operation of the household, the life chances of its members, and, ultimately, its reproduction (or demise) over time. Yet, while the primary unit of analysis is the household, broadly conceived, the research concerns must therefore be addressed at other levels as well. It is also important to note that how households respond to the prevailing circumstances is both cause as well as effect of the development process.

The overarching consideration of this study, as previously noted, revolves around the unevenness of the development process. Although this phenomenon is interpreted in many ways, social scientists remain in disagreement over the continued presence, even resilience, of what is commonly termed the peasantry or smallholders. The theoretical issue that shapes the general orientation of this study is intended to help specify the nature of rural transformation through an understanding of households, as well as the processes that affect changes in their productive activities and social organization. The point is, some households/householders are seemingly able to effectively cope with these changes, albeit in different ways and with different results, while others simply cannot. More importantly, over time significant and sometimes wrenching changes do occur that may expand or undermine the viability of particular types of households.

Regional Context

Though commodity production and participation in market activities are not new to the Nuba Mountains, in the past these were largely intermittent and sporadic. Regularized commodity production, along with the routine sale of labor, began in earnest only in the past few decades (especially after the early 1970s) with the development of mechanized, rainfed farming under the auspices of the Mechanized Farming Corporation (MFC) and the Nuba Mountains Agricultural Production Corporation (NMAPC) (Mahmoud, 1984; Kursany, 1983; and Mohammed, 1982). These state-sponsored schemes were designed to modernize "traditional" agriculture. Earlier British colonial investment in Sudanese agriculture was primarily concentrated in the Gezira Scheme between the two Nile rivers near Khartoum and was aimed at expanding cotton cultivation for export to Manchester textile mills (Barnett, 1977). In the main, the Nuba Mountains remained outside British economic interests, with the exception of limited attempts to promote cotton production through the distribution of seeds and collection of cotton (O'Brien, 1980). Presently, agricultural practices include a complex pattern of production strategies, ranging from complete commercialization to household subsistence. Across the spectrum, however, farming has generally remained a small-scale enterprise.

The major crops of this area are sorghum (which is grown on eighty percent of the cultivated land), millet, sesame, groundnuts, cotton, and gum-Arabic (Mohammed, 1982). Although many basic agricultural activities have not changed, they have taken on added meaning within the context of a market economy. Sorghum and cotton serve as the main cash crops, while sesame and groundnuts primarily supply the local oil handicraft industry (Kursany, 1983). Sorghum is also important in the village exchange-barter system, is used for labor payments-in-kind, and is central to the *shayl* (money lending system).

Similarly, sesame has other "noneconomic" functions and is used for such ceremonial purposes as dowry and brideprice (Badigian and Harlan, 1983). And, while ruminant production remains important, it is probably becoming less so as a symbolic source of wealth and dietary supplement than as a marketable commodity in the regional markets and a hedge against the vagaries of the future.

Located in Southern Kordofan Province, the Nuba Mountains occupy an area about 250 km by 165 km. A plain of clay soil, broken by rugged granitic boulders and mountains (*jebels*) that vary in height and distribution, covers the region. The Nuba Mountains receive about 500 mm annual rainfall, with the rainy season lasting from May to October (Mohammed, 1982). Although annual rainfall is not large and evaporation rates are high, water supply generally has been sufficient to supply crops to maturity (Badigian and Harlan, 1983). Nevertheless, the region is ecologically fragile, as recurring drought conditions emphasize, and thus requires highly diversified agricultural practices to avoid disaster.

Recent studies have shown that the basic structure of agriculture, and of rural life in general, is undergoing significant alteration. Traditionally, the most common form of land tenure was communal ownership, with land distributed among village members, usually along lineage or kinship lines (Khalafalla, 1982; Hadari, 1974). Under this system, land is heritable but cannot be sold. Farmers usually cultivate two or three nonadjacent plots, which combined are less than 10 feddans—1 feddan = 1.038 acres (Mohammed, 1982). A small supplemental garden plot (*jubraka*) near the household compound is generally worked by women. During the past decade, state and private ownership of land have increased (Mahmoud, 1984; Kursany, 1983). In these forms, land usage is restricted to tenants of the Mechanized Farming Corporation or the Nuba Mountain Agricultural Production Corporation schemes, or to private owners. In addition, some private and, especially, state landholdings, that occupy thousands of feddans of arable land, are creating increasing conflict over access to land and have resulted in the displacement of numerous pastoralists and peasant agriculturalists (Shepard, 1983). Finally, the expansion of mechanized farming has squeezed resources, pushing small cultivators into areas that have become marginal as their natural fertility is sapped.

The composition of the labor force is also undergoing major changes. Although family labor is still the most important source, wage labor is slowly replacing the communal labor exchange system (*nafir*) (O'Brien, 1980). Increasingly, some household members are finding it necessary to devote more of their time to laboring away from the farm. In fact, according to Kursany (1983), more than fifty percent of active family members sell their labor power at some point in the year, while more than one-quarter resort to hiring outside wage labor for production activities. Reasons for this include the increasing nuclearization of the family household unit, competing off-farm employment opportunities, and production of commodities for market. For example, the nafir is generally used only to assist in the production of subsistence crops and not in crops for sale in the market, payment being in-kind. Moreover, nafir, as a rule, is limited to labor-intensive activities such as weeding and harvesting, while wage labor can be used for all activities. As a result, "push" factors are reenforced, while "pull" factors multiply.

Technological changes are also evidenced by the spread of both government-sponsored mechanization schemes and privately rented tractors directed at small farmers. This has altered the traditional division of labor, although its full implications have not been well documented (O'Brien, 1983). These changes—plus the spread of small village-based mechanized flour mills, relatively inexpensive consumer goods, the commercialized sale of water, and state taxation—have created a greater need for cash income (Khalafalla, 1982). In effect, this necessitates the sale of labor and/or commodities for cash. As a result of increased cash needs, many farm households find that even after a good harvest, seldom is there enough to see them through to the following year. Some households find that they must "mortgage" their crop for credit to the village merchant (*shayl*) at a price below market value (Kursany, 1983). In many instances, this practice leads to the merchant's gaining control over the household's production and marketing decisions.

Theoretical Perspectives

One of the difficulties in analyzing rural transformation is in deriving categories that reflect the exigencies presented by the wider structural, cultural, and historical contexts, yet also accounting for local specificity (including individual agency). As is becoming increasingly obvious, development does not proceed in a straightforward manner; rather, it is a multidimensional and complex process that is fraught with conflict and tension. In the course of fieldwork this becomes immediately evident. In such regions as the Nuba Mountains, the rich diversity in the organization of production and exchange—both capitalist and noncapitalist—has proven to be a recurrent enigma in development studies (Vandergeest, 1988). Problems inevitably arise when integrating theory with empirical observation, and they are especially evident in underlying explanations of rural transformation. Disagreements center around how to conceptualize these multiform societies, particularly when

TABLE 1.1
Size of Plots Cultivated in the Nuba Mountains Area, 1979/80[3]

Total Area of Cultivated Plots in *Feddans* (N=161)					
0.0–5.0	5.1–10.0	10.1–15.0	15.1–20.0	20.1–30.0	>30.0
31.8%	36.0%	15.5%	9.3%	3.1%	4.3%

(*Source*: Mohammed, 1986).

most economic activities are undertaken by small-scale household-based enterprises, or what is commonly referred to as the peasantry in Third World situations. The Nuba Mountains region is no different. Research indicates that agriculture in this region remains dominated by "traditional smallholders," with nearly sixty-eight percent of farmers cultivating 10 feddans or less (table 1.1) (Mohammed, 1986). Manufacturing, too, has made little headway, with Kordofan accounting for a mere 3.3 percent of Sudan's industrial labor force (Ali, 1980:167).[2] Within such societies, just how do people cope? And, more importantly, what is the "logic" behind their coping strategies?

The debate over the tenacity of smallholders, or the peasantry, resides largely in the effects of modernization and the ensuing integration of households and enterprises into a specifically market economy. Scott (1976), for example, forwarding the cause of moral economy, suggests that the transition to a market-oriented economy further reduces the economic viability of the poorer families in a village, enhancing only the life chances of the wealthy. Popkin (1979), on the other hand, argues the case of rational economy and concludes that the commercialization of agriculture increases opportunities for rural families to improve their welfare and security. I suspect that the answer cannot be easily reduced to questions of moral vs. rational economy. For our purposes, then, we need to come to terms with two seemingly contradictory tendencies: (1) the subjectivist logic of household production where commodity sales/purchases (especially wage-labor) present adaptive strategies to the then prevailing circumstances and where resource allocation remains, on the whole, a family affair, and (2) the increasing economic differentiation among the rural populace and the attendant decomposition of household-based production as evidenced by the increase of on-farm wage-labor, off-farm employment, and increased scale of operation.

What the development debate also suggests is that the issues involved in rural transformation—particularly those associated with modernization—are extremely complex and require far more sensitive theorization, moving beyond a single deductive logic "which identifies variation as systematic, but which theorizes it as unique or anomalous" (McMichael and Buttel, 1990:97). In other words, empirical evidence points to the fact that rural transformation belies propositional outcomes or axiomatic universals. Research in advanced industrial countries alone points to the unevenness of the development experience; there is no reason why it should be less so in the Third World. Unquestionably, the intensification of commodity production and market activities imparts definite and distinct implications for smallholders. Yet, the long-term outcomes of this process remain tentative. Most of the classical theorists (Marx, Weber) contend that market forces and competition will cause the demise of small-scale producers, leading eventually to the formation of a bifurcated system comprised of a small entrepreneurial class of property owners and a large class of wage earners dependent solely upon the sale of their labor. In contrast, the persistence perspective (Chayanov, Sahlins) emphasizes the internal dynamics of small-scale producers to effectively resist the rationalization of production through their ability to reduce consumption and use unpaid household labor.

Despite obvious differences, both perspectives suffer similar shortcomings in their ability to illuminate. Aside from a singular deductive logic, there is a tendency within the former perspective, particularly structural versions, to err towards linear, teleologic, and deterministic explanations of socioeconomic change (Davidson, 1989; Benton, 1984). On the other hand, the latter perspective, focusing solely on the internal dynamics of the household, forces a homogenous depiction of the peasantry and explains "changes in the composition and economic organization of the household mainly in terms of internal demographic and social processes" to the neglect of the "impact of forces external to the household itself" (Long, 1984:6). Certainly, household operations, where much of the labor derives from family members and where labor costs can be held to a minimum, are quite adaptable and tenacious in the face of unfavorable prices and economic hard times. Observed instances, however, reveal that neither scenario is necessarily inevitable; neither the decomposition nor persistence of smallholders is preordained as a determinant outcome of contemporary development (see Davidson and

Schwarzweller, 1995; Whatmore, et al., 1991; and Marsden, et al., 1990). Imposing such rigorous consistency on rural transformations tends to obscure more than it reveals about developmental processes. What must be borne in mind is that the local basis of economy is being continuously redefined in various ways and with different results such that the current modernization of rural life reflects a multitude of different trajectories across time and space. As Cooper (1981:309) recognizes in the African context:

> It is...questionable to see 'proletarianization' as the last stage of a direct sequence: independent cultivator to peasant to impoverished cultivator to worker. Some peasants did not become workers; some cultivators became workers because they could not become peasants; some workers became peasants. Some areas that were the least connected to export markets before the colonial era became the leading suppliers of workers, while some of the most incorporated were the least 'proletarianized.'

Thus, if we are to move beyond preconceived notions of rural transformation, we must account for a variety of organizational forms and directions in rural change in order to lend credence to historical and locational specificities.

Out of the impasse posed by the two seemingly incompatible polemics, Friedmann (1978, 1980, 1986a, 1986b), in particular, has attempted to revitalize the debate over small-scale household production by reconstructing and synthesizing the theoretical arguments advanced by both the decomposition and persistence perspectives. Such an endeavor traverses the discrepancies between macro- and microlevel approaches and combines elements associated with market domination and the noneconomic characteristics of household-based production units. Friedmann's reconceptualization of small-scale household production in terms of "simple commodity production" both maintains the integrity of the household by use of "double specification" of the internal characteristics of the household and the external characteristics of the wider society. Her approach thus allows for a household form of production based on the household's internal relations, while recognizing the importance of pressures exerted by the encompassing socioeconomic complex that impinges upon the household and sets limits to the range of livelihood possibilities (Bouquet and de Haan, 1987).

Nevertheless, Friedmann's ideal-type fails to effectively allow for a more discreet variability, does not adequately identify the major types of units subsumed under "simple commodity production," nor does it facilitate a closer examination of how various economic and noneconomic elements interrelate. What is required is a better understanding of the manner by which households begin to rationalize production and the effects this has on the household's form and function. Hence, a more useful starting point is to consider how people organize and secure their subsistence and, more generally, how they secure their livelihoods (Moore, 1988; Fernandez-Kelly, 1982). In these terms, different livelihood practices, including social networks and other cultural devices, command different loyalties among their adherents, not just between different localities but within the same locality as well. While recognizing that substantive inquiries do have certain inherent limitations, it is important to recognize that people do act according to different "logics," though logics ineluctably grounded in broader considerations.

Broadly, this type of approach focuses on the critical technical, economic, and social variables operating within households, as well as on the extra-household relations in which they are embedded. This way, even residence of household members, demographic composition, and kinship can be potential elements of strategies, not just what is planted and who engages in what type of labor. Thus, at the village level, this approach specifies the structural linkages that internally differentiate and externally connect variant households, while within the larger society it vertically positions these households. Depending upon circumstances, then, changes within the wider society may broaden or limit opportunities for diversification of livelihood strategies and may reinforce or weaken older forms of social organization. Each element of a household's strategy, in turn, is conditioned by the other. The presence of external opportunities, however, provides competing alternatives within which households may diversify, change, or abandon current strategies. The ability to alter present strategies is, nonetheless, shaped by strategies previously adopted in response to then-prevailing socioeconomic and physical conditions, so that, once pursued, livelihood strategies create their own social and organizational constraints to the expansion or intensification of various economic activities.

Not only will such an approach free us from preconceived constructs of development and livelihood strategies, but it frees us from fixed definitions of household forms in the narrow sense and opens up the variability in its concrete manifestations that we seek to explain (Spiegel,

1986). Thus, we can speak of different types of households and strategies, not only through empirical construction, but by systematically detailing the various contexts within which household livelihood strategies unfold.

Field Research and Village Selection

The information gathering approaches chosen for this study were tailored to meet the specific requirements of doing research in the Nuba Mountains, about which there is very scanty data. The information collected represents a rich blend of qualitative and quantitative information; the former help strengthen generalizations derived from the latter by fleshing out the analysis. While quantitative data lend themselves to uncovering patterns of structure, we run the risk of overrunning their deeper contextual meaning without collaborating qualitative information, which serves to verify the validity of quantitative data as well as to underscore the importance of human agency.

In the course of fieldwork, the researcher is faced with a dilemma: when does the point of diminishing returns mitigate the benefits gained from enlarging the study area. In part, this rests on the types of questions the research seeks to answer. For me, one village, a case study, was not sufficient. While understanding household strategies in a single village, it was not possible to generalize outside of that context or to fully explore the significance of different household strategies. In drawing conclusions, two villages lend more confidence by enabling a deeper understanding of important structural variations. Still, there is insufficient variation to provide adequate insight into larger processes that shape strategies. This comes only with increased variation in structural conditions. And while four villages may have contributed to increased ability to generalize, advantages fell short of the additional headache encountered in managing such a project, let alone in analyzing the data.

The three villages studied were Somasem, Shair Tomat, and Shatt Damam (see figure 1.1). The villages lie roughly on a north/south continuum extending from Dilling, a primary market town, to Kadugli, the provincial capital. At first glance, the most visible differences among the villages have to do with their topography, which partially tells the story of their settlement, of their inhabitants departure from their mountain havens. Somasem and Shair Tomat stand out on the expansive plains, while the construction of Shatt Damam reflects its residents' continued ambiguity towards the world outside. The majority of householders here reside on the rugged slopes of the protective jebels, with only a few living quarters erected on the plains floor near the market center. In part, the answer abides in the fact that the Shatt have few farms located at a distance to draw them further afield, as did the Ghulfan of Somasem. Nor were they relocated as were the original inhabitants of Shair Tomat. Still, the Shatt remain leery of alien intrusion and retain a high cultural attachment to their ancestral *dar,* or homeland.

Upon careful observation, the routine of everyday life discloses the integration of the villages into the outside world. Village inhabitants readily recognize the effects of integration as new ways of doing things: tractors plough vast tracts of land, which necessitates the hiring of labor; lorries haul commodities and villagers to market; tea is steeped for those too busy to do so themselves; brideprice increasingly requires the addition of store-bought goods; family, friends, and neighbors periodically or permanently leave the village confines in search of education or employment; and so on. More importantly, all of these changes involve the mediation of money and, hence, the need for it. Some people look contemptuously on these changes, fearful of the consequences for the old way of life. Others see them as wonderful opportunities and avidly pursue them with the zeal of missionaries, labeling apostates as "backwards." Still others feel uneasy with the new economic realities and, finding few alternatives, reluctantly enter the labor and product markets. No one is without an opinion on the subject, and few have escaped its effects altogether. Table 1.2 depicts the broad means by which the three villages were integrated into the wider economy, taking note of the primary types of outside employment opportunities open to the villagers and the dominant source of capital available to them as well.

TABLE 1.2
Primary Means of Economic Integration of the Three Villages

Village	Outside Employment	Source of Capital
Somasem	semiskilled labor	local merchant capital
Shair Tomat	skilled labor	government capital (NMAPC[4])
Shatt Damam	unskilled labor	outside merchant capital

The selection of the three villages centered primarily on the basis of differences in access to and utilization of land, labor, and technology. As agriculture is the dominant activity in this region, it was assumed that factors affecting its organization would exert the greatest impact on household livelihood strategies. Labor thus provides an immediate insight into the developmental processes shaping the villages and indicates a household's general socioeconomic orientation. Table 1.3 displays for each village percentages for primary types of labor used for main farm cropping activities and the mean size of the main farm—wage labor in Somasem, family/household in Shair Tomat, and nafir in Shatt Damam.[5] (Somasem farmers employing tractors do not perform a first weeding, as plowing makes this task unnecessary.) Certainly too, the historical and cultural backgrounds of the three villages differ markedly, as suggested by their means of integration into the wider Sudanese complex. Nevertheless, the three villages were matched in all other respects insofar as possible. Commonalities included approximate distance to regional markets (market and employment opportunities), agricultural services (such as extension), village services (education, flour mills, and water), and the presence of a general store (local merchants). Of the three villages, Shatt Damam appears to be the least directly affected by modernizing pressures, while Somasem exhibits extensive elements of modernization. Shair Tomat lies somewhere in between.

The basic characteristics of the three villages are summarized as following:

TABLE 1.3
Source of Household Labor for Main Farm Cropping Activities by Village
(Percent of feddans cultivated and sacks of sorghum/millet threshed by type of labor.)

	Somasem	Shair Tomat	Shatt Damam
Activity	Wage	Family	*Nafir*
clear	29.3	91.1	16.9
plow	90.7	65.7	8.3
1st weeding	2.4	67.2	35.4
2nd weeding	53.6	82.4	5.5
harvest	61.0	82.1	34.3
threshing	74.2	67.1	18.4

1. Somasem: The inhabitants of Somasem are "Arabized" Nuba and have lost much of their earlier "Nuba" past. At 16.2 feddans, the mean size of main farms is the largest of the three villages. Not surprisingly, the use of tractors is widespread. Farmers generally rely on wage labor for most but the easiest agricultural tasks. By lorry, this village lies four hours north of Kadugli and one and a half south of Dilling on the tarmac road connecting the two. Somasem is situated on the plains, though the majority of its settlers relocated here from surrounding jebels to be near their main farms. This occurred only after the cessation of violence permitted a degree of security for those opting to remain on the more fertile land.

2. Shair Tomat: Shair Tomat was established around 1932, when the British relocated a group of Hawazma Arabs residing in Daloka with instructions to "take up farming" and desist from slave raiding. The mean size of main farms is 13.2 feddans and are worked primarily with family labor. While the use of tractors is considerable, their use remains limited to cotton fields plowed by the Nuba Mountains Agricultural Production Corporation (NMAPC) at Kadugli. This village, one and a half hours north-northeast of Kadugli by lorry, is the most difficult to reach of the three. While it is possible to get there by lorry during the dry season, generally one gets off at the tarmac road running between Kadugli and Dilling and walks in.

3. Shatt Damam: Although it is changing, Shatt Damam still retains strong vestiges of its matrilinear past and remains predominantly "African" in its cultural orientation. The mean size of main farms is the smallest of the three villages, at 5.4 feddans, and is worked by hand with extensive use of nafir labor, although family labor is also important. This is a relatively old village, approximately one hour by lorry south of Kadugli on a seasonal road. The villagers relation with the non-Shatt outside world remains tentative at best.

Three Village Household Survey

A difficulty in analyzing household strategies is the confusion over unit of observation and unit of analysis. Residence is a unit of observation, while the unit of analysis is a household. What I am suggesting is that residence is only the starting point for unraveling and constructing a household. Our ultimate goal, however, is not to dwell on residence per se but to deconstruct residence and reconstruct household as a meaningful unit of analysis. Residences are merely a physical boundary, while household must allow us to explore the meaning of that boundary and, therefore, to shift from physical proximity as the criteria of the household to the concept of membership itself as a foundation of the household. What this allows is going beyond an a priori construct of household to exploring the variability of that boundary.

Initially, each residential unit was questioned as to membership, age, and sex of members; number of feddans farmed/owned; and number and types of ruminants.[6] In order to ensure accuracy of the enumeration of residential units, the results were checked against the village sugar rationing lists and any discrepancies discussed with the village *sheikhs*. At this time, I also separated male from female headed residences. Female headed residences included divorcees, widows, and females whose spouses either were long-term migrants or who had abandoned them. Following this, I stratified residential units by landholding size and/or by numbers of ruminants, as well as by those with substantial business interests. A purposive sample was thus possible for the selection of the respondents by sex of residential head and by this crude wealth indicator.

During this phase I began to recompose residential units into households, moving beyond the requirement of physical residence to a criteria that reflected a certain regularized degree of consumption, production, and reproduction, as well as a shared feeling of "belongingness." The major difficulty of such a task cannot be overstated because since the criteria themselves are also part of livelihood strategies, they do not remain constant. This necessitated careful questioning on both quantitative and qualitative dimensions with both residential heads and local village informants. In this manner, I picked up some migrants who otherwise might have been excluded, grouped together separate residences into single households, and split residences into separate households even though they were located within the same compound.[7] The recomposed households make the analysis of livelihood strategies more comprehensible and subsequent patterns of residence more reflective of the dynamic and fluid quality of households. Aside from the occasional migrant, the bulk of the recomposition of households was accomplished during the enumeration of residences. Table 1.4 illustrates the final sample drawn from the population of households.

TABLE 1.4
Sampling Distribution of Household Heads by Village and Sex
(Population figures are in parenthesis.)

	Somasem	Shair Tomat	Shatt Damam	Total
Male	46 (128)	23 (32)	50 (187)	118 (348)
Female	14 (36)	7 (12)	10 (27)	32 (74)
Total	60 (164)	30 (44)	60 (214)	150 (422)

The core of data provided a basis for establishing patters of relationships. Information was collected on individuals, but as members of households. Individuals or individual behavior per se, in and of themselves, reveal little of consequence for social analysis, rather my concern is with social relationships set against the backdrop of structure and process. In the end, the unit of study is social relationships and not the individual.

The Problematic Revisited

To resummarize the problematic, I am arguing that household, despite its conceptual vagaries, sustains sufficient commonality in usage to derive an effective unit of analysis. As a specific cluster of social relations, household assumes a universal presence, though not necessarily in its organizational forms, nor in the activities its members undertake in its name. Needless to say, households appear in a remarkable array of diversity across space and time. Consequently, we begin with household as a generalized notion rather than attempting a composite image that can account for all households—past, present, and future. In other words, although households may share certain basic similarities, they are not necessarily historically the same, nor should we expect them to be. At this level of abstraction, I propose that household be characterized as a site of biological and social reproduction. Beyond this, appropriation of empirical material enables us to discern specific types of households. Clarification of this comprises an important aim of this study.

Household presents one means by which individuals are grouped, although an especially important one where small-scale production predominates and the household is an effective unit of both production and reproduction, business enterprise and domestic group. In addition, by approaching household as a middle-level construct, empirical variations can become more manageable and still accommodate theoretical exigencies. This requires that we understand the peoples who make up households, as well as the setting of their daily lives. In this way we expect to see different household forms and functions. Above all, household formation and dissolution is an active process, identifiable through its constituent activities that are reflected in the livelihood strategies adopted by the respective households.

The case of the Nuba Mountains also presents an opportunity to understand various aspects of development processes. And for our purposes, how individuals as members of households respond to the opportunities and constraints presented by newer forms of social organization and productive activities is particularly revealing. Accordingly, we will be able to shed light on the general process of rural transformation and on the notion of peasantry. I thus seek to illustrate a means for the theorization of the effects of modernization on small-scale production, providing a way to conceptually differentiate types of households. And, since my goal is to analyze the basis of the parameters regulating the conditions within which household livelihood strategies are formed, historical specificity demands the study of real instances. Hence, the shift from household forms to the consequences of livelihood strategies necessitates a shift from conceptual to historical analysis. Moreover, my focus on household and livelihood strategies as active processes generates a means to interpret development without disregarding human agency.

Organization of the Book

The foremost task is to develop a broad understanding of what households look like and what its members do. Chapter 2 provides a brief theoretical discussion of household as well as initial empirical observations of the surveyed households in the three villages. The historical description in chapter 3 provides a basis to formulate a framework within which to locate our empirical starting-point by outlining the historical development and ecological context of the Nuba Mountains. Chapters 4, 5, and 6, respectively, deal with: (1) the Nuba Mountains as a social complex, paying particular attention to the formation and transformation of lineages; (2) the extent of modernizing pressures, including the spread of capitalism in the region, through examination of twelve villages; and (3) construction of categories of household (re)production and social differentiation. The preceding chapters supply the grounding and categories of households necessary to effectively analyze livelihood strategies in Somasem, Shair Tomat, and Shatt Damam. The results are reported in chapters 7, 8, and 9. The concluding chapter is not really a conclusion in the sense of a perfunctory summation but an effort to weave together the disparate threads of the various chapters so that important inferences can be drawn.

Notes

1. But as Roxborough (1988:756) reminds us: "the word 'capacity' does not imply that this capability is actually used, nor that it is used in any sense 'optimally'." There is, thus, considerable room for variability in the modernization process; hence, we can talk of uneven development.
2. Kordofan includes both North and South Kordofan provinces. Most of the industrial labor force is outside of the Nuba Mountains in El-Obeid, Dilling, and Babanusa.
3. Table 1.1 is abstracted from Mohammed (1986:126). He lists landholdings by region and, essentially, considers all farmers outside of the government-operated schemes to be smallholders. Mohammed (p. 116) estimates that "traditional agriculture" provides the livelihood for some 380,000 smallholders.
4. Nuba Mountain Agricultural Production Corporation.
5. For a more detailed account of source of household labor by each of the three villages, see Appendix 1.
6. This included pigs for the village of Shatt Damam. Getting an accurate number of animals, especially cows, can prove very difficult. In order to cross check this, I frequently went to the *seraf* (watering hole) and question the young men as to whose animals they were tending and then make a count. At other times it was possible to cross check this with information gained from other relatives or neighbors. Needless to say, sometimes I was left with deflated numbers.
7. This point cannot be overstated. In the Nuba Mountains, for example, many husbands are forced to seek their livelihoods in distant locations such as Khartoum. Due to the difficulty of domestic travel, travel to their home villages may be infrequent. Yet, this should not automatically preclude household membership. Moreover, a migrant may maintain a household in his village and yet be part of a separate household in the capital.

2

Households, Activities,
and Livelihood Strategies

At first glance, the identification of households in the Nuba Mountains seems to be a straightforward, if not perfunctory procedure. On the surface each domestic compound imparts the sense that they are readily isolable into household entities and, hence, readily understandable. Perhaps it is the repetitive, obvious appearance of domestic compounds that renders their enumeration seemingly problematic. There are observable differences—in the number of sleeping quarters and granaries, composition of membership, productive activities, and kinship networks. But on the whole, these seem to be minor variations that are secondary to the household itself. Closer inspection clearly reveals that this is wrong. What this assumes is that we are able to detach households from the wider empirical setting, to atomize them, and still to theorize their existence. In effect, by separating households from the environment within which they are located, we lose perspective on the very meaning of household and, consequently, on the reason households assume different forms and take on different activities.

In order to transcend this assumption, two interrelated approaches are necessary. The first requires the explication of household; that is, a broad description of the organizational structure—including composition, boundary, and activities. The second, to be taken up in later chapters, entails a consideration of the wider forces that impinge on each household, allowing greater understanding of the cumulative patterns of household forms and functions. What will lend coherence to these seemingly disparate tasks will be the analysis of the livelihood strategies advanced by these households through its members, strategies manifested as household-based activities. In short, we must relate what households look like with what individual members do in order to gain insights into household as both an active entity and a dynamic process.

Theoretical Considerations: Rethinking Household

In recent years the analysis of "livelihood strategies" has received considerable attention from a diverse range of social scientists.[1] Attempts to understand livelihood strategies, in turn, have led increasingly to a focus on the household as a meaningful unit of analysis. A review of the literature, however, quickly reveals that household is at once a multidimensional concept that seems to defy attempts to analytically fix its meaning, particularly in such areas as the Nuba Mountains, with its turbulent history and diverse sociocultural milieu. As an organizing concept, household nonetheless retains certain analytical appeal. In part, it is assumed that the household bears some sort of universal presence, that it is "more cross-culturally comparable than many more frequently studied institutions" (Netting et al., 1984:xxvi; see also Netting, 1993). But that is just the point. It is not necessary that we establish a rigid, universal definition of household, merely that we agree on a working definition that takes into consideration its dynamic and fluid nature. And for us, household is characterized as a site of biological and social reproduction, whose members, broadly speaking, attempt to ensure some sort of "mutual" survival (at least in the short-run and however defined).

We expect variations in households according to what is popularly termed life cycle or life course. But what is of even greater interest is why some households evidence substantive differences in their life course experiences while others do so in anticipated chronological ways. Why, for example, is the hiring or selling of wage labor a condition of existence for some Nuba Mountain households, while others continue to meet their labor needs through nafir, and still others with a mixture of both? Rethinking the problem of household, Wilk and Netting (1984:4) assert that such "questions involve relating both the morphology *and* functions of household groups to each other and to wider social, economic, and cultural realms." Rather than concentrate on household variations as simply arising from life cycle, then, analysis must view the development cycle of the domestic group as "a movement governed by its relations to the external fields" (Fortes, 1958:2).

Furthermore, most analyses of life cycle tend to harmonize household interests and goals which, in effect, naturalizes the domestic division of labor to the particular stages. This reveals little about the actual social relations through which activities are organized, labor is deployed, and resources are distributed within the household, and even less about the material practices and ideologies that underpin these relations (Whatmore, 1991). When placed alongside the household, for instance, relations of authority and dominance produce distinct outcomes. Decisions, for example, may be imposed through heavy handedness, arrived at through consensus, or pursued independently, depending on the changing configuration of household members that individuals relate to over the course of their lives and the institutional sources of authority (Davidson, 1991). Thus, if we are not to treat the household as an unproblematical, internally coherent entity, it is necessary to understand variabilities both within and beyond households. As noted, this requires an account of a household's internal characteristics, dynamics, and activities, but in conjunction with the external pressures brought to bear on this unit.

What must be continuously borne in mind is that various social relations exert strong pressures on households that are differentially realized and experienced by household members. There is, therefore, the need to "distinguish roles and positions of the various household members" in order to grasp the implications of household as a structuring agent (Hareven, 1987). More importantly, economic and noneconomic social relations must be considered as equally significant in their own right; together these can provide the analytical tools necessary to unlock the concept of household. The fate of individual members diverges since "imperatives and choices are shaped by their position in the family, by the economic and social structures in which the household is located, and by the processes of change which these structures are undergoing" (Tilly, 1975:138). How a household and its constituent members are eventually situated in the context of the wider environment has much to do with such principles as ownership of resources, rules of inheritance, the sexual division of labor, and age-based seniority. These, in turn, provide a foundation for household norms and set parameters on the possible structural forms households may assume and, in addition, to the types of activities its members may or may not perform. The household, in effect, mediates the opportunities and constraints with reference to these wider parameters but according to the internal division of labor and the differential distribution of resources by such lines as marital status, gender, and age.

Household Reformulated

Despite some calls for the abandonment of household as a conceptual construct (see Aijmer, n.d., and Guyer, 1981, 1984), household can provide a useful entry point for social analysis. In light of criticisms, the explication of household must begin with modest aims and requires that we exercise great caution, and some daring as well. Throughout this discussion, the concept "household" is understood to be a structured process and not a thing apart. Therefore, the question of invariable boundary is unconscionable; it remains a matter of logical and empirical credence. Boundaries in the quantitative sense can exist only as an existential moment in time, secure only at specified instances. "What the boundaries of any given unit of analysis are," comments Roxborough (1979:52), "is therefore an historical question and cannot be settled before hand by theoretical deliberation except in an abstract way."

What must be understood is that we unravel households in the phenomenal forms in which they appear. Accordingly, we begin with households broadly conceived and, by differentiating them according to their means of integration into the larger system, we are able to systematically establish their criterion of existence. Even after establishing a household relation, its precise nature is not always immediately clear.[2] Cash remittances by migrating members of split-labor households, for example, may strengthen a household or signal its imminent breakup. Or, the presence of wage labor on family farms may signify the dominance of capital relations or simply an irregular means of exchange. Here historical movement based on empirical fact-finding remains important for subsequent theoretical generalizations, fleshing out the organizational logic of the various households. By this, and at variant analytical levels, we are able to differentiate households into increasingly more manageable units.

In order to proceed to an understanding of the household that is discursive rather than intuitive, then, formal structure and rules give way to fluid, interactive sets of social relations. Households thus require investigation into the meaning of boundary, advancing from physical proximity to an understanding of membership itself as the basis of the household. What this means is that members do not have to be physically present to be part of a household, nor does an individual's membership in one household automatically preclude membership in another. On the other hand, individuals sharing a physical residence may not constitute a household. By transcending the arbitrary isolation of household it becomes possible to include such members as migrants, those with multiple residences, and individuals with membership in more than one household.[3] Households, in other words, are expressed in social relationships (which are realized in activities), while residence units supply physical indicators.[4]

The universal necessity for organizing residence should merely underscore the sheer diversity in the ways this can be accomplished and not set an absolute limit through ideal types. By breaking out of the strict confines of physical residence, we will be able to grapple with the following concerns:

1. Under what conditions is household a useful entry point from which to proceed to understanding livelihood strategies?
2. What clustering of social relations does household encapsulate?
3. What are the conditions of existence for differing households and their effect on livelihood strategies?
4. How do various processes differentially incorporate households into the wider system and to what effect?

Households and Livelihood Strategies

Human responses to social situations are seldom—if ever—crafted in isolation from life experiences. Individuals confront the social terrain from different perspectives and formulate livelihood strategies on the basis of past decisions,[5] present needs, and future expectations. And if the subject is structure, these very parameters set limits, always reformulated to the actor's knowledge and actions, however. At the household level, different structures impart commensurate social relations that encapsulate broader patterns of cooperation and conflict, domination and subordination, and, consequently, provoke a variety of livelihood strategies. Unquestionably, the individual is important, but, for our purposes, within the framework of the household and in the context of the social complex in which life is ultimately lived.

It is primarily through the elucidation of livelihood strategies, then, that the meaning of structure and household becomes intelligible. As L. Tilly (1975:138) insightfully observes: "Analysis of strategy tries to uncover the principles which lead to observable regularities or patterns of behavior among households"—not individuals per se. Although individuals conceive strategies, we are concerned with the effects of strategies on the household—not with individual psychological motivations, but on the immediate social consequences of particular actions on the household as a specific clustering of social relations. "Like the concept of adaption," Schminck (1984:95) notes, "that of strategy can lose its meaning to the extent that it becomes a mere functionalist label applied post-facto to whatever behavior is found." Hence, while thinking, struggling, active subjects shape their lives and the course of events, they do so within the boundaries imposed by structures that emerge as coherent sets of social relationships.

By looking at livelihood strategies we are positioned to uncover the connection between residence and household, individual and structure, working from unit of observation to unit of analysis. Given different activity groups of varying degrees and intensities, Wilk and Netting (1984:5) claim that "we can begin to visualize households as groups in which there is a high density of activity." Not all of these activity spheres will necessarily be undertaken by a household; nonetheless, some will be. This involves decomposing household activities into constituent elements. How these activities are accomplished and by whom—if indeed they are accomplished by individuals as members of households—unites the form the household actually assumes with the livelihood strategies followed in order to ensure its continuity (or affect its demise). In other words, we must recognize that inter- and suprahousehold networks may also be a distinguishing characteristic of households and, hence, livelihood strategies. The strategies pursued will, in turn, affect the form and operation of the household and, ultimately, its material and social reproduction over time. Some strategies may lead to dead ends while others offer new opportunities. Yet, once those doors are opened or shut, the possibilities for subsequent strategies are irrevocably altered. It is within this context that we attempt to isolate and understand household livelihood strategies.

Initial Observations of Households in Somasem, Shair Tomat, and Shatt Damam

The empirical description of the household begins with "simple residence," with the enumeration of the individuals physically dwelling there. Throughout this initial exercise, we must be sensitive to how the "immediate household" secures its livelihood. In this manner, it is possible to detect individuals residing outside of the household who, nevertheless, contribute on an ongoing basis. Depending on the degree, intensity, and impact of their participation, we can determine whether or not they should be included as household members.[6] Certainly, we must also be sensitive to the household as a subjective reality, as a unit with which its members identify their particular interests. For example, by recognizing the differences between household responsibilities and kinship obligations, we can determine if we have an actual member of the household who has migrated and is sending remittances, a former household member sending remittances under filial obligations, or if we have a member who has left during the dry season, not necessarily to send remittances, but to relieve the household of a resource-consuming member during the "hungry season." Admittedly, this is no easy task and entails qualitative assessment through informed judgement, but at the end we have derived households.

We are now in a position to begin to describe the household's basic characteristics, bearing in mind that detailed analysis addressing the whys requires locating households in the wider socioeconomic environment, a topic taken up later. Accordingly, the task at hand is to provide an overview of the households in Somasem, Shair Tomat, and Shatt Damam, considering such aspects as size, age and sex distribution, residency pattern, type of household heads, occupations of members, and so on.

Household: Organizational Structure

Table 2.1 summarizes household sizes in the three villages. The majority of households in each village contain between two and nine members. In part, this is attributable to the high infant mortality rate and low life expectancy in general (49 years for the Sudan as a whole), as well as to the overall low level of productivity that tends to set the upper limits of demographic reproduction. Furthermore, within each village the op-

TABLE 2.1
Household Size by Village

Household Size	Somasem	Shair Tomat	Shatt Damam	Total
1 Person	8.3%	3.3%	.0%	4.0%
2–5	36.7	33.3	36.7	36.0
6–9	38.3	50.0	41.6	42.0
10–13	15.0	10.0	15.0	14.0
14–18	1.7	3.3	6.7	4.0
Total	100%	100%	100%	100%
(N=)	(60)	(30)	(60)	(150)
(Mean)	(6.1)	(6.4)	(7.2)	(6.6)

timal situation is for newly married young men to remain in their ancestral village and to begin their own households, albeit in the vicinity of their relatives.[7] The mean household size in each village is roughly similar, although the mean size in Shatt Damam is slightly larger than the other two. Lastly, incidences of single individual households are absent in Shatt Damam which, not surprisingly in light of this, also contains more households of ten or more members.

Overall, the gender distribution is more or less equal but with important variations between age categories within and between the three villages (table 2.2). In line with the typical age pyramid evidenced in other Third World countries, approximately 49 percent of household members in these villages are 15 years of age or less, while fewer than 7 percent are 50 years or older.[8] Males, however, in the first two age categories outnumber females and comprise, respectively, about 28 to 21 percent of the total population. Certainly we can attribute some of these variations to the fact that the population of each village is relatively small,[9] yet the next two age categories reveal the opposite: females outnumber males 21 percent to 12 percent; reversing the trend again, males 50 years or older account for 4.3 percent of the population, while females amount to only 2.5 percent. Some of the reasons for this disparity include intervillage mobility, such as the fostering of children where female children join the household of a widowed grandmother or a newly married sister in order to assist in daily activities and/or to help ease the transition to married life; the earlier age of first marriage of most fe-

TABLE 2.2
Age/Sex Structure of Households in Each Village

Age category by gender	Somasem	Shair Tomat	Shatt Damam	Total	(N)
Male					
<8	29.9%	28.0%	23.5%	26.7%	(132)
8–15	29.3	24.0	31.2	29.1	(144)
16–23	8.6	16.0	19.0	14.7	(73)
24–35	6.3	9.0	11.3	9.1	(45)
36–50	13.8	9.0	11.8	11.9	(59)
>50	12.1	14.0	3.2	8.5	(42)
Total	100.0%	100.0%	100.0%	100.0%	
(n=)	(174)	(100)	(221)	(495)	
(Mean)	(21)	(22)	(18)	(20)	
Female					
< 8	19.9%	17.4%	24.5%	21.4%	(105)
8–15	23.6	21.7	18.8	21.2	(104)
16–23	17.3	21.7	23.1	20.6	(101)
24–35	16.2	15.2	20.2	17.7	(87)
36–50	16.2	20.7	9.1	14.1	(69)
>50	6.8	3.3	4.3	5.1	(25)
Total	100.0%	100.0%	100.0%	100.0%	
(n=)	(191)	(92)	(208)	(491)	
(Mean)	(23)	(23)	(20)	(21)	
Grand Total	100.0%	100.0%	100.0%	100.0%	
(Grand N=)	(365)	(192)	(429)	(986)	
(Grand Mean)	(22)	(22)	(19)	(21)	

males (14 to 16 years of age); and male out-migration, usually to urban areas, to seek a better life. Additional reasons include the lower life expectancy of women due to the rigors of domestic activities coupled with the strains of childbirth,[10] and a higher mortality rate of female infants under the age of 5, particularly in Somasem and Shair Tomat.[11]

In most groups there is inevitably one or more individuals with the final word, those able to exert greater suasion by virtue of status. Within the household this is no different. What is important, however, is who these individuals are. At this point, it is worthwhile to consider the types

TABLE 2.3
Type of Household Head by Sex and Village

Type of Household Head	Somasem	Shair Tomat	Shatt Damam	Total
Single Head	95.0%	96.7%	78.4%	88.7%
Male	73.3	76.7	65.1	70.7
Female	21.7	20.0	13.3	18.0
Joint Head	5.0	3.3	21.6	11.3
Females	1.7	3.3	3.3	2.6
Males	3.3	.0	1.7	2.0
Male/Female	.0	.0	16.6	6.7
Total	100.0%	100.0%	100.0%	100.0%
(N=)	(60)	(30)	(60)	(150)

of household head (table 2.3), bearing in mind that there is a difference between de jure and de facto designations. Optimally, our task is made easier where the distinction is collapsed within a single individual; where it is not, our interest lies more with the enduring household head and less with temporary and perfunctory considerations. Identifying the household head is not always a straightforward matter and requires that we distinguish nuances of meaning between local categories. *Rab al-usra* refers to the head of family or lineage affairs, while *Rab al-manzil* denotes the head of domestic operations. The former designation carries more weight in household concerns. For our purposes, then, the specification of the household head is the individual(s) whose word sustains ultimate authority within the household, and assessment of this invariably involved careful evaluation of those decisions affecting the household over time.

The majority of households evidence a single head (88.7 percent), with a variety of jointly headed households comprising slightly more than 11 percent. Of greater interest, joint heads account for nearly 22 percent of the households in Shatt Damam and, in the main, connote a more consensual and less rigid form of decision-making. On the other hand, although the predominant means of reckoning descent in Shatt Damam is matrilineal, 66.8 percent of households are headed singularly or jointly by males. It should be made clear from this that questions of female subordination cannot be traced directly to the form of inheritance, nor is sexual egalitarianism assured within a matrilinear system. Somasem and Shair Tomat, however, are no less patriarchal; they merely have more household heads who are widows or divorced (13.3 and 20.0 percent respectively) than does Shatt Damam (5 percent). And since each village is patriarchal, we can expect the orientation of the household to be biased towards males at the expense of females. That is, household strategies will tend to favor males over females, with females undertaking the bulk of the arduous domestic chores (including maintenance of the jubraka or house garden) and receiving a smaller share of resources.

Evaluation of households and, consequently, of their livelihood strategies must be considered, not within an hourly or annual period as is a common trend among neoclassical economists, but over the life course of a household. It is a matter of observation that individuals, as members of households, determine their activities by the then realities of their household's demographic situation. For this reason, the age of the household head provides an important indicator of the developmental cycle of a household (table 2.4). As the data reveal, the majority of household heads are in the 36 to 50 years of age category—45.8 percent of male household heads and 47.9 percent of female. Interestingly, 37.3 percent of male and 42.9 percent of female household heads in Shatt Damam are in the younger age category of 24 to 35. In Somasem, these figures decline to 10.9 and 21.1 percent respectively. Some 17 percent of male household heads in Shair Tomat are in this younger age category, but there are no female equivalents.

The absence of female household heads in the 16 to 23 and 24 to 35 age ranges in Shair Tomat suggests a more extreme form of patriarchy in this village, disclosing its *Hawazma* Arab/Muslim heritage, with male elders holding firmly to the staff of power; the lack of male household heads in the 16 to 23 age range further attests to this. In terms of young males, these figures also point to a later age of first marriage and the start of a new household; these life course trajectories generally occur earlier in Somasem and Shatt Damam. At the other end of the age spectrum, household heads aged 50 years or more in Somasem account for 37.0 and 10.5 percent of male and female household heads respectively, 56.5 and 25.0 percent in Shair Tomat, but less than 10 percent for both categories in Shatt Damam. In part, the discrepancies in age categories of household heads are due to a lower life expectancy in Shatt Damam and to the fact that an

TABLE 2.4
Age of Household Head by Sex and Village

Age category of household head	Somasem	Shair Tomat	Shatt Damam	Total
Male				
16–23 2.2%	.0%	3.9%	2.5%	
24–35	10.9	17.4	37.3	23.3
36–50	50.0	26.1	51.0	45.8
>50	37.0	56.5	7.8	28.3
Total	100.0%	100.0%	100.0%	100.0%
(n=)	(46)	(23)	(51)	(120)
(Mean Age)	(49)	(53)	(38)	(45)
Female				
16–23	21.1%	.0%	9.5%	12.5%
24–35	21.1	.0	42.9	27.1
36–50	47.4	75.0	38.1	47.9
>50	10.5	25.0	9.5	12.5
Total	100.0%	100.0%	100.0%	100.0%
(n=)	(19)	(8)	(21)	(48)
(Mean Age)	(39)	(50)	(34)	(39)
(N=)	(65)	(31)	(72)	(168)
(Grand Mean Age)	(46)	(52)	(37)	(43)

aged parent is more apt to live with an adult child and to cede the mantle of authority. The mean age of male household heads is older than that of females in each village, as well as for all three villages combined—45 as opposed to 39 years of age. The data also suggest evidence of the fact that female headed households are probably a relatively recent phenomenon, the upsurge coming as a result of general socioeconomic insecurity and vulnerability as well as of a breakdown in long-standing kinship networks.

Since we are interested in the household as a collective unit, an additional task requires fixing its basis of membership and physical boundary. Moreover, while the mechanisms of kinship (or family) and propinquity appear typically to many households, the possibility of nonkinship bonds and spatial separation remains. With this in mind, further examination of households is accordingly: (1) a basis of social

TABLE 2.5
Household Member's Relation to Household Head[13]

Member's relation	Somasem		Shair Tomat		Shatt Damam		Total	
Spouse	18.8%		16.8%		17.3%		17.6%	
Child	71.2	(1.0)	76.5	(2.5)	64.2	(0.5)	69.2	(1.1)
Parent	4.3		0.6	(0.6)	3.8	3.3	(0.1)	
Grandchild	1.3		3.7		1.4		1.8	
Sibling	3.1	(0.7)	1.2	(0.6)	7.0	(1.7)	4.5	(1.1)
Uncle/Aunt	0.3		0		0		0.1	
Nephew/Niece	0.7		0.6		4.9	(4.9)	2.5	(2.2)
Cousin	0		0		1.4	(1.4)	0.6	(0.6)
Nonkin	0.3		0.6		0		0.2	
Total	100.0%		100.0%		100.0%		100.0%	
(N=)	(303)		(161)		(370)		(834)	

organization within the household; (2) a structural composition of households; and (3) a spatial arrangement of household residences.

The language of lineage in the Nuba Mountains speaks loudly. Kinship remains an important means around which households are organized (table 2.5). We should not assume, however, that it signifies the same thing for each village or within each village, or that it automatically supersedes economic considerations. On closer inspection the kinship criteria for household membership reveals a rich assortment of relations. Evidence of Shatt Damam's matrilinear background begins to surface in the magnitude of nonnuclear family household members. What is notable is the number of siblings, nieces, nephews, and cousins residing with the household head(s) (13.3 percent), as well as the higher incidence of in-laws within the household (8.5 percent).[12] Households in Somasem and Shair Tomat, on the other hand, are essentially nuclear, composed primarily of spouses and their children (90.0 and 93.3 percent respectively).

Closely associated with membership characteristics are the types of household residential arrangements (table 2.6). These range from single person units to complex households. While kinship remains central, it is not the sole basis of household organization. Of the sample, seven households were based on nonkinship ties for the simple fact

TABLE 2.6
Household Residential Type by Village

Household Type	Somasem	Shair Tomat	Shatt Damam	Total	(N)
Single adult	(25.0%)	(13.2%)	(13.4%)	(18.0%)	(27)
Male	3.3	.0	1.7	2.0	(3)
Female	5.0	3.3	.0	2.7	(4)
Male w/dependent(s)	1.7	3.3	1.7	2.0	(3)
Female w/dependent(s)	15.0	6.6	10.0	11.4	(17)
Nuclear	(53.3%)	(60.1%)	(40.0%)	(49.3%)	(74)
No dependents	5.0	6.7	1.7	4.0	(6)
W/dependent(s)	28.3	36.7	31.6	31.3	(47)
Polygamous w/dependent(s)	20.0	16.7	6.7	14.0	(21)
Complex	(21.7%)	(26.7%)	(46.6%)	(32.7%)	(49)
Extended w/dependent(s)	11.7	20.0	13.4	14.0	(21)
Ext. polygamous w/dep.(s)	1.7	.0	1.7	1.3	(2)
Joint w/dependent(s)	3.3	6.7	10.0	6.7	(10)
Joint poly. w/dep(s)	1.7	.0	8.3	4.0	(6)
Extended-joint w/dep.(s)	3.3	.0	6.6	4.0	(6)
Ext.-joint poly. w/dep(s)	.0	.0	6.6	2.7	(4)
Total	100.0%	100.0%	100.0%	100.0%	
(N=)	(60)	(30)	(60)	(150)	

that they were single member units, while only one household, in Shair Tomat, was a complex (joint) household based on nonkin ties of friendship (although they were sisters-in-law, this was not a deciding factor in their decision to form a household and share household-based activities). In the main, the dominant type of household in Somasem and Shair Tomat is the nuclear family, while in Shatt Damam the most common is the complex type (46.6 percent). Complex households include joint (adults of the same generation), extended (adults of different generations), and joint/extended. Nuclear and complex households are further differentiated by polygamous marriage bonds. The different patterns of household residential arrangements also provides further indication of socioeconomic vulnerability induced by increasing male out-migration, changing kinship systems and stressful conjugal relations, and the restructuring of agriculture at the village level, especially in the number of single (particularly) female headed households, with or without dependents.

We must further account for the ways in which actual residency patterns and households intersect (table 2.7). Spatial arrangements consist of coresidence, dispersed residence, multiresidence, and dispersed/ multiresidence. Except for Shatt Damam, coresidence with household members sharing a single common residence is the most frequent type of arrangement. In Shatt Damam, however, household members tend to be dispersed (53.3 percent) as a result of temporary out-migration for employment or (less frequently) education, and age-grade rituals where young men live together apart from the village confines. In this case, one or more members reside "temporarily" away from the household and secure separate "shelter." Multiresidence includes instances where one or more household members reside in an additional "primary" residence. For example, Moustafa maintains two permanent residences— one in Shair Tomat for one wife and children and a second in Kadugli for another wife and children. Incidences of multiresidence are low in Somasem (5.0 percent) and Shair Tomat (6.7 percent) and absent in Shatt Damam. In each village 3.3 percent of the households are dispersed/ multiresidence, which combines elements of both types. In general, these latter two types of residential arrangements require large household

TABLE 2.7
Household Spatial Residency Type by Village

Household Residency Pattern	Somasem	Shair Tomat	Shatt Damam	Total
Coresidence	56.7%	53.3%	41.7%	50.0%
Dispersed	26.7	33.3	53.3	38.7
Multiresidence	5.0	6.7	.0	3.3
Disp./multiresidence	3.3	3.3	3.3	3.3
Single member	8.3	3.3	1.7	4.7
Total	100.0%	100.0%	100.0%	100.0%
(N=)	(60)	(30)	(60)	(150)

membership and, more importantly, ample resources. Nonetheless, they constitute important minority forms.

Household Dynamics

We now turn to the basic assets owned and activities undertaken by household members in an attempt to shed light on the material reproduction of households. It is essentially from assets and activities that we will develop an immediate concrete understanding of livelihood strategies. Needless to say, households are in many ways refractory to analysis, in much the same way as other structures, because of their mutability, especially over time. Household has to do with rights, responsibilities, and obligations over such areas as marriage, parenting, transmission, residence, and labor—and subsequently with the constraints all of these place on individuals.

Considerations over the creation, control, and allocation of resources within the household is equally important and highlights gender and age issues. We cannot assume, for example, that resources are controlled and accumulated solely by males. But even in cases where men and women control their own incomes, their relative positions usually differ. What our analysis requires is an understanding of household as sets of exchange relationships based on social power. Within the idiom of patriarchy, women are not effectively empowered, making it difficult for them to accumulate wealth or to acquire education. Differences also exist among women according to their respective communities: *Ghulfan* women in Somasem have more power than do *Hamar* women in Shair Tomat, but less than Shatt women in Shatt Damam. Nonetheless, patriarchy ensures that across the board men exercise greater market and nonmarket access to important resources such as labor. Furthermore, since a male's income is greater than is a female's he typically enjoys better access to market and nonmarket sources of labor. As a result, the acreage cultivated by females remains smaller than that of her male counterparts.

Household Assets

The routine of everyday village life centers around agriculture. Consequently, for most households, land is everything. Although the meanings people attach to land may differ, overall it provides the means

TABLE 2.8
Size of Main Farm Owned by Household

No. feddans owned	Somasem	Shair Tomat	Shatt Damam	Total
none	8.3%	.0%	6.7%	6.0%
0.1-5.0	13.3	10.0	50.0	27.3
5.1-10.0	11.7	3.3	30.0	17.3
10.1-20.0	25.0	26.7	10.0	19.3
20.1-40.0	18.3	50.0	3.3	18.7
40.1-60.0	1.7	10.0	.0	2.7
60.1-100.0	6.7	.0	.0	2.7
over 100.0	15.0	.0	.0	6.0
Total	100.0%	100.0%	100.0%	100.0%
(n=)	(60)	(30)	(60)	(150)

necessary for daily and generational reproduction. Table 2.8 indicates the importance of land, with very few households having no main farm (6.0 percent). Most households in Somasem (43.3 percent) and Shair Tomat (76.7 percent) own between 10.1 and 40.0 feddans, while only 13.3 percent do in Shatt Damam. The size of landholdings is significantly smaller in Shatt Damam, with 80.0 percent of households owning ten feddans or less. On the other hand, 15.0 percent of households in

TABLE 2.9
Number of Feddans Cultivated by Household

No. feddans cultivated	Somasem	Shair Tomat	Shatt Damam	Total
none	6.7%	3.3%	3.3%	4.7%
0.1-5.0	31.7	13.3	60.0	39.3
5.1-10.0	20.0	23.3	30.0	24.7
10.1-20.0	18.3	36.7	5.0	16.7
20.1-40.0	11.7	23.3	1.7	10.0
40.1-60.0	3.3	.0	.0	1.3
60.1-100.0	6.7	.0	.0	2.7
over 100.0	1.7	.0	.0	.7
Total 100.0%	100.0%	100.0%	100.0%	
(n=)	(60)	(30)	(60)	(150)

Somasem own more than 100.0 feddans of land.[14] This fairly unequal distribution of land among the three villages (particularly Somasem) suggests that households can be divided into distinct strata on the basis of access to land.

Rarely do households cultivate every feddan at the disposal of its members. Aside from the need to periodically let land lay fallow, intermittent labor shortages, changing consumption requirements, market expectations, and variable weather patterns preclude the full usage of the main farm. In this respect, land ownership represents an important "store of wealth"—land claimed now for future anticipated needs. Table 2.9 shows the number of feddans under cultivation in each village. Few households cultivate no land, although nearly 40 percent of households

TABLE 2.10
Number of Parcels Household Cultivates

No. parcels cultivated	Somasem	Shair Tomat	Shatt Damam	Total
One	62.4%	3.4%	19.0%	32.8%
Two	30.4	41.4	43.1	37.8
Three	3.6	37.8	25.8	19.6
Four	3.6	17.2	12.1	9.8
Total	100.0%	100.0%	100.0%	100.0%
(n=)	(60)	(30)	(60)	(150)

TABLE 2.11
How Household Cultivates Main Farm

How main farm cultivated	Somasem	Shair Tomat	Shatt Damam	Total
No land cultivated	6.7%	6.7%	.0%	4.0%
Tractor used	50.0	.0	.0	20.0
Digging stick used	3.3	13.3	98.3	43.3
Mostly tractor	40.0	6.7	1.7	18.0
Tractor for cotton only, Digging stick for rest	.0	73.3	.0	14.7
Total	100.0%	100.0%	100.0%	100.0%
(n=)	(60)	(30)	(60)	(150)

in Shatt Damam cultivate five feddans or less. In fact, 90.0 percent of households in this village cultivate 10.0 feddans or less, indicating its small-scale character. In contrast, 30 and 60 percent of households in Somasem and Shair Tomat respectively cultivate between 10.1 and 40.0 feddans. As with land ownership, the largest cultivators reside in Somasem, with one household planting roughly 131 feddans.[15]

Moreover, with the exception of Somasem, the majority of households do not cultivate contiguous plots (table 2.10). Essentially, this represents a hedge against the vagaries of nature, including insects, weeds, and extremely localized rainfall. The likelihood of simultaneous crop failure on separate plots is thus minimized. Specific crops also require certain types of soil, hence the need for access to different fields. Groundnuts, for example, require *gardud*, or sandy-clay soil, while *dura* grows best in *hadaba*, or cracking clay. On the other hand, the mechanization of agriculture in the form of tractors requires the engrossment of land (contiguous fields), and the traditional landholding pattern retards the use of a tractor. Given the number of land parcels farmers cultivate in each of the three villages, it is not surprising that half of the households in Somasem rely solely on tractors for plowing their main fields (an additional 40 percent mostly rely on tractors); about 73 percent use tractors in Shair Tomat, but in the cotton schemes only; while in Shatt Damam, more than 98 percent rely solely on digging sticks (table 2.11).

Domestic animals, aside from land, constitute an important agricultural asset. A brief look at the number and types of animals owned by households reveals that most households possess at least chickens (table 2.12). In general, cattle, goats, and chickens are the more commonly kept animals, with slightly more than half of sampled households owning cattle, while nearly 73 percent have goats, and 88 percent keep chickens. The size of herds is small such that approximately 33 and 48 percent of households have between 1 and 10 cows and goats respectively. Larger herds of both are found in Somasem and Shair Tomat, although one household in Shatt Damam owned 99 cows.[16] As a source of meat or cash, sheep are of relatively little importance, primarily because goats require less attention and are better suited to local forage. Donkeys and camels provide important means of transport for people and goods. In addition, camels are also used to power oil presses. Householders in Shair Tomat have more of these animals than do householders in the other two villages. Pigs remain prominent in Shatt Damam, with nearly

TABLE 2.12
Type and Number of Animals Owned by Households (percent)

No. owned	cattle	sheep	goat	camel	donkey	chicken	pigeon	pig	TOTAL
SOMASEM									100%
none	43.3%	100.0%	25.0%	93.3%	81.7%	13.3%	96.7%	100.0%	(n=60)
1-5	16.7	.0	20.0	6.7	18.3	21.7	3.3	.0	
6-10	11.7	.0	20.0	.0	.0	31.7	.0	.0	
11-20	13.3	.0	21.7	.0	.0	25.0	.0	.0	
over 20	15.0	.0	13.3	.0	.0	8.3	.0	.0	
SHAIR TOMAT									
none	56.7	96.7	10.0	96.7	76.7	3.3	93.3	100.0	100%
1-5	16.7	.0	23.3	3.3	23.3	33.3	6.7	.0	(n=30)
6-10	10.0	.0	26.7	.0	.0	33.3	.0	.0	
11-20	10.0	3.3	33.3	.0	.0	20.0	.0	.0	
over 20	6.7	.0	6.7	.0	.0	10.0	.0	.0	
SHATT DAMAM									100%
none	51.7	83.4	38.3	98.3	98.3	15.0	100.0	58.4	(n=60)
1-5	30.0	5.0	30.0	.0	1.7	45.0	.0	38.3	
6-10	10.0	8.3	23.3	1.7	.0	28.3	.0	3.3	
11-20	3.3	3.3	8.3	.0	.0	10.0	.0	.0	
over 20	5.0	.0	.0	.0	.0	1.7	.0	.0	
TOTAL									100%
none	49.2	92.7	27.3	96.0	87.3	12.0	97.3	83.3	(N=150)
1-5	22.0	2.0	24.7	3.3	12.7	33.3	2.7	15.4	
6-10	10.7	3.3	22.7	.7	.0	30.7	.0	1.3	
11-20	8.7	2.0	18.7	.0	.0	18.0	.0	.0	
over 20	9.4	.0	6.6	.0	.0	6.0	.0	.0	

42 percent of households keeping between 1 and 10. While respondents in Somasem admitted to keeping pigs in the past, the inhabitants of Shair Tomat (predominantly Arabs) emphatically asserted that they never did. As with land, the unequal distribution of animals supposes distinct categories of households.

Landholdings and animals, clearly important resources, by no means constitute a household's entire set of assets. Aside from these, 36 percent of households own one or more other business enterprises (table 2.13). These enterprises comprise a broad range of endeavors, from vending goods in the local shop to a tractor for hire, from cut-

TABLE 2.13
Number of Enterprises Owned by Household

No. of enterprises	Somasem	Shair Tomat	Shatt Damam	Total
none	46.7%	66.7%	80.0%	64.0%
one	38.3	16.7	13.3	24.0
two	8.3	13.3	1.7	6.7
three	5.0	3.3	3.3	4.0
four	1.7	.0	1.7	1.3
Total	100.0%	100.0%	100.0%	100.0%
(n=)	(60)	(30)	(60)	(150)

TABLE 2.14
Education of Household Members by Sex (7 years old or greater)

Education	Somasem		Shair Tomat		Shatt Damam		Total
	male	female	male	female	male	female	
illiterate	48.8%	68.4%	39.7%	79.5%	75.1%	95.7%	70.8%
read/write	4.7	.0	9.6	1.2	3.4	.0	2.6
some elementary	30.2	20.9	30.1	10.8	15.3	1.9	17.0
completed elementary	7.0	3.2	8.2	6.0	2.8	1.9	4.2
some intermediate	2.3	4.4	5.5	2.4	2.3	.0	2.6
completed intermediate	1.6	.6	1.4	.0	.6	.6	.8
some high school	4.7	1.3	1.4	.0	.6	.0	1.3
completed high school	.0	.6	4.1	.0	.0	.0	.5
some college	.8	.6	.0	.0	.0	.0	.3
TOTAL	100.0%	100.0%	100.0%	100.0%	100.0%	100.0%	100.0%
(n=)	(129)	(158)	(73)	(83)	(177)	(162)	(782)

ting wood to collecting gum arabic, and from hauling water to providing tea and coffee. Nonagricultural businesses are most notable in Somasem, with around 38 percent of households operating at least one. In addition, 15 percent of households in Somasem and nearly 17 percent in Shair Tomat own more than one business enterprise. Ownership of business enterprises is less significant in Shatt Damam, with only 20.0 percent of households having one or more nonagricultural business enterprises.

Arguably, formal education can be considered a household asset. With the expansion of a capitalist economy, the ability to read, write, and perform numerical computations is increasingly important. Table 2.14 indicates the level of educational attainment for household members over the age of seven. Overall, the three villages evidence a high degree of illiteracy (70.8 percent). Significant variations exist between villages as well as between males and females, however. In general, males tend to be better educated than are their female counterparts, although females in Somasem have more education than do those in the other two villages. The category of read/write (basic literacy) reflects greater male employment opportunities, especially in the military and police, where these skills are learned outside of formal schooling. Few individuals extend their education past elementary school, most noticeably in Shatt Damam, where only 3.5 percent of males and less the 1 percent of females have more than an elementary education. Only household members from Somasem have studied at the college level.

Household Activities

The reproduction of households and their members is a complex undertaking, revealed in the diversity of the primary work statuses cited by household members (table 2.15). Bearing in mind the mean size of households and the increasing importance of education, it is not unexpected that 43.7 percent of males and 27.7 percent of female respondents were not employed since they are children or are in school.[17] Percentage differences in the "child" category by sex within each village is, in part, due to the fact that females customarily begin work at an earlier age than do males, usually helping in household chores. In addition, the disparity in male and female students corresponds to the level of education of household members; as noted, females tend to have less education than males. Lastly, variance between villages also suggests that the age at which childhood ends is changing.

Given the prominence of agriculture in the Nuba Mountains, it is not surprising that approximately 31 percent of males and 22 percent of females cite their primary occupation as self-employed farmers. Also, nearly 45 percent of females labor predominately in domestic activities,

TABLE 2.15
Ratio of Productive to Unproductive Workers

	Somasem	Shair Tomat	Shatt Damam	Total
ratio	1.2:1	1.5:1	2.2:1	1.6:1

TABLE 2.16
Primary Work Status of Household Members by Sex

Work status	Somasem	Shair Tomat	Shatt Damam	Total
Male				
Nonemployment				
retired	2.3%	3.0%	1.4%	2.0%
unemployed	.6	.0	.5	.4
student	21.3	25.0	10.0	17.0
child	31.0	27.0	23.1	26.7
Self-Employment				
farmer	30.5	27.0	33.5	31.1
tend livestock	5.7	3.0	15.4	9.5
merchant	2.9	1.0	.9	1.6
free enterpriser	.0	.0	.5	.2
shop keeper	.6	1.0	.0	.4
HH operations	2.3	4.0	1.4	2.2
Public Employment				
civil servant	.6	2.0	.0	.6
teacher	.6	.0	.0	.2
clinical tech.	.0	.0	.5	.2
army	.0	1.0	.0	.2
Private Employment				
menial laborer	1.1	3.0	12.7	6.7
run flour mill	.0	1.0	.0	.2
shop clerk	.0	.0	.5	.2
driver	.0	1.0	.0	.2
electrician	.6	.0	.0	.2
guard	.0	1.0	.0	.2
Total	100.0%	100.0%	100.0%	100.0%
(n=)	(174)	(100)	(221)	(495)

TABLE 2.16 (continued)
Primary Work Status of Household Members by Sex

Work status	Somasem	Shair Tomat	Shatt Damam	Total
Female				
Nonemployment				
retired	1.6	.0	1.9	1.4
student	17.3	9.8	1.4	9.2
child	16.8	13.0	22.6	18.5
Self-Employment				
farmer	11.5	29.3	29.3	22.4
tend livestock	1.6	4.3	1.4	2.0
merchant	.0	4.3	.0	.8
tea stall	1.0	.0	.0	.4
shop clerk	.0	1.1	.0	.2
HH operations	49.7	37.0	43.3	44.6
Public Employment				
teacher	.5	1.1	.0%	.4
Total	100.0%	100.0%	100.0%	100.0%
(n=)	(191)	(92)	(208)	(491)
Grand Total	100.0%	100.0%	100.0%	100.0%
(N=)	(365)	(192)	(429)	(986)

including food preparation, hauling of water, and tending of the jubraka, or house garden. Few males or females engage primarily in private or public employment, with the exception of Shatt Damam, where 12.7 percent of males claim menial labor as their primary work status. The initial picture that emerges of village life, then, is one of relative independence from the outside world, of self-sufficient small-scale farmers. The ratio of productive to unproductive workers appears to underscore this, with an overall ratio of 1.6:1 (table 2.16). Lastly, each village has a full-time merchant provisioning manufactured goods—five in Somasem, one in Shatt Tomat, and two in Shatt Damam.

Table 2.17 indicates greater participation in nonagricultural activities by household members reporting a secondary work status. Needless to say, these pursuits are less time-consuming than is primary work, yet they cannot be assumed to contribute less to the household's reproduction. In fact, secondary occupations are frequently important sources

TABLE 2.17
Secondary Work Status of Household Members by Sex

Work status	Somasem	Shair Tomat	Shatt Damam	Total
Male				
Self-Employment				
farmer	31.1%	66.7%	44.8%	43.3%
tend livestock	28.6	8.3	15.5	19.9
merchant	2.6	5.6	.0	2.3
free enterpriser	15.6	13.8	8.6	12.9
smith	1.3	.0	.0	.7
carpenter	1.3	.0	1.7	1.2
run mech. farm	7.8	.0	.0	3.5
shop clerk	1.3	.0	.0	.7
HH operations	7.8	2.8	6.9	6.4
Private Employment				
menial laborer	1.3	2.8	18.9	7.0
run flour mill	1.3	.0	1.8	1.4
tailor	.0	.0	1.8	.7
Total	100.0%	100.0%	100.0%	100.0%
	(77)	(36)	(58)	(171)
Female				
Self-Employment				
farmer	57.0	45.3	51.1	52.2
tend livestock	3.0	1.3	2.9	2.6
merchant	.7	.0	.0	.3
free enterpriser	1.5	.0	2.2	1.4
HH operations	30.4	49.3	37.2	37.2
Public Employment				
teacher	.7	.0	.0	.3
nurse's aid	.0	1.3	.0	.3
Private Employment				
menial laborer	6.7	2.8	6.6	5.7
Total	100.0%	100.0%	100.0%	100.0%
	(135)	(75)	(137)	(347)
Grand Total	100.0%	100.0%	100.0%	100.0%
(N=)	(212)	(111)	(195)	(518)

of cash income and can mean the difference between household continuity and dissolution. Farming still remains the dominant activity, with
43.3 percent of males and 52.2 percent of females specifying this as
their secondary occupation. In general, these individuals farm intermittently and provide supplementary household labor during peak periods
of the agricultural production cycle. Tending livestock is also an important activity, occupying the spare time of roughly 20 percent of males
and 3 percent of females. In addition, 7.8 percent of males in Somasem
also operate mechanized farms in the nearby Habila mechanized scheme.
Slightly more than 6 percent of males and 37 percent of females occasionally help in household operations, usually in carrying water, fetching wood, and watching children.

The number of household members engaged in secondary off-farm,
nondomestic work is considerably larger than reported in table 2.15,
accounting for roughly 30 percent of males and 8 percent of females.
With the exception of Shair Tomat, nonagricultural/nondomestic self-
employment is particularly important, accounting for some 27 percent
of the male's secondary work (but for less than 2 percent of the female's).
Clearly, free enterprisers dominate this category and consist of collectors (gum, thatch, wood, water) and artisans (saddles, bowls, marissa,
beds, gates). On the other hand, more than 22 percent of males in Shatt
Damam seek private employment, with almost 19 percent working as
menial laborers in their secondary occupations. Aside from farming and
tending to household operations, females, overall, find themselves toiling as menial laborers. What tables 2.15 and 2.17 also suggest is the
gender bias in economic opportunities, such that 33.3 percent of males
engage primarily in farming or household operations as opposed to 67.0
percent of females. This gap widens in secondary employment to 49.7
and 89.4 percent, respectively.

As is becoming apparent, off-farm employment, whether working
for oneself, the government, or for another individual, is increasingly
an important source of cash for many households. Table 2.18 refers to
the general types of off-farm employment—daHwa,[18] agricultural piece-
work, and nonagricultural—and the percent of household members engaged in each type of activity.

Off-farm agricultural labor applies specifically to laborers being
paid by the number of feddan completed (piece-work) and is more
profitable than daHwa, which is by fixed payment. Few individual

TABLE 2.18
Number of Household Members Working Off-Farm

Number of workers	DaHwa	Agriculture	Nonagriculture	Total
Somasem				
None	66.7%	96.7%	83.3%	100%
One	18.3	3.3	13.3	(n=60)
Two	3.3	.0	1.7	
Three	8.3	.0	1.7	
Four	1.7	.0	.0	
Five	1.7	.0	.0	
Shair Tomat				
None	93.3	83.3	63.4	100%
One	.0	10.0	33.3	(n=30)
Two	3.3	6.7	3.3	
Three	3.3	.0	.0	
Four	.0	.0	.0	
Five	.0	.0	.0	
Shatt Damam				
None	56.7	91.7	51.7	100%
One	16.7	8.3	33.3	(n=60)
Two	11.7	.0	13.3	
Three	8.3	.0	1.7	
Four	3.3	.0	.0	
Five	3.3	.0	.0	
Total				
None	68.0	92.0	66.7	100%
One	14.0	6.7	25.3	(N=150)
Two	6.7	1.3	6.7	
Three	7.3	.0	1.3	
Four	2.0	.0	.0	
Five	2.0	.0	.0	

workers prefer daHwa, although it is the more common means of employing wage labor for agricultural tasks. At 17 percent, the village of Shair Tomat has the largest percentage of household members working periodically off the farms as agricultural laborers. Most villagers tend to look down on people (especially adult males) working for cash on another farmer's field and believe they are neglecting their own farms. Interestingly, 33 and 34 percent of households in Somasem and Shatt Damam have at least one member working as a day agricultural laborer (daHwa), whereas only 6.6 percent of households in Shair Tomat do. This is due, in part, to the Arab background of Shair Tomat such that women are discouraged from working publicly. In general, employers prefer to hire adult males as agricultural laborers since they tend to work fastest, while daHwa is reserved for females, children, and the aged. Nonagricultural labor is the more popular pursuit for individuals in Shair Tomat and Shatt Damam, with approximately 37 and 48 percent of households having one or more members employed in these activities. Fewer people in Shatt Damam engage in non-agricultural labor, in part because there are fewer opportunities open to them.

An additional point regarding off-farm employment involves the number of labor days spent in each undertaking and provides an indication of their importance to households (table 2.19). Time devoted to working in household-owned businesses is also considered since it, like the other activities, potentially diverts labor away from household agriculture. Most labor days are expended in nonagricultural employment and in working in a household-owned business. These account for most of the labor days, as contractual employment is less flexible and, thus, usually demands more long-term commitment, although it should be noted that some household owned and operated businesses also require members to be absent from the village for extended periods of time.

Although agricultural employment and daHwa can permit a greater measure of flexibility in terms of duration of employment, these jobs are significantly limited by their seasonal nature and thus account for far fewer labor days. Moreover, household members will generally only work as agricultural and daHwa laborers as a last resort. Certainly, too, public opinion dissuades all but the poorest from engaging in these types of employment activities. Not surprisingly, then, approximately 30 percent of households in Shair Tomat and Shatt Damam report that nonagricultural labor accounts for between 181 to 450 labor days per year, while over 33 percent of households in Somasem devote between 31 to 300 labor days to household businesses. Only 4 percent of households spent more than 30 labor days in agricultural labor, with Somasem and Shair Tomat accounting for most of these.

TABLE 2.19
Number of Labor Days Spent in Off-farm Activities

No. labor days	daHwa	ag.	nonag.	business	Total
Somasem					
none	66.7%	96.7%	86.5%	61.7%	100.0%
1-7	13.3	.0	.0	1.7	(n=60)
8-30	11.7	.0	.0	.0	
31-90	8.3	1.7	1.7	11.7	
91-180	.0	1.7	.0	13.3	
181-300	.0	.0	1.7	8.3	
301-450	.0	.0	6.7	3.3	
451-660	.0	.0	1.7	.0	
over 660	.0	.0	1.7	.0	
Shair Tomat					
none	93.4	83.3	63.3	66.7	100.0%
1-7	3.3	.0	.0	.0	(n=30)
8-30	3.3	10.0	.0	10.0	
31-90	.0	6.7	3.3	13.4	
91-180	.0	.0	.0	3.3	
181-300	.0	.0	10.0	3.3	
301-450	.0	.0	20.0	3.3	
451-660	.0	.0	.0	.0	
over 660	.0	.0	3.3	.0	
Shatt Damam					
none	56.7	91.7	51.7	80.0	100.0%
1-7	15.0	1.7	.0	.0	(n=60)
8-30	28.3	3.3	.0	.0	
31-90	.0	1.7	.0	1.7	
91-180	.0	1.7	5.0	8.3	
181-300	.0	.0	10.0	3.3	
301-450	.0	.0	20.0	6.7	
451-660	.0	.0	8.3	.0	
over 660	.0	.0	5.0	.0	
Total					
none	68.0	92.0%	68.0	70.0	100.0%
1-7	12.0	.7	.0	.7	(n=150)
8-30	16.7	3.3	.0	2.0	
31-90	3.3	2.7	1.3	8.0	
91-180	.0	1.3	2.0	9.3	
181-300	.0	.0	6.7	5.3	
301-450	.0	.0	14.7	4.7	
451-660	.0	.0	4.0	.0	
over 660	.0	.0	3.4	.0	

Household Income

Most would agree that autarky has never been a dominant feature of any household in securing its reproduction requirements. Some household needs are met through trade. The expansion of capitalism into the Nuba Mountains has tended to expand the circuits of trade and has generally been accompanied by an increase of cash money as the preferred medium of exchange. Therefore, even in households that provide for most of their needs through dint of their own efforts, the need arises for cash, even if only occasionally. Furthermore, household-based agricultural activities frequently are not sufficient in meeting a household's cash needs and requires a strategy of multiple income streams. And besides, not every household member remains satisfied with farming, while some hopeful farmers need to first acquire sufficient resources. Only 22 percent of households acquire cash solely through the sale of crops and/ or livestock. The point is, the majority of sampled households have at least two or three means to obtain cash income, with 60.0 percent of households in Shair Tomat, 56.7 percent in Somasem, and 51.7 percent in Shatt Damam having three or more sources of income (table 2.20).

A final point concerns household income (table 2.21). This table reveals the unequal distribution of cash incomes within and between the three villages. In these terms, Shatt Damam is by far the poorest village, with nearly 62 percent of households earning Sudanese £500 or less and approximately 87 percent of households making £1500 or less. Significantly fewer households earn £500 or less in both Somasem (38.3 per-

TABLE 2.20
Number of Sources[19] of Household Cash Income

No. sources	Somasem	Shair Tomat	Shatt Damam	Total
One	13.3%	13.3%	11.7%	12.7%
Two	30.0	26.7	36.7	32.0
Three	35.0	30.0	30.0	32.0
Four	16.7	26.7	15.0	18.0
Five	5.0	3.3	6.7	5.3
Total	100.0%	100.0%	100.0%	100.0%
(n=)	(60)	(30)	(60)	(150)

TABLE 2.21
Household Net Income in Sudanese Pounds

Net income	Somasem	Shair Tomat	Shatt Damam	Total
under 100	13.3%	.0%	15.0%	11.3%
100–500	25.0	33.3	46.7	35.3
501–1500	23.3	46.7	25.0	28.7
1501–3000	18.3	3.3	6.7	10.7
3001–10,000	16.7	16.7	3.3	11.3
over 10,000	3.3	.0	3.3	2.7
Total	100.0%	100.0%	100.0%	100.0%
(n=)	(60)	(30)	(60)	(150)

cent) and Shair Tomat (33.3 percent). On the other end of the income scale, about 17 percent of households in Somasem and Shair Tomat enjoy annual incomes of between £3,001 to £10,000; a mere 3.3 percent of households in Shatt Damam boast similar incomes. Lastly, 3.3 percent of households in Somasem and Shatt Damam earn in excess of £10,000 per annum, while none do in Shair Tomat. What the data suggest is that social differentiation and capitalist class formation is on-going, with the creation of an economic elite dominating the economic benefits.

Concluding Comments

Once revealed, households seem to emerge as relatively unequivocal units of analysis, whose livelihood strategies merely await precise delineation. One can already begin to question the merits of such an approach. Although we now have a better understanding of what households look like and what their members do, our initial observations have been necessarily schematic and superficial. This exercise points to the need to look more closely at the wider socioeconomic environment in which households are located, as well as to their internal dynamics. From this perspective, various opportunities and constraints figure differently for households and household members. We could simply stop at variations in land size, animals owned, agricultural and nonagricultural occupations, and household size and composition, yet still fall short of our goal. Simple stratification and demographic analysis fails to adequately explain variations in livelihood strategies because these approaches underemphasize the variability of Third World societies in other than capitalist terms and homogenize household interests outside of life cycle.

The analysis of household livelihood strategies thus requires careful consideration of more than just the household as an independent inclusive entity; it forces us to investigate the significance of different combinations of household resources in conjunction with opportunities and constraints presented by the wider economy at the individual level. Moreover, we must also admit that members may be involved in social relations at odds with each other, relations that may ultimately lead to the demise of a particular household.

If we are to proceed constructively, we must achieve a purposeful way of formulating a conception of the household in reference to the wider society, while at the same time remaining sensitive to individual agency. To the degree that we can distill the structural essence of the household, we will have helped fix the logic of individual rationality. But the backdrop of this is nothing less than the encompassing social complex in which people live out their lives. The presence of both capitalist and noncapitalist economic forces account for tensions and conflicts that can exert powerful affects on household forms and activities. And, when viewed in conjunction with equally contradictory forces such as kinship (patrilinear and matrilinear), religion (Islam, Christianity, and animism), and gender, significant variations in households abound. If the goal is to understand household livelihood strategies—not the household as individual actors but as a coherent set of social relations—we need to connect changes in households to the larger ongoing processes at work within that society. What we term the formation of household livelihood strategies, then, is more reasonably the transformation in the range and structure of available options.

Notes

1. These have alternately been termed subsistence, sustenance, survival, reproduction, and life strategies.
2. Too, throughout this process, it is incumbent upon the researcher to admit that the household may not be the essential category for particular lines of inquiry, such as the organization of agricultural production. This facet, for example, may require either an individual-level or community-level focus.
3. This point cannot be overstated. In the Nuba Mountains, for example, many husbands are forced to seek their livelihoods in distant locations, such as Khartoum.

Due to the difficulty of domestic travel, travel to their home villages may be infrequent. Yet, this should not automatically preclude household membership. Moreover, a migrant may maintain a household in his village and yet be part of a separate household in the capital.

4. By opening up residence, in all likelihood, the household member count will not equal the census count.

5. The role of "tradition," or received knowledge, can also not be ignored. Tradition is used to interpret everyday occurrences and to guide daily activities. This can help explain why some find comfort in tradition because not every event must be processed and analyzed anew. Tradition is neither stagnant nor constant, but always the subject of change. The traditions of one generation, for example, may or may not be those of the preceding one. This in no way invalidates one or the other, or sets them at opposite ends of a "development" pole; it merely underscores the fact that references change with the then realities.

6. Needless to say, by the end of fieldwork some household members were deemed nonmembers, while other individuals were added. The point is, identifying household members is an ongoing activity.

7. In Shatt Damam, for those enmeshed in matrilineal relations, the new household is established near the husband's mother's relatives. In patrilineal instances, it is with the husband's father's relatives. Somasem and Shair Tomat are both patrilineal.

8. Hadari (1974:161)), in a survey of 282 villages in the Nuba Mountains, achieved similar results: "Children up to the age of 12 years comprise 43 percent of the total, while adults (19 years and over) comprise only about 45 percent of the total."

9. The "law of large numbers" within the small populations of the respective villages does not hold and, therefore, we cannot expect a rough balance in males and females. When the village populations are combined, however, 50.2 percent of the population are male and 49.8 percent are female.

10. The widespread custom of female circumcision in Shair Tomat and Somasem makes childbirth difficult. Circumcision is commonly associated with Islam in the Sudan, so its practice is adopted with the conversion to Islam.

11. The matrilinear customs in Shatt Damam elevate the status of females and, thus, female infants are afforded the same attention and resources as are male infants.

12. The majority of nieces, nephews, cousins, and in-laws in Shatt Damam are from the maternal side of the family and is indicative of matrilinear cultures. In the other two villages, the majority are from the paternal side.

13. Percentage in parenthesis indicates in-law status, and child includes foster children.

14. Eight households in Somasem respectively own 100.8, 102.4, 108.8, 124.8, 126.4, and 185.6 *feddans*, with two households each owning 131.2.

15. One household cultivates 60.8 *feddans* and another 72.8, while two households each farm 63.2 *feddans*.

16. In Somasem, one household owned 50 goats and another 84 goats.

17. The age upper limit in the concept of child varied, as this is culturally determined and, hence, the age at which work is commenced varies. In the main, however, child extended to the age of 8 years, with few exceptions, although some children under the age of 8 worked.

18. *DaHwa*, or day labor, is usually from 7 A.M. to 2 P.M., and is a common way weeders are hired, and is by fixed wage. It is very low-paying.

19. Sources include crop sales, animal sales, household businesses, agricultural labor, *daHwa*, nonagricultural labor, and remittances.

3

The Nuba Mountains in Space and Time

Questions concerning human interaction are never easily resolved. This is especially true with regard to both its proper spatial and temporal context. Contributions within the development debate over the past twenty years have compelled social scientists to reconsider the broader macrolevel issues in an effort to refine their theoretical and methodological approaches. Macroforces can and do exert enormous pressures, which activate variant responses at the microlevel. Moreover, wider environmental trends also work to influence the course of events, affecting the lives of a local populace. On the other hand, case studies are essential in order to elucidate the diverse range of responses and initiatives found at the local level, to forge the "necessary link between personal experience and the flow of history" (Tilly, 1984:64). Thus, while this research is concerned with the formation of livelihood strategies in three particular villages in the Nuba Maintains, it cannot be conceived of in isolation to wider events—both present and past. After all, the unfolding past has left an indelible impression on present conditions and acts to place parameters on future alternatives.

Physical Setting and Ethnographic Origins

The Nuba Mountains, located near the geographical center of the Democratic Republic of the Sudan in southeastern Kordofan Province, covers an area approximately 30,000 square miles[1] and is situated between 29°00′E and 31°00′E latitude and 10°30′N and 12°30′N longitude.Geographically, this region presents a diverse range of geomorphic conditions and is called the Nuba Mountains more from common convention than geologic accuracy. The Nuba Mountains lies on the semiarid summer-rain savannah belt some 2,000 feet above sea level, and its plains are broken by residual massifs (such as Heiban group in the center, Nyima in the northwest, and Otoro in the southeast), as well as by a number of isolated obtruding outlies scattered intermittently across the region. The highest elevations extend some 3,000 feet above the floor at Jebel Temading and Jebel Dair. Most of these mountains, however, are little more than multiple hills and isolated granitic or diorite boulders that rise abruptly from the plain's floor, with little apparent systematic grouping except for the large masses at Tegali and Miri. Many of the mountains are pocketed with caves connected by precipitous footpaths and, thus, historically afforded welcomed protection from hostile aggressors. A number of the intermontane basins are deeply incised by *khors* (seasonal riverbeds), a few of which continue to trickle throughout the dry season, while in others water is usually obtainable by digging holes in the bed (March, 1948:834).

The population of the Nuba Mountains is approximately 1.2 million people, of which 800,000, or two-thirds, are classified as Nuba.[2] If the use of "mountain" to describe the topography is questionable, the appellation of Nuba to denote its inhabitants is a misnomer. Both the origins of the people and the etymology of the word to describe them are unclear, and it usually brings forth a cry of consternation from ethnographers and historians alike. Unfortunately, the state of Nuba historiography is more tentative than established, consisting of tangential statements, conjecture, and assumptions (e.g., Seligman, 1932; Nadel, 1947; Stevenson, 1984; and Spaulding, 1985a). In general, scholarly inquiry remains confined to anthropological inquiry[3], describing certain aspects of particular groups without attempting to grapple with the knottier historical issues. In part, this is due to the necessity of piecing together the history of the Nuba Mountains from the records of Sinnar, separated from Kordofan by the Blue Nile, and Darfur, lying to the west, as well as from the respective oral histories of the area (MacMichael, 1967:4). This latter activity can prove especially difficult. As stressed by S.F. Nadel (1947:5):

> It often seems as if historical traditions had been cut short by the overpowering experience of the Mahdist regime (1881–1898), which must have severed all links with a more distant—and possibly less disturbed—past. In some tribes the tradition of past movements or previous places of settlement are summarized in one sentence: 'We have always lived here.'

Although the Nuba exhibit distinctiveness in relation to Nilotic and Arab cultural traditions that dominate the surrounding countryside, they also demonstrate great discrepancies among themselves. Aside from the "bewildering complexity" of languages (Nadel, 1947:2), which Stevenson (1984:8–9) classified as ten, along with upwards of fifty linguistic subgroups and dialects, Nadel (1947:1) claimed "over fifty different ethnic groups."[4] Part of this ethnographic quandary resulted from the promise of sanctuary, albeit only partially realized, offered by the Nuba Mountains' terrain. The very problem thus lies in the tumultuous history of the Kordofan plains as witnessed by the many incursions, which succeeded over the centuries in rolling back various plains communities to what is now commonly known as the Nuba Mountains. As noted by MacMichael (1967:1):

> In the earliest days and for thousands of subsequent years the ancestors of the Nuba probably held the greater part of this country (Kordofan), excepting the northernmost deserts. Beaten back by other races that ruled the Nile banks in successive generations, or by tribes from the interior, and finally by the nomad Arabs, the Nuba have now retired to the mountains of Southern Kordofan (Nuba Mountains).

The history of the Nuba, then, is a chronicle of alien intrusion, enslavement, and impoverishment.

Various theories abound on the origin of the present-day inhabitants of the Nuba Mountains. Suffice it to say "that the 'ethnic type' presented by many of the Nuba today was formerly more widespread in the Sudan" (Stevenson, 1984:32). Most agree that many of the Nuba groups are descendants of Nubians pushed south[5] by the incoming penetration of Muslim groups claiming Arab ancestry, but the exact relationship between these homonymous groups remains a matter of controversy. Others, like the Shatt, are purportedly a branch of the Daju, who migrated from Darfur before reaching their present locations by way of the Nile valley near Malakal. What is at stake, however, is whether "there exists something like a 'Nuba culture', a cultural make-up common to all the various groups," notwithstanding the "diversity of the Nuba hill tribes" (Nadel, 1947:3). Or, is this perceived commonality merely a kind of "regional stamp or cachet" (Stevenson, 1984:11), forged in historical exigencies?

Without question, the name Nuba gained popularity as a pejorative label affixed by Arabic speakers to all black Africans from the Sudanic belt. Burckhardt (1822:279), from his travels in the early 1800s, informs us that "The name Nouba is given to all Blacks coming from the slave countries south of Sennar." Other accounts indicate that Arab sources from the ninth century A.D. used the words Nuba and Sudan (literally meaning blacks) interchangeably and that the "term *al-Nuba* became almost synonymous with 'black slaves'" (Hassan, 1967:8–45). The term Nuba, then, did not originate among the various Nuba groups but is an alien conception derived externally. Nuba "commonality," in all probability, arose in necessary contradistinction to Arabs, and any feeling of "Nubahood" assumes a response to mutual understandings acquired vis-à-vis Sudanese Arabs of the region and not from any strongly held traits among Nuba groups.[6]

Further difficulties arise when attaching tribal labels to specific Nuba groups. One of the difficulties in the concept of tribe stems from the use of tribal names as if they retained a meaning constant through time (O'Fahey and Spaulding, 1974:318). Tribe, in and of itself, is essentially a product of European colonialism that brought with it "certain ways of reconstructing the African reality" (Mafeji, 1971:253). This poses a sense of ambiguity because while the concept may be fixed, that which it intends to demarcate is fluid and dynamic. In light of this, throughout my discussion I will use the Arabic word for tribe. The Arabic word *gabila* is usually translated as tribe, but as Ahmed (1976) points out, affinity offers a closer approximation. This way the phrasing of tribal meaning shifts from the ideological mechanisms of "natural" or immutable statements to socially constructed facts.[7]

Contemporary names of various gabila usually reflect place location such as Ghulfan, Miri, or Dilling. The names may also merely mean people as Shatt (saat in the local language) or the Nyima's name for themselves, *ama mede kolat*, people of the seven hills. Currently, when a Nuba is asked about his or her ethnicity the response will vary according to whom asks the question. An Arab, for example, will elicit the response of Nuba, while a Nuba will respond to another Nuba with the Jebel from which they come. The point being, gabila (as with ethnicity, race, etc.) must be tied into larger historical trends before its saliency can be comprehended. And in the case of the Nuba, "It is only very recently.... that some sense of a common 'Nuba-ness' has developed," or that specific gabila names have emerged (Stevenson, 1984:11).

Aside from the respective Nuba groups that inhabit the region, there are a number of important Arab groups. In many respects, the categories *Arab* and Nuba are generic terms used to designate inhabitants of what is now called the Nuba Mountains and their respective homelands, such as

Dar Hamar (plains area) and Dar Nuba (mountains area). Beginning in the sixteenth century the region witnessed the southward expansion of the Baggara cattle nomads, Hamar and Messiriya camel nomads, and others such as the Hawazma, associated with the expansion of the Funj. Later incursions by Baggara horsemen from the west and northern *jallaba* (merchants) in the nineteenth century saw the influx of even more groups. In addition, Arab also embraces northern and western administrative officials and military personnel, appearing first with the arrival of the Anglo-Egyptian Condominium, including the Shaigiyya and Shendi. It is important to remember that many Arabs, such as the Baggara, did not always fare well, as is evident during Turkish rule throughout much of the 1800s. They, too, have been victims of historical forces that served to divide Arab from Nuba in the dictates of enmity, giving "cultural" meaning to the distinction of tribe (and ethnicity). Lastly, other groups, such as the *fellata* and *khawajat*, also played significant roles in the area.[8]

Tributary Status and Institutionalized Insecurity

The history of the Nuba Mountains is essentially the history of a buffer territory and labor reserve, first the prey of its eastern, then of its western, and finally of its northern neighbors. Debate centers around the existence of a "state form of government among the Nuba in precolonial times" (Spaulding, n.d.:1). The majority opinion argues against any form of state in its entirety, pointing to "the great lack of firm tribal traditions of history, origins, migrations, etc." (Stevenson, 1984:31; also Seligman, 1932; Nadel, 1947; and Baumann, 1987). Against this interpretation, a second view contends that the Nuba Mountains was appended to one or another of the pre-Islamic monarchies of the northern Nile or, more specifically, to the Funj kingdom of Sinnar via the provincial governate of Kordofan and the tributary fiefdom of Tegali (Spaulding, 1985a). As Spaulding demonstrates, employing documents from eighteenth-century Sinnar, the Nuba operated under some form of state hegemony and have, for a long time, been forced to operate within the context of a "law-abiding, tax-paying society" (Spaulding, 1985b).

It is the nature of that contact, however, which is of interest and more importantly, the effect that contact exerted on the consequent economic organization of respective Nuba groups. Where Spaulding is correct in his major assertion, doubts cloud the matter of degree of incorporation into the formal administrative structure of the state. In the main, the Nuba Mountains was never directly incorporated into a state structure in terms of direct rule but served as an adjunct in multifarious tributary systems.[9] The Funj governor of Kordofan, for example, received tribute from and conferred investiture upon rulers of various Nuba groups.[10] The kingdom of Tegali did, however, extend direct rule over a wide number of Nuba communities, but the extent of that dominance as well as its quality remain problematic.[11] Moreover, Tegali was not always able to retain its independence, but found itself appended periodically to Sinnar in the east. With the usurpation of Kordofan by the Sultanate of Darfur in 1790, that hold became even more precarious, with a number of Nuba communities rebelling against a weakened Sinnar and a besieged Tegali.

Popular legend has it that Tegali, in the extreme northeast of the Nuba Mountains, was founded by a migrating holy man of the *ja'alyyin* by the name of Mohammed al-Ja'ali, who came preaching Islam around the year 1530. The chief of Tegali, impressed by the stranger's piety and wisdom, granted him the right to settle there, and eventually he married the chief's daughter, thereupon establishing the dynasty of Tegali kings known as Ja'ali (Elles, 1935:7–8). The tradition of the coming of a "Wise Stranger" who founds a dynasty, however, is not unknown to Sudanic Africa and is the basis for a number of such occurrences.[12] Though the initial chronicle of the origins of the Tegali kings may lodge in folklore, there is no doubt that the royal lineage of Ja'ali existed for at least twelve generations and that Islam was introduced into Tegali some three to four hundred years ago (Stevenson, 1963:10). At this time, Islam made important inroads into the Nuba Mountains, especially with the arrival of Islamic teachers as visitors or settlers in Tegali (Stevenson, 1963:10).

The wealth of the Tegali kings, as with the Funj kings and Darfur sultans, depended, in part, on apportioning trade concessions or trading zones to select individuals in return for a share of the profits,[13] and from the exaction of tribute from communities in their domain (Stevenson, 1984; Spaulding, 1985; and Kapteijns and Spaulding,[14] 1988). Kapteijns (1984), writing on the organization of trade in precolonial western Sudan, distinguishes three levels of exchange: local barter or face-to-face interactions based on reciprocity in goods or services; regional trade, partially employing limited-purpose currencies and exerting greater state control; and foreign or international commerce stringently controlled by the suzerain. International trade was inevitably restricted to royally sanctioned bearers of license in return for first right of refusal and a monopoly of certain goods like firearms (Kapteijns and Spaulding, 1988). Transactions were conducted in kind and consisted primarily of luxury items of local provenance, including gold, ivory, iron, leather, civet, and, above all, slaves. In the regional spheres of exchange, noblemen assessed market user fees in concordance with established convention, part of which passed upward to the king as tribute. Trade practices generally excluded commoners, in part by strictly enforced sumptuary laws,[15] but also because of the danger inherent in travel. Commoners who left the comforting confines and security of the community frequently found themselves "subject to robbery and enslavement" (Kapteijns and Spaulding, 1988:61).[16]

The general stipulation governing tribute commanded payment in locally available goods suitable for export, although cattle and slaves were of primary importance from the dominated areas within the Nuba Mountains.[17] In addition, tribute in the form of labor obligations was not unknown. For example, nafir labor could be mobilized to fulfill labor obligations that the subjects owed their rulers, as in the case of gold mining at Tira Mandi (Dunn, 1921). The cooptation of this type of communal labor for labor projects resulted in the Sudan Arabic proverb: "The *nafir* without a master accomplishes nothing" (Spaulding, 1985b). A proverb like this would not have been coined in the strict sense of nafir as communal reciprocity and, therefore, points to this second function. Tribute was not always delivered regularly (Stevenson, 1984:41), but as Spaulding (1984:98) points out, recalcitrant individuals were subject to immediate enslavement, while uncooperative groups attempting to avoid submission were hunted down until they sought protection from the lord.

Within any type of tributary system the ruling class must be able to assert its authority over its subjects, preferably through nonviolent institutions but certainly by force, if required, and to protect its domain from external aggressors. Once the power to enforce its rule is found deficient, the procurement of tribute (as well as the protection of trade) becomes problematical. This is particularly true for many of the Nuba groups, whose position within the orbit of various tributary kingdoms proved intractable at best. Historical accounts reveal many attempts to evade payment, either through direct confrontation or escapement to the jebels. In order to safeguard their interests, then, the kingdoms depended upon their armies, armies inevitably comprised of slaves (*jihadiyya*).[18] According to MacMichael (1967:8), Sinnar captured many of its slaves in southern Kordofan, especially from Dair and Tegali and "almost entirely recruited its army therefrom." While the truth of this is difficult to ascertain, the traveler Bruce (1873:317) describes the sight of Nuba soldiers ringing Sinnar city: "These are all Nuba soldiers of the Mek of Sinnar; and the villages which they occupy at a distance of four or five miles." He further states that "settlements and provisions (are) given to them." Slaves were also important for other activities, primarily domestic activities in royal houses and, to a more limited degree, in production (usually agricultural estates).

A climate of institutionalized insecurity[19] blanketed the Nuba Mountains as a result of slave raids. Not only were slaves hunted by the government,[20] but also by the Nuba themselves. Government policy directly facilitated this latter activity by allowing, even encouraging, payment of taxes in the form of slaves and cattle, most easily, if not exclusively, obtained by raiding one's neighbors. Consequently, many Nuba communities engaged in low-grade internecine warfare. Not only did this have the effect of demographic dislocation, but it also fractured the Nuba, further impeding regional political organization. Hence, it is not surprising for travelers of the day to describe the Nuba as living in isolated communities distrustful of all from the "outside world." Moreover, agricultural and pastoral production declined among particularly hard-hit communities, instigating even more raids. Nevertheless, the presence of "vast piles of simsim" stored "some 10 miles north of Jebel Ghulfan" indicates that at least some Nuba groups "could cultivate at such a distance from their own homes" (Sagar, 1922:140; also Stevens, 1912). Further deprivations and discontinuities awaited the irruption of the Turkiyya and the onrush of colonialism.

The Rise of Slavery and Institutionalized Terror

Essentially, these precolonial kingdoms were feudal-based social formations that augmented their treasuries through trade and taxation in the form of tribute. Trade, and the tribute that helped enable it, allowed nobility to wallow in conspicuous consumption, redistribute goods to favored vassals,[21] and/or engage in yet more trade. Darfur, like the other kingdoms, also participated in trade and, in many ways, this (as with the others) served to undergird its sense of social superiority and moral rectitude in the conduct of its affairs. Of interest for the Nuba Mountains, however, was the rising importance of a certain item necessary to Darfur's economy, namely slaves. For this reason, Darfur impinged on the Nuba Mountains and, by 1790, supplanted the Funj as the predominant power within the region. As previously mentioned, slavery existed in Tegali and the Funj, but its use in production remained minimal and was largely confined to an area surrounding their respective capital cities. In the northern stretches of the Funj there were only "about 4,500 slaves between Wadi Halfa and the Fourth Cataract, amounting to approximately 4 percent of the total population" (Spaulding, 1982:9).

The expansion of the estate system within Darfur greatly added to the demand for slaves. For example, "Sultans Tayrab (1751–85) and Abd al-Rahman (1785–1801) settled slaves on agricultural estates near their capitals, at Dar Fongoro, and on Jabal Marra and its foothills" (Lovejoy, 1983:113–14). Estates were also allotted to court officials, wealthy jallaba, military commanders, and important religious leaders. The need for slaves proved great, especially among the hereditary royalty: "Sultan Ali Dinar is said to have employed five hundred women (slaves) simply to bring water to his palace" (O'Fahey, 1985:88–9). In addition, the ruling elite of Darfur were firmly entrenched as suppliers of slaves to merchants, with one result being that Darfur became a major supplier of slaves to the Egyptian market.

All of these developments boded poorly for the inhabitants of the Nuba Mountains. The primary hunting grounds for slaves lay on a path that traversed the Nuba Mountains. Slave raids were conducted with military precision by horse-mounted cavalry, sweeping in across the plains, striking fear into the hearts of the unfortunate victims. Over time, as O'Fahey (1985:85) notes, "Within this inner arc relations between raided and raiders were to become in some cases stabilized and formalized into tributary status." Once again, various Nuba communities warred on weaker neighbors in order to meet demands derived externally. They were also the subjected to seizure by various Baggara groups who had begun drifting into the area from the 1800s onward in search of suitable grazing lands and security. Although references to slaves captured in the Nuba Mountains are rather scanty in earlier times, accounts of incidences increase during this and later colonial periods. The real extent of

geographic and demographic dislocation associated with slavery, however, was to await the period called the Turkiyya.

This period of "Oriental mercantilism" operated in much the same way
as did its European counterpart during its initial period of capitalist development (Amin, 1976:322). It helped lay the groundwork for rationalizing
the economy by minimizing trade restrictions, popularizing the use of
currency, privatizing land (though not in all areas), and expanding production for the market. This brand of mercantilism, nonetheless, failed to
fully rationalize the economy because they remained unconcerned over
the ways goods were actually produced. And besides, the real intent of
Turkish rule remained the crude extraction of resources in the most expe-
ditious way. As a result, the merchant (jallaba) ascended to the helm of the
Sudanese economy and cared little how that wealth was forthcoming, as
long as they were not fettered in its pursuit. As Spaulding (1982:18) cor-
rectly points out, the jallaba did not venture south out of some innate
desire for trade, but from the very objective socioeconomic conditions set
in motion by the Mohammed 'Ali and the Turko-Egyptian empire in 1821.

The resources of eastern Sudan were certainly not unknown to
Mohammed 'Ali's Egypt, as the Mediterranean trade had been ongoing
periodically for centuries. An image of the superabundance of gold and
slaves drove 'Ali to invade the Sudan in his desire to attain a measurable
degree of independence from the Ottoman suzerain in Istanbul (Hill,
1959:7–8; Holt and Daly, 1988:47–9).[22] One set of resources was to
provide the requisite finances, the other to man his army. Ultimately,
the abundance of wealth proved somewhat disappointing, as did his
ambition to create a large-standing army in Egypt comprised of foreign-
born, Egyptian-trained Nilotic Sudanese. Still, Mohammed 'Ali managed to unleash a reign of terror throughout the Sudan, but a reign
especially brutal in the Nuba Mountains (and southern regions).

The slave trade dramatically expanded during the first twenty years
of Mohammed 'Ali's rule. Pursuant to the viceroy's desire to create a
jihadiyya, large numbers of slaves were captured through regularized
raids by government forces and later in the southern zones through the
services of Sudanese, European, and Turkish concessionaires. Additional
slaves were also collected through a heavy tax burden levied by the
Turkish administration, which commissioned taxes in slaves due to the
absolute paucity of specie.[23] Pallme (1844:39), in his *Travels to Kordofan*,
describes the results of this practice:

When a village has nothing left wherewith to pay its taxes, it is obliged to find a certain number of slaves, who are drafted as recruits into the various regiments, or publicly sold…the government receives these slaves at a value of 150 to 300 piasters…a head; children at 30 piasters, or more; but always below the market price, in order that Mehemed Ali, the great slave merchant, may gain something by the bargain, at the expense of his oppressed subjects.

Such procedures magnified feelings of resentment towards the foreign intruders and eventually undermined their rule.

After securing northern Sudan, 'Ali sent his son-in-law, Mohammed Bey Khusraw, the *Defterdar*,[24] south to conquer Kordofan and the sultanate of Darfur. A contingent of "4000 cavalry and infantry, ten pieces of artillery, and about 1000 Bedouins" accompanied the Defterdar and enabled him to sack El-Obeid and bring all of Kordofan under his heel, with the exception of the Nuba Mountains (MacMichael, 1967:19; also see Petherick, 1861:272–75). Initially, the southernmost administrative boundary extended to Jebel Kadiro, approximately due east of Dilling (MacMichael, 1967; Stevenson, 1984). Turkish expeditions met intense resistance from Tegali and Dair; nonetheless, Turkish force managed to capture a number of slaves. Irruptions into the jebels were no longer an intermittent occurrence and came as no surprise. Both Petherick (1861) and MacMichael (1967:24) report that Dair "was never subdued though assaulted time and time again" and that its inhabitants "lived by robbery and raided successfully as far north as Melbis (near El-Obeid)." Holroyd (1839) spoke of Tegali as independent, but by 1863 Petherick (1869) says that Tegali had succumbed to a loose tributary status paid in gold and slaves. The Turks were thus able to effect a tributary relation with Tegali, but the latter resisted payment whenever the opportunity arose and eventually ceased altogether. The establishment of tributary systems in the Nuba Mountains, as elsewhere, was never given priority; confiscation rather than revenue marked the true intent, and this could be accomplished through more direct means (Holt and Daly, 1988). From the outset the unrelenting acquisition of slaves assumed primary importance, as witnessed by a letter from 'Ali to the Defterdar in September of 1825: "You are aware that the end of all our effort and this expense is to procure negroes. Please show zeal in carrying out our wishes in this capital matter" (Holt and Daly, 1988:45). The Nuba Mountains was thus steadily drawn into the ambit of an externally located power, whose insatiable demand for slaves seemed unlimited (see Bjorkelo, 1989).

The Turkish government's ability to amass slaves was remarkably successful but created unforeseen difficulties in the coordination of slave hunting with the government's ability to create new regiments. Consequently, redundant slaves were used to pay the salaries of the distressed Turkish troops in-kind. Pallme (1844:306) reports:

> The Viceroy of Egypt institutes annually, once or twice in the course of the year, an actual hunt in the mountains of Nuba...and seizes upon a certain number of the negroes by stratagem or force, in order to pay the arrears due to his troops in Kordofan with these unfortunate men, instead of with ready money, or to increase his revenues by the sale of his fellow creatures.... The burden of this sanguinary fate falls most heavily upon the miserable inhabitants of the Nuba mountains.

He further adds that in 1825 approximately 40,000 slaves were captured and that by 1839 this number swelled to 200,000[25], notwithstanding the thousands taken by the Baggara and bought by jallaba. Similar observations were recorded by Holyroyd (1836:177) in El-Obeid upon the successful return of a slave-hunting party: "The handsome women were sold for the harems of the Turks and Arabs; the able bodied men were placed in the ranks; the decrepit of both sexes, the pregnant females, and young children, were allotted to the soldiers in lieu of money to the amount of moiety of their arrears."[26] Since the soldiers had no need of slaves and could scarcely more than afford themselves, they immediately sold them, adding to the already swollen public market.

Aside from cattle, there was little else of immediate value in the Nuba Mountains, with the limited exception of honey, ivory, and civet. Cattle were obtained to augment Egyptian herds that had been depleted by epizootics and warfare, for leather, and to provision the occupying troops. Gold deposits, on the other hand, at Jebel Sheibun (and Fazughli) showed to be more fable than fact, a point made evident by European experts urged on by 'Ali. Iron prospects fared slightly better and, by 1829, iron was used to make nails for the government shipyard at Manjara on the White Nile. An attempt to improve its exploitation with the aid of English iron founders was short-lived, as six of eight died within two months of reaching Kordofan (Hill, 1959:56).

The Baggara also raided for slaves, partly for personal use but primarily to replenish stock paid to the government in tax, a practice in which they were given a free hand to raid in the Nuba Mountains.[27] These activities initiated certain changes in the socioeconomic organization of the Baggara. Territorial claims (dar) in the Nuba Mountains were quickly established, demarcating various Baggara enterprise zones under the leadership of a type of warrior aristocracy (Amin, 1976:323). Within these respective domains many Nuba communities paid in slaves for protection, leaving the Baggara to raid other areas. Making matters worse, the raiders not only seized members of Nuba communities, but inevitably burned crops and frequently villages too. Accounts by Stevens (1912) and McLoughlan (1962:365) claim that the Nuba, in their misery, were even forced to sometimes "sell on the open market their own unprotected people such as orphans, widows, and other destitutes."

As previously mentioned, the Nuba prior to this time could be found cultivating the plains and grazing their livestock, albeit increasingly closer to the jebels as the pace of slave raids quickened. A further development was also evident in the reorganization of Nuba agriculture into "ribbon farms," elongated plots arranged side by side. This afforded better protection, as the farmers could present a relatively compact line posed between any raiding party and the village. Weapons and hoes could be used interchangeably, according to the prevailing conditions. It was also at this time that the conventional image of Nuba agricultural holdings into far farms, near farms, and house gardens apparently developed. Slave raids also increased the power of male elders since it fell under their purview to coordinate protection as well as organize their own raiding parties, especially after the shift from small-scale intermittent raids to well-organized regularized raids. In terms of this latter activity, the more important elders certainly received a larger share of any plunder. In addition, elders could always deepen their dominance by selling recalcitrant juniors to passing jallaba or Baggara.

Nadel (1947:55–6) discusses the incorporation of captives into respective Nuba kinship groups and states that "In most groups slaves, whether they had been captured or purchased, were readily adopted into the family and became fully fledged members of the kinship group." He does note that other groups, such as the Nyima and Dilling, did acquire slaves as a "capital investment;" that is, "wealth as potential labour." The truth of these claims is difficult to assess. Meillassoux (1983:51) points out that since the law of large numbers does not operate within small "domestic" groups, sex and age ratios must be balanced through conscious policy. These may include circulation of women between allied groups or through raiding, incorporation of sons-in-law without bride-price, and the introduction of prisoners or captives (p.51). Baumann

(1987:77) also suggests the integration of slaves into kinship networks in his study of Miri Bara but clearly understood the difficulty in obtaining useful information: "Geneological enquiries often had to be abandoned for a respectful acceptance of people's sensitivities, when the questions asked would have led to admission of unfree descent." This in itself reveals, more by omission, the opprobriousness of slave ancestry. One informant quietly told me of instances of marriage to captives in his village, but when pressed to discuss his own family, he loudly complained of a bout of rheumatism, demanded aspirin to supplicate his pain, and promptly feigned sleep. He never talked about it again.

Outside of the confines of the Nuba Mountains in northern Sudan the issue is much more straightforward. Questions of labor need is not confused with kinship, gainsaying those who wish to paint a more benign image of African slavery (see Kopytoff and Meirs; 1977). Meillassoux (1973, 1983, 1991) argues that this confuses rhetoric with reality, labor exploitation with its rationalization, and that slaves were systematically nonkin. For example, in order to ideologically reenforce their subordinant class location, slave names were frequently derogatory—Good Morning and Leather Sack (Burckhardt, 1822:293) or Sea of Lusts, Patience is a Blessing, and Increase in Wealth (Spaulding, 1982:12).

Initial Turkish efforts directed slaves towards external markets, most notably Egypt and Arabia. Events further afield also strengthened the demand for slave labor within Egypt, such as the global cotton boom lasting through the American Civil War. With the injection of substantial numbers of slaves into the Sudanese market and consequent to the government's removal of restrictions on slave owning after 1840, most slaves were retained for internal use. Coupled with the privatization of agricultural lands, most pronounced in the riverain areas and Gezira (though not in the Nuba Mountains), a rapid upsurge in agricultural slavery occurred.[28] By the close of the nineteenth century, McLoughlan (1962:361) suggests that slaves performed the bulk of all agricultural activities in the north and comprised one third of the population. Clarifying the central importance of slavery to the Sudanese economy, Spaulding (1982:13) draws attention to speculators who played the slave market in hopes of turning a profit. This would hardly have transpired in times past.

If slavery helped create a new order, it also facilitated the meteoric rise of an indigenous merchant class, the jallaba. The migration of north-

ern merchants to the southern slave-catchment zones was a direct out-
growth of the socioeconomic changes affecting the north. These individuals came to places like the Nuba Mountains in hopes of securing a
fortune with which to return to their homes and resume their lives.[29]
Many, to be sure, remained in the south, having established profitable
trading concerns, though certainly al-Zubayr Pasha Rahma Mansur (a
Ja'li from the north) best exemplifies this. Ten years after beginning
slave trading in Bahr al-Ghazal, he became virtual ruler of the province.
Concomitant to the weakening of Turkish governance and its usurpation in Sudan by Europeans,[30] pressures were brought for "free trade"
and, by the mid-1840s, various state monopolies had been abolished,
further encouraging the flow of potential traders south.

The jallaba also functioned as conduits of "manufactured" goods to
Nuba communities, primarily iron blades for axes and hoes, beads,
knives, spear tips, and rifles. The Nuba's need and ability to trade was
inexorably connected to the incessant warfare enveloping the jebels.
Weapons were essential for village defence—protection from Turkish
or Baggara raiding parties and from other Nuba groups as well. The
dominant "currency" of this trade involved slaves and cattle. Some Nuba
groups, like the Kadugli, Miri, Moro, and Nyima, redoubled and regularized their raids on weaker neighbors in order to maintain an adequate
supply of weapons and, thus, avoid being enslaved themselves. In fact,
Nadel (1947:393) characterized the Nyima slave raids as very efficient
and ruthless. Trade with the jallaba also expedited the extension of the
infamous shayl system, a practice that exists to this day. The point is,
the slave trade affected everyone, but certainly none had as great an
economic stake in it as the jallaba or, though certainly to a lesser degree,
the war-leaders, Nuba and Baggara, whose power developed in response
to exigencies of turbulent times. So, when the Turkish administration,
acting under British pressure, attempted to suppress the slave trade, the
time was ripe for a "deliverer"

The Mahdist uprising began in 1881 and "was particularly appropriate for 'the oppressed' for situations in which they have not only become conscious of oppression but are willing to respond to a movement
which seems to offer a way out" (Hodgkin, 1971:110). Many reasons
are offered for this phenomenon but each essentially concerns the undermining of Turkish authority by powerful slave interests like al-Zubayr,
which created a power vacuum; dependency on foreign creditors, such

as the British and French in financing the Suez Canal; and the super-
exploitation of the Sudanese themselves. The movement was led by a
certain Mohammed Ahmed ibn 'Abdullah, who, in 1881, proclaimed
himself the Expected Mahdi, the divine leader chosen by god at the end
of time to bring justice and equity to humankind. He largely drew his
followers (*ansar*) from three disgruntled sections of the population: (1)
religious and pious men, who largely believed in the eschatological
purpose of the Mahdi's mission; (2) those harboring "practical grievances," such as the "Ja'aliyyin and Danaqla of the dispersion," who had
been pushed south to the fringe of Arab Sudan and came to depend,
directly or indirectly, on the slave trade; and, (3) Baggara nomads, who
neither claimed religious piety nor held political grievances but merely
distrusted all forms of centralized government, which may be summed
up simply as "Kill the Turks and cease to pay taxes" (Holt, 1961:79).
The Baggara, however, formed the backbone of the Mahdi's army under their able leader 'Abdallahi ibn Mohammed, who later ruled as the
supreme Khalifa upon Mahdi's death from typhus in 1885 and until the
successful reconquest in 1898. But, if the Mahdist rebellion began as a
nationalist movement, under Khalifa 'Abdallahi it reverted to the quest
for sectarian interests, and the rise of the Baggara aristocracy.

As Stevenson (1984:56) appropriately notes, "The Mahdist rising
meant new problems and troubles for the Nuba, new decisions for some
tribes as to allegiance, and in many cases attacks by Mahdist forces."
The Mahdi began his long march towards Khartoum by way of Jebel
Gadir, located in the remote periphery of southeast Nuba Mountains.
There he gathered his forces and drove towards El-Obeid, the premier
city of Kordofan. The Mahdi managed to strike an uneasy truce with
King Adam Dabbalu of Tegali, who swore an oath not to hinder his
efforts in return for a pledge to leave Tegali unmolested, and he then
proceeded north to attack El-Obeid. Following King Adam's detention
by Khalifa 'Abdallahi and his death in El-Obeid in 1884, however, jebels
Tegali and Dair came under assault by Mahdist forces in their constant
pursuit of slaves, both for the jihadiyya as well as for other uses. Although slaves comprised only 15 to 18 percent of the army during the
Mahdiyya, the dependence of the local population on slaves increased
as "free men" responded to the Mahdi's call of *jihad* and formed the
bulk of labor in agriculture, herding, and domestic work (Nakash,
1988:52).

The legitimacy of the institution of slavery was never an issue during the Mahdiyya, although the enslavement and export of slaves failed to be renewed on the scale it had previously assumed under the Turkish regime (Warburg, 1981:253). Internal demand for slaves remained strong, especially by the military, but constant wars with foreign enemies inhibited the Mahdist regime's ability to acquire them.

(The Mahdist state) fought the Turko-Egyptian army in 1885–86 and again in 1891 along the Red Sea coast; the Ethiopians and the Darfur Sultan between 1887–89; rebellions in Kordofan and Darfur in 1891; the British-supported Italians from Ethiopia in 1893–94; and the Belgians in the southern region in 1894…. By 1896, the British and French governments both dispatched expeditions to seize control of the Nile headwaters (Collins, 1976:5).

Consequently, slave procurement languished in Equatoria and Bahr al-Ghazal, important catchment zones in the south, as well as in other areas. In addition, the Mahdist government maintained rigid control over the slave trade and imposed a strict trade embargo on the transportation of slaves to Egypt, in part to prevent their military usage there.

Mahdist forces did manage to enslave many Nuba, causing further socioeconomic disruption and driving the remaining inhabitants deeper into the jebels. The Nuba were not acquiescent, however, and instances of fierce resistance, though often futile, color the literature. In 1885, jihadiyya troops primarily from Jebel Dair mutinied in El-Obeid, killing the deputy governor and looting the town before fleeing south to Jebel Nimma (a Ghulfan redoubt). Their success proved short-lived. After beating off two attempts to subdue them, the mutineers and their protectors were brutally defeated, with the survivors enslaved or dispersed. Meanwhile, unable to storm Jebel Dair, Mahdist forces traveled south to Talodi, where they conducted "extensive raids on the surrounding neighborhood and captured large numbers of slaves which (were) sent in convoys to Omdurman" (Wingate, 1968:291). These actions, ironically, stirred the Baggara to revolt, due to the perceived infringement on their rights by interlopers engaging in slaving in the area. The Baggara were defeated in a "terrible slaughter," with a loss of approximately 10,000 men (Wingate, 1968:291). But, the real devastation to the Nuba Mountains occurred in 1896, when the Khalifa summoned the bulk of his army to Omdurman. The army slowly made its way, gathering all who lay in its path, "driving men, women, and children before the extended detachments of (the) army, who, to render desertion impossible, destroyed every village and settlement as they passed and left a wake of utter destruction in their train" (Kordofan Handbook, 1912:89, quoted in Stevenson, 1984:60). Entire areas were decimated and peoples scattered in all directions. Particularly hard hit were Ghulfan, Namma, Miri, and Debri. This final assault was to leave an indelible impression. The release of slaves and the disbandment of the jihadiyya, upon the fall of Omdurman, by the reoccupation forces in 1898, nonetheless, proved an important element in the spread of Islam to certain regions of the Nuba Mountains.[31]

The Rise of Capitalism and Institutionalized Security

Foremost among British intentions for reoccupying the Sudan was the need to forestall French designs in extending its own empire from the Atlantic coast to the Indian Ocean. French occupation of the upper Nile waters would have severely handicapped British interests in Egypt, principally in cotton production. In a clever ruse, the British claimed they were merely acting on the Khedive's behalf, thus mollifying French, Belgian, and Italian suspicions over Britain's true territorial interests in conquering the Sudan. This whiff of legality provided all the necessary pretext the British government needed and was further reinforced by the subsequent Condominium Agreement which, theoretically, formed the basis of joint Anglo-Egyptian sovereignty. In reality, the more important administrative positions, such as governor-general,[32] provincial governors, and district commissioners were held by British subjects. Egypt, on the other hand, was forced to absorb the lion's share of the financial burden in meeting Sudan's budget deficits prior to 1913 and loaned money, without interest, to cover development projects (predominately railroad construction). The costs of maintaining the Egyptian army, however, remained Egypt's responsibility until 1924–25, when they rebelled and the British forcefully evacuated the last tangible vestiges of Egyptian rule.[33] Previous to this time, junior-level Egyptian administrators had been interposed between the British rulers and the Sudanese masses, but now were replaced with educated Sudanese, primarily from the north. This legacy was to have a lasting impact on the composition and quality of Sudanese governance.

In the years that immediately followed reoccupation, the need for Sudan to be financially self-sufficient became a pressing colonial priority. The consolidation of Condominium rule required the restoration of Sudan's population and economy to provide goods necessary to Britain's expanding global empire. To this end, Britain developed a rail network[34] to connect important regional centers, initiated new tax regimes, and laid the foundation for the dependency on cotton monoculture (Collins, 1976). Fear over the ready supply of Egyptian long-staple cotton led Lancashire textile manufacturers to found the British Cotton Growing Association (BCGA), with the expressed purpose of promoting cotton production in the Gezira.[35] Concurrent with the Condominium government's need to create an economic basis within the Sudan in order that its administration become self-supporting, a lasting union was formed whereby both the interests of British businessmen (spearheaded by the BCGA) and those of the Condominium government could be satisfied.

The viability of cotton plantations had already been established by an American millionaire entrepreneur, Leigh Hunt, and by 1914, under the aegis of the Sudan Plantation Syndicate (SPS), work was begun to dam the Blue Nile at Sinnar. The project was completed in 1925, creating the world's largest gravity-irrigated cotton plantation—the Gezira Scheme.[36] The Gezira Land Ordinance of 1921 empowered the government to turn proprietors into tenants, whose management came under the SPS. But, in order to keep the "wages-bill" down, it was mandatory that a portion of the tenancy be set aside for sorghum cultivation, ensuring that tenants would meet their own basic food requirements. Nonetheless, as the Gezira Scheme expanded, a secure supply of seasonal labor (to the Gezira and elsewhere) became a chronic problem. This was partially alleviated through British policy, which loosened immigration laws to allow a large influx of West Africans, including Hausas, pushed out by the British conquest of northern Nigeria and the subsequent breakup of the Fulani sultanates, and others such as Chadians. As a Sudanese notable remarked to Wingate: "Allah took away our slaves, but sent us the Fellata" (Annual Sudan Reports, 1909:55, quoted in Warburg, 1981:266).

The development of Britain's capacity to accumulate wealth was delimited by the wide variety of production forms found in divergent parts of the Sudan. Hence, solutions in one area were not always amenable to others, including the Nuba Mountains.[37] Labor acquisition and its control proved a formidable task, rendered more so if slave labor was to be eschewed in the immediate future. Sudan, after all, was not India, where labor was abundant and land scarce, but the opposite, multiplying the difficulty in creating a ready supply of labor. The various land ordinances (1899, 1905, and 1921) both reinforced rights of private ownership (a trend begun earlier) and accorded legal authorization for the state expropriate land, but still failed to create sufficient labor supplies.[38] Other strategies remained to be devised. Moreover, dependence on West Africans was not always judicious policy because, as "outsiders," they posed additional sources of ethnic and nationalist unrest.[39] "Free" labor had to be coerced by other means.

The downfall of the Mahdist State thus posed a particular problem for the British—how to balance the abolition of slavery with an acute labor shortage. Population estimates in 1903 show that, in Kordofan alone (north and south), the population during Mahdist rule decreased from 1.8 million to 550,000, with 600,000 succumbing to disease and 650,000 to warfare (McLoughlin, 1962:387).[40] In addition, "Before the Condominium," writes Daly (1986:231), "the economy of the Sudan was based upon slavery." Slavery was of critical importance along the Niles and, in general, for tending the herds and growing food for the nomads (Daly, 1986). O'Fahey (1985:95) alleges that "it is possible that the cattle and camel herders of Dar Fur and Kordofan were more nomadic in the 19th century and before than in recent years and that slavery was a crucial factor in this change." The solution advanced by the British thus reflected a strong sense of pragmatism and a complete disregard for their own moral pronouncements.[41] Formal policy "decried slavery, took some steps to root out the trade, but simultaneously upheld and even enforced the continuation of domestic slavery" (Daly, 1986:231; also see Khalafalla, 1982).[42]

Initially, then, Condominium rule accommodated slavery, preferring to regard slaves as "Sudanese servants."[43] Above all else, reopening the Sudan to investment suffused its policies which, in turn, necessitated minimizing internal turbulence. To this end, British machinations focused on institutionalizing "security" to provide a stable context for capital accumulation. In this light, the immediate abolition of slavery proved impractical.[44] In the Nuba Mountains, British administrators were confronted with the twin dilemmas of facilitating surplus extraction with the abolition of the slave trade.[45] Table 3.1 gives some indication of the ambivalent nature of British attempts to suppress the slave trade.

TABLE 3.1
Number of Individuals Arrested and Convicted in Slave
Cases in the Nuba Mountains, 1905–1913

	1905	1906	1907	1908	1909	1910	1911	1912	1913	TOTAL
Arrested	17	18	6	—	10	22	23	8	8	112
Convicted	16	5	4	—	6	15	16	8	6	76

Source: Compiled from McLoughlan (1962:388).

This ambivalency probably stemmed, in part, from the fact that it was difficult to retain Nuba and Baggara participation in a commercial market, however limited, when an important medium of exchange—slaves—was no longer accepted. In addition, isolation from being remanded to the jebels eroded social relations between various Nuba Mountain communities and led to a continued pattern of communal warfare, the intent of which was to settle disputes and to enrich the community in both animals and people. According to Ibrahim (1985:12), the government tended to avoid interfering in "inter-tribal quarrels," unless they directly posed a threat to governmental authority in the region.[46] This divisive policy helped preclude a united front against the Condominium government. Subsequently, initial government policies chose to ignore slavery while stepping up the exaction of taxes.

Certainly too, British racism cannot be discounted. Perhaps Jackson (1953:94), a political officer during the Condominium, best sums up British attitude: "to have freed all slaves would have meant letting loose upon society thousands of men and women with no sense of social responsibility who would have been a menace to public security and morals."[47] Similar accounts reflect British perceptions of the Nuba Mountains, particularly *Savage Life in Black Sudan,* where the Nuba are characterized as "these queer people" or "(I) came face to face with not only one but a small group of the most repulsive-looking and completely naked savages" (Fife, 1927:55–6 and 218). Mann (1954:39) depicts of the Nuba Mountains, in *Where God Laughed: The Sudan To-day,* as the most primitive area of Sudan and probably of Africa as a whole. Racism's corollary, paternalism, is equally evident in a colonial administrator's role in containing an outbreak of cerebrospinal meningitis:

> The Nuba behaved like badly frightened animals and huddled together around each new victim, the most dangerous thing they could do. In extreme cases we had to

resort to burning their huts to get them into the open.... At that moment I think I realized more clearly than ever before what a worth-while job was ours. At least it steadied my hand to set light to the thatched roof and destroy the home of a poor savage in the interest of his future welfare (Strachan, 1951:267).

Together, racism and paternalism shaped the ideological carapace rationalizing British rule in the Sudan.

The ability to collect taxes is a reflection of the extension of a government's rule. Taxation and "law and order" were thus two sides of the same coin. In the eyes of the assessed, both Nuba and Baggara, taxes were perceived as tribute and, except for the absence of enslavement, were collected in much the same way as had been done in the past. At first, taxes were collected from weaker communities in the Nuba Mountains, those primarily associated with accessible jebels. Ironically, those able to resist paying tribute increased their attacks on other communities with contrived impunity.[48] By 1910, however, British troops were positioned to bring "security" to the Nuba Mountains, a fact made necessary by the intransigence of many Nuba Mountain communities in meeting their imposed tax obligations. For example, after the British succeeded in interdicting Baggara raids on the Nuba, the latter ceased to pay tribute because, for them, it constituted protection money and safeguarding from the Baggara was no longer needed. The Nuba had to be taught the meaning of "civilization" and, as such, the British responded with "measured punitive reprisals." To this end, the British utilized "fiercely repressive means of pacification," freely employing machine guns and artillery, before burning crops and villages (Daly, 1986:129).

Following government military actions, whole villages were forcefully relocated from their aeries to the plains below, and the Nuba's rifles were confiscated, either forcefully or through fines imposed for raiding.[49] In this way, agriculture could be made over into the image of the English yeoman farmer, of small independent farmers selling part of their crops on the market in order to secure those items they were unable to produce themselves. But, in the case of the Nuba Mountains, that item increasingly became cotton[50], and there was no corresponding "free" market. Farmers had to contend with either government monopolies, as with cotton, or with the jallaba and his shayl system. As for independent farmers, they were at once subject to the reformulation of political authority, which envisaged a multitiered system of a *mek* as a paramount chief, an *omda* as an intermediate chief in larger villages, and a *sheikh* in each settlement (Baumann, 1987). Meks were allowed considerable leeway in the conduct of their affairs, so long as they acquiesced to the demands placed on them by the Condominium government. The first was to pay the yearly tribute, which they were entrusted to collect (as well as fines), and the second was to cease raiding for slaves and cattle. In many instances, new patterns of dominance were fashioned and older ones abraded.

Major outbursts of armed resistance to government authority during the first three decades precluded the systematic extension of cotton production into the Nuba Mountains. The first serious challenge to Condominium rule came at Tegali in 1903, followed by other uprisings at Talodi in 1906,[51] Miri in 1915, Nyima in 1917, and jebels Julud, Timayan and Tullishi in 1926 (see Ibrahim, 1985; Jackson, 1955; and Daly, 1986). The institutionalization of security was complete by the end of the 1920s, although isolated instances of banditry continued to plague governmental authorities. In many Nuba communities, banditry became ritualized as a rite of passage. Among the Tira, for example, usual proof of a youth's manhood and marriage eligibility was success in cattle raiding (Ibrahim, 1985:50). In current times, a similar basis for cattle raiding exists, a fact that was related to me by informants in other communities, such as Kalulu. These goods could best be readily obtained by raiding. In addition, spears, guns, and cattle increasingly comprised a large part of the bride price, a necessity that further extended elders' power as recipients of valued possessions. Other artifacts of importance included tobacco, salt, sugar, and tea, also indicative of the growing nexus with the jallaba, as well as of out-migration for wage labor. Finally, any act of successful banditry construed a source of village pride, especially since part of the spoilage was distributed among fellow villagers.[52]

With the cessation of truculence, the government, in conjunction with the Sudan Plantations Syndicate, the Empire Cotton Growing Corporation, the British Cotton Growing Association, and a group of Lancashire textile manufactures, conspired to extend cotton production to selected areas in the Nuba Mountains. Experimental plots during the rainy season of 1924 showed that American type cotton could be grown, and plans were laid to establish a cotton growing industry under the aegis of the Nuba Mountain Cotton Industry (NMCI) (March, 1948:842; Mohammed, 1986:117). The NMCI retained firm control; cotton seeds were distributed free of charge; but farmers could dispose of their crop only to government agents at a predetermined "official price." The NMCI also provided nomads with (cotton) seed cake in order to stimulate cotton cultivation among this segment of the population. Aside from lint cotton, the government's aim was to introduce a cash crop to "supplement people's income and to acquaint the Nuba (and nomadic) people with money."[53] Money went to pay taxes (e.g., poll), with the remainder used to purchase cattle and goats.[54] The NMCI also insisted that cotton production supplement grain-based agriculture, underscoring British intentions to keep wage levels low while ensuring adequate food supplies.

The Nuba Mountains were thus drawn into the world market through the active intervention of the government to facilitate cotton production.[55] Accordingly, the government set up mobile heavy machinery teams to excavate *hafirs* (reservoirs) and to maintain roads. Subsequent promotion of complementary industries points to the depth of British interests. Ginning factories were established at Kadugli, Talodi, Kalogi, Lagowa, Abu Gibeiha, Um Birembitah, and Simieh. Contractors were commissioned to transport the raw cotton to the ginning factories and to store it in the yard. There it was ginned and hauled to the railheads at Simieh or Dibeibat for shipment to Port Sudan. The cotton was then sold at auction to British agents. In addition, the government set up enterprises to manufacture oil, soap, and seed cake from cotton byproducts (see n. 56).

As in other European colonies, the Sudanese were compelled to render payment of taxes in cash, an obligation that necessitated emigration for many inhabitants of the Nuba Mountains.[56] Migrants leaving their local areas usually were soldiers in the army, policemen, railroad guards, and young men searching for employment. Significant portions of the Condominium military and, later, police were comprised of Nuba. It is estimated, for example, that 75 percent of the Tenth Sudanese Battalion and nearly all of the Shendi company were Nuba (Ibrahim, 1985:62). Apart from the construction of Sinnar Dam, the expansion of the Gezira Scheme required large numbers of seasonal workers (Henderson, 1987). Huddleston, Governor of Blue Nile Province in 1924, reasoned that:

> an assured supply of casual labour up to 50,000 men will be required. Local sources of supply will by then have been largely eliminated, and reliance will have to be placed on some Sudan source of supply, for example, the Nuba Mountains.... (National Records Office, Khartoum, Blue Nile Province; cited in Duffield, 1981).

TABLE 3.2
Natives of the Nuba Mountains Passing through Kosti in 1927

District	Men	Women	Children	Total
Dilling	124	6	1	131
Talodi	45	—	—	45
Kadugli	4	—	—	4
Rashad	17	2	1	20
Total	190	8	2	200

The scale of out-migration from the Nuba Mountains reached such an extent that many meks complained of insufficient numbers of able-bodied men left for local cultivation (Ibrahim, 1985:61). In the absence of regular records detailing this phenomenon, Nasr (1971:31), nonetheless, provides a clear indication of the trend (table 3.2).

By 1937, the district commissioner, Western Jebels, estimated the number of migrants from Dilling district alone to be 800 (Nasr, 1971:31). This population drain continues to exert a powerful influence on the course of development in the Nuba Mountains.

Nuba emigration also magnified British worries over the spread of Islam and the Arabization of the Nuba. "Some detribalized Nuba had already been Arabized" says Sanderson (1963:236), "but, in the opinion of British officials, the resulting blend tended to combine the shortcomings of both cultures with the virtues of neither."[57] Essentially, the British wished to stem Islamic and Arabic influence and to provide a bulwark against their further spread to the southern regions.[58] In an effort to curtail Nuba-Arab contact, the government adopted a policy of Indirect Rule and instituted two forms of governance, one to administer Arabs, the other Nuba. From this developed a separate legal system and set of laws, which were continuously modified to meet the exigencies of the day. Subsequently, the Nuba Mountains was proclaimed a Closed District in 1924,[59] in effect closing trade to all but "natives," unless one had a special permit from the authorities, and placing restraints on Nuba migration. Nuba migrants, for example, could be repatriated if unemployed and were encouraged to reside in Nuba "villages," outside areas of employment. With regard to cotton cultivation, it was hoped that this policy might act as a deterrent to further Nuba migration by providing a means to acquire cash (apart from its economic benefit to the government).[60]

Education policy was formulated along the same lines and reflected the urgency to segregate Arab and Nuba students, after the decision to provide pedagogic instruction to the latter in 1920. *Khalwas* (Islamic schools) were left intact and met the educational needs of predominantly Muslim areas. Elsewhere, the administration sought to provide education through the tutelage of the Sudan United Mission and later the Church Missionary Society, predicated on the pattern of missionary education in Southern Sudan. Mission schools, for the most part, failed due to recurrent lack of financial and staffing resources, vacillating government policies,[61] and gross underestimation of Christianity's appeal. In the end, inconsistencies in British policy of separation in the Nuba Mountains unraveled; this is underscored in Nadel's summary (1947:487):

> That we invest them (Nuba *Meks*) with swords and robes of honour, offer them tea in Arab fashion, and encourage them to visit Arab cities or Government offices staffed by Arabs, endorses their own leanings (inclinations towards "assimilation").

There would be no "Christian-inspired Nuba renaissance." It would not be until 1940, however, that government schools in Dilling, Talodi, and Kadugli would admit Nuba students from the rural areas (Sanderson, 1963).

Government policy for the Nuba Mountains was, unfortunately, beset with contradictions that forestalled initiative and blunted reason. Faced with the necessity to coordinate the extraction of Sudan's resources, the isolation of the Nuba proved impractical from the outset. Moreover, the economies of the Nuba Mountains and the rest of Kordofan were ineluctably intertwined through the activities of the jallaba, the transportation network, and the flow of commodities. At its worst, British policy severely restricted economic opportunities for the Nuba vis-á-vis the Arabs by creating an arena of competition, but then withholding the wherewithal to compete. More importantly, many Nuba were squeezed out in the intense struggle for scarce resources by men wielding considerably more influence. The decided lack of opportunities at the village level forced many Nuba to relocate to regional market towns and national centers of commerce. The results of this have had a profound impact on the course of change and the ensuing struggles in the region as a whole.

In the final analysis, the economist P.T. Bauer (1984:90) provides the quintessential apologia for *Pax Britannica* when he writes:

In British India, as elsewhere, colonial conquest had often been accompanied by bloodshed and early colonial rule frequently involved the levy of forced labor. This phase was largely over by the end of the nineteenth century, and by the late nineteenth and early twentieth centuries, British colonial administrations governed firmly but lightly. They did not attempt to control closely the lives and activities of their subjects. Taxation was modest and people enjoyed virtually complete personal freedom, including the freedom to choose their own activities, to move around the country unheeded, and to dispose of their incomes as they wished.

Hiding behind this rhetoric, Bauer fails to fully comprehend the more onerous effects of colonialism—the destruction of communities, the subjugation of people to the narrow concerns of an insular ruling class, and the orientation of economies to benefit foreign interests. This is hardly a laudable position one would choose to champion.[62] In the end, British policy in the Sudan, as Turkish rule before it, encapsulated a callous disregard for the masses of Sudanese.

Old Ways and New Days: Independent Sudan

World War II formally marked the territorial demise of Britain's global hegemony, and this was first felt in the crown jewel of the empire—India. Thereafter, the sun swiftly set on its far-flung dominions, with full political independence accorded to the Sudan on 1 January 1956. Lamentably, little changed for the majority of Sudanese, whose expectations of the benefits of independence fell far short of its reality, especially with regard to the popular jargon espousing a cornucopia of munificence for all to share in once the chimera of colonialism was slain. But, when the echoes of slogans had settled in the dust, foreign capital had simply been reenforced by an indigenous nascent variety. The only problem for struggling Sudanese entrepreneurs was that capital was not sufficiently national enough. As a result, no significant structural changes occurred in the inherited system of economic organization. In short, economic miracles were based on a continued policy of utilization of agricultural resources for export rather than for domestic consumption (table 3.3).

Although the first five-year plan promised diversification and an end to privileged concessions, structural reforms quickly faltered due to vested class interests. Instead, the government adopted a policy of "modernization of traditional agriculture," advancing the use of tractors together with seasonal wage labor. A policy of cheap labor required the

TABLE 3.3
Composition of Exports (as a percentage)

Commodity	1971/72	1980/81
Cotton	58	28
Gum Arabic	8	7
Sesame	8	8
Groundnuts	8	16
Edible Oil	4	3
Oilcake and meal	4	5
Sorghum	2	15
Others	8	18
Total Exports	100	100

Source: IBRD, (1982:17).

continued disjuncture between domestic consumption and production.[63] In the case of the Sudan, no market developed for mass consumption, nor has an internal capital goods sector emerged. Moreover, there are relatively no intraindustrial or intersectoral linkages. "Not more than 6.8% of the agricultural output," write Oesterdiekhoff and Wohkmuth (1983:15), "were processed by the industrial sector despite the latter's bias towards agro-industries." National integration lay prostrate, a problem plaguing Africa and low-income countries in general, as evidenced by table 3.4.

Scarce government monies continued to finance the expansion of capital-consuming, large-scale irrigated cotton schemes in addition to the opening up of vast tracts of land for mechanized rain-fed agriculture under private arrangement. Although the area under cotton grew mea-

TABLE 3.4
Sectoral Composition of GDP (%) in 1984

Country Group	Agriculture	Industry[64]	Services
Sudan	36	14	50
Sub-Saharan Africa	33	27	40
All low-income countries	37	32	31
Industrial market countries	3	36	61

Source: World Bank (1984:59).

TABLE 3.5
Sudan's Foreign Trade, 1960 to 1974

Year	1960	1965	1970	1974
Exports	63.7	68.0	102.2	153.4
Imports	63.0	72.2	108.2	228.3
Difference	+0.7	-4.2	-6.0	-74.9

Source: ILO (1976:29).

surably following 1956, the expansion of state-sponsored and private mechanized schemes was astronomical, increasing from 200,000 feddans to more than five million by 1983 (Affan, 1984:23). The latter, however, amounted to little more than agricultural stripmining, destabilizing vast tracts of land that ultimately invited desertification. Coupled with narrow international and national interests, as well as fluctuating world markets, agriculture stagnated, resulting in increased food deficits, exacerbated terms of trade, and a widening trade gap (table 3.5).

As of 1984, Sudan's external debt was estimated to be in excess of 11 billion dollars, while deficit-financing policies and domestic borrowing pushed the rate of inflation to a rate of 38 percent per annum (Fadlalla, 1986:196). The corresponding average annual growth rate for the Sudan between 1960 and 1982 recorded a growth rate of negative 0.4 percent (World Bank, 1984:57).[65] This picture, however, is currently worsening, with the civil war entering its seventh year. Now, scarcities have become a rule rather than an exception.[66] In addition to sectoral imbalances and stagnation, regional disparities deteriorated, with the Western (especially the Nuba Mountains) and Southern regions suffering the greatest deficiencies respectively (see El-Din, 1983 and Fadlalla, 1986).[67] The central-eastern region (primarily Gezira, the northern riverain lands, and Khartoum areas), however, benefited the most, but these were also the areas most integrated into the global market and from a much earlier date. These areas, as a result, also evidence the greatest economic disparities between classes. Although the creation of wealth was made possible from this connection, prosperity quickly became dominated by a few privileged individuals.

Select groups profited politically and economically from the withdrawal of the British—established gabila and religious leaders, high-level administrators and ranking military officers, and, above all, the jallaba of

northern Sudan.[68] Each stood poised on the eve of independence to manipulate religious, ethnic, and secular symbols—inevitably some combination of Islam, Arabism (and Arabic), and nationalism, but with the latter
defined in relation to the first two. Consequently, many groups were circumscribed in their quest for a political voice and, except for their potential labor power, soon became peripheral to the development process.[69]
Depending on the specific nature of the instituted relation to the Condominium government and the resulting basis of their puissance, each group
promoted different sets of economic interests. Initially, after independence,
they were bound by shared commonalities expressed in the creation of a
state firmly committed to rationalizing the economy. Factional conflicts,
nevertheless, periodically erupted, leading to new economic crises. In the
long run, however, international and state communities have shown themselves to be remarkably resilient in containing the groundswells of discontent voiced by the Sudanese masses.

Gabila leaders drew early political support from colonial rule.[70] The
system of "native administration" instituted under Turkish rule was re-
vived by the British with the Nomads and Shaykhs Ordinance of 1922
and 1927. Gabila leaders were invested with powers that originated outside of the domestic community. More importantly, their authority was
reinforced by a powerful central government. This presented a different
picture, in many cases, than that which operated in previous times. Ba-
sically, gabila leaders were assigned the tasks of collecting taxes, imposing fines on miscreants, adjudicating local disputes, and allocating
land in their communities. In many instances, this protected sphere of
authority led to economic self-aggrandizement. For example:

> It is not unknown for a villager to pay dues to the Shaykh for the privilege of
> tapping (gum Arabic), but a stranger is known to do so. Gum gardens outside the
> boundaries of a village are regarded by custom to be at the disposal of the tribal
> chief who as the agent of the Government is entitled to collect these dues from
> tappers (Bolton, 1948:7).

Numerous gabila leaders in the Nuba Mountains were thus able to translate political positions of authority into economic prominence. In post-
independent Sudan, some were thus able to take advantage of the new
economic opportunities, such as the various agricultural schemes, expanded government employment, and business ventures. Those who
failed to do so were unable to have been relegated to talking of past
power as these roles waned, especially during the rule of Numieri.[71]

Religious leaders benefited similarly under Condominium rule, especially after the decision to rapidly expand cotton production necessitated greater control of agricultural smallholders. Like gabila leaders, support of religious leaders was also crucial to neutralizing local resistance to foreign occupation. Consequently, various religious leaders, such as Sayyid 'Ali al-Mirghani, Sharif Yusuf al-Hindi, and Sayyid 'Abd al-Rahman al-Mahdi, experienced a resurgence in their influence and, more importantly, their economic fortunes.[72] Wealth would eventually be turned into political leverage with which to bend the incipient state to their respective wills. The British permitted Muslim leaders to continue to collect zakat[73] from their adherents and, in the case of some, large landholdings were invested in their hands. For example, the British, seeking to forestall any revival of Mahdism, initially granted al-Mirghani vast lands in the Northern Province, preferring him to Sayyid al-Mahdi for his pro-Egyptian stance and faithfulness during the Mahdiyya. With the onset of World War I and nationalist unrest in Egypt, the British turned to al-Mahdi, bequeathing him substantial lands on Aba Island,[74] raising his stipend from £15 per month to £2,000 per annum, allocating him lucrative wood contracts, and lending large sums of money that were never repaid. Ironically, in their quest to bind these leaders economically to Condominium rule, the British merely succeeded in providing a powerful basis for their political control of large segments of the populace that eventually formed part of a substantial nationalist movement. The real effects of this policy were immediately apparent after independence, as the al-Mahdi and al-Mirghani families quickly rose to political preeminence.

Another group that proliferated under colonial rule was the educated Sudanese civil administrators (and later military officers). The power of this group—called *effendiya*—increased by the mid-1930s, as several of its members acceded to the upper divisions in the administration. Educated primarily at Gordon College (renamed University College of Khartoum and then University of Khartoum), Sudanese civil servants were largely drawn from the leading religious, gabila, and jallaba families from the north. The composition of the effendiya illustrates the immediate and total control northerners held at independence, and it is not surprising that many regions like the Nuba Mountains were ignored in the government's attempts to develop the Sudan. The Nuba Mountains remained a labor reserve and a source of

cheap agricultural commodities, while even basic services continued
to be a distant dream.

Foremost among the powerful groups at the outset of independence
was the jallaba. Trade routes had been established by the jallaba since
the Turkiyya and before and penetrated most areas of the Sudan. During
British rule, however, the jallaba were primarily restricted to intermediary positions unless directly sanctioned by the British, such as the al-
Mirghani and al-Mahdi families. As the oft-quoted writing from Beshir
(1970:32) illustrates:

> that in spite of frequent requests to the contrary, large quantities of "Arab" clothing
> are still being made and sold. Please note that in the future, it is *forbidden* to make
> or sell such clothes...No more Arab clothing is to made from today...This
> order applies to all outside agents and owners of sewing machines (Beshir, 1970:52).

Indicative of the role of the jallaba in 1921, a Sudan directory shows
that of 259 business firms in the Sudan, only 1 was owned by a Sudanese
(Khalafalla, 1981:89). Nonetheless, the jallaba made the Sudan run,
acting as the all-important link between foreign business representatives and the actual producers. Merchants interested in "buying cheap
and selling dear" have been and continue to dominate Sudanese business enterprises. In the Nuba Mountains, the jallaba extended their presence through the provision of weaponry, agricultural, and consumption
goods, at first through the medium of slavery and then, more importantly, through cash or kind. With the increased stress on agriculture
following independence, the jallaba, were thus able, through such time-
proven systems as the shayl, to monopolize the trade network and, thus,
coerce agricultural products from indebted farmers. The jallaba also
opened stores at the village level, providing tea, sugar, salt, cloth, coffee, tobacco, and so on. Not only did this promote increased trade, but it
also widened what were considered to be necessities (as opposed to
luxury goods). For example, coffee in the past was generally considered
a woman's drink and now it is a drink enjoyed by both men and women.

The prominent gabila, religious, administrative, and jallaba leaders
were not discretely separable on the basis of these respective endeavors, rather these individuals tended to coalesce into recognizable class
fractions on the basis of their integration into the economy as well as on
their ideological orientations. A glance at Niblock (1987) reveals the
merging of these individuals into one powerful fraction or another, each

TABLE 3.6
Primary Occupations of Leaseholders of Um Seitat Mechanized Farms

Occupation of Holders	No. of Schemes	Percentage
Merchants	117	58
Pensioners (Civil/Military)	46	23
Civil Servants/Gov't Officials	23	11
Cooperative Societies	7	3
Farmers	4	2
Companies	2	1
Others	4	
Total	203	100

Source: O'Brien, 1980:107.

attempting to control the state and ensure access to its revenue.[75] In the Nuba Mountains, government rule with northern administrators led to its economic control by these groups. Mechanized schemes begun in places like Habila, for example, were quickly dominated by those with connections to the government. According to Affan (1984), Shepherd (1983), and O'Brien (1978), the vast majority of leaseholdings in the schemes went to civil servants, military officers, and jallaba, and not to local farmers (table 3.6).

In fact, local farmers were forced off fertile lands and left to cultivate marginal soils, while pastoralists lost precious grazing lands and frequently found traditional migratory routes blocked. In most instances, leaseholders did not have farm backgrounds but relied on managers and cheap wage-labor. Moreover, the overriding need to keep wages down led to the maintenance of subsistence-oriented agriculture. According to Mohammed (1986:341), "traditional agriculture" accounts for 54 percent of the total agricultural area and 28 percent of major crop production, and, in the Nuba Mountains alone, provides the livelihood of some 380,000 smallholders.

At this juncture it is easy to locate the blame for Sudan's misguided development policies squarely on its leaders, as is often done by practitioners and theorists alike. But, as the Sudanese quickly discovered, independence can be illusive, especially when it concerns economic matters. Various colonial interventions structured the Sudan's economy according to the precepts of rapid resource extraction, minimal expenditures, and low maintenance costs. Redirecting national development, however, in a modern nation-state is costly and depends either on infusions of finance in the short-run or its long-term domestic accretion

Intenational financial institutions were eagerly assisting the Sudanese government, pressing the general prescription of comparative advantage in terms of extractive resources as the best means to achieve economic growth, while maintaining popular support. Within the global context, the World Bank, International Monetary Fund, European Economic Community, U.S. Agency for International Development, Arab Agricultural Development Bank among others view the Sudan as a ready source of cheap agricultural goods and tailor their aid programs to continue the extraction of agricultural commodities.[76] Development was thus directed towards those commodities needed, first by the West and later by the Middle East. Consequently the demands of commercializing agriculture, initiated by earlier colonial regimes, absorbed the interests of the new government. Profits, for those able to secure pump schemes, mechanized schemes, or monopolize agricultural trade were high; unfortunately, few were positioned to reap the benefits (O'Brien, 1978). In the end, the Sudan finds itself pressured by external demands to the detriment of meeting domestic needs. Compounding matters, the Nuba Mountains struggles at the crossroads between northern domination and southern aspirations and thus has been increasingly drawn into a devastating civil war.

Ecological Context and Environmental Degradation

Aside from the environmental degradations wrought by many agricultural practices, especially tractorized farming, climatic fluctuations also contributed to an already declining agricultural productivity. Rain and water supply are crucial to support both crops and animals, as well as to sustain people. Throughout the rainy season, surface water is relatively abundant, replenishing hafirs, filling numerous khors, and raising the water tables. During the dry season, domestic water supply is usually a problem. At this time, water is found in hafirs, springs (seraf) primarily located near jebels, and wells of varying depths. Some khors also retain some water during the dry season, but usually water is obtained in these by digging holes in the bed. Nonetheless, permanent water supplies can be problematical, and this raises the difficulty in its transportation. In some villages it is delivered by lorry (at a cost), but predominantly water is carried in five gallon jerry cans on the heads of women. Nomads, too, face similar difficulties, especially as they find themselves increasingly in competition with sedentary settlements.

Southern Kordofan forms part of the vast savannahs extending across Africa. The plains consist of a variety of fertile soils, ranging from the *goz*, or sandy soils, primarily in the northern reaches, *tin*[77], or black and red cracking clay soils located throughout the plains, and *gardud*, or noncracking compact clays interspersed on the plains, which tend to be impermeable in their "natural" state, and a second variety made up of reddish-brown gritty loam or fine gravel abutting the mountains. The heavy clay soils are the richest and are locally described as *fawa*, cracking clay soils found in depressed areas subject to seasonal flooding or swampiness, and *hadaba*, cracking clay soils that are not fawa. The jebel tops and slopes have little soil and consist mostly of rock, sand, and occasional sandy loams. Most are unsuited to anything but grazing, except for a few, such as Jebel Ghulfan, which has soil on top. The pediments, or gently sloping surfaces at the foot of steep slopes, contain alluvial soils, which are the site of intensive cultivation. In the main, the richness of the soils coupled with adequate summer rains make the area suitable to crop raising and ruminant grazing.

Rainfall, however, has increasingly become a critical factor to the sustainability of the Nuba Mountains. Throughout the period of 1916 to 1978, the mean annual rainfall at the Kadugli station in the southern

TABLE 3.7
Mean Rainfall in mm by 10-Year Intervals at Dilling and Kadugli Stations

Dilling	Mean	Kadugli	Mean
1916–25	628.5	1916–25	701.6
1926–35	690.2	1926–35	777.0
1936–45	713.3	1936–45	782.0
1946–55	631.6	1946–55	751.2
1956–65	635.6	1956–65	763.0
1966–75	519.0	1966–75	637.0
1976–78[79]	726.3	1976–78	734.6
Grand Mean	641.0	Grand Mean	741.0

Source: Government of Sudan, *Draft Report on the Hydrometeorology of South Kordofan Province*, 1979.

Nuba Mountains recorded 741 mm, while Dilling in the north registered 641 mm (table 3.7).[78]

Overall, the southern region receives 13.5 percent more rain than does the north. North of Dilling, the amount of rainfall drops precipitously, increasingly so in recent years. Although rainfall has been relatively stable during this period, the Nuba Mountains, nonetheless, experienced the drought felt throughout the Sahel from 1968 to 1973. The most distinct drought years in Dilling occurred in 1970, 1971, and 1972 and in Kadugli in 1968 to 1970 and 1972 to 1973.[80]

The drought enveloping much of Africa in the early 1980s is well known, with images of swollen stomachs, fly-encrusted eyes, and the walking dead dominating the media around the globe. Personal conversations in the Nuba Mountains confirm the severity of this drought. It led to massive out-migration (many assume permanently, especially given the political climate), especially of young males; decimation of herds; and tremendous human suffering. If calamity can bring people together, it also presents fortuitous opportunities for some. Stories of corruption in "relief" efforts abound: the drivers of lorries carrying sorghum charged villagers to unload precious grain; international relief foodstuffs were sold outright in various markets; gifts of grain disappeared from warehouses; individuals were forced to sell their animals at a mere fraction of their value; and grain was hoarded by merchants in hopes of even higher prices. But, as Tully (1988) makes clear from his study of Dar Masalit, the drought of the 1980s should have come as no surprise in light of the evidence available in the 1970s, which indicated a long-term decline in rainfall. This is readily apparent in the northern, more arid, zones and imparts graver consequences for the fragile ecological balance. Although there have been good years since 1973, the more recent drought supports the theory that some losses of soils and forests is irreversible and that the regeneration of other areas will take decades to accomplish under optimal conditions (Tully, 1988:55).[81]

Table 3.8 indicates the severity of the 1984 drought in both North and South Kordofan, especially during the key agricultural months. The rainfall data for 1987 indicates that the predrought rain levels have yet to return to "normal." In the El-Obeid area alone, crop failures have been estimated at 75 percent, and further north at 100 percent. Crop failures further south in the Dilling area (Kortala, Touqma, and Somasem) were not as grave, with less than 50 percent failure reported (Nour et al., 1987:26).

TABLE 3.8
Rainfall in mm During Selected Months in El-Obeid
and Kadugli in 1984 and 1987

El-Obeid	May	June	July	August	Total
1984	5.4	5.9	75.5	10.3	97.1
1987	4.0	18.0	12.0	156.5	190.5
[1951–80]	10.1	23.2	111.7	137.1	282.1
Kadugli					
1984	53.3	92.7	86.7	143.5	376.2
1987	108.5	58.9	229.6	56.0	453.0
[1951–80]	67.5	104.3	142.1	161.8	475.7

Source: Nour et al., 1987:11.

There are four seasons (and two subseasons) in the Nuba Mountains. The approximate timing of each, depending on whether one is in the north or the south, is as follows:

Shita	December to February	dry and cool
Sayf	March to May	hot, increased humidity
(Rushaash	April to May	early rains)
Kharif	May to October	rainy season
(Subna		dry spell between rains)
Derat	October to December	hot and dry

In general, rainfall is confined to the *Kharif*, although light scattered showers occasionally occur both before and after this time. *Subna*, or brief dry spell, usually occurs sometime in the middle of the rainy season. A drought is simply an extended subna. A prolonged subna, of between 40 and 70 days, with little to light rains, has a disastrous effect on crops and pastures. Although August rains may be sufficient, in the northern reaches of South Kordofan and in North Kordofan, these rains are too late. The growing season in South Kordofan (and elsewhere) is limited by the seasonality and distribution of rainfall and begins when the moisture storage of the soil is raised permanently above the wilting point. A potential soil moisture deficit, nonetheless, exists throughout the growing season, as evaporation rates tend to be higher than the rainfall supply. Potential evaporation rates reach their peak during *sayf*, when monthly values of around 220 mm can be expected (associated with low relative humidity) and drops to about 170 mm per month during kharif (Government of Sudan, 1979:1.1.4).

One point that seems clear is that famine associated with drought is not an "act of God." Rather, it is a social phenomenon not to be written off in the most pretentious of cant phrases—"natural disaster." Hunger and food shortages seem to have always been a part of the Sahelian region, but in the past they never approached the catastrophic consequences of the 1973 and 1984 droughts. Drought-induced famine, it is argued, is further exacerbated by hopelessly outdated agricultural practices perpetuated by the peoples of the region. In viewing famine as a "natural" condition made worse by "irrational" behavior, the social parameters that influence human behavior are denied. To fully comprehend what is presently happening in the Nuba Mountains (and the Sahel in general), it is necessary to locate the Nuba Mountains firmly within the wider socioeconomic environment. Recognizing the links between environmental fluctuation, level of technology, and famine is insufficient without recourse to including consideration for the organization of social life, particularly relations of reciprocity. Together, these may lessen or magnify environmental conditions. This way, human actions may be considered as a response to environmental conditions, albeit circumscribed by the way in which social relationships are being transformed.

With the rapid changes in the daily lives of the inhabitants of the Nuba Mountains came a growing need to exploit resources. Accompanying Condominium rule, and later, independence, cash needs increased and became regularized to pay various taxes as well as to purchase market goods and production inputs. In addition, government and merchant towns such as Dilling, Kadugli, and Talodi swelled, placing greater demands on their surrounding areas for food, wood fuel, and land. The expansion of mechanized farming schemes also added to the exploitation of the environment. Agricultural cultivation expanded, forests were cut down, trees pollarded, and herd sizes grew.[82] Once cash needs are established, they are difficult to forswear. In light of this, it is easy to understand why people have come to discard past practices adopted to maintain soil fertility, like multicropping (especially with sesame) and land fallowing. Moreover, those dependent on tractors in field preparation frequently must plow according to its availability rather than on soil conditions. Rainfall in the Nuba Mountains is generally produced by isolated thunderstorms and is often preceded or accompanied by high winds that can produce a *haboob* (dust storm), which carries away unprotected soil. The leading edge intensities of these convective storm cells often exceeds 30 mm of rainfall per hour which can lead to further soil erosion in the absence of sufficient ground cover. Recent drought periods thus propelled people to intensify resource exploitation to make up for cash shortfalls, all of which leads to deforestation, desertification, and soil infertility. And, in the face of falling agricultural labor wages due to increased competition and higher food prices, this cycle of environmental abuse continues.[83]

Notes

1. The Nuba Mountains occupies an area approximately the size of South Carolina or of Scotland.
2. The demographic data on the region, like those for most of Sudan, are sparse and their reliability is open to question. These figures are taken from the 1983 *Census*.
3. One of the dilemmas of anthropology is an ethereal sense of timelessness imparted to the subject of inquiry. In the case of the Nuba Mountains, little (if any) attempt is made to draw a particular village into the orbit of greater historical conditions that indelibly affix the organization of life at a given time and place in that social formation.
4. A common phrase in the Nuba Mountains is that there are ninety-nine hills and ninety-nine languages. This phrase has also been used to describe specific ranges, such as Tegali, and merely connotes an unspecified number of each.
5. In fact, Kordofan is a Nubian word and initially was the name given to a Jebel ten miles southeast of El-Obeid (Lloyd, 1910; MacMichael, 1967; and Stevenson, 1894).
6. Stevenson (1984:11) argues that some of the shared traits invoked by Nadel "are not particularly common to the Nuba over against other peoples."
7. In terms of a biological basis to tribe (or race), Bayoumi (1985:368), in a study of genetic characteristics of the Fur and Baggara, indicates a large degree of "admixture" that is part of a "larger process...taking place between the Baggara, other western Africans, and the rest of the Sudanese population," thus derailing the myth of the presumed primordial purity of so-called tribes.
8. The term *fellata* is a denigrative term used to label people who originated from west Africa, while *khawaja* (sing.) specifies pale complexion and foreign origin, such as Europeans.
9. The general absence of specific treatments of the Nuba, except their primary role as a source of slaves, suggests the peripheral nature of the Nuba Mountains to the various kingdoms and that it probably remained outside of the direct rule and institutional incorporation into their state structures (with the exception of Tegali, of course).
10. The Ghudiyat comprised the last dynasty of Funj rulers in Kordofan. Nadel (1947:360–62) further establishes that the Ghudiyat (Ghadayat) received tribute from the Nuba groups of Ghulfan, Nyima, Tabaq, and Kadero.

11. Spaulding (1985a, 1985b, and n.d.) locates an extensive boundary to the Tegali kingdom, while Ewald (1982) contends that Tegali's size was delimited to its capital and immediate surrounding environs. This second interpretation lends itself to a more indirect rule of the Nuba Mountains.

12. For example, the "Wise Stranger" legend lies behind the founding of the "Kara" dynasty by a "Hilali or Abbasi" in Darfur and Wadai by a Ja'ali from Shendi (Hasan, 1967:154). Other instances are recounted by Trimingham (1959) for West Africa.

13. One extreme characterized by Coqery-Vidrovitch (1978:266) argues in favor of an African mode of production characterized by the "combination of patriarchal agricultural economy with a low internal surplus at the village level and of the great international...trade at the State level" upon which the state is based. Terray (1974), to the contrary, asserts that only through control of productive slavery was trade possible in the first place, by providing the necessary commodities with which to attract traders.

14. Kapteijns and Spaulding (1988) assert that although significant differences between state systems did exist (as well as regional variations within them) it is possible, when approached with caution, to draw meaningful generalizations about them with regards to the mechanisms of tribute extractions and the institutional organization of trade.

15. In a passage, worth quoting at length, describing sumptuary law in the Funj kingdom, Spaulding (1985a:78-9) writes:

> To southern subjects, their rulers were "the clothes wearing people".... When a nobleman traveled through the countryside, people should "rejoice at his passing as if it were the greatest of feast days for them" and expose their bodies according to custom. The attempt to rise above one's commoner status, for example, through the acquisition of sewn garments or other objects of conspicuous value, was a crime called *sibla*, and such illegitimate social climbing was severely punished.

16. In fact, this is what made banishment from a village particularly onerous and helped assure compliance with "the law of the land."

17. Once again, a more critical analysis is delimited by the paucity of available information. Either tribute is referred to in a brief cursory comment or in a generalized account of a wider geographical area.

18. Scholars of precolonial Sudanese history share a common problem in the limited nature of available sources to the effect that subsequent analyses tend to be static. Commenting on the institution of slavery, Kapteijns (1985:5) laments: "Although one may query the relevance of generalizations on this level and of this ahistorical, functionalist type, for the time being they might be the only generalizations about African slavery possible."

19. Spaulding (1985a:98) asserts that in order "To secure the labor of their subjects the southern (Sinnar) nobleman imposed a condition which may be called 'institutionalized insecurity.'"

20. As the size of standing armies increased, the responsibility for provisioning them became increasingly intolerable to their retainers so that they were expected to be self-sustaining (Spaulding, 1985a:207). Military excursions thus became profit-seeking ventures and had to be regular and successful since they functioned as pay checks. A favorite area for these activities was the Nuba Mountains.

21. Redistribution of subsistence goods to commoners was also necessary during hard times and was part of the sovereign's responsibilities. Failure to fulfill these obligations cast a pallor over the sanctity of that rule.

22. In 1811 Mohammed Ali managed to break the power of the Mamluks in Egypt. Ali believed that the wealth of the Sudan would ensure his uncontested power as viceroy of the region and would further establish the independence of the sultan.

23. According to Spaulding (1985a:142), for example, at the dawn of the Heroic Age of Sinnar the "use of specie in exchange was almost exclusively confined to those involved in the sultanic caravan trade to the outside world." By 1836 Holyroyd (1836:176) observed a wide variety of specie in use in El-Obeid, including "Pasha's money, Spanish dollars, and English gold." The wide variety of coinage reveals that it was not a standardized medium of exchange. In all probability it remained limited to major market towns under the viceroy's sovereignty and certainly was not prevalent in the Nuba Mountains to the degree where taxation in this form could proceed.

24. *Defterdar* literally meant keeper of the register of the lands and the defterdar was the most important fiscal officer.

25. In 1836 one such raid into the Nuba Mountains returned with 2,187 slaves (Issawi, 1966:485).

26. Interestingly, Holyroyd uses the words negro and slave interchangeably.

27. This ploy was also adapted by the Khartoum-based traders and used against the Dinka after the bead market had been satiated and the Dinka refused to trade or exert themselves on behalf of the traders. The traders then resorted to widespread cattle theft in order to create a demand for which the Dinka would exert themselves (Mire, 1985:107).

28. Only along the Blue Nile did agricultural slaves come to replace free labor to any degree before the arrival of the Turks (Spaulding, 1985a:209).

29. Describing the merchant systems that developed, O'Fahey (1973:33) writes:

    A credit system operated whereby the traders would supply the slavers with goods...in exchange for slaves to be captured. A slaver with good reputation could obtain goods on credit worth as much as five to six hundred slaves. But the traders covered their risks by a system of differential payments; thus if they accompanied the raid to the south and took payment there, they received five of six slaves for goods worth one slave in the al-Fashir market. If they were content to wait until the slaves returned, they received only two or three slaves. These transactions were confirmed in writing.

30. "The Englishman Samuel Baker was granted the administration of Equatoria province and soon controlled the lucrative ivory trade. He was succeeded by General Gordon, who was appointed Governor-General of the Sudan by the Khedive in 1877, and soon after appointed his European collaborators as governors of other Sudanese provinces. An Italian ruled Kordofan, an Austrian administered parts of Darfur, and an Englishman, Bahr al-Ghazal, Swiss and Danish adventurer-merchants fought in the Khedive's Ethiopian campaigns" (Collins, 1976:4).

31. A number of informants in Somasem also stressed this to me when I asked when the people adopted Islam: they all declared that when relatives fought with the Mahdi they became Muslim.

32. And, as Holt and Daly (1988:118) emphasize: "Supreme military and civil authority in the Sudan was vested in the governor-general, who could rule by de-

cree." In theory accountable to the other codomini, the governor-general, in fact, reported to the Foreign Office in London through the British representative in Cairo, allowing far more independence of action than accorded to other such individuals (120–21).

33. After this date, the only remaining tie Sudan maintained with Egypt was the Sudan Defence Force, an all Sudanese force financed through Egyptian funds but under a British commander. By this time, Britain's presence in the Sudan was a fait accompli to other European powers.

34. The rail network connected Khartoum with Atbara to the north, Port Sudan to the east, Sinnar to the south, and El-Obeid to the west. Southern Sudan and Darfur, aside from taxes and limited attempts to promote cotton production in the former, functioned as buffer zones between the Belgians and French colonies.

35. Essentially, Egyptian over-taxation drove many *fellahin* from their lands, reducing the cultivation of long-staple cotton. At the same time, American textile industries absorbed their own domestic supplies. All of this added to an astronomical rise in the price of raw cotton. The BCGA thus realized the paramount importance in establishing a reliable source of cotton, a source that they would be able to control. By securing a monopoly in cotton, the Lancashire industry remained viable for a few more decades (see Barnett, 1977 and Tait, 1988).

36. "A gross area of 240,000 feddans was irrigated in the Gezira in 1925, rising to 300,000 in 1926, 667,000 in 1931, 852,000 in 1938, and almost one million in 1956" (Niblock, 1987:14).

37. According to O'Brien (1980:81–2): "The government was able to amass a cumulative surplus of over £16 million on its direct Gezira share after debt service by 1950. Moreover from 1925 to 1956 cotton exports represented about 70% of Sudan's export earnings, over 80% of which came from Gezira. The total profits to the SPS by 1950 also exceeded £16 million, with average annual dividends to its shareholders of 15% plus a capital profit of 25 shillings on every 20 invested upon liquidation and distribution of reserves." All in all, it provided a very tidy profit indeed.

38. Sudan's area is 596.6 million feddans and, except for six million privately owned feddans, is owned by the state. Private landholdings are primarily restricted to the main Nile and to some of its tributaries (Awad,1987:39).

39. A similar solution had been devised within other British colonies; for instance, Tamil "coolies" were brought to Malaysian rubber plantations and to Ceylon's tea estates.

40. The British consul-general in Egypt in 1903 estimated that Sudan's population during the Mahdiyya shrank from 8.5 to 1.9 million (Nakash, 1988:53–4).

41. In fact, Gordon advocated bringing Zubair back to the Sudan as governor-general, believing him to be the only man who could save Sudan from the Mahdi. Strange bedfellows—Gordon, an avowed abolitionist, Zubair, an inveterate slaver.

42. Runaway slaves, for example, during the first two decades of the Condominium, were routinely returned to their "masters."

43. In order to appease public opinion in Britain, Arabs in general and Islam in particular were isolated as the culprit in the perpetuation of slavery in the Sudan (and elsewhere). This cynical manipulation has helped to perpetuate many stereotypes regarding both Arabs and Islam.

44. Britain needed to make the Sudan self-supporting as quickly as possible. Besides, the Sudan was not among the more important colonies. After all, when the British

colonized Sudan, its power was ebbing, which became increasingly apparent after World War I. There would be no Delhi Durbar in Sudan.

45. A 1902 report characterizes the situation in the Nuba Mountains: "a deplorable state of internecine conflict between the Nuba Meks of the various mountain districts has been revealed, whilst these unfortunate blacks are in turn the object of constant raids on the part of Nomad Arabs, who carry off their women and children into slavery" (McLoughlin, 1962:364).

46. Quite simply, the Condominium government did not have the manpower to subdue the Nuba Mountains at this time. Moreover, various Nuba were now well armed with rifles gotten from Baggara in trade for cattle and from the deserting troops of the Mahdiyya.

47. Examples of racism abound. In more general remarks, Slatin Pasha, inspector-general of the Sudan, wrote that "by nature all blacks are lazy," while the governor of Kordofan states "personally I am not a great admirer of the black man at his home and am certain that you see him best as a slave or a soldier" (Warburg, 1981:260–62).

48. Major O'Connell, in 1902, described a series of raids in the Nuba Mountains in which Hawazma (Baggara) and Nuba alternately raided several Nuba Villages and, in most cases, burned the crops and village structures (Jackson, 1955:172).

49. As summarized by the governor of Kordofan in 1926: "I feel most strongly that nothing can be done in the way of administering these communities (the Nuba) as long as they are allowed to remain on the tops of their hills, not only does this render them immune from all Government authority, but the very fact of their position tends to produce in them a rebellious and independent spirit" (cited in Ibrahim, 1985:45).

50. To a lesser degree in this area, gum arabic was an important product sought by the British, as it was by regimes antedating them. In 1926–29, Sudan exported 79.2 percent of the world's gum supplies and by 1954–57, its share increased to 85.0 percent.

51. The truculence of the "Talodi Arabs," runaway slaves who had begun a community at Talodi, was blamed for the incident. Essentially, they continued to vigorously engage in the trafficking of slaves, much to British chagrin.

52. Nuba raiding of "outsiders" is the basis of a common Arab-Sudanese stereotype that the Nuba are, by nature, inveterate thieves. I heard the Nuba described in this way many times in such places as Khartoum, El-Obeid, and Kadugli.

53. Personal interview with the former general-director or the Nuba Mountain Agricultural Corporation and present member of the Gezira Board of Directors.

54. The magnitude of the spread of cotton cultivation is evidenced by the fact that "sums amounting to £128,000 in 1938 and £136,000 in 1940 were paid out for rain grown cotton to an Arab and Nuba population estimated at 400,000 souls" (Henderson, 1946:23).

55. During World War II, the numbers of feddan under cotton cultivation shrank as the British pressed for greater quantities of sorghum needed to feed its troops. Following the war, the people were once again exhorted to cultivate cotton.

56. O'Brien (1988:140) argues that "The time of rural tax collection in key labour supply provinces was shifted from the end of the dry season (May-June) to the beginning of the cotton-picking season (January-February) by 1943 in order to ensure that peasants and pastoralists were relieved of their cash at the most opportune time."

57. In 1927, the governor of the Nuba Mountains, Major Northcote, conducted a general survey of the region and classified the districts according to their degree of Arabization: Class I, "pagan naked" Nuba; Class II, "tainted" pagans; Class III, "pagans with more Arab influence than I and II;" Class IV, "mixture of pagan and Muslim;" and, Class V, "pure Nuba Muslims" (Ibrahim, 1985:57-8). Note how Islam and Arab are treated as synonymous, also a recurring problem today when discussing the "Arab" countries.

58. It is interesting to note that in one breath the Nuba were disparaged and, in the next, "authentic Nuba culture" praised, although the latter was done vis-á-vis the Arabs.

59. Other Closed Districts included Darfur, most of the rest of Kordofan, Bahr al-Ghazal, Mongalla and Blue Nile, and parts of Dongala, Kassala, and Halfa.

60. In the words of one British administrator, "if the Nuba can make money within the province instead of having to go abroad for it a considerable tendency towards Arabization is automatically removed" (Ibrahim, 1985:63).

61. Language of instruction provides an appropriate illustration of this problem. At one time or another, students were taught in their vernacular, in English, in Arabic with Romanized characters, and in Arabic in its original script.

62. It is like apologists for the Turkish regime arguing that slaves were ultimately taken in order to best teach them necessary skills. In point of fact, slavery was abolished in Jamaica in 1834, but planters secured a four-year grace period by the provision of "apprenticeship" of the ex-slave (Post, 1978:22). As if they needed to learn the art of cane cutting!

63. Food continues to exhibit a high elasticity of demand, accounting for 71.6 percent of household consumption expenditures, followed by housing, textiles, and miscellaneous at 7.6, 8.1, and 12.6 percent respectively (Oesterdiekhoff and Wohlmuth, 1983:14).

64. Manufacturing, as a subsystem of industry, is equally bleak, accounting for 7% of Sudan's GDP, 8% of Sub-Saharan Africa, 14% of low-income countries, and 24% of industrial market economies (World Bank, 1984:59).

65. The Sudanese pound has suffered severe devaluation.

66. In December of 1987 the government was forced to raise revenues for its war efforts by sponsoring a "telethon," where viewers were urged to pledge money.

67. Two civil wars have resulted from the oppression of the southern regions; the Ana Yaya and the Sudanese People's Liberation Movement. The latter has increasingly picked up popular momentum in many parts of the country, as the other impoverished regions have realized their bond of commonality.

68. Niblock (1987:60-81) underscores this in his detailed depiction of the composition of the Legislative Assembly and the first Parliament. Mahmoud (1984) draws similar conclusions in her research on the Sudanese bourgeoisie.

69. Evidence of this is readily seen in the inability of some political groups (e.g., Umma Party) to eschew the creation of an Islamic Republic centered around *Sharia* law. This continues to provide a seemingly insurmountable barrier to a settlement of the current civil war.

70. The colonial government, for example, gave Sultan Mohammed Bello Mai Wurno the land rights surrounding Maiurno in 1915 in order to bind him to the state and to present an opposition to urban-based nationalist movements. By 1949, realizing the coming shift to nonterritorial forms of imperialism (neocolonialism), the land was taken back and sold to local jallaba (Duffield, 1978:66-7).

71. A major complaint voiced to me by a number of sheikhs in the Nuba Mountains was the lack of authority that position carried and the attendant lack of profitability.
72. Other families able to translate their positions of religious leadership into economic strength included al-Majdhub (agricultural schemes around Ed Damer), Nur al-Da'im (pump schemes on the White Nile), Siwar al-Dahab (pump schemes around Dongola), and al-Makki (trading concerns covering Kordofan and Darfur). Without question, however, none proved as adept in business as did Sayyid Mahdi, whose family has become a dominant force in the Sudan.
73. Literally a tithe, but in many ways it approaches tribute in cash or kind.
74. Sayyid Mahdi later expanded his area of cultivation to other areas in the White and Blue Niles and, by 1935, controlled some 15,000 feddans. More importantly, Mahdi enjoyed a virtually costless labor supply provided by the Ansar. In return for clearing or cultivating one square meter of his land, for example, they were promised one square meter in paradise (Khalafalla, 1981:86).
75. Some men, such as Sayyid al-Mahdi, headed religious sects (Ansar), political parties (Umma), and large business enterprises.
76. The major portion of the loans made by the World Bank during the 1960s and 1970s were earmarked for agricultural schemes, leaving the delivery of such basic items as clean water to UNICEF. Following this, the development banks in Saudi Arabia and Kuwait became the creditor of choice in their desire to turn the Sudan into an "Arab breadbasket."
77. The cracking clay soils occupy approximately 50% of the plains area. The most common extends to a depth of 2 meters, with cracks reaching down some 1.5 meters. These soils can be difficult to cultivate, as they are extremely hard during the dry season and very gummy during the rainy season, so that aside from slickness, it tends to cling to the feet in large clumps.
78. Further south of Kadugli, Talodi recorded a mean average rainfall for 30 years of 860.2 mm, while Lagowa in western Nuba Mountains received 623.9 mm.
79. Data is for three years only for both Dilling and Kadugli.
80. The year 1966 registered the lowest rainfall of the decade in Dilling, with 303 mm. For Kadugli, 1968 recorded the least amount of rainfall, with 457 mm.
81. During the period of 1970 to 1984, recorded rainfall in Kadugli indicates that below normal rains fell in ten of the fourteen years.
82. One result of deforestation is the rapidly dwindling supply of wildlife. Not long ago the Nuba Mountains area supported a wide variety of wildlife, including lions, elephants, giraffes, gazelles, leopards, ostriches, hyenas, and monkeys. Now, aside from an infrequent monkey, one espies an occasional guinea fowl or hare, but certainly encounters nothing more ferocious than the desert rat or white ant.
83. In 1987, for example, the Subna made weeding unnecessary in some areas. In others, such as Rahad, weeding rates fell to £10 per 1.6 feddan and, in Wad Ashana, dropped to £20 from a "normal" rate of £40 respectively. The market price for cereals, however, in norther South Kordofan and the El-Obeid area increased 50 to 200 percent from May to August of that year. Further reduced wage labor opportunities were due to fluctuating rain supplies, rat and grasshopper infestations, a shortage of tractor fuel and spare parts, and delayed loans from the Agricultural Bank; only 10 percent of the schemes in Kortala and Habila were planted as of August (Nour et al., 1987).

4

The Formation of Society in the Nuba Mountains

Our investigation, if we are to move beyond general statements, must detail the complex historical patterns encountered in the Nuba Mountains and account for the diversity in structural arrangements. This requires that we reconsider the larger historical context outlined in chapter 3, but now with an effort towards outlining its structural dynamics. Above all, our investigation must be accomplished with the purpose of furthering our understanding of household and the formation of livelihood strategies. This task underscores the intersection of various socioeconomic and cultural dimensions, including the organization of production activities, consumption, social and generational reproduction, distribution of resources, patterns of exchange, and social networks. In this way we will begin to know the deeper meaning of what a household is, the strategies that ensure household survival, and the sources of variability.

Given the present historical and geographical frame of analysis it is difficult to precisely delineate social change in the Nuba Mountains because it does not stop politely for regional or national boundaries. Yet, clearly the history of the region reveals the importance of modernization and the integration of the Nuba Mountains into various socioeconomic and political entities. Nevertheless, lineage-based groups in the Nuba Mountains continue to provide an important means of social organization. We know from the region's history of some of the more remote gabila, but information prior to these accounts is scanty, if not lacking altogether. Nevertheless, for our purposes we simply need to provide a brief contextual history of the area, paying particular attention to what is commonly termed the lineage or domestic community. This will be accomplished through a blend of the existing literature, both theoretical and empirical, and my own fieldwork, especially the oral histories of the area.

Conceptualizing Lineage

The aim here is to sketch out the basic principles of social organization underpinning lineages. What distinguishes a lineage from other types of societies is the central character assumed by kinship and an attendant hierarchic age-based structure—the division between elders and juniors, and the particular role of women. In general, the elders' authority over juniors is affirmed in the strict control over pubescent women and through the exercise of a monopoly over prestige goods such as cattle, ironware, and guns.[1] Needless to say, there can be considerable variation between lineage-based societies such as those found in the Nuba Mountains and elsewhere. The coherence of the Keiga and Moro elders' authority, for example, varies in their ability to organize production, regulate labor, and accumulate wealth. Kinship groups also exhibit a multiplicity of compositions; patrilineal among the Ghulfan, matrilineal among the Shatt, and duolineal among the Kao. These variations, however, are discerned at the historical level and need not compromise its conceptual usefulness.[2]

According to Meillassoux (1981, 1983), the "domestic community," or lineage, is principled primarily on demographic concerns and centers on the circulation of people and prestige goods in such a way that a demographic balance is maintained. Environmental conditions and demographic dynamics cause lineage groups to split or, for newer members, to be incorporated through marriage, fostering, or force. To this end, domestic communities enter into political alliances with each other, establishing a "matrimonial area" in order to ensure an even distribution of pubescent women throughout the participant communities. The large number of mutually distinct languages in the Nuba Mountains, nevertheless, points to the inability to forge any significant regional political affiliations. An additional mechanism to guarantee an adequate number of productive laborers includes extensive rules for adoption, either through peaceful means or raids on bellicose villages. Thus, the domestic community is, in general, a closed system that can be penetrated only through birth or its equivalent, fostering (Meillassoux, 1991).

Intimately attached to the concept of seniority is the control over territory "of which the perpetual 'property' (is) symbolically held by the ancestors, and in reality by their representatives, the elders" (Jewsiewicki, 1981:95). The territory over which a group lays claim and has access to is the sum total of the natural resources available to the group. It is not surprising that, within lineages, agriculture comprises the dominant activity—arable land is relatively abundant,[3] technology and techniques remain simple, and human labor supplies the most important source of energy (Sahlins, 1972). Moreover, the major portion of food required to sustain the community is domestically produced, minimizing the need for trade. Hence, the domestic community tends towards self-sufficiency with the exception, as noted above, of the need to maintain a suitable demographic balance between productive members and unproductive dependents, as well as between males and females. Upon this edifice is constructed a social system of inequality based on status, privilege, and prestige.

The availability of land and the simplicity of techniques precludes social differentiation on the basis of task specialization; rather social differentiation is grounded in kinship and its linchpin—marriage. As depicted by Meillassoux (1991:25), "Rank and status are expressed in kinship...congruently with the lifelong evolution of each individual in the double cycle of material production and human reproduction." Of central importance to understanding the construction of inequality within Nuba lineages, then, is the elders' control of biological reproduction as "a young man can pay bridewealth and marry a wife only through the intermediary of his elder" (Geschiere and Raatgever, 1985:15). No social substitution exists for a fecund woman; a man must have a wife if he is to become a full-fledged member of the community; i.e., an elder with the accompanying privileges such status affords. Within this arrangement, a junior must work for his elders in order to secure the required brideprice. In effect, the payment of bridewealth provides juniors with a claim against the future labor of the proceeding generation. Nevertheless, a junior is dependent upon the goodwill and largess of his elders. Thus, by controlling the conditions of assimilation into the basic groups, the elders gain access to and control of wealth.

Privileged access to lineage surfeit stems from being physically and, above all, socially an elder. Accordingly, a potential elder is a male with kin in good community standing.[4] This fact alone enables a junior to acquire ancestral lands and confers entitlement to a nubile woman, following payment of bridewealth, of course. Full fellowship in the community of elders thus demands that a junior establish his own family. Concomitantly, the family is the subsequent source of an elder's wealth, as he will benefit from the productive activities of his dependents, including wives, children, and other social juniors (in the past this included slaves).[5] Each junior consequently holds a profound stake in "remaining in his basic group of production/reproduction, which he [views] as a kin group, on pain of losing his recognized status" (Jewsiewicki, 1981:96).

Aside from the idiom of kinship, the authority of the elders is codified and ritualized in an elaborate age-grade system that regulates the participation of individuals in social, political, and economic life. Briefly, age grades demarcate the life course of age mates, specifying generational relationships and functions at various junctures.[6] Normally, females occupy parallel age grades, but in contrast to males they get married at a younger age and, consequently, make an earlier change in their social status. In addition, apart from the potential for conflict between generations, de Jonge (1985) draws specific attention to additional asymmetries between the sexes. Most revealing, and in accordance with the general system of patriarchy, the status of females is less than that of males throughout the course of their lives:

> A boy still had the chance of one day attaining the status of adult man, if only he lived long enough. But a woman was destined to be in a position subordinate to that of an adult man for the rest of her life. (de Jonge, 1985:56)

This remains true regardless of the type of lineal group in the African context, although empirical variations occur such that women in some lineages have more leeway in their personal affairs.

Economic differentiation within lineages is a particularly contentious subject, primarily because empirical instances of inequality are not always readily observable and it is frequently assumed that relationships between moieties is complimentary and symmetrically reciprocal (Kelly, 1993). This is especially true when the superordinate group, as a result of consolidating its own dominant position, invokes the powerful ideology of kinship. Idea systems, after all, as the socially-established framework of meaning, often impart elements of the dominant group's values that can obscure relations of inequality. Under the pretext of kinship, the appeal to blood is frequently so profound that juniors may not consider challenging the elders' position of authority. Moreover, elder/junior relations are also firmly patterned in patriarchal pretense, further binding them in an ideology of gender. The role and power of ideology to orient social action, thus, should not be minimized or reduced merely to economic principles or "false consciousness." Still, "an empirical or phenomenological approach cannot fail to discover limitless 'inequality', but raises the question of the significance of what is being described and explained" (Kelly, 1993:478). Hence, we would add that a major determinant of inequality must include effects on individual life chances and not simply a system of moral evaluation. After all, "people at work with their fellows produce ideas about their social relations along with their products, they 'manufacture consent'" (Friedmann, 1986c:191).

Lineages in Historical Perspective

The Nuba Mountains is a hilly area, with most settlements extending from the slopes of the hills out towards the plains. Farming comprises the dominant economic activity and remains primarily a small-scale undertaking. The prevailing form of production provides the basis for what is termed "traditional smallholder agriculture...consisting of small operating units, low levels of capital inputs, dominance of hand labour, and generally low and unstable production" (Mohammed, 1986.116). Superficially, this assessment is correct, but to stop here belies significant structural imperatives. Hence, we must draw on the organizational principles of the lineage or domestic community in order to comprehend so-called traditional society in the Nuba Mountains. The aim here is to present general historical abstractions or ideal-types, outlining commonalities in some of the lineages found in the Nuba Mountains.

The Organization of Economy

Farming implants the life-blood of the Nuba Mountains, although animal husbandry is also of some importance. The life rhythms of the village—ceremonial rituals, celebrations, marriages, and migrations—are intimately part of the agricultural cycle. The typical villager reckons time according to the demands of cultivation and, to a lesser extent, the requirements of their animals. In fact, farming is held in such high esteem that an individual who does not farm never really attains full membership within the village community. In this respect, the very act of farming conveys an indissoluble bond among villagers and provides the basis of "moral economy." At the heart of village life, agriculture thus obligates communal welfare and harmony. Although self-reliance is considered to be an important individual virtue and quality, villagers also believe that mutual cooperation in agriculture (and other labor intensive activities) is an ever present responsibility. Feelings of good will generated by such close association in agriculture invariably carry over to other activities such that rarely, if ever, do villagers do anything alone; company is always welcomed and expected.

The most important factors of production in the Nuba Mountains are land and labor. Land is claimed and controlled by the respective gabila and constitutes their dar, or domain. Quite often land plays an integral role in gabila mythology and colors accounts of their origin (Nadel, 1947). Access to land occurs through a variety of mechanisms but is primarily limited to clearing virgin land, inheritance, borrowing, and gifts among relatives. Purchase of land may also occur between lineage members and historically carries a nominal, standardized price, such as one or two goats (Stevenson, 1984). Fields are generally cropped for five to eight years and then put into fallow (sometimes for as long as ten to fifteen years), depending on land availability and fertility. Loss of soil fertility is recognized by the spread of certain weeds such as *buda* (striga). Farmers frequently have two or three dispersed plots of varying quality and distance from the village at their disposal. In part, this helps minimize crop losses from variable rain, insects, fire, or cattle by spreading the risks. Of course, distance to the village as well as the fertility of the soil also reflect an elder's seniority and status within the village.

Intercropping is common, usually mixing dura (sorghum) varieties with *simsim* (sesame) or *lubia* (cowpea). Without question, dura is the most important crop and is differentiated by maturation time, size, storability, resistance to pests, usage, taste, and color. *Dukhn* (millet) is of lesser importance in most areas of the Nuba Mountains, due to its growing conditions, and is distinguished along the lines of dura. *Ful* (groundnuts) is primarily limited to *qoz* and *gardud* (sandy soils), as is dukhn (millet).

In addition, each household cultivates a jubraka (house garden) to provide food during the "hungry period," which extends approximately

TABLE 4.1
Primary Crops Grown And Characteristics

Name	Characteristics	Maturation	Storage	Planted	Primary Use
Dura (sorghum)					
Karaamaka Hamr	red, medium, heavy	120 days	3–4 months	main farm	eat (best)
Karaamaka baida	white, medium, heavy	120 days	3–4 months	main farm	eat (best)
GadamaHaam	white, short, light	45 days	3–4 months	main farm	sell
Jak	white, short, light	40 days	3–4 months	main farm	sell
Kulu kulu	white, short, light	45 days	3–4 months	main farm	sell
Safra	yellow, tall, heavy	45 days	4–5 months	main farm	sell
Kaluum	red, medium, heavy	60 days	4–5 months	main farm	sell
Kurgay	yellow, short, heavy	60 days	4–5 months	main farm	sell
Dabar	yellow, medium, medium	40 days	4–3 months	main farm	eat
Najad	brown, tall, heavy	90 days	eat as get	jubraka	eat
	white, tall heavy	60 days	eat as get	jubraka	eat
	white, tall, light	45 days	eat as get	jubraka	eat
Simsim (sesame)					
Simsim AHmar	red, heavy	90 days	5 years	main/jubraka	oil/sell
Simsim AbayD	white, heavy	60 days	5 years	main farm	eat
Dalaamiid	brown, heavy	45 days	5 years	main farm	oil
Lubia (cowpeas)					
Aina Wahad	white, NA, medium	150 days	4–5 months	main/jubraka	eat
Ful Sundani (groundnuts)					
Ful Sudani kabir	NA, NA, heavy	90 days	2 years	jubraka	eat/sell
Ful Sudani sagir	NA, NA, heavy	75 days	2 years	main/jubraka	eat/sell
Barabati	NA, NA, heavy	60 days	2 years	main/jubraka	eat (best)
Karkadeh (hibiscus)					
AHmar	red, NA, heavy	90 days	sell as get	main/jubraka	sell
Abiyad	white, NA, medium	90 days	3 years	main/jubraka	drink

from July until the first harvest from the main fields. Every jubraka is enclosed by either a stone wall or thorn fence (*shok*) to keep out animals and inattentive people. Crops include quick maturing strains of dura (such as *nagad*), *tibish* (cucumber), tomatoes, maize, simsim, *bamiya* (okra), *battikh* (watermelon), *garaa* (squash), lubia, ful, *karadeh* (hibiscus), *meloukhia* (greens), and *basul* (onions). Table 4.1 shows the characteristics of the major crops now grown in the area, as well as their primary uses (characteristics include color, plant size, and yield).

Agricultural technology and techniques, though effective, are rudimentary. An ax is employed for hewing larger trees during the initial clearing of a field, although a few shade trees are left for shelter during the growing season. Underbrush and small trees, as on land following an extended bush fallow, are cut with an *antabob* (sickle). If there are sufficient dead grasses covering the land it is burned following early rains and the first flush of weed growth. The *harig* method usually kills weeds and delays the first weeding. On land cultivated the previous year, crop residue left over from grazing livestock is collected and burned. If the grass covering is insufficient, a preplanting weeding must be done using a *hashasha* or *sulokab*.[7] Planting is accomplished with either a sulokab or *geria* (long pointed pole with a hardened or metal tip). Weeding is accomplished using the tools mentioned above and is performed one to three times, depending on the weed growth.[8] Harvesting lasts for several months, with dura and simsim cut with a small knife, while lubia and ful is harvested by hand. Threshing activities employ a *mudgaba*[9], which is used to pound the dura grains from the heads. Most crops must then be dried and/or winnowed before storage in sacks or clay granaries that are raised on supports to minimize losses due to rats and termites. Different crops are stored separately, and simsim is usually ground into oil.

Labor is also an important element of the production process, particularly as agricultural activities tend to be labor intensive. Typically, the basic economic unit or group that works together throughout the production cycle is the household group, consisting of a man, his wife (or wives when polygamous), and unmarried older children under his guardianship (agnatic or affinic relations).[10] Other sources include labor from obligations of brideservice and age-grades, as well as nafir. As part of the obligatory brideprice, a young man must work on his prospective in-law's fields. Quite often similarly betrothed age-mates labor together, reinforcing the social separation between elders and juniors.

In addition, in lineages with well-defined age-grades, labor can be mobilized to work the fields of particularly influential elders (Nadel, 1947; and researcher's own observations in Shatt Damam).

Nafir is also an important source of labor, especially during peak labor periods such as *hash murr* (first weeding; literally, bitter weeding), harvesting, and threshing. Recruitment is based on kinship ties, age-mates, and/or locality (close neighbors).[11] The host or convener compensates the participants with *marissa* (beer is the essential ingredient), *'asida* (porridge), *mulah* (stew), and sometimes meat, such as goat or chicken. Whereas the host is under obligation to later assist the participants if they, in turn, call a nafir, reciprocity varies in intensity and is not always strictly followed.[12] The timing and size of nafir parties also expresses differential status rankings among the elders themselves. Nafir labor is also utilized for constructing domestic buildings. Lastly, females also may organize their own nafir for work on the jubraka or in their own fields (in some gabila women have rights to their own land).

Nafir also serves as a mechanism that enables community members to express communal self-sufficiency, as well as to express feelings of belongingness. Frequently, for example, a nafir party will decompose into small groups, with one singing words that good-naturedly disparage the working abilities of the other groups, while quickening their own work tempo. As the one group finally slows down another picks up the song as well as the pace. This occurs throughout the day, breaking intermittently for marissa and food, and, aside from bringing gaiety to an otherwise monotonous activity, individuals reconfirm their mutual dependence and feelings of communal attachment. Analysis of the institution of nafir thus cannot be wholly explained by an overriding economic logic. Some individuals, for instance, are invited to join a nafir, not for their agricultural skills or endurance but for their ability to tell humorous stories or sing favorite ballads.

Although occupational specialization is minimal, it exists to some degree within most villages. Individuals, in addition to being farmers, may also be smiths, rope makers, artisans, healers, or priests. Of greater importance, however, is the division of labor based on sex and age. In many instances these divisions are both formally codified and highly ritualized into age-grades, with age-mates addressing each other in terms that signify a tie stronger than friendship.[13] Nevertheless, as Kelly (1993:418) notes, "A division of labor characterized by qualitatively rather than quantitatively different patterns of activity provides little scope for the grounding or elaboration of gender differences."

Age-grades are highly symbolic and ritualistic, marking rites of passage and instilling gabila solidarity through various practices, such as cicatrization, circumcision (male and/or female), and ornamentation in the form of jewelry and skin coloring. With limited exceptions, few tasks fall exclusively within the domain of one sex, although females appear to labor more arduously than do males and have a greater array of daily tasks. As young children, boys watch small animals (typically goats and calves) and young girls care for the smaller children. Older boys tend the cattle of the elders, frequently residing at the community's cattle collective (*zariba*).[14] At this time boys begin to learn the art of warfare, physically conditioning themselves through wrestling, stick fighting, and, in the southeastern Nuba Mountains, bracelet fighting. Males roughly between the ages of 18 and 35 are warriors, responsible for protecting the village from outside intrusion and for maintaining internal order. Females, following menarche, are integrated directly into the labor force, working a small jubraka, assisting in the fields, and participating in the exclusively female activities of carrying water, load carrying, fetching wood, marissa brewing, and grinding dura. Females wed between the ages of 14 and 16, whereas males do so between the ages of 25 and 30, after receiving their own lands. Tasks exclusively male include digging wells, herding cattle, and hunting. More importantly, married women have control over the domestic food supplies.

The Authority of the Elders

As in other lineages throughout Africa, the authority of the elders stems from their monopoly over the circulation of fertile women. This, in effect, enables control of the labor of male age-mates, females, and offspring.[15] Arrangement of a betrothal occurs between the elders of the respective lineages. A marriage contract entails the husband's lineage presenting the bride's with an agreed upon sum of cattle, goats, and/or pigs and other prestige goods like spear tips, iron blades, and guns, as well as dura and simsim oil. Brideprice frequently varies according to the physical prowess and courage of the groom (proved through warfare, banditry, or intervillage sports) and the ability of the bride to brew exceptional marissa, which adds to a husband's prestige and image of hospitality when receiving his age-mates. Moreover, marissa as the central element of nafir can attract larger work parties on its taste alone.[16] The bridewealth is kept and distributed among the elders of the bride's lineage (the father and his real and classificatory brothers), although the father normally retains the lion's share for himself.

Tensions between elders and juniors can run high over the latter's desire for marriage and independence. It is not uncommon for a father to postpone his son's marriage for as long as possible. A father, for example, may not acknowledge that his son deserves a wife because he has not worked a sufficient amount of time or shown due respect. Aside from the loss of his son's labor, the father also incurs the lose of the labor of the lad's age-mates (e.g., as among the Otoro). Furthermore, friction frequently develops out of a father's own ambition to wed an additional wife in order to enlarge his own lineage, augmenting his personal prestige and political prominence through widening his base of wealth accumulation. In all of the gabila polygamous marriage is an ideal, although only those elders in a position of affluence are able to realize it.

A prospective father-in-law may prove equally recalcitrant. Brideservice, common among a number of lineages such as the Shatt, Tira, and Moro, customarily lasts until the final installment is made and the girl joins her husband. A father-in-law may attempt to lengthen this period and continue to benefit from the labor of the young man and his similarly betrothed age-mates. Throughout this time, due to certain avoidance taboos, the bride remains with her family and continues to help with the agricultural and domestic chores. The personal objectives of both father and father-in-law are, nonetheless, kept within bounds by the marriage rules obtaining in different gabila.

The existence of age-grades thus provides a moral hierarchy that consolidates the authority of the elders over juniors and relegates females to a lifetime of subordination to males. Women have limited opportunities to earn prestige and must contend with far more constrained life chances; thus, women can never be equal to males. In many respects, it is culturally envisioned that women (and children) possess different capabilities than males; hence, the engendered (and age) pattern of differentiation. It should be noted, however, that women do have access to male products and services according to socially determined obligations and responsibilities. Nonetheless, male seniority is everything, rationalizing and legitimating the inequitable division of political authority and attendant material enjoyment.

Theoretically, males move from one age-grade to the next until they attain the status of elder. The progression from one status to another, however, depends, among other things, on longevity of life and the customary age of marriage. Due to high mortality rates (more so in the past), not all juniors attain the status of elder. And, of those who do, fewer yet become privileged seniors (over 50 years of age). Moreover, the sanctity of the elders' status is safeguarded by maintaining a difference between the marital ages of males and females (ten to fifteen years on average). What this means is that, while social inequality may be quite minimal, these societies are not necessarily egalitarian. Such a model requires a balanced reciprocity over a relatively long period of time in labor and products.

Relations among the elders is not always harmonious. Influential leaders and "priests" are able to mobilize labor from certain age-grades not available to every elder (e.g., Nyimang). In gabila practicing adelphic inheritance of cattle, like the Ghulfan of Murong, the position of older brothers strengthens at the expense of younger brothers (as well as of sons). Personal ambition exists; after all, leaders have to prove themselves time and time again in order to ensure that their insights will prevail among the council of elders. Although elder status is ascribed, there is room for achievement; prestige can be enhanced through individual efforts. Too, obedience outside of one's familial circle is not automatic and must be continuously reaffirmed. Among the Shatt, for example, people know who the influential elders are and can readily explain why, pointing out land holdings, number of wives and children, and the abundance of food and marissa. In sum, a type of competition prevails among elders, creating a hierarchy of status among them and their respective lineages. If disagreements grow too heated, however, a group can always go elsewhere and begin anew. The village of Shimal Murta was founded in this manner, when a disgruntled individual and his family left Miri Bara over a land dispute.

Nevertheless, social inequality within lineages is less onerous than it is in other forms of social organization, primarily through the existence of various leveling mechanisms, which curtail excessive displays of self-interest, ambition, and aggression. One such function of the many gabila celebrations is to share one's good fortune with fellow villagers. These festivities are always occasioned by ample food and drink. An additional mark of prestige is the ability to assist those less fortunate in their time of need, either through largess of food or labor. Occasionally, influential individuals within neighboring villages will organize a joint nafir to weed the fields between the two. The participants then feast on freshly prepared meat (usually beef) and bounteous supplies of marissa. But, that is a key to understanding the lineage; individuals gain status not from the accumulation of material goods but from their social consumption.

The Cultural Nexus of Religion

Religion exerts a powerful force over village life, affirming communal unity and rationalizing social differentiation. Religion, perhaps, is a poor choice of words in attempting to describe the indigenous belief systems and ritual practices of the various lineages found in the Nuba Mountains. These local religions are experiential rather than scriptural and are realized through personal attitude rather than social ordination. The various beliefs combine a sense of respect and fear, awe and order, which are interwoven within the spiritual, human, and natural worlds (Baumann, 1987:162–73). Although each variant expounds a supreme spiritual being of creation/destruction in one form or another (as well as the presence of other spirits), religious manifestations assume numerous forms and styles.

The unifying elements connecting the various religious expressions found throughout the Nuba Mountains is the belief in a spiritual medium who speaks though the oracles of a *kujur*, or possession priest; a rainpriest, who is responsible for agricultural rituals and annual festivals (*sibir*), such as that which occurs prior to the first rains; and a healer[17], who possesses powers of recovery (Nadel, 1941, 1947; Stevenson, 1940, 1984; Martini, 1961; and Baumann, 1987).[18] Some gabila also include a grainpriest who, before the initial sowing of the fields, contributes a small portion of grain to each cultivator to mix with their own seed stock (Bell, 1938).[19]

Although most Nuba religions have lost their outright appeal in the face of Islam and, to a lesser extent, Christianity, they nonetheless provide an on-going backdrop in the daily lives of most villagers. It is difficult for either Islam or Christianity to completely dispel earlier belief systems because these local religions are fluid and affect people in ways that neither contradict nor threaten Islam or Christianity (Baumann, 1987). *Allah* may be the One God—few Nuba would bother to dispute this—but this in no way depreciates the universal oneness or connection with nature experienced by the Nuba at a deeper level. Nuba professing the Islamic faith, for example, can readily recite the basic canon of One God as revealed to the Prophet Muhammad, as well as the fundamental practices and principles of Islam, but for many Nuba the distinctions separating Islam from their indigenous beliefs seems rather nebulous. As one elderly Kadugli woman in Shimal Murta related to me when asked to explain which religion she believed to be "true": "They are all the same, there is no difference" ("*Kulu wahid, ma farq*").

Unquestionably, the complex set of beliefs found throughout the Nuba Mountains are inexorably intertwined with the life-sustaining activities of agriculture. In fact, this inseparable bond between religion and agriculture is countenanced and confirmed throughout the year by a procession of village festivals and ceremonial rituals that not only initiate, regulate, and sanctify agricultural activities, but reenforce the "moral economy." In this manner, key seasonal agricultural activities, such as planting and harvesting, are afforded every opportunity of success.[20] Some of the more common sibirs, or festivals, include: (1) *Sibir al Diboia*, a rain-making festival that both marks the start and end of a year. (*Diboia* is also one of the times that "*anima mundi*" is manifested through the medium of the kujur, who, after falling into a trance and speaking in the voice of the spirit, prophesizes about future occurrences and discloses the causes of past misfortunes.) Another rain-making festival is *Sibir al Lungang*. (2) *Sibir al Bokhsa* is a harvest festival, first for the near farms and later for the far farms, noted for its intricate music played on pipes of differing caliber, with distinct notes and accompanied by a singular drum to mark the tempo. The dancers form two concentric circles around the band, with the women on the inside, dancing counter-clockwise, and the men on the outside, dancing clockwise. (3) *Sibir al Farig* comprises an initiation festival for males in which the men bind bull's horns to the tops of their heads and with *kosh kosh* (leg rattles) tied to their calves, dance the *kambala*. Women stand around the perimeter in a circle, while elders lash the backs of the initiates with whips. (4) *Sibir al Prum* is a festival featuring wrestling, usually pitting youths from different villages against each other. This festival also furnishes an important opportunity for young men to enhance their status through displays of physical prowess. Each villager eagerly anticipates the coming of the various sibir, as they are a time of socializing, song, dance, food, and libation. (Although various Nuba Gabila know these sibir by other names, for simplicity, when referring to a particular sibir in the text, the above names will be used.)

The Nuba system of spiritual beliefs, and despite its many layers, forms a coherent world view, linking together thought and practice, life and death, and chance and destiny. More importantly, these beliefs enable villagers to cope with an otherwise unmanageable reality. Agriculture is a precarious endeavor throughout most of the Nuba Mountains region; hence, as every Nuba stands in reverence of nature's munificence, each shrinks in fear of its retribution. In the eyes of the Nuba, any violation of the natural order through shirking or dismissal of sacral observances can have profound consequences and can readily invite disaster on the fields and into the village. Baumann (1987:169) eloquently relates this in a pointed exchange between two villagers.

> A Miri Bara farmer suspected of violating a natural observance was questioned by the son of a rainpriest in the presence of half a dozen men of all ages. One of the older men, an outsider by birth and known for his sardonic humour, challenged the rainpriest's son: "You can't cut this tree before this festival, and that tree before that festival, and grass before any festival.—Next you will invent a festival before which you can't even fuck your wife!" His rebuke was as immediate as it is telling: "The fuck that you came from was done in Nyimodu village, so cut whatever tree you like when you are there. While you live here, respect our observances and don't bring disaster to our fields!"

The various belief systems of the Nuba also provides a basis for social differentiation. Respect for seniority is established at birth, with children of the same mother being named according to gender and order of birth. (Up to seven names are given—if there are more than seven children the naming begins anew.) As older children are responsible for the well-being of younger siblings, they can demand obedience. On a different level, everyone must accord deference to the aged, particularly male elders. Lastly, priests with their ability to control the village's destiny command respect from the entire community. This is evident in the fact that, aside from being elders, they have access to additional village labor and goods. Not only is a priest's field planted and harvested first, but he or she is frequently the beneficiary of many bequests. According to the Seligmans (1932:378), in the old raiding days the rainpriest of the

Dilling "took a large portion of any plunder as well as certain fines (and) he takes a portion of the bride-wealth."

Unquestionably, kinship is the paramount principle in the social order of the lineage but in power relations another principle plays a crucial role—the belief in magic. Consequently, the kujur is especially revered by the community for his of her mystical powers. The story of kujur Kamali in Shimal Murta portrays the awe in which a kujur is commonly held.

> The Arabs were very afraid of *kujur* Kamali. One time when the Arabs came to steal slaves and cattle *kujur* Kamali sent bees on them and drove them away. He also had a spear which he threw at Arabs from the top of the *jebel*. After it had killed an Arab it would return to his hand. Even his brother caught Arabs with Kamali's power and sold them as slaves. He was a powerful *kujur*. Kamali went hunting with a gun without bullets. He pointed the gun at the animal, made the sound of a gun with his mouth, and the animal died. When Kamali grew old he told the people to make *marissa* and prepare for a feast. Kamali killed many cows and the people ate and drank the whole day. When evening came he was approached by a white horse. Kamali told the people that he was leaving them and began to ride up the *jebel*. When it became too steep the horse flew over the top. Kamali was never seen again.

Few question whether or not to obey a priest; with such power the community can be protected or endangered, rains fall on fields or the ground is scorched by the sun, and individuals remain healthy or take ill.

The diversity and volubility in the types of leadership help to restrain centralization of power and, consequently, new leaders continuously come and go. In addition to priests, each gabila contains what may be termed chieftains. The most influential of these is known as the "master of the path" (*sayyid al darb*) and oversees relations between the village and outsiders.[21] Historically, the master of the path negotiated peace settlements, arranged ransom of captives, ensured the safety of visitors or emissaries, and launched raids on other settlements (Ewald, 1990:25–6). As Ewald notes (1990:26), in the past the roles of the master of the path and priests (primarily the kujur) often blurred, merging into a single powerful individual. In general, the "offices" remained separate, albeit mutually dependent, with neither wielding central authority. Today, the position of master of the path is largely symbolic, if not absent altogether.

Multiple Systems and Social Complexity

Today, the Nuba Mountains presents an extremely complex society. Depending upon the historical trajection of a particular lineage and the manner by which it was integrated into various tributary/ slave and capitalist systems, different practices were strengthened and others diminished. More often than not lineages were altered by the newer socioeconomic and political contexts, which effected new forms of organization. Without a doubt, lineage-based social relations became more complicated, leading to competing sources of authority and inequalities within the villages themselves. Certainly, the Turkiyya and Mahdiyya conquests must be noted as turning points, with the later Anglo-Egyptian Condominium further rupturing lineage groups.

What remains at issue is specifying the current nature of the Nuba Mountains society. Multiple complex cultures and intricate social structure present knotty problems for bounded historical inquiry in the Nuba Mountains. The various colonial impositions, as noted, remade long-distance trade and its connection to the Nuba Mountains. Its reordering and expansion were forged in a cauldron of social disorder engendered by the slave trade and its eventual cessation, pestilence and disease, internecine warfare, and new forms of governance and control. These developments (and others) fostered far-reaching consequences against which the various local groups had to refigure livelihood strategies in the aftermath of new socioeconomic and political realities.

The Tributary/Slave Systems

In the first instance of inclusion, the tributary/slave systems altered settlement groupings, agricultural practices, and trade patterns. The overwhelming need for security drove the Nuba further into the mountains, where they were forced to increasingly terrace and cultivate hillsides.[22] According to Wood (1971:36): "The amount of formerly terraced land...is much greater than most researchers have suspected." Nevertheless, hill land cultivation proved insufficient to meet all of the community's food needs, compelling farmers to venture onto the immediate surrounding plains.[23] This reorganization of agriculture production into near and far farms fostered the *kalunki* system—long elongated fields side by side. This kept farmers in close proximity and near to defensible sites. During times of warfare, the vulnerable lowland fields were abandoned, while the near farms could be better defended against raiding parties of all kinds.[24]

Trade among the various Nuba communities is not a recent phenomenon and certainly precedes the nineteenth century. Periodic grain shortages long favored exchange among the Nuba, although emigration and
raids presented equally viable options. Agricultural yields vary from
year to year, but it is difficult to maintain sufficient food stores, in part
due to the assorted leveling mechanisms and also owing to the storage
life of the numerous grain types (Nadel, 1947:49–50). In addition, the
physical diversity of the Nuba Mountains encouraged trade between
those communities that relied on useful "items produced in micro-
environments outside of their own villages," such as iron for tools and
weapons, fiber for mats and ropes, hardwood for digging sticks and,
mimosa wood and poison for spears (Ewald, 1990:22). Outside traders,
too, were hardly new to the area and brokered their wares in exchange
for goods of local provenance (including slaves). Despite the retreat of
the Nuba into mountain refuges, trading practices continued. Trade after this time, however, differed in that it adopted a distinct medium—
human chattel—arising from the voracious demand for slaves. The
currency of slaves afforded both freedom from enslavement and famine, except for those unfortunate enough to be tendered.

Forces originating far beyond the Nuba Mountains dramatically affected conflicts within lineages. The inrush of traders and raiders placed
the Nuba on a permanent war footing, either in defence from maraud-
ers who threatened the region as never before or in initiating their own
raids in search of food and slaves. In either case, the turmoil enveloping the Nuba Mountains lent a new importance to lineage elders and
brought about the need for a more stable coordination of leadership,
either in the form of a single powerful chieftain or a collective body.
Unquestionably, the master of the path and kujur profited most from
this situation. The master of the path benefited from his ability to successfully deal with itinerant jallaba, to coordinate raiding parties, and
to organize village defenses. The authority of the kujur likewise grew
with the ability to prophesize the results of raids and afford protection
to the community through occult powers. Certainly, each received a
greater share of any tribute or plunder.[25] One traveler in the late 1800s
recounted that among the Dilling, captives were "taken to the (kujur),
who makes his choice, leaving the rest for the victors" (Martini,
1961:125). Often an ambitious elder would attempt to assume both
roles, although instances of this were rare (Ewald, 1990). The author-

ity of other war leaders probably also increased, mitigating against trends towards centralization.

The essential relation between elders and juniors/women became more inequitable and, thus, exploitative during this period and further facilitated social differentiation. The addition of multiple wives was a significant symbol of the prerogative of chieftainship among gabila, exacerbating competition between elders and juniors for cattle and nubile women. In the more predatory gabila, the infusion of wealth through plunder and tribute paid by weaker communities for protection probably began the inflation of brideprice, especially the inclusion of guns in addition to an increase of cattle and goats.[26] Enterprising young men could meet the larger demands only though raids on their neighbors, jallaba, or pastoralists, bringing yet more wealth into the ambit of elders.[27] Thus, the flow of goods and services from the juniors and women enhanced the power position of many elders. In gabila subject to repeated victimization, the reverse held true. In all probability the stature of the elders diminished along with a deflation in bridewealth. Consequently, the elders' ability to control juniors and women in these situations decreased.

The period of the Turkiyya also pushed a number of Baggara pastoralists further into the Nuba Mountains, first to find refuge from pressing tax collectors and later in search of cattle and slaves. Assisted by their knowledge of the environment, they proved extremely effective, operating in small, fast raiding parties. In fact, by the mid-1800s pastoralists provided El-Obeid jellaba with most of their slaves (Pallme, 1844). Within these patrilineages, certainly, the power of elders increased, similar to the increase in power of their Nuba counterparts. During the Mahdiyya, however, many pastoralists lost their cattle to raids and the general chaos that ensued. As a result, many took up agriculture out of economic necessity, although some Baggara groups continued to raid, such as the Hamar, who operated out of Daloka and Shatt Safiya. Further elaboration will be given in Chapter 8, with the analysis of the Hamar village of Shair Tomat.

Modernization and the Rise of Capitalism

The impacts of modernization and the rise of capitalism proved equally dramatic in their effects on lineages. During the first two decades of

Condominium rule administration remained in the hands of the military, whose mission was to establish governmental authority and stabilize the region. Early contacts with Condominium forces evidenced little change over most previous relations with outsiders; taxation retained its tributary form, with the government extracting payments from the more vulnerable Nuba and Arab communities, while the stronger resisted. Cattle raids, kidnapping, and trafficking in slaves continued unabated as the government looked the other way. It was against this background that the colonial state needed to break open older lineage relations in order to draw villages into a market economy. The main obstacle to the success of capitalism lay in freeing up both labor and agricultural products, first by direct coercive means and later, indirectly, through the expansion of a specifically market economy. In short, what was needed for capitalism to effectively remake lineages was the monetization of lineal obligations and exchanges.

A crucial moment of economic change in the Nuba Mountains (as elsewhere on the African continent) proved to be the monetization of bridewealth. Even today, a major preoccupation of young men is how to acquire enough money to pay for a bride, forcing many young men to migrate in order to earn sufficient bridewealth.[28] According to older informants among the Shatt, Ghulfan, Kadugli, and Miri, cash money and luxury goods like tea, coffee, cloth, and sugar did not routinely enter into the circuit of brideprice until the 1930s, although the required number of cattle and goats did decrease. Fines and taxes, too, played a significant role. At first, both were paid in cattle and guns, but gradually money assumed greater importance. In addition to drawing villagers into a cash economy, the loss of guns reduced the threat of raids and intransigence, whereas the deprivation of cattle increased the need for money and began the trend towards unforced out-migration.

As previously mentioned, Condominium administrators faced a difficult problem in deciding how to integrate the Nuba Mountains into its rule and make it profitable.[29] At first the British responded by resettling the Nuba away from their formidable redoubts and onto the fertile plains below. Resettlement aided in the collection of taxes as well as in the general aim of pacification. In some instances this was accomplished by Maxims, in others communities voluntarily descended, opting for closer proximity to more fertile soils (Ibrahim, 1985; Roden, 1972). This in itself, however, does not instill the "Protestant ethic and the spirit of capitalism." Armed with previous experiences on the continent and elsewhere, however, the British knew how to control the lineage-based communities.

The initial task of involving villages in a capitalist economy required coercive measures. To this end large-scale labor levies were made against villages to recruit the manpower essential to construct infrastructure, including roads, administrative buildings, and hafir for newly developed government cotton schemes. Elderly men in Somasem, for example, still talk about having to work on the Dilling to Kadugli road. But the key to British successes ultimately lay in drawing people voluntarily into a market-based economy. In the above case, workers received a nominal wage for their labors, which had a type of multiplier effect on local economies, obvious in the acquirement of such store-bought goods as tea, sugar, jewelry, and clothing.[30] In addition, workers not from the Somasem vicinity purchased food and drink from the local women. Cash incomes, however, primarily went to defray taxes, to purchase livestock, and to meet brideprices. Once capitalism made suitable inroads into the villages, young men were increasingly willing to engage in wage-labor on their own volition and with the expressed encouragement of their elders.

The state in the Sudan also played an important role in restructuring agricultural relations, first during the Condominium period and later in independent Sudan. Within the framework of development policy, parastatal organizations determined the overall strategy for agricultural development and, in this function, oversaw the construction of regional infrastructure. The expansion of capitalism required new markets in labor, products, and investment opportunities. The development of cash crops (i.e., cotton) was intended to meet these needs by stimulating production for the market, while simultaneously solving the problem of securing revenues from the local populace. This reorganization of agriculture, however, took place within the older patterns of production; i.e., "traditional agriculture."

The Khartoum government established the Nuba Mountains Cotton Industry (NMCI) in 1923 to disseminate the growing of cheap lint cotton destined for the mills in Manchester. Moreover, the introduction of a cash crop was intended to "supplement people's income and to acquaint the Nuba people with money," though primarily for poll and crop tax purposes (Al Tilib, 1987).[31] By 1929 the NMCI was in full operation, with eight ginning factories: two in Kadugli and one each in Dilling,

Talodi, Lagowa, Abu Gubeiha, Umm Berembeita, and Semeih. Farmers handed their cotton crops over to local weighing centers, where they were paid a fixed government price. Cotton production reached its peak during the 1950s and remained strong up through the 1962/63 season of 1,029,000 *kantars* of seed cotton.[32] The NMCI had also wanted to set up industries for processing cotton byproducts (oil, soap, and seedcake for fattening cattle) but lost interest as Sudanese independence loomed closer.

The postcolonial state differs little from its predecessor in its general orientation to development. State intervention in the form of agricultural schemes remains the primary tool in controlling the Nuba Mountain economy. Cotton production is currently under the auspices of the Nuba Mountain Agricultural Production Corporation (NMAPC), which operates mechanized schemes throughout the region, but which now allows for a rotation of dura and cotton.[33] Large gaps still remain between the prices farmers receive for seed cotton and the government's export price. Baumann (1987:207) estimates that from 1969 through 1979, producer prices for seed cotton prices fell 49 percent. Al-Tilib (1987) concurs, stating that "Although the price [for seed cotton] has increased, it is still way below the world market price."

In 1969 the government began another parastatal organization, the Mechanized Farming Corporation (MFC). In accordance with its original goal, the MFC has established six schemes throughout the clay plains, with the largest at Habila in the eastern reaches of the Nuba Mountains. Each scheme is apportioned into plots ranging between 1,000 and 1,500 feddan. In the beginning short-staple cotton occupied part of the crop rotation but in recent years has fallen out of favor due to the decreases in world-market prices. The planting of dura presently receives primary consideration, as the government hopes to lower the market costs for the dominant food grain and, thus, the overall wage-bill of workers.[34] According to the General Director of the MFC (1987):[35]

> Those capable of running schemes by themselves are given priority. They must be a proper tenant...judged by their ability to get credit from the Agricultural Bank. Every year the tenants must come to the MFC for a certificate to show the Agricultural Bank for credit. An MFC inspector visits every scheme and notes if the land is cleared and ready for planting.

He later acknowledged that jallaba monopolized the schemes, relying on the wage-labor of Nuba, Dinka, and others for the actual cultivation.[36] In addition, Nuba villages in the midst of the schemes find themselves hemmed into a circular area with a diameter of six kilometers, necessitating labor migration as the expansion of their own agricultural production proves impossible.

Other recent parastatals include the Nuba Mountains Rural Development Project (NMRDP), the Western Sudan Agricultural Research Project (WSARP), and Agricultural Extension.[37] NMRDP and WSARP have strong ties to the international economic community; the EEC and World Bank/USAID respectively. Their efforts are directed towards the modernization of Nuba Mountain agriculture through: (1) the use and restructuring of productive capacities; (2) the extension and expansion of factor and product markets; and (3) the replacement of traditional methods of economic organization such as nafir.

All of these agencies are, in the main, entrusted with "getting traditional agriculture moving" through increased productivity and sale of products. Owing to the enlarged scope of competition, farmers are increasingly forced to rationalize and mechanize their production. Aside from some of the more technical merits of the intermediate technologies being made available, such as the NMRDP's animal traction project, these agencies have intensified the farmers' dependence on agricultural inputs, including DDT and other herbicides/pesticides, treated seeds, tractors, etc.[38] The growing need for money to purchase production factors has led to a rise in out-migration and a reliance on the shayl (moneylender). In addition, changes within agriculture have instigated a different and more pronounced pattern of social differentiation at the village level. A major complaint voiced in rural communities is that development agencies usually target the prosperous farmers for assistance and ignore the contributions of women all together (with the exception of an occasional jubraka project).

The multiple points of intersection between the old and the new represent a subtle and complex blend of social relations, political authority, and value orientation. Various actors appear to compliment each other in the convergence of their interests. This convergence, however, is probably not a consciously thought-out strategy or a part of the decision-making process. Nevertheless, this uneasy alliance highlights rather stark differences. Capitalist entrepreneurs, for instance, often find themselves at odds with what they consider to be the elders' unproductive uses of cattle and bridewealth. Elders, to the contrary, consider the seemingly authoritarian prescriptions advanced by government administrators as insulting to their dignity and threatening to their authority. And, while the continuity of lineage relations guarantees a voice for the elders, it is increasingly limited to the realm of their extended families. On the other hand, many villagers—particularly juniors—who have gained favorable access to external resources (including education) have been able to transcend the confines of the village and the ensuing obligations imposed by older organizational principles. Nevertheless, parvenus still find that they must translate their new-found wealth into the local idiom of kinship.

As indicated, major changes took place in the relations between elders, juniors, and women. Some have opened up new avenues of power for the elders, while others have led to the deterioration of their positions within the community. With the transformation of bridewealth and its subsequent inflation, many young men were propelled into labor markets or found it increasingly necessary to cultivate cash crops such as cotton.[39] Incomes were used to purchase "prestige" goods, which went to village elders along with money payments. Initially, migration was seasonal or lasted only a few years, but since the early 1970s its duration has steadily lengthened and some never return to the village except for the occasional visit. In part, this is due to the expansion of employment opportunities outside of the fields of agriculture, herding, and military/police service, especially in the construction industry and the service sector in the Khartoum conurbation. In these circumstances, remittances are frequently forwarded by migrants but are channeled differently than is bridewealth, usually limited to immediate kin. A further erosion of the elders' power is evident in villages where young men, against accepted practice, wed a wife from outside of the matrimonial area while migrating. Moreover, young men are increasingly able to gain access to village lands without the requirement of first establishing a family of their own. In effect, this circumvents and, thus, undermines the monopoly of the lineage elders over marriageable women and land, the cornerstones of the elders' authority.

Ironically, what adds to the wealth and status of the elders in many villages also contributes to its demise. The increased absence of young men creates labor shortages and contributes to the breakdown in nafir, resulting in the greater exploitation of women. In most areas of the Nuba Mountains competition for agricultural labor is fierce, and farmers vie against each other to attract workers. They must manipulate and cajole every claim and obligation in calling a nafir party. In this aggressive quest to attract laborers, competition has popularized the ethos of nafir beyond its prior meaning, even to the extent that it requires cash outlays. As obligations between age-mates or consanguine kin gave way to cooperation among neighbors and friends, sumptuary principles underwent inflation. Now it is difficult to arrange a nafir without serving meat (especially goat), tea, sugar, and, in some instances, *saut* (chewing tobacco). And, in the case of a specifically cash crop like cotton, that is at odds with the culture of nafir, wage labor is hired, opening the door to its regular utilization on other crops. Of all the potential labor resources, however, extra burdens of cultivation fall unevenly on women, who find they must intensify their work load to make up for shortfalls.

The very act of expanding agriculture onto the plains necessitated the acquisition and clearing of new land and cut into the authority of elders. These new lands lay outside of the elders' domain and, in most communities, the elders were unable to stake their claim of ancestral guardians to those lands. Only those juniors still reliant on the hillside claims of their elders are inspired with filial obedience. In addition, migrants lend (or lease in some areas) their lands to other villagers while they are absent from the village. These transactions also lie outside of the purview of elders.

Money is now a fact of village life—needed for education and medical services, agricultural inputs and labor, and taxes and bridewealth. Consequently, there is always the possibility of going into debt. The shayl has always been extremely generous with cash advances. The aim of the largess is soon apparent; the individual is obliged to sell the crop to him at the end of the coming season. There are limits to the power of the shayl—an individual cannot be separated from the land, as this is enmeshed in the authority of the elders and communal rights. The shayl, therefore, finds it very difficult to gain direct control over production and must remain content with simple usury. Nevertheless, the shayl limits the ability of the debtor to accumulate wealth (or simply savings) and, hence, can undermine the bridewealth system. The debtor's fear of an uncertain future and the shayl's predominant position in the marketing system ensure repayment of debt.

The new system of governance likewise presented competing bases of authority. In some gabila, like the Ghulfan of Somasem, the position of elders and priests was entirely undermined. Initially the British appointed a village chief (sheikh), a completely new type of leader, to collect taxes and maintain civil order, but accorded him no substantive power of enforcement. Consequently, only the weak paid, while the collector had to make up the difference himself (Ibrahim, 1985:46). Not surprisingly, at first villagers viewed this new civilian administration with distrust, as it went against the grain of the lineage elders. The sheikh functioned as a lightning rod for village discontent, with elders carping about disclosure of cattle for tax purposes, insubordination to priests, and collusion with outsiders. In spite of their beginnings, the rise of the politico-administrative elites, wealthy farmers, and successful entrepreneurs provides an independent power base and, thus, offers a way out from under the oversight of the elders.

Notes

1. Prestige goods incorporate goods that cannot be exchanged for commonplace consumption goods, underscoring the elders' monopoly over the former.
2. The lineage or domestic community depicted here is, in many ways, what Weber termed an ideal-type. For a further discussion, see Chapter 6.
3. This is not always the case, as in North Africa, where land shortages affect yet more historical variations.
4. Conversely, a slave is an individual without kin.
5. Hence, the basis for the common adage among Africanists that control over people is the key to wealth and power. Consequently, males need control over a wife and over her offspring.
6. Age-mates refers to institutionalized groupings of individuals assigned a common age, with special prerogatives and specific tasks (Bernardi, 1985:2).
7. A *hashasha* is a short handled implement with a flat metal blade, and a *sulokab* is a longer version. Both are pushed into the ground and turned at a right angle.
8. When weed growth is particularly vigorous, or weeding has been delayed, and rises above the crop, it generally must be pulled by hand. In addition, thinning is done in order to remove inefficient plants.
9. A wooden implement consisting of a flat board attached at a 45 degree angle to a long pole.
10. Even today, children under the age of 15 rarely work in the fields. My previous field experience had been in India and the Philippines, where child labor is quite common. When I asked why younger children did not perform agricultural work, people incredulously responded: "Because they are children!" The rare exception is during planting, especially the *jubraka*, where they will follow adults preparing the ground and plant seeds.
11. In the main, males and females participate alike, although females are responsible for carrying the water, *marissa*, and food to the *nafir* site.
12. For example, an individual may possess insufficient stocks with which to recompense the laborers because of previous illness or poor harvest.

13. The organization of age-grades varies considerably throughout the Nuba Mountains. Consequently, the following will offer a cursory overview; a more detailed account of the Shatt age-grade can be found in Chapter 7.

14. In some areas these were like separate "villages." Young men spent most of their time here under the tutelage of aged elders, who inculcated the youth in lineage lore and instilled obedience.

15. This is highly variable in the case of boys in a matrilineage, where a male assumes responsibility for his sister's sons.

16. During a celebration I attended in one village, I was told that each marriageable girl was preparing her best *marissa* for wide and liberal public sampling. The next day I asked my friends which of the girls had made the best *marissa,* and I was given the names of three girls.

17. Often the *kujur* is also the healer, able to divine the cause of particular illnesses.

18. "Witchcraft" in various forms also seems to be universal in the Nuba Mountains. Most individuals wear an amulet around their necks to ward off the "evil eye." Jealousy is one factor that is considered to provoke a witch and, consequently, operates as a leveling device, as successful individuals do not want to provoke a witch. On the other hand, prosperous people are assumed to have the support of witches by the very fact of their success.

19. In some communities females held responsibility for ensuring rains, healing the sick, and speaking in a spirit's voice as a *kujur.*

20. No Nuba in the past would have thought of initiating an agricultural activity on his/her own without the proper time being proclaimed by the rainpriest and celebrated by the village en masse.

21. Nadel (1947:4) refers to this as the "Chief of the Path" and notes the prevalence of this position among the various *gabila.* Also see Ewald, 1990.

22. According to Pallme (1844), in the wake of the *Defterdar's* campaign, whole villages fled Kordofan to seek refuge in the Nuba Mountains and Dar Fur.

23. One consequence of the reliance on hillside cultivation was the very real possibility of famine. It was the threat or reality of starvation that fueled intergabila raids throughout the Nuba Mountains.

24. This necessity also fostered a stronger division of labor between men and women, as men went to the far farms by themselves in order to leave the women and children in the safety of the mountains.

25. Certain groups became the prey of their more powerful neighbors and, as a result, paid protection, or ransom, for the return of captives. The Kurungu, Tumma, and Katcha, for example, seem to have had this type of relationship with the Miri (Baumann, 1987), while the Shatt were often raided by the Kadugli and Hamar. *Jallaba* also provided the master of the path with gifts in order to assure his safety while in a particular community.

26. Most accounts of the Nuba from the 1930s describe a decline in the number of cattle and goats from the past. Stevenson (1940), for example, records that the number of cattle fell from seven to three.

27. Baumann (1987:100) relates that the "Miri raiders and warriors were soon feared throughout the region" and that "An official British estimate of 1925 states that the then paramount chief of the Miri commanded no less than 500 riflemen."

28. A major complaint voiced to me by young men was the cost of marriage, especially in furnishing a house with urban-style furniture: metal table and chairs, metal frame bed, glasses, and so on.

29. At any rate, by this time the exchequer required that all colonies at a minimum be self-supporting, which Khartoum extended to all provinces within the Sudan.
30. The adoption of clothing entered the Nuba Maintains with the Islamic and Christian/European concept of shame of nakedness and the requirement to cover one's body.
31. The history of cotton in the Nuba Mountains was gathered primarily from interviews on August 24 and 26, 1987, with Abdul Rahman Al-Nour Al-Tilib, who was on the Gezira Board of Governors. Previous to this appointment, he was the general director of the Nuba Mountain Agricultural Production Corporation in Kadugli and also worked for the Mechanized Farming Corporation in Dilling, Damazin, and Gadaraf.
32. One *kantar* is equal to 99 pounds. During the 1930s farmers were paid 60 piasters per *kantar*, £1.20 in the 1940s, and £3.50 in the 1950s (Al-Tilib).
33. Al-Tilib lamented the fact that, with the use of tractors and the uprooting of trees, rather than chopping them down for better fallowing, "we are destroying our environment."
34. According to Oesterdiekhoff and Wohlmuth (1983:14), expenditure on food represents 71.6 percent of household consumption expenditures.
35. Information on the MFC was gathered, in part, from an interview with the General Director in Dilling, September 13, 1987.
36. The General Director informed me that "native people" (i.e., the Nuba) were not very adept at this type of agriculture, so that most schemes had to be given over to people from outside of the area, although he assured me that they were from Kordofan. In general, his bias regarding the Nuba was painfully evident in such comments as: "the inhabitants of the Nuba Mountains are unwilling to work," "the Nuba don't work," and "the Nuba aren't very good farmers."
37. There are also a number of international firms working in South Kordofan. The General Director of Agricultural Extension commented: "There are so many institutions, so many departments working (in South Kordofan), doing similar jobs but without any cooperation. And the foreign ones, they come for a while, do something and then leave, while another institution or group takes their place. And we don't always know what they are doing."
38. Unfortunately, these production factors are not produced in the Sudan, which poses a further drain on scarce funds.
39. This was and is, by no means, an even process among the various *gabila* and Arab groups. Among the Nuba, for example, the Ghulfan, Miri, and Nyimang, having adopted Islam and Sudanese-Arab customs earlier than others enjoyed better jobs and firmly established migration routes for later migrants to follow.

5

Multiple Structures and a Complex of Villages

Evidence of uneven development, documented through detailed field-work, underscores the problems explaining and substantiating the nature and tempo of modernization. Hence, our empirical level of analysis now shifts to the region in order to examine the extent and type of changes in the Nuba Mountains. This discussion thus brings back into the fore the persistence of older forms of social organization, and it highlights the difficulties in sweeping these away. It is our contention that households within the Nuba Mountains were initially shaped by lineages and later refashioned by modernizing pressures emanating in entirely different circumstances and forms of social organization. The primary purpose of this chapter is to provide additional understanding to matters of household through clarification of how the Nuba Mountains has been integrated into the wider Sudanese complex, as well as the form, and to what degree, such developments assume locally. This has great import for our understanding of household variations through considerations of patterns of social differentiation, market integration, and overall extent of change.

Traces of Mediation

One of the more troublesome tasks associated with fieldwork involves the recognition, simplification, and classification of information. Optimally, the researcher enters the study site with ready categories, then diligently sets about collecting data, and eventually struggles with analysis. But we know better. Preconceived categories are rarely self-evident in the field, nor are they entirely appropriate outside of their original setting. In the present case our problem centers around identifying the various manifestations resulting from the integration of the Nuba Mountains into the wider environment, as well as the character and extent of those processes.

Where historians tend to emphasize sequences of events, sociologists look for patterns of interaction. Taken together, it becomes possible to trace the effects of specific processes that come to dominate at particular junctures in space and time. Household formation, like commoditization, migration, social differentiation, or mechanization, is a process that occurs in a coherent and identifiable manner. Each process, however, exacts distinct outcomes at different empirical levels and, consequently, their shared connections are not always readily discernable nor intuitively apparent, leaving us with seemingly unconnected phenomena.[1] Processes, nonetheless, disclose evidence of their existence— elements of mediation—that can link seemingly dissimilar phenomena (Post, 1978). In this way, various mediations permit us to isolate critical processes at various empirical levels and to differentiate them into increasingly more manageable units. This task will later allow us to construct concrete categories within which to locate and typologize households.

What is of primary interest here is the overall type and nature of change in the Nuba Mountains, including the forms it assumes through traces of mediation imparted by the forces of modernization affecting the region. Certainly, as noted, the modernization of agriculture and the rise of a specifically capitalist economy have proven to be important forces of change. So, too, has been the spread of Islam, government institutions, modern technology, educational centers, and the like. Thus, we will briefly examine the twelve villages of Shatt Damam, Shair Tomat, Somasem, Kortala, Touqma, Keiga Lubin, Keiga Al-Khail, Umm Sardeiba, Umm Jabralla, Demick, Kalulu, and Miri Juwa, scattered throughout the Nuba Mountains (see figure 1.1). On the whole, the material presented here underscores the lack of uniformity and unevenness in the developmental processes, as evidenced through a variety of indicators. While these indicators are not conclusive evidence supporting the endurance of lineages, nonetheless, they point to the continued importance of direct production in meeting domestic needs; such needs are met through a multitude of nonmarket relations—communal, kinship, and familial. These indicators also point to the overall pattern, depth, and intensity of modernization in general.

Elements of Mediation

In *Peasants and Capital*, Trouillot (1988:198–230) characterizes elements of mediation "by their function at particular moments…rather than by their functional nature" (p. 199). He distinguishes spatially "fixed" and "mobile" elements of mediation, with the latter further differentiated into "material" ("instruments of mediation") and "human" elements ("agents of mediation"). For our purposes, spatially fixed elements include shops, mosques, churches, oil presses, clinics, schools, roads, markets, agricultural schemes, and the like. Material elements encompass various items such as tea, marissa, matches, oil, batteries, remittances, spears, rifles, hoes, tractors, mechanical threshers, taxes, bridewealth, money, and so on. Human elements comprise such individuals as sheikhs, jallaba, shayl, farmers, laborers, tractor drivers, tea vendors, and teachers.

Alone, traces of processes are merely "things" and have no real significant social meaning. Taken together, however, elements of mediation link individuals in specific patterns of social relations, although ensuing events hold differential relevance for the actors involved (Trouillot, 1988). In this way elements of mediation both refer to and reflect particular processes, but to the effect that singular elements do not affect everyone equally; hence, their importance varies. The importance of elements of mediation, therefore, lie in the clues they impart relating to "human behavior" and its options.[2]

Fixed Elements of Mediation

The central question here is: What broad patterns and trends have modernization affected that have transformed the physical environment of the Nuba Mountains? The analysis of such relevant items as shops, commodity markets, roads, water sources, and agricultural schemes demonstrates clear evidence of modernity as well as its recent temporal advancement. Fixed elements are also important loci around which people cluster because they draw people in as sellers, buyers, and producers of commodities, citizens of the Republic of the Sudan, practitioners of global religions, adherents of local beliefs, or social denizens enjoying camaraderie. These elements bring together diverse people who, on a personal level, share information that may confirm old ideas, alter present perceptions, or foster future plans. In short, it is here where the inhabitants of the Nuba Mountains find identity within the Sudanese state, as well as their place in the world outside their immediate borders. What fixed elements also reveal is that even relatively remote villages are not far removed from the modern world.

Institutions and Services

Table 5.1 shows the spread of selected institutions and services within the twelve villages. On the whole, each village witnessed a substantial increase in the number and types of institutions and services, with the exception of Kalulu and Shair Tomat.[3] The extension of certain government institutions and services (health clinic, primary school, police station, flour mill, and village council) indicate Khartoum's commitment to incorporate these villages into its general vision of a national Sudan, especially the larger economy, although the table indicates nothing of motive. Primary school instructors, for example, teach in the Arabic language. In itself this may indicate the need for a mutually comprehensible lingua franca, but the medium of instruction is increasingly the content of *The Koran*.[4] In addition, People's Councils tend to undercut the authority of village elders (unless they also dominate these institutions) and, in conjunction with Islam, minimize the authority of the local kujur and priests. In some villages, like Shatt Damam, Umm Jabralla, and Miri Juwa, however, the kujur and priests are not subject to the civil jurisdiction of local sheikhs.

It should not be implied that equal access to local institutions and services exists; this requires more in-depth considerations, such as ethnicity, gender, and class. The presence of cooperatives, nonetheless, evinces what Baumann (1987:189) terms "redintegration," such that a cooperative establishing a *tahona*, or flour mill, can restore a village's "viability, self-reliance, and communal pride." On the other hand, a flour mill, regardless of its source, also frees up the labor of women for other activities such as wage-labor and farm work, as they no longer need to spend hours pounding dura, just as it necessitates the need for money.[5] Cooperatives, such as a flour mill or a village shop, are usually created in conjunction with the collaboration of village people, labor migrants, and the Department of Cooperatives. The existence of regular weekly markets provides a ready outlet for cash sales of crops and, conversely, their purchase.

TABLE 5.1
Institutions and Services, Now and 20 Years Ago

Institution/service	Now	Diff.	Now	Diff.	Now	Diff.	Now	Diff.	Now	Diff.	Now	Diff.
	Shatt Damam		Shair Tomat		Somasem		Keiga Kortala		Lubin		Kalulu	
Mosque	1	—	1	+1	2	+2	2	+1	2	+1	0	—
Church	1	+1	0	—	0	—	0	—	0	—	0	—
Health clinic	1	—	0	—	0	—	1	—	1	—	1	+1
Primary school	1	—	0	—	0	—	3	+1	1	+1	0	—
Police station	0	—	0	—	0	—	0	—	0	—	0	—
People's Coun.	1	+1	0	—	1	+1	1	+1	1	+1	0	—
Weekly market	1	—	0	—	0	—	1	+1	0	—	0	—
Four mill	2	+1	0	—	1	+1	2	+1	2	+2	1	+1
Cooperative	1	+1	1	+1	1	+1	1	—	1	+1	0	—
Electric gen.	0	=	0	=	0	=	1	+1	0	=	0	=
Number change		+4		+2		+5		+5		+6		+2
	Umm Sardeiba		Demick		Touqma		Keiga Al-Khail		Umm Jabralla		Miri Juwa	
Mosque	3	+2	4	+3	3	+2	2	+2	1	+1	1	—
Church	1	+1	0	—	0	—	0	—	4	+4	0	—
Health clinic	1	—	1	—	1	—	1	+1	1	+1	1	—
Primary school	3	+2	2	—	1	—	2	+2	1	+1	1	—
Police station	1	+1	1	—	0	—	1	+1	0	—	0	—
People's Coun.	1	—	1	+1	1	+1	1	+1	1	+1	1	+1
Weekly market	1	—	1	—	0	-1	1	+1	0	—	0	—
Flour mill	1	—	3	+2	1	+1	2	+2	1	+1	1	+1
Cooperative	0	—	1	+1	0	—	0	—	0	—	1	+1
Electric gen.	0	=	0	=	0	=	0	=	0	=	0	=
Number change		+6		+7		+3		+10		+9		+3

The number of mosques and churches in each village, with the exception of Kalulu, which adheres solely to its indigenous spirituality, imparts concrete evidence of the penetration of "foreign" ideologies and belief systems. The manner by which Islam and, more importantly, Northern Sudan Arab Muslim culture have become so pervasive in many ways speaks as a metaphor for the trade that helped create and sustain the need for outside goods.[6] Without question, Islam has also changed local values in the Nuba Mountains, fostering shame of na-

kedness; proscriptions against alcohol (marissa) and pork; female seclusion (when economically feasible); denial of matrilinear customs;
displacement of the "natural order;"[7] alteration of rituals surrounding
birth, marriage, and death; and the generally perceived superiority of
Islam. More cynically, conversion to Islam, at least the cessation of
keeping pigs and the public imbibing of marissa, frequently is a touch-
stone for a village's acquiring government services, such as a school
or flour mill, and in gaining government employment.[8] The expansion
of Christianity is associated with the Anglo-Egyptian Condominium,
primarily through the early organizations of the Church Missionary
Society, Sudan United Mission, and Catholic missionaries such as
Bishop Danielé Camboni.[9] Since independence, Christian proselytization has been effectively held in check. Nonetheless, acceptance of either religion by the faithful acknowledges membership into
a global fellowship of like-minded believers. And, for any devout
Muslim, making the pilgrimage to Mecca represents the capstone to a
pious life.

The presence of police posts is primarily restricted to large,
centrally-located villages and provides a powerful symbol of
Khartoum's hegemony. The police are entrusted with maintaining
civil order, especially in serious crimes such as homicide, cattle theft,
or arson. Like many other institutions, the police force (and security
forces in general) is deeply politicized, as the following story reveals. In a dispute between the Nuba of Shatt Safia (a village near
Shatt Damam) and Arabs over grazing rights, seven Nuba were killed.
The Arabs claimed that the Nuba had stolen 400 head of cattle, while
the Nuba maintained that Arab cattle had destroyed their dura fields.
The government police, acting as a mediator, decided that the Nuba
should pay 460 cattle, while the Arabs would pay 31 cows per slain
Nuba, as well as £250,000 Sudanese in compensation for the destroyed crops. Still, the Nuba persistently denied that they had stolen any cows, and in all likelihood it would be very difficult, if not
impossible, to steal quietly away with 400 cows. On the day that the
exchange was to be completed, the Arabs took the Nuba cattle, returned 217 of the worst to the Nuba, paid no money, and left smil-
ing. It seems that on this day the government mediators were not
only "insignificant" police officers but were forces dispatched from
the Security for Southern Kordofan in Kadugli.

TABLE 5.2
Number of Shops, Now and 20 Years Ago

Village	Now	≥20 years	Village	Now	≥20 years
Shatt Damam	5	3	Kortala	21	9
Shair Tomat	1	0	Keiga Al-Khail	6	5
Somasem	5	2	Umm Jabralla	3	1
Keiga Lubin	11	3	Touqma	7	3
Kalulu	3	0	Demick	29	5
Umm Sardeiba	5	2	Miri Juwa	1	0

Infrastructure

The village shop (table 5.2) is an important conduit for the transmission of commodities in and out of villages. Each village contains at least one shop, while larger villages on regular thoroughfares boast many. Not only are goods available from other parts of the Sudan, but they frequently come from distant countries as well. The village store (*dukkan*) is the source for satisfying the now social necessities of local life, including tea, coffee, matches, spices, beads, cloth, soap, tobacco, and (especially) sugar. These goods, more than anything else, attest to the observable incorporation of villages into the larger capitalist world. In most villages the shops are specialized: general stores, tea stalls, and eating establishments, while larger ones like Keiga Lubin, Kortala, and Demick also feature a marissa house(s). Shops also comprise sites where outside news is passed along, gossip and information exchanged, and where young men sit playing dominos.

The medium of exchange utilized in most shops in smaller villages like Shatt Damam, Somasem, Kalulu, Umm Jabralla, and Miri Juwa suggests the limited nature of transactions. In the larger villages and towns of Kadugli, Dilling, Lagowa, and Talodi paper currency predominates as the medium of exchange; fifty pound notes down to twenty-five piaster notes. In villages such as Shatt Damam coins between five piasters and one pound still prevail for small purchases, exhibiting the "closed" nature of money circulation at the local level and the paucity of money in general (as well as escalating urban prices).[10]

Roads are essential in carrying the life blood of the market—commodities. Without adequate access to markets, the outflow of goods

TABLE 5.3
Road Access to the Twelve Villages

Village	Road Type	Village	Road Type
Shatt Damam	seasonal	Kortala	seasonal
Shair Tomat	variable	Keiga Al-Khail	variable
Somasem	year round	Umm Jabralla	seasonal
Keiga Lubin	year round	Touqma	year round
Kalulu	seasonal	Demick	variable
Umm Sardeiba	seasonal	Miri Juwa	seasonal

bound for the *suq* are choked off at the source. The principle route connecting the Nuba Mountains to the Khartoum area runs from Kadugli to Omdurman via Dilling and El Obeid. With the exception of the tarmac road linking Kadugli and Dilling, conditions are tough and the roads are poorly maintained, especially in the qoz areas and where bisected by khors. Long stretches of the tarmac road have also fallen into disrepair, forcing buses and lorries to drive alongside the deeply cratered surface. Another popular route leading from Kadugli permits passage through Habila and reaches up to Kosti on the edge of the vast Gezira scheme.[11] In addition, the network of dirt roads constructed between 1948 and 1951 are deeply eroded and now merely mark the way to various villages. Other rudimentary tracks radiate throughout the Nuba Mountains, although these, too, are frequently impassable.[12] Table 5.3 indicates the type of road connecting the sampled villages to regional market centers, especially Kadugli or Dilling. Depending on the terrain, the roads can be year round, seasonal, or conditional (variable roads are dependent on daily weather, regardless of season).

Within capitalism, the exchange of commodities conveniently takes place in formal, fixed markets. Where commerce currently differs from the past "is the nature of the involvement of the common people" (Tully, 1984:224). From an administered and restricted practice, open markets have now penetrated even the remotest village. Agricultural products and livestock comprise the primary commodities of a system of trade dominated by merchants (jallaba and *tajir*), allowing some individuals to acquire needed goods and others to accumulate capital. Market transactions are undertaken with differing motives. From the perspective of the "typical" farmer in the Nuba

Mountains, for example, exchange presents itself as C_1-M-C_2; that is, commodities (C_1) are exchanged for money (M), which, in turn, is exchanged for different commodities (C_2). A farmer may sell dura in order to buy sugar. The motive underlying such a transaction assumes selling one set of use-values for purchase of another. For those desiring to realize exchange-value rather than a good's use-value, trade presents itself as M_1-C-M_2, where (M_1) represents money used to purchase a commodity (C) in order to generate more money or profit (M_2). In this case, for example, a merchant uses his money to acquire sugar to sell at a profit.

In principle, market transactions assume that products exchange at equivalent values.[13] In reality, the situation in the Nuba Mountains is one of merchant monopoly and monopsony, which enables them to "buy cheap and sell dear." According to Mandel (1968:80–81), initially the appearance of professional traders from "a more advanced trading civilization…appear alongside owners of commodities who merely want to get rid of these commodities in order to meet some needs." Hence, the latter are unaware of the "real" value of their goods, while the former are. Certainly this finds familiarity in the first waves of khawaja and, later, the jallaba, who found their way to the Nuba Mountains. Now, however, other mechanisms also account for the decided lack of competition: a poor transportation system, small quantities sold by villagers over an extended period, the shayl preempting a farmer's options, and the vertical and horizontal integration of the merchants themselves. It is not surprising, then, that most villagers I questioned believed that merchants were duplicitous, less than honest in their dealings with them.

Table 5.4 outlines markets available to the respective villages, the day(s) of operation, and the mode of transport individuals utilize to bring their goods to market. The "informal on demand" market available in each village, at first glance, may appear trivial compared to the larger suq in Kadugli or Dilling, or even to the markets in Keiga Al-Khail, Kortala, and Demick. This marketing arrangement, however, constitutes the core of the entire system and, in fact, is what primarily connects the village to the wider economy. The tajir, or proprietor of the village dukkan, literally brings the market to an individual's front door. Most farmers enter the market as needs arise and/or as agricultural surpluses become available.[14] The tajir purchases the usually small amounts of-

TABLE 5.4
Market Location, Days Operated, and Transport Mode

Village	Market Domain: Days Operated: Transport Mode
Shatt Damam	1. local: informal on demand: variable. 2. local: weekly: variable. 3. Kadugli: daily: *reikha* (basket); rarely lorry.
Shair Tomat	1. Kadugli: daily: donkey and lorry.
Somasem	1. local: informal on demand: variable. 2. Kurgel: daily: lorry. 3. Dilling: daily: lorry.
Keiga Lubin	1. local: informal on demand: variable. 2. Demick: Sat./Mon.: 2—5 by *reikha*, 3. Al Bardab: Sat./Mon.: bicycle, donkey. 4. Koweik: daily: oxen or lorry. 5. Kadugli: daily: oxen or lorry
Kalulu	1. local: informal on demand: variable. 2. Kadugli: daily: *reikha*; rarely lorry.
Umm Sardeiba	1. local: informal on demand: variable. 2. local: daily: variable. 3. Kadugli: daily: donkey, oxen, or lorry.
Kortala	1. local: informal on demand: variable. 2. Agricultural Bank: local: variable. 3. El-Obeid: daily: lorry.
Keiga Al-Khail	1. local: informal on demand: variable. 2. local: Mon./Thurs.: variable. 3. Kadugli: daily—*reikha*, oxen, and donkey.
Umm Jabralla	1. local: informal on demand: variable. 2. Umm Sardeiba: daily: 2—4 by donkey. 3. Umm Dolo: daily: oxen and lorry. 4. Kadugli: daily: oxen and lorry.
Touqma	1. local: informal on demand: variable. 2. Dilling: daily: lorry.
Demick	1. local: informal on demand: variable. 2. local: Sat./Mon.: variable. 3. Kadugli: daily: *reikha*, donkey, camel, & lorry.
Miri Juwa	1. local: informal on demand: variable. 2. Miri Bara: daily: *reikha* and donkey. 3. Kadugli: daily: lorry; rarely *reikha*.

fered periodically by farmers. When a tajir amasses sufficient quantities, he transports them to regional markets or continues to hoard until prices rise. Although farmers fare better in the larger regularized markets, they still find the market controlled by the commercial networks of merchants. Not surprisingly, the bulk of the goods offered in the markets do not remain in the Nuba Mountains.

Contemporary Sudan was integrated into the world economy through the global agro-technical system, as a primary exporter of short-staple cotton and, later, of dura.[15] Overall, agricultural development has concentrated on large-scale mechanized schemes cultivated by contractual tenants (Gezira and the MFC schemes), but with cotton in the Nuba Mountains cultivated within the framework of the "village economy" (NMAPC).[16] The various schemes (especially MFC schemes) can be an important source of cash, although agricultural wage-labor employment on the schemes is less popular now, with the emergence of other opportunities.[17] Generally, villagers will only seek work on the large MFC schemes rather than the small NMAPC plots when the pay is better. Kortala village is in the midst of Habila scheme, while Touqma and Somasem are 1 hour away by lorry. Miri Juwa is 12 km from the nearest NMAPC schemes at Al-Mashisha and Al-Kedik, and Shatt Damam is some 40 km away from the NMAPC scheme at AbuSunun.

Table 5.5 notes the agricultural schemes directly located within village domains. As part of the arrangement between farmers and the NMAPC, farmers receive access to land and agree to plant half in cotton every other year.[18] In return the NMACP tractor discs the land, supplies seeds, and purchases the cotton at the end of the season. Most participants in this arrangement, however, expressed displeasure with the NMAPC, claiming that fields are frequently ploughed late, management is heavy-handed, and government prices are too low. As one individual told me: "Farmers are philosophers by nature; if anything is not justified by the labor in the fields, they won't sow it" (Al-Tilib, 1987).[19] Nevertheless, cotton cultivation can be a commanding cash crop and, besides, the participants prefer having their dura or simsim fields ploughed, as it reduces the amount of time spent weeding. Umm Sardeiba, as part of the NMRDC, receives HYV seeds, which significantly increases sorghum yields. It is also the site of an animal traction project.

TABLE 5.5
Agricultural Scheme within Each Village[20]

Village	Scheme	Village	Scheme
Shatt Damam	none	Kortala	none
Shair Tomat	NMAPC	Keiga Al-Khail	NMAPC
Somasem	none	Umm Jabralla	NMAPC
Keiga Lubin	NMAPC	Touqma	NMAPC
Kalulu	NMAPC	Demick	NMAPC
Umm Sardeiba	NMRDP	Miri Juwa	none

Resources

Given the dominant type of agriculture practiced in the Nuba Mountains, it is difficult to increase production without recourse to fertile lands since agricultural practices are extensive rather than intensive. The presence of the large mechanized schemes may offer a source of employment for agricultural labor, but they also compete for land. In many ways the expansion of mechanized farming may be likened to the enclosure and the engrossing movement that occurred in Great Britain more than 300 years ago. Relocation of whole villages or their encirclement, with the loss of their "traditional" farming lands, occurs under the guise of a perverse eminent domain, whereby no compensation is forthcoming, as the government technically owns all of the land. Kortala is not directly part of a scheme, but it is located within Habila and has lost some of its stock of agricultural lands to the MFC. Touqma and Somasem, also near Habila, feel indirect pressure. As the MFC schemes grow, villages come increasingly into direct conflict with each other over land-use rights.

Land availability is shown in Table 5.6. Kortala, Somasem, and Miri Juwa reported that there were no unused, unclaimed lands available. Inhabitants of Miri Juwa, hemmed in by rugged jebel, reported that available lands were extremely difficult to access during the rainy season because of a rain-engorged stream impeding the way. The remaining villages indicated that new and unclaimed lands were available. These lands, however, are not always convenient to the villages: Kalulu is 1 hour away by foot and also requires crossing a khor; Umm Sardeiba is 2 hours away, Demick, 2 1/2 hours, and Keiga Al-Khail, 3 hours.

TABLE 5.6
"Unclaimed" Lands for Agricultural Expansion,
Availability, and Distance from Village

Village	Avail./Dis.	Village	Avail./Dis.
Shatt Damam	yes/far	Kortala	no/claimed
Shair Tomat	yes/near	Keiga Al-Khail	yes/3 hours
Somasem	no/claimed	Umm Jabralla	yes/near
Keiga Lubin	yes/near	Touqma	yes/near
Kalulu	yes/1 hour	Demick	yes/2½ hours
Umm Sardeiba	yes/2 hours	Miri Juwa	no/claimed

In general, the traditional means of acquiring arable land continue to predominate at the village level. Table 5.7 displays the low mobility of land through land rentals and sales now and twenty years ago. The enduring belief equating land rights and gabila membership limits its rental and deters outright land sales. An outsider might rent land for a short period of time but can effect no long-term claims on it. After a couple of years they must vacate the land and move on. Most land rentals occur between villagers, where an absent migrant needs dura for his household or where an individual is unable to cultivate due to illness or age.

TABLE 5.7
Land Rented and Sold, Now and 20 Years Ago

Village	Rental		Sale	
	Now	≥20	Now	≥20
Shatt Damam	no	no	no	yes
Shair Tomat	no	no	no	no
Somasem	no	no	yes	no
Keiga Lubin	yes	yes	no	no
Kalulu	no	no	no	no
Umm Sardeiba	yes	no	yes	no
Kortala	yes	no	no	no
Keiga Al-Khail	yes	yes	no	no
Umm Jebralla	yes	yes	yes	yes
Touqma	yes	no	no	no
Demick	yes	no	no	no
Miri Juwa	no	no	no	no

Typically this involves a "sharecrop" agreement, but there is no established sum and it does not entail direct cash payments.

As the above table reveals, land sales are much less common, especially cash sales involving outsiders. This entails the actual transference of land rather than just rights to its cultivation.[21] The Nuba of Umm Sardeiba were quick to point out that it was the Arab residents who rented and sold land. To them this seemed a very bad act, a denial of the sanctity of land and, thus, the village. There was one incidence of land sale in Somasem, but many villagers were reluctant to discuss it because they were still angry with the individual who did it. People felt that it would cause others to follow suit and would diminish the land supplies of the village. More revealing, one old man in Somasem sadly shook his head when asked to comment on the story and grieved: "In the past we used to be a village, but not any more." In another case, the elders of Shatt Damam made an exception and allowed a "Fellata" merchant to purchase land on a one-time basis and settle within the village.

In a semiarid region, water perhaps constitutes the most important resource. Sources of potable water (table 5.8) determine the location of villages in large measure, regulate women's work load as the prime carriers, and affect the well-being of the community through water-born diseases such as *frendit* (guinea worm) and amoebic dysentery. In the past, villages were limited to springs (*saraf*), streams, wells, and hafir. Many villages now boast hand pumps, which not only reduce the time women spend ferrying water, but provide safe drinking water.[22] Only Somasem did not have a pump and had to rely on a hafir, which they shared with their cattle and goats. Both Somasem and Touqma also have water delivered, but most people are unable to afford this luxury.

Mobile Elements of Mediation

Mobile elements of mediation are equally important and continuously reflect the manner by which the Nuba Mountains was integrated into the modern world. These elements are ubiquitous, from the marissa purchased by field laborers in Habila, to the agricultural inputs designed to increase yields; from the radio blasting the latest ballads popular in Khartoum, to the poster of Michael Jackson taped to the wall of a small shop in Kadugli; from the lorries transporting their cargo, to the UNICEF plane landing on the gravel strip at the Western Sudan Agricultural Re-

TABLE 5.8
Water Sources and Distance, Now and 20 Years Ago

Village	Source Now: Distance	Source ≥20 years: Distance
Shatt Damam	1. well: 15 min. 2. spring: 20 min. 3. pump: inside	1. well: 15 min 2. spring: 20 min
Shair Tomat	1. surface well: 30 mins. 2. deep well: inside 3. pump: inside	1. surf. well: 30 min. 2. deep well: inside
Somasem	1. *hafir*: inside 2. pump: 3 hours 3. delivered: inside	1. *hafir*: inside
Keiga Lubin	1. stream: 15 min. 2. pump: inside	1. stream: 15 min. 2. surf. well: 10 min.
Kalulu	1. spring: 5 min. 2. stream: 15 min. 3. pump: 1 hour 4. surface well: 1 hour	1. spring: 5 min. 2. stream: 15 min.
Umm Sardeiba	1. stream: 15 min. 2. pump: inside	1. stream: 15 min. 2. surf. well: inside
Kortala	1. *hafir*: inside 2. pump: inside	1. *hafir*: inside 2. surf. well: inside
Keiga Al-Khail	1. surface well: 10 min. 2. pump: inside	1. surf. well: 10 min.
Umm Jabralla	1. surface well: inside 2. spring: 15 min. 3. stream: 15 min.	1. surf. well: inside 2. spring: 15 min. 3. stream: 15 min.
Touqma	1. deep well: inside 2. stream: 10 min. 3. spring: 10 min. 4. delivered: inside	1. deep well: inside 2. stream: 10 min. 3. spring: 10 min.
Demick	1. spring: 20 min. 2. deep well: 15 min. 3. surface well: 10 min. 4. pump: inside	1. spring: 20 min. 2. deep well: 15 min. 3. surf. well: 10 min.
Miri Juwa	1. spring: 15 min. 2. stream: 15 min. 3. pump: inside	1. spring: 15 min. 2. stream: 15 min. 3. pump: inside

search Project; and, from tablets of chloroquine to combat malaria, to the remittances sent back by family members laboring outside of the Nuba Mountains. Material elements of modernity are too numerous to list and are ever present in their often sharp contrast to the supposed bucolic life of the village. But these are just inanimate objects, inconsequential without the people whose lives they touch. People are thus the crux of social reality, and by giving meaning to the physical world, they set their stamp on space and time. Here it will be useful to briefly highlight some of the more important material and human mobile elements of mediation.

Material Articles

Every good produced presupposes an eventual use-value. Most use-values at the village level go to satisfy subsistence needs. While it is possible to delineate an absolute minimum necessary for human existence, this quickly unravels when applied across the board. More revealing are relative standards that are historically and culturally defined. Accordingly, goods offered in the dukkan provide evidence as to what satisfies the social average of basic needs.[23] Yet, while some may appear to be luxuries, tell that to the young woman in courtship desiring a bottle of scent or to an older man relaxing with his friends and enjoying saut (snuff). Table 5.9 lists various commodities on (or under) the shelves of most shops. The prices in 1969 and 1977 are for the village of Fungor, located in the southeastern section of the Nuba Mountains. The prices in 1987 come from the suq in Kadugli and Dilling.

Price rises from 1969 to 1987 are quite dramatic. While these comparisons have no absolute validity, they nevertheless convey the image of an expanding capitalist economy, but an especially volatile one. Even the Nuba Mountains was not shielded from inflation, although some increases are probably attributable to Sudan's sagging economy in general. The disparate prices also reveal an inherent problem of market instability, primarily induced shortages from hoarding and from Sudan's chronic lack of foreign exchange, as well as the increased dependence on external sources for necessities (with the exception of oil, salt, and onions, these products must be secured from sources outside villages). On the other hand, the rise in importance of certain commodities mirrors the expansion in transport services needed to get these products to market. Lastly,

TABLE 5.9
Selected Commodity Prices in the Nuba Mountains, 1969, 1977, and 1988**

			prices per unit		
Year	1969	1977	1987	1987	
Commodity	unit	Fungor	Fungor	Kadugli	Dilling
1. coffee	kg	0.36 0.80	2.80 4.45	25.00– 37.50	22.50
2. hoe, axe, spear, knife blades	1 0.15 each	0.10– NA	0.25 10.00	4.00– 15.00	7.00–
3. cloth (plain white)	meter 0.08	0.05– 0.25	0.15– 12.00	6.00– 17.50	7.00–
4. sugar	kg	0.15	0.15	4.25– 10.00	4.50– 6.75
5. salt	kg	0.08	0.11	1.00	1.00
6. scent	bottle 0.25	0.15– 0.50	0.25– 10.00	16.00	6.00–
7. oil	kg	0.30	0.45	6.75	6.75
8. dates	kg	0.15	0.25	8.00– 20.00	4.50– 19.00
9. *matches	box	0.03– 0.05	0.02	.25– .75	.50– .75
10. flashlight	1	0.50	1.00	25.00	23.00
11. batteries	1	0.08	0.15	5.00– 7.50	6.00– 8.00
12. bulbs	1	0.05	0.05	.50	.50
13. mirror	1	0.25	0.50	4.50	5.50
14. beads	strand	0.10	0.20	2.50	2.50
15. blueing	pack	0.10	0.15	.25	.25
16. snuff	kg	NA	2.20	15.75	18.00
17. cigarette	10	NA	0.20	3.00– 7.50	5.00– 10.00
18. soap	powder/bar	NA	0.07	.75– 1.50	.75– 1.00
19. tea	kg	NA	2.30	27.00	22.50
20. onions	kg	NA	0.10	2.25	1.85

** Unadjusted prices for 1969 and 1977 are from Iten (1979:81).
* Matches in 1969 were primarily used for making bullets. Now they are primarily used for lighting fires.

TABLE 5.10
Type of Agricultural Labor by Order of Importance**

Village	Labor	Village	Labor
Shatt Damam	N,F,W	Kortala	W,F*
Shair Tomat	F,W,N	Keiga Al-Khail	N,F,W
Somasem	W,N,F	Umm Jabralla	F,N,W
Keiga Lubin	F,N,W	Touqma	F,N,W
Kalulu	F,N,W	Demick	F,N,W
Umm Sardeiba	F,W,N	Miri Juwa	F,N,W

N = *nafir* F = family W = wage labor * do not use anymore ** rank order, from left to right.

escalating prices also indicate an increase in the money supply, although not in the numbers of people with effective market demand.

In its broadest sense and, as an historical abstraction, capitalism characterizes a particular relation whereby "free" and "unutilized" labor is bought and sold through contractual relations; the laborer receives a wage while the employer owns the product of that labor. Within lineages, labor in the main is communal and familial based. A useful summary of the rationalizing process within the local economies, then, is revealed in the source of labor in the fields. Table 5.10 profiles the types of agricultural labor used by order of importance.

Villagers in Kortala abandoned nafir in the early 1970s. People claimed that arranging nafir became too taxing, owing to out-migration and lack of time, which limited participation in other's nafir parties. Villagers also cited its expense and preferred to replace it with wage-labor. Besides, as one informant explained, "People come and they just want to drink marissa, so it is easier to use wage-labor." The villages of Shatt Damam, Kalulu, Umm Sardeiba, and Umm Jabralla, on the other hand, reported an increase in the use of nafir labor. In part, this is attributable to difficulties in securing wage-labor at reasonable rates, but hiring wage-labor also involves the tacit admission that one has no kinsmen, age-mates, and friends to count on to help. Reliance on nafir remained constant in Somasem, Touqma, and Demick, as farmers who expanded production took advantage of any type of labor regardless of its perceived costs.

The ethos of nafir has changed in some instances. In addition to receiving the traditional foods, some nafir participants receive "nontraditional" inducements, such as cash or saut in Shatt Damam, Kalulu, Somasem, and Umm Jabralla. Essentially, this is a form of wage-labor, but without the pejorative labels that accompany it.[24] Most males believe their community standing would be compromised if they worked for a fellow villager and that it would also indicate a cavalier attitude towards their own fields. Consequently, the majority of villagers laboring on their neighbors' fields for cash are women, children, and the aged. This not only points to chronic labor shortages affecting villages, due to the excessive out-migration of young men, but also to the economic plight gripping many villages. Farmers in Shatt Damam, Kalulu, Keiga Al-Khail, Umm Jabralla, and Miri Juwa employed labor from within the village, while those in Touqma, Keiga Lubin, Umm Sardeiba, Somasem, Shair Tomat, and Demick hired labor both from within and from outside their respective villages. Only Kortala residents hired labor exclusively from outside.

Capitalism requires rationalization of production. Part of this process involves increased productivity achieved through technical inputs. All of the villages, except Umm Jabralla, reported that recent harvests have been less bountiful than they were twenty years ago. While some of this can be attributed to a tendency to view the past with wistful nostalgia, there are very real constraints. Rain dominates any topic of conversation, more so since the drought of 1984, and everyone concluded that the rains were better twenty years ago. Additional barriers given for "poor" agricultural production were pests (birds, locusts, bullworms, beetles, ants, termites, and rats), weeds (*umm chakko, abu lissek, moletta,* and *buda*), and "tired" soil.[25] Few inputs were available to combat these problems and, when they were, the farmers had little knowledge of proper usage.[26] Chemical fertilizers were rarely used, although DDT and Aldrex T[27] were commonly utilized by large-scale village farmers. Diseases affecting cattle include anthrax (*fahima*), rinderpest (*judri*), other bacterial diseases, such as *safra* and *umm zagala*, and *umm brijango* (a poisonous plant). Farmers still trek their herds northward during the rainy season in hopes of avoiding these. Other problems that deflate productivity included human illness, such as malaria and guinea worm.

Marissa must also be mentioned. Historically, as the primary source of nutrition and calories, marissa is the "cultural superfood" of the Nuba Mountains.[28] It also carries strong cultural and symbolic connotations.

Marissa comprises the primary food of nafir parties; it is offered to all guests as a measure of hospitality, and it is central to religious rituals and village festivities. The enjoyment of marissa is very much a communal affair such that few people (if any) drink it alone. Although marissa is intoxicating, it is a mild libation that, in the moderate quantities consumed, does not cause drunkenness, merely a "lightening of the human spirit." Therefore, when a Nuba no longer partakes of marissa on religious grounds (Islam), they are rejecting, in large measure, a part of Nuba culture. Moreover, marissa holds an important place in a cash economy, especially for the women who control its brewing. Marissa also allows a male access to female labor; a man cannot force his wife to work in his fields, but he can make legitimate requests for marissa.

Human Instruments

Although we have already discussed elements of human mediation, especially people with power, such as the kujur, rainpriest, elders, small-scale farmer, etc., we must return briefly to the merchant. Merchants (the tajir and jallaba) are an important linchpin in the capitalist economy, although they remain content with making their living in the realm of circulation and, for the most part, do not attempt to control or rationalize the agricultural production process.[29] The tajir operates at the village level, buying crops from the villagers and selling them manufactured goods in return. The jallaba functions at the regional level, dealing in wholesale markets. One indication of the paucity of capital in the Nuba Mountains is the minimal cash outlay required to enter into trade. A hopeful trader, however, must first attach himself to a jallaba in order to establish the right connections and to ensure the flow of commodities. The marketing system thus centers around a two-tiered system of dependence: the village retailer on the jallaba for transport, manufactured goods, and government rationed items,[30] and the local populace on the retailers for their purchases and sales (Salih, 1984). Ironically, what also facilitates this dependence is the desire to avoid taxes that must be paid to the government agent in the larger markets—*ushuur* (paid by the seller) and *gibaana* (paid by the merchant).

Where more than one dukkan exists, the tajir usually are relatives or fast friends, thus maintaining a close reign on the market. Similar ties bind the local retailers to the jallaba and enables a relatively inclusive market structure. In addition, the more successful tajir and jallaba own the lorries that transport people and goods to market, as well as the off-scheme tractors needed by farmers if they hope to expand their production. Differences of opinion do exist between merchants, and relations are not always harmonious among traders. Nevertheless, it is in the economic interests of all to minimize discord.

The local merchant also functions as the shayl. It is difficult to obtain information on this informal credit system—not on how it works but on its specifics. Most people will acknowledge knowing someone who has borrowed money, grain, or seed from a shayl, yet only a handful will admit to having done so themselves. It is not a point of social honor to be forced to do business with a shayl. Not only does debt bring into question an individual's farming ability, but one's ability to adequately care for one's family. In short, debt imparts a loss of respect. As noted, the shayl system requires a farmer's mortgaging future crops or, less frequently, repayment in cash at exorbitant rates (commonly 50 to 75 percent interest rates).

Unquestionably, agricultural activities dominate village life. Although limited specialization predates modernity and capitalism, what differs is its scope. In the past, skillful artisans generally produced goods like saddles, wooden bowls, or baskets to meet a limited need. These avocations still exist, but equally important in shedding light on changes in the local economy is the growth of nonagricultural wage labor employment. The general local shortage of money compels some to look for alternate sources of cash outside of farming. Table 5.11 presents these occupations within villages both now and twenty years ago.[31] The rapid increase in the number of civil servants mirrors the general trend in Sudan as a whole. These include omda, sheikh, guard, police, *katib as-suq* (market clerk), and so on. Although a school teacher may still cultivate a small plot, teaching indicates the local desire to gain new opportunities. Nevertheless, teachers are usually townspeople who rarely remain past their initial appointment. Tailors sew garments by order on pedal-operated machines owned, in most cases, by the local tajir. Cobblers, similarly, make or repair shoes on demand, primarily for town dwellers who have adopted the habit of footwear. Carpenters, blacksmiths, and builders ply old trades to people with money who no longer have the time to undertake these chores themselves and are unable or unwilling to call a nafir. Butchers cater to the local demand for meat,

TABLE 5.11
Nonagricultural Wage-Labor Occupations within Villages, Now and 20 Years Ago

Occupation	Now	Diff.	Now	Diff.	Now	Diff.	Now	Diff.	Now	Diff.	Now	Diff.
	Shatt Damam		Shair Tomat		Somasem		Kortala		Keiga Lubin		Kalulu	
Carpenter	0	—	1	—	8	+8	0	—	3	—	0	—
Tailor	5	+4	0	—	0	—	6	—	6	+4	0	—
Cobbler	1	+1	0	—	0	—	0	—	0	-1	0	—
Builder	6	—	0	—	2	+2	0	—	6	+3	0	—
Butcher	3	+3	0	—	1	+1	5	—	4	+3	1	+1
Midwife	0	—	1	+1	1	+1	1	+1	5	+5	0	—
Blacksmith	4	+2	0	—	0	—	6	+5	3	+1	0	—
Teacher	1	+1	2	+2	1	+1	6	+5	3	+3	0	—
Civil servant	0	=	2	+2	0	=	52	+52	25	+17	2	+2
Number change		+11		+5		+13		+63		+35		+3
	Umm Sardiba		Demick		Touqma		Keiga Al-Khail		Umm Jabralla		Miri Juwa	
Carpenter	0	—	3	—	0	-1	3	+3	0	—	1	—
Tailor	2	+1	11	+8	5	+5	4	-16	0	—	0	—
Cobbler	0	—	2	-19	1	+1	4	+3	0	—	0	—
Builder	0	—	6	+3	0	—	10	+10	0	—	0	—
Butcher	1	+1	6	+3	2	+2	4	+3	1	+1	0	—
Midwife	1	—	2	+1	1	+1	1	+1	1	+1	1	—
Blacksmith	1	—	1	—	1	—	2	—	2	—	0	—
Teacher	6	+6	3	+2	0	—	3	+3	3	+3	3	+3
Civil servant	21	+21	40	+22	6	-2	18	+18	18	+18	35	+12
Number change		+29		+20		+6		+25		+23		+15

where an individual has no animals or does not want to slaughter one of his own animals. Although people enjoy eating meat, its expense has pushed it out of the daily diet of most villagers.

From the above discussion, it is clear that modernizing pressures, including the rise and spread of capitalism, have been experienced unevenly within the Nuba Mountains. Some insights have also been revealed regarding the various mixtures of noncapitalist and capitalist structures and the forms of social organization, but the relationship of these for households has yet to be clarified. Clarification of this will lead to an explication of households and of useful means to construct a typology of household forms.

Notes

1. A hierarchy of mediations intervenes between phenomena and essence and tends to obscure the linkage. Thus, while it is untenable to draw direct correlations by way of crude reductionism, neither is it warranted to argue independence of form.
2. It is not always easy to follow these slender threads (order, simplify, and classify data), especially in a complex social formation rent with structural contradictions and human struggles. Events and patterns hold different outcomes for the various actors involved. Some are affected directly while others are only indirectly. How the actors "fit" into a sequence of events serves to shape subsequent patterns of interaction.
3. The inhabitants of Kalulu have remained in the hills and are distrustful of outsiders. In fact, when some children spied me coming they fled, shrieking, into the "bush," sure that the "bogey man" had come for them. Shair Tomat, on the other hand, is a small village that must rely on the surrounding villages for needed services.
4. This point was first made to me by a Dinka youth in Kadugli, who told me: "I don't mind learning Arabic: we have to be able to talk to different people. But I do not want to become a Muslim; I don't want to study *The Koran*."
5. It takes approximately twenty minutes for three women to pound a *malwa* (4.125 litres) of *dura* into edible grain. Women typically sing "grindstone songs" while working.
6. Islam, from its inception, arose in a mercantile capitalist culture, originating in the vast trade centers of the Arabian peninsula. The success of Islam, from its beginnings in Mecca, lay in its combination of urban mercantile elites with Bedouin nomadic warriors. Similar patterns are equally evident in the Sudan (as well as the Nuba Mountains). Rodinson (1974) argues that Islam is not antithetical to capitalism and, in fact, capital sectors developed in the "Arab world" similar to their Christian European counterparts. Muslim merchants, however, remained content with trading and not with producing commodities (see Turner, 1974).
7. Islam, like Christianity, is a "temple-bound" religion rather than "nature-oriented" (Campbell, 1988). Consequently, "animist" religions are considered to be displays of magic in their attempts to place themselves in accord with nature. Temple-bound religions break with nature, such that nature must be dominated and controlled.
8. In the hills around Kadugli, I witnessed Christian church workers offering food and clothing to those who would "embrace Christ." Consequently, depending upon whom some Nuba were addressing, they would respond with the "correct" religious orientation.
9. Christianity is bound up with the twin missions of spreading Christ and capitalism, although the relationship between the two in the Nuba Mountains is not as clear-cut as it is with Islam, where Islam and trade are closely intertwined.
10. After I had returned to Khartoum for a brief stay I stopped to purchase a cup of tea and paid with coins. The tea vendor laughed and asked me where I had come from. When I replied, "the Nuba Mountains," she looked knowingly at me.

11. Kortala is a bus/lorry stop on this road.
12. One road on which I traveled from Kadugli to Miri Juwa passed over an extremely rocky *jebel*. One stretch of the road was constructed using a lining of small boulders. On the return trip the front tire slipped, causing the front drive shaft to snap in half.
13. In neoclassical terminology, there is a perfectly competitive market, with perfect knowledge of prices and costs.
14. The *shayl* system operates on the premise that household consumption is squeezed to the maximum such that there are no surpluses with which to meet the needs of household reproduction.
15. It was hoped by the World Bank, the International Monetary Fund, the U.S. Agency for International Development, the European Economic Community, the Arab Bank for Economic Development, and the Faisal Islamic Bank that the Sudan would become the "breadbasket of the Middle East."
16. Presently, many international agencies criticize the Sudan for its mechanized schemes, especially their agricultural strip-mining. Ironically, the World Bank played a key role in their inception, as did the Arab Development Bank.
17. As Al-Tilib (1987) informed me, most of the laborers on the MFC schemes are Dinka and Arabs from North Kordofan.
18. This appears to be the typical arrangement, although others exist, such as 15 *feddan*; 5 for cotton, 5 for *dura*, and 5 left fallow. Cotton is grown on a yearly basis within this type of scheme.
19. According to Al-Tilib, the optimum sewing time follows the first ample rains. A month past this reduces the crop anywhere from 30 to 50 percent.
20. NMAPC is Nuba Mountain Agricultural Corporation and NMRDC is Nuba Mountain Rural Development Corporation.
21. Nadel (1947) noted land sales as the transfer of use rights within a *gabila* for a nominal fee. Hawksworth (1932) and Wood (1971) found no incidences, while I found it to be very minor.
22. Most of the pumps were installed by UNICEF, which trains local people in their maintenance.
23. Class considerations are apparent in satisfying consumer demand. Therefore, what one class may consider a necessity, another will deem a luxury, although equally desirable.
24. Bad farmers (as well as good) are frequently the subject of local songs. One element of being a good farmer is the willingness to share one's bounty, evident in sumptuous *nafir*. In this case hiring wage-labor, even if a farmer has the cash, would appear vulgar and dismissive of one's communal obligations.
25. Also cited was the poor system of NMAPC, which caused late planting and stray animals in the fields.
26. This was particularly frightening, especially with such toxic chemicals as DDT. One farmer quit using it because it made his cattle ill, but he made no mention of its effect on himself or his family. Moreover, the chemicals were handled with bare hands.
27. *Suweit* is a substitute that is manufactured locally in the Sudan.
28. Rice provides most calories in Asia, corn meal in Central America, bread in North America, and so on. These are what may be termed "cultural superfoods."
29. Merchants seem to own and control everything except the immediate production process. In part, there is too much uncertainty in the main, except on MFC schemes, where money capital and government-subsidized land minimizes risk.

30. The *jallaba*, through their connections in the Rural Council and cooperatives, are relegated the responsibility of dispersing goods covered by the government rationing system—essentially food goods like sugar and wheat-flour. I rarely saw any commodity sell at its fixed government price. Consequently, there is a lively black market, and when real shortages appear in the markets, it is essential that a person know somebody with "connections."

31. Not included is the position of operating a flour mill. With the exception of Shair Tomat, which has none, each village has a local individual who operates one.

6

Household Forms and Social Differentiation

Questions concerning the dynamics and the differential effects of the integration of households into the modern world are not easily resolved. Within the Nuba Mountains, the unevenness in developmental processes and the preponderance of household-based production units merits special consideration. In part, problems arise from "an emphasis on broadly generalizable features of Third World formations [which] has led to a lack of attention to understanding the tremendous heterogeneity of less developed countries" (Vandergeest and Buttel, 1988:685; also see Moore, 1979). Too often, theorization consists of formal models that propose to represent rather than interpret reality. As such, when applied to developing countries, these models become self-determining, specifying a priori the outcomes they, in fact, seek to explain. To the contrary, one cannot argue from a general set of propositions; rather, general statements must be firmly based on grounded historical work (Tilly, 1984). Given this, certain ambiguities in the analysis of development suggest a need to seriously rethink what we mean by transformation, especially the modernization of village life in the Nuba Mountains and its impact on household formation, organization, and function. Against this, our task unfolds with the aim of devising categories that can empirically differentiate and clarify household types and livelihood strategies.

Social Transformation and Modernization

Debates over the nature of social transformation have long dominated the field of development sociology. Most notably, transformation has been conceptualized from the classical sociologists onward in terms of dichotomous ideal-types—traditional/modern—which are placed in binary opposition. These antinomies have then been used to describe

157

and contrast past and present human social structure and to explain the processes of change from one form of society to another. In this manner, Marx described the transition from feudalism to capitalism, Durkheim the shift from mechanical to organic solidarity, and Weber the rise of bureaucracy and formal rationality. Despite a number of well-known problems, this type of formulation maintains certain analytical appeal. Tönnies, for example, envisaged transformation in terms of *"Gemeinschaft"* (community) and *"Gesellschaft"* (association), Maine of "status" and "contract," Zimmerman of "localistic" and "cosmopolitan," Becker of "sacred" and "secular," Frank of "satellite" and "metropolitan," and de Janvry of "peasant" and "capitalist." Notwithstanding differences in theoretical approaches, such accounts can be useful by painting a broad-brush picture of the nature of changes brought about by modernization and the consequences of those changes over time— namely, the process of social differentiation evident in the rationalization of social behavior and organization (Moore, 1979).

One of the difficulties in employing a traditional/modern dichotomy, however, is in the strong tendency to sacrifice historical specificity for conceptual purity. This is unfortunate. Weber (1949:90) termed a construct of formal theory an "ideal-type" or a "conceptual pattern [bringing] together certain relationships and events of historical life into a complex, which is conceived as an internally consistent system."[1] More importantly, as Weber was quick to note, "In its conceptual purity, this mental construct *(Gedankenbild)* cannot be found empirically anywhere in reality" (90). It is hardly surprising, then, that the failure to effectively incorporate contextual and historical analysis has proven to be a recurrent problem in development studies. An ideal-type cannot demonstrate or verify the reality of a particular case—nor identify a particular stage in an assumed tradition/modern continuum—but simply provides a useful tool to discern variations. In this respect, an ideal-type as a theoretical model is clearly "subjective or interpretive and may be used to 'understand,' but not 'explain,' an empirical case" (Vandergeest and Buttel, 1988:687).

Accompanying the emphasis on broadly generalizable features depicting traditional and modern societies has been the discomforting propensity to force particular cases into a predetermined model of modernization. Concomitant with the trend in the social sciences for deductive theorization is the assumption that what occurs in the course of modernization is not only necessary, but inevitably unfolds according to certain objective laws of development—invariably modeled on that which has happened in the West. This, too, is misplaced; there is no "natural" course of social change. Unquestionably, all aspects of human life have been profoundly affected by the "great transformation" begun in Europe during what Fernand Braudel has called the "long" sixteenth century. Indeed, the creation of the modern world or industrial-based society is still on-going. But, is such a model appropriate for understanding contemporary societal development in the Third World? In other words, will the historical record of such regions as the Nuba Mountains necessarily match that of the West? Probably not; but, if we concede that modernization was never a smooth process in the West, devoid of conflict and uncertainty, then major objections diminish. According to Moore (1979:26-7), for example, "Exaggeration of commonalities among premodernizing societies and the neglect of different historical paths" ignores "major value differences, along with differences in resources, organizations, and normative structures [that are] significant for both the course and the destination of change." The same is true in the West, where accounts of uneven development are well documented (see, for example, Lyson and Falk, 1993; Davidson and Schwarzweller, 1995). The point is, both ideal-types of society display an impressive range of historical and structural variation that is central to understanding what is happening in developed and developing countries alike.

From this perspective, then, not all traditional or premodern societies need be fundamentally alike. Nor is convergence a foregone conclusion of modernization. To ignore this confuses concept with process, abstraction with context. Furthermore, social differentiation and rationalization in no way suggest stable-end states, either at the beginning or end of the modernization process; to the contrary, we should be sensitized to the fact that there are a variety of social structures and, thus, multiple paths of development. All that modernization signifies is the capacity for social transformation, where modernizing societies are becoming increasingly complex and their component social processes more calculable (Roxborough, 1988). In other words, linear evolutionism and teleology are not inherent to the notion of modernization. This becomes especially evident once we acknowledge the importance of the human actor. As summarized by Vandergeest (1988:23), "in understanding agrarian transformation and how peasants are likely to react, it is important to look at both losses and gains in control, power, and agency, and in particular, at the choices peasants are able or not able to make as the economic, political, and cultural institutional context in which they live changes." And with respect to household, it soon becomes obvious that neither the persistence nor the decline of small-scale family-based enterprises is an inevitable outcome of modernization; to the contrary, the local basis of society is being continuously redefined in various ways and with different results.

Household, Smallholder, and Modernization

While recent assessments of rural transformation acknowledge the increasing importance of economic rationalization and means-end orientation in the transformation of contemporary society, the impact on the organization and function of households remains unclear. At what point, for example, do noneconomic considerations diminish and the rationalization of production begin? Certainly, households evincing a firm distinction between "economy and society"—business enterprise and domestic unit—are both quantitatively and, above all, qualitatively different from households where these are joined. "Before capitalist production was fully developed," writes Perelman (1983:20), "one could not locate a clear boundary separating those activities directed toward the production of commodities for sale on the market from those other activities performed to reproduce the household." Ostensibly, then, expansion and intensification in the marketing of goods and services magnifies and sharpens this distinction. Nevertheless, households can assume a variety of forms and can engage assorted activities, but for different sets of reasons and with different consequences. But, this says nothing of what households actually look like, nor about what household members do.

At the risk of redundancy, Weber's use of an ideal-type is pointedly one-sided, used for understanding social change and not for forcing the interpretation of complex reality into pregiven models. Households are not historical isolates but must be contextualized and operationalized within a wider framework of analysis. In this respect, there are no specific household forms that we can confidently label "modern." Much of the confusion over the perceived nuclearization of the household stems, in part, from Parson's (1943) supposition that the fragmentation of the household (family) cohered with industrialization, as well as from Le Play's "error of order about the original universality of large and extended households" (Laslett, 1987:270). Others argue that changes occur not so much within the household but within the community. Tönnies (1957), for example, contends that modernization involves a loss of three kinds of *Gemeinschaft*; locality (common habitat), kinship, and mind (friendship); that is, the loss of "communityness." Hence, the depersonalization of social relations at the community level leads to changes at the household level. This becomes obvious in the Nuba Mountains through the breakdown of such community institutions as nafir and care for the aged. But, in terms of specific household forms, Segalen (1984:169) notes with respect to Europe that historians have long since "demonstrated that households were nuclear in a large section of Europe before industrialization started" and that, ironically, "The stability of the nuclear household in the nineteenth century was generally a sign of great poverty." But, if there are no specific household forms, where does this leave household activities? Is it possible to distinguish specific patterns of household activities according to economic orientation?

Without question, capitalism has proven to be the primary force driving world modernization. The processes of economic rationalization and differentiation that capitalism engenders have impacted most aspects of social organization and behavior, including the household. According to Weber (1978), in the course of capitalist development "household and occupation become ecologically separated, the household is no longer a unit of common production but of common consumption" (p. 375). In other words, there is a marked shift in rationality from substantive, which takes into account nonrational considerations such as ethical or egalitarian goals, to formal rationality, which is purely quantitative in "calculable terms" (85).[2] Of course, sifting though empirical complexities is relatively straightforward at the extremes, where we have households that either own the necessary factors of production and employ wage-labor, or else, lacking resources, engage in wage-labor. It is in the middle, with the smallholder or peasant, where conceptual problems arise regarding the unity of production and consumption; that is, business enterprise and domestic group. This middle level poses certain analytical difficulties. Despite a categorical logic that conceptualizes small-scale household-based producers in terms other than an essential capitalism, neither smallholder nor peasant represent particularly coherent theoretical categories in themselves. Across time and space, smallholders or peasants are simply too varied and cover too wide and diverse a range of households. In the end, what we are left with are matters of degree and not of kind.

The construction of a typology, particularly if we are to clarify what we have termed the smallholder, must go beyond simple observable differences in households in order to avoid a retreat into empiricism. Hence, the need for devising historically grounded theoretical categories. Too, only theory can provide the necessary validity check for our typologies. "The method by which a typology is constructed," write Whatmore et al. (1987:23), "derives from and embodies a set of epistemological assumptions about how we conceptualize and explain social phenomena and thus how theory and empirical work are related." In other words, we cannot always assume that all small-scale household-based producers share the same criterion of existence? Even though two such households may own the same number of feddan and/or cattle, and their members participate in similar nonagricultural activities, they may not be classified as the same because they operate under different logics.

What is needed is a reconceptualization of smallholder that departs from its exclusive identification with capitalism and modernity. True, production for the market is part of economic rationalization brought about by capitalism, but it is equally correct that it is a necessary, though not a sufficient, condition of that process. What must be remembered is that production for the market is not a recent phenomenon brought about solely by the advent of world modernization; rather, it developed with the creation of "a sufficiently extensive market" and has been especially preponderant in periods of urban civilization, such as in the sixth century B.C. Greece, the eighth century A.D. Islamic world, and the eleventh century onward in western Europe (Mandel, 1968:65-6). Modernizing peasant agriculture has been difficult, indeed, because peasants tend to relate to the market very inconsistently (Cooper, 1981; Vandergeest, 1988). And, with regard to the monetization of the economy, it should be recalled that:

> non-capitalist institutions act to restructure the monetary elements introduced into the system, and so long as peasants retain a relatively independent basis for the operation of their economic affairs, then capitalist relations and principles will not prevail in all situations. Non-capitalist forms are not, of course, outside the capitalist framework but represent the way in which local or subordinate social structures mediate the effects of capitalist penetration. (Long, 1984:13-4)

What this means is that the market and money are not exclusive to capitalism but impart different meanings and significance, depending upon the intensity and extent to which they organize production units; i.e., the quality of economic rationalization (or "irrationalization"). In order to facilitate a more effective analysis of households, we thus need to reassess and refine our analytical tools. The formulation of household must provide a framework with which to analyze the degree and kind of economic organization and market orientation; such a formulation, however, must be grounded in historically specific contexts that allow for different outcomes within and between various localities. Depending upon the particular historical situation, we can identify different types of households that have their conditions of existence within different contexts. This way, while recognizing the effects of modernization, credence is afforded to local particularities and, specifically, to how various households respond and adapt to changes.

The conceptualization of small-scale household-based production units proposed here revolves around a distinction between various types of smallholders through the quality and quantity of their market interaction. As noted, market activities are not unique to capitalism; hence, not all smallholders can be considered capitalists. Rather, their conditions of existence can derive from different contexts that invoke different meanings and concede different outcomes. What this entails is a more careful examination of the household's labor process and economic activities in order to establish the precise ways in which production for the market and exchange mechanisms shape specific households. And, while income-generating activities, scale of operation, and work-force composition are important considerations, so too is the need to know "how historically-specific relations have structured control of access to factors of production in non-capitalist social formations" (Vandergeest, 1988:23). Thus, the nature of the household, social networks, cultural mechanisms, and the like are equally as important and help clarify the degree and extent of market orientation, as well as do local particularities.

Such an orientation is important, since attention now shifts to the causes and consequences of the development process. And, when we arrive back at the household, pressures exerted by the wider social complex become all the more apparent in the multitude of household forms and functions. The diverse array of economic, political, and ideological forces, depending on how these interrelate, creates a number of household alternatives and types, and thus a broad array of livelihood strategies. To be sure, we could simply attribute household differences to individual behavioral characteristics and motivations. These are important, but for us, only with respect to the internal and external conditions of existence of any household, and these are best determined at the level of structure.

Towards a Household Typology

We begin the construction of our categories with the assumption that the household is a primary locus of people's daily and generational reproduction in the Nuba Mountains. The household, structured predominantly by family or kinship, still provides a basis of reproduction in the demographic sense and ensures the creation of future labor. Of course, with the advent of modernizing pressures, including capitalism, this changes, especially in places like Kadugli where, for example, males cohabitate and form a household for the purpose of residence and consumption on a daily basis (there is no minimal family unit of mother and infant). Still, in Nuba Mountain villages the economic and ideological necessity of "family" predominates. Hence, variations in the life cycle of a household are attributed more to the life course of individual members than to any systematic breakdown in the family or domestic unit.

Reproduction also involves household labor as an institutionalized process through which the household provides its material sustenance. Not only does this include agricultural activities but also nonagricultural undertakings such as cottage industries and off-farm employment. We talk of household labor in that it excludes other sources of labor such as nafir and wage, although these also may prove important to the household's reproduction, but for different reasons. In addition, the household is a site of socialization, where members are oriented towards the world and given instructions for deportment.

The conceptualization of household as a consumption unit in association with the ways that it meets those consumption requirements simultaneously creates categories of households as effective sites of production. This assumes that household composition and function, including the cultural (kinship, inheritance) and political practices (marriage responsibilities, control of resources) that buttress them, are intimately connected to specific economic or production practices—

albeit, production in its broadest sense. Each household has members who engage in productive activities, whether for the market or not, that are essential for household reproduction. For this reason, we classify households according to the primary means households activate and ensure that (re)production. This is especially effective in a complex modernizing society, where households evidence different types and combinations of social organization—those based on rationalization principles of capitalism and those predicated on noneconomic precepts of the lineage system. To this end we have identified five household (re)production forms: three capitalist forms—capitalist entrepreneur, small-scale capitalist, and wage-labor; and two lineage forms—lineage market and lineage subsistence. Yet, we are in no way resurrecting a theoretically opposed dualism. To the contrary, it is necessary to increasingly link variant household forms together into an integrated framework of analysis.

Capitalist Household Forms

As a first step for differentiating smallholders, it is our contention that some are small-scale capitalists. More importantly, like the operator of any other capitalist enterprise, this form is equally subject to pressures of economic rationalization that is realized in competition, economic calculation, and the depersonalization of social relations in general. As stated by Thompson (1966:416): "Each stage of industrial differentiation and specialization struck also at the family economy, disturbing customary relations between husband and wife, parents and children, and differentiating more sharply between 'work' and 'life.'" In this sense it is especially problematical to envision small-scale capitalists as "not acting at least as income maximizers, if not profit maximizers, given that they must invest in expanded means of production to stay in business" (Deere, 1990:9). The conditions that allow for small-scale capitalism are thus the conditions for fully capitalist or rational production. The two are differentiated primarily by scale and all that scale implies; namely, the size of operation and labor marshaled through the market rather than through "family" or communal ties. To be sure, the rationalization of household production through specific historical processes occurs with varying degrees of completeness, so that not all small-scale capitalist households necessarily appear to be the same.

A distinguishing factor differentiating entrepreneurial and small-scale capitalist households is the degree of economic or enterprise rationality and, thus, the degree of separation between business enterprise and family unit—substantive rationality in small-scale capitalist and formal rationality in capitalist entrepreneurial households. Each form entails a slightly different "logic," owing to the difference in economic rationality and relation to the market. The capitalist entrepreneurial household is organized solely along the lines of rational calculation and profit maximization, while the small-scale capitalist form allows for noneconomic considerations. Nevertheless, both forms are subject to similar pressures, albeit to different degrees. The use of a tractor, for example, involves an irreversible commitment to land size that can lead to a built-in dependence on specific inputs of labor. In this case, the acreage under cultivation does not necessarily fluctuate with the life cycle of the domestic unit—the acreage under cultivation generally remains constant regardless of the domestic labor supply. On the other hand, over time, a tractor can undermine the viability of a small-scale capitalist household, given the tenuous separation of business enterprise and family household, leading to a fully capitalist enterprise or to dispossession. And, if the employment of wage-labor is required, even if only periodically though on a regular basis, we are saying something further about the intensity of production. As a result, although we expect differences in livelihood strategies according to these two forms, they share a certain basic commonality in the logic of their production.

The third capitalist household form is made up of households that rely primarily, if not completely, on its members working outside of the household, either by choice or circumstance. This form is a relatively recent phenomenon in the Nuba Mountains and, in large measure, is an indicator of the growing inequality in access to resources and the decline of the lineage system. Of course, some individuals prefer not to farm or to engage in other household-based production activities, but in the main, members of these household forms frequently have little choice but to work for other people. In short, these are the people that modernization dispossesed.

Lineage Household Forms

It is only through understanding the lineage system in the Nuba Mountains that we can differentiate other historical household forms and provide theoretical coherence to our analysis of households and livelihood strategies. Market exchange, as noted, is not limited solely to capitalism; hence, the need to discern alternative forms of smallholders that are not prefaced solely in terms of an "essential capitalism." As an ideal-type, substantive rationality is too ambiguous to effectively analyze smallholders. Perhaps in this instance it would be better to consider the organizing logic of some households as "presubstantive" rationality.[3] In this way, we can have smallholders who manifest the conditions but not the substance conveyed by substantive rationality, which requires a measure of economic calculability and all that this entails. Still, practical experience indicates that we must avoid definition by default and comprehend the conditions under which lineage households operate. For our purposes, the form that relates more "regularly" to the market is termed lineage market household, while the form minimally connected to the market (if at all) is labeled lineage subsistence household.

It is generally not possible or feasible to determine a household's economic orientation from economic practices alone, especially in instances where the production unit is structured by kinship and community, as in lineages. Most would agree that autarky has seldom, if ever, been a dominant feature of any household in meeting its reproductive requirements. An important consideration for lineage-based households, therefore, is the social complex within which it is embedded. The utilization of brideservice and wage-labor, for instance, are based on entirely different mechanisms of recruitment, such that the network of social relations that enables the former will not support the latter. Furthermore, as noted, the division of labor and the distribution of products within lineages are governed by kinship, patriarchy, age, and gender. Nevertheless, the reproductive cycle of an individual household producing a narrow fixed range of goods on demand and that technically pass through a market is different than that of a small-scale capitalist. Lineage market and lineage subsistence household forms remain dependent upon nonmarket social relations for their (re)production. The two forms differ in that the subsistence form rarely markets goods or services and continues to provide for most of its needs through communal and domestic labor.

Certainly at one point the lineage market household form in the Nuba Mountains was minimal, depending more or less on the extent of trade and artisinal specialization within and between specific gabila. Unlike the small-scale capitalists, however, the lineage market form is not reliant on regularized market activities, and the sale of goods and services is conditioned by the household's life cycle and not by considerations of economic rationality. In other words, this form is not a profit maximizer and is dominated by noncapitalist economic principles. In this way lineage market forms can manifest the conditions but not the substance of small-scale capitalism. This holds important consequences for our understanding of a complex society like the Nuba Mountains. The largely intermittent production and sale of goods comprises only a small part of the overall logic of the lineage market household and thus is not definitive of its organization. In addition, since lineage market households do not relate directly to markets, individually or competitively, they have no "market strategy," as evidenced in their difficulty in adapting or responding to market changes such as fluctuations in commodity prices.

Lineage market households, thus, differ substantively from small-scale capitalists. The latter form is subject to market competition, although its effect may be limited or extreme. The manner by which lineage market (and lineage subsistence) households relate to the market, then, is mediated by noneconomic considerations, which can mitigate the need to rationalize production. This does not mean that this form remains unaffected by the market. To the contrary, contradictions between the old and the new are frequently galvanized. When the shayl assumes at least indirect control of the production process, he can force the production of cash crops or restrict their cultivation and propel people increasingly into wage-labor, both of which can erode existing lineage relations. Or, at a certain juncture, the hiring of wage-labor to replace the contributions of migrating members, especially as the duration of migration increases, figures significantly into the reproduction of the household. And, if migrants are unable to send cash remittances to offset their absences, those left behind may find it increasingly necessary to work off of the farm for other individuals. Therefore, over time we may see a lineage market household transform into a small-scale capitalist or wage-labor household.

On an empirical level, the key lines of inquiry economically differentiating lineage market from small-scale capitalist household forms are:

1. Withdrawal from the market without adverse effects over time, such as absolute consumption shortfalls and/or intensification of domestic labor

(e.g., drop out of school, work at younger ages than social norm, bring women more to main farms).
2. Market calculation (e.g., shift between types of labor (nafir, family, and wage), specialization of production, flexibility in goods produced, and so on.
3. Orientation to the market (use-value vs. exchange-value).
4. Scale of operation, technology and techniques of production, and access to resources.

Unquestionably, the development of a capitalist market in the Nuba Mountains amplified a household's economic orientation, but not necessarily to the extent that the buying and selling of goods and services dominated the reproduction of the respective lineages as a whole or of the various households themselves. That does not mean that the slave/tributary systems left no trace of their presence or that the effects of capitalism somehow exist outside of the lineage systems; the presence of contradictory pressures and convulsive changes attest to this. Nevertheless, individuals within a lineage are involved in an encompassing network of social relations that can blunt pressures towards rationalization. Nevertheless, the slave/tributary systems and, later, capitalism infused differing types of political control, organization of agricultural production, expansion of trade, and wealth accumulation. In particular, the rise of capitalism has both crystallized and eroded the older lineage systems. It initially crystallized them through accentuating the circulation of women and the power of elders, and eroded them through the monetization of prestige goods and taxes, which forced juniors to migrate from their villages. And, later, with the expansion of opportunities, both within and outside of the villages, still other changes have occurred that continue to erode at the base of lineages while simultaneously making many villagers increasingly dependent upon each other for survival. So, too, with females, whose roles changed with the absence of young men, affording them an economic independence previously unknown, but often at the cost of a greatly increased work load and financial uncertainty.

A Typology of Household (Re)production Forms

Livelihood strategies engendered by the capitalist entrepreneurial, small-scale capitalist, and wage-labor households are inexorably shaped by the processes of modernization and economic rationalization, while strategies conceived by lineage commodity and nonlineage commodity producers are fashioned by "communal" needs, responsibilities, and obligations. And, since livelihood strategies devised to meet a household's reproduction requirements are formulated within different sets of opportunities and constraints, they will also convey specific values and meanings. For example, cattle owned by those in a lineage are kept essentially as a "store of wealth," but within capitalism they assume the form of capital. What is of interest, however, are the tensions the pursuit of specific strategies creates, how those tensions are resolved, and to what result. This does not imply a state of equilibrium between various strategies, but accentuates points of contradiction and tension. As we shall see, the lineage is not infinitely elastic, and eventually irrevocable consequences occur that lead to its demise.

At the level of typological formulations, households in the villages of Somasem, Shair Tomat, and Shatt Damam are differentiated categorically according to their resource base and form of economic (re)production. The following categories guide the village analyses.

1. Capitalist entrepreneurial households (CE), generally with substantial off-farm economic interests.
2. Small-scale capitalist households (SC) that are not able to voluntarily withdraw from the market and that, as a routine matter, regularly sell agricultural and nonagricultural products, the members of which regularly engage in off-farm employment, though to a far lesser degree than does the first group. Differences between this and the capitalist entrepreneurs is one of degree of market participation and not of kind.
3. Lineage market households (LM), which are able to withdraw from the market and which irregularly sell goods, members of which only intermittently work off the farm. Differences between this group and small-scale capitalists is one of kind and not of degree. That is, SC and LM are differentiated by quality of market ties and by the routinization of the sale of goods and services.
4. Lineage subsistence households (LS), which, when they do engage in market activities, trade and barter. When money is involved, it is merely another item for barter that never assumes the form of "capital" for future investment.
5. Wage-labor households (WL), the livelihood of which is gained off the farm through the sale of the labor of household members, but which generally operate a jubraka to supplement that income.

We expect each (re)production form to exhibit different "behavioral characteristics" due to differential exposure to the constraints and op-

TABLE 6.1
Households By (Re)Production Form In Somasem,
Shatt Damam, And Shair Tomat

| Village | Household by Form of (Re)Production | | | | | Total | (N) |
	CE	SC	LM	LS	WL		
Somasem	3.3%	65.0%	10.0%	10.0%	11.7%	100.0%	(60)
Sh. Tomat	3.3	66.7	13.3	6.7	10.0	100.0	(30)
Sh. Damam	3.3	31.7	35.0	30.0	.0	100.0	(60)
Total	3.3%	51.3%	20.7%	17.3%	6.7%	100.0%	
(n=)	(5)	(78)	(31)	(26)	(10)		(150)

portunities present within the wider society. Theoretically, choice may be infinite but, in reality, given structural parameters are imposed by the particular household (re)production form in which people live and operate on a daily basis. Table 6.1 summarizes households by their (re)production forms. From this perspective, we will analyze household livelihood strategies as they reflect the household's internal structure, but always in conjunction with consideration of external pressures.

Admittedly, the boundaries between our categories tend to blur. Yet, as the subject matter is empirical in nature, the boundary of household requires delineation. In order to establish credible household boundaries, the categories must be refined by constant appeal to empirical material and theoretical precepts. At the historical level, analysis entails detailing interrelations between categories while, at the theoretical level, analysis involves further differentiation on historical-logical grounds. Furthermore, we are in position to situate individuals in terms of household-oriented social relations. The important point to note from this argumentation is that we must look at the types of households encountered and try to understand the pressures that result in the observed patterns. From the above attempt to establish a typology of households, at least in principle, the livelihood strategies pursued by various households begin to make sense.

Household and Social Differentiation

As a last step in understanding the dynamics of household formation and livelihood strategies, we must briefly consider the frequently contradictory nature of social differentiation and its significance at the household level. For purposes here, our concern is with the totality of social life and the intersection of various social relations that illuminate a household's access to and control of resources as well as of other livelihood generating activities. The ways individuals are situated within local and regional contexts has both direct and indirect implications for the viability of households and their reproduction over time. Relationships between household members are also determined by economic, political, and cultural relations outside of the household and not from the household itself. Yet, the Nuba Mountains, as a society involving both capitalist and noncapitalist structures, reveals a complex interweaving of social relations that originate in diverse systems that are differentially realized and experienced.

The macro-level pressures of differentiation that shape and define the character of social relations often refer to inequalities and the subordinate position in an asymmetrical power or resource sharing relationship. As a structured process, social relations of inequality inevitably comprise opposing interests between, for example, capital and wage-labor, elder and junior, male and female, Arab and Nuba, and Muslim and animist. More importantly, individuals can and are differentiated on the basis of multiple dimensions of inequality. Ultimately, these dimensions impose parameters to individual action through the provision of rules for behavior, directions to motivation, and determinants of life chances. In this sense, the range of possible options available to individuals is not unlimited but involves "the interplay of the entire ensemble of political, economic, and ideological relations" (Keith and Keith, 1988:13).

Within the totality of production, class and its attendant category of status are important lines of differentiation and express the manner by which individuals gain access to resources and thus secure their livelihoods. Class and status also concern the manner by which "wealth" is created and distributed.[4] In a creative approach to economic inequality and household formation in the Peruvian highlands, Carmen Deere (1990) draws on the work of Stephen Resnick and Richard Wolff, which enables her to move beyond the constraining boundaries of a dichotomous two-class treatment and account for multiple class configurations. It is for this reason that it is not feasible to differentiate households on the basis of a single class attribute. Modifying their approach, a key to understanding economic differentiation and class formation is the distinction between primary and secondary classes.

Primary classes refer to individuals who are direct producers, those who either control the labor process or perform the actual labor. Secondary classes, on the other hand, encompass individuals who do neither, yet provide certain functions necessary to the labor process and, as a result of their activities, receive a portion of what is produced (in cash or kind) from one or more of the primary classes. It should be noted that economic inequality does not prevent mobility, either up or down the social scale. Nevertheless, an individual's and, by implication, a household's position in the economic hierarchy does favor some groups while constraining the life chances of others.

The complexity of the interconnections of class relations at the empirical level cannot be understated. For example, in the lineage epoch the kujur, priests, and master of the path derived their economic power and ability to demand benefits on the basis of their ideological/political roles. These class (or status) positions, as previously mentioned, took on additional functions when confronted with the slave/tributary epoch of production. In this period, these individuals found new means to demand benefits in the form of "tribute." Of course, they could still continue to accumulate wealth in the capacity of their more traditional roles of elders. With the initial expansion of capitalism, Condominium rule added yet a third layer of inequality through the creation of the position of sheikh, who had the responsibility of collecting taxes and requisitioning labor. Later, opportunities for commercial agriculture, business ventures, and off-farm employment added additional opportunities for economic advancement, which further differentiated communities. Some individuals were better positioned to take advantage of the new situation, while others were not. Figure 6.1 shows the multiple bases of economic inequality in the Nuba Mountains and the broad range of primary and secondary classes. At the extremes we will get "capitalist" and "working" classes, in addition to lineage elders and juniors. But, there is also a blurring of class considerations, as individuals often occupy more than one class position. And, when an individual holds multiple class positions, pressures frequently result in conflicting demands, increased tensions, and erratic strategies.

While class is certainly an important dimension of inequality, it by no means accounts for all inequality. One of the critical issues in the study of inequality concerns the nature of noneconomic relationships. The causal factors responsible for social differentiation originate in di-

FIGURE 6.1
Bases of Economic Inequality in the Nuba Mountains

Capitalism	*Primary classes*:	
	performer	wage-laborer
	controller	capitalist
	Secondary classes:	
	controller	state functionaries (sheikh)
		merchants/businessmen
		bankers
Tributary	*Primary classes*:	
	performer	service laborer
	controller	master of the path
		kujur
		priests
	Secondary classes:	
	controller	merchant/trader
		usurer/shayl
Lineage	*Primary classes*:	
	performer	juniors/women
	controller	elders
	Secondary classes:	
	controller	jujur
		priests
		master of the path

verse domains and generally yield mutually reinforcing configurations of inequality. An understanding of this involves further examination of the division of labor, bases of control over the labor process, and distribution of resources within and between households, as well as the relation of the village community to the wider society. The implications of inequality at the household level can only be understood by analyzing social relations as mutually determining systems of differentiation that find different expressions, depending upon how they intersect. Other dimensions of inequality, particularly in terms of the communities' relation to the outside world, include ethnicity and religion, a point made painfully clear in the protracted civil war. These dimensions unquestionably affect the structure of life chances confronting household members, particularly in terms of education, off-farm employment and business opportunities, and governmental services to the village. Without question, the type of employment or education individuals are able to access outside of the village depends primarily upon their wealth, gender, ethnicity, and religion.

Within the household, gender and age relations present important foci of differentiation that are expressed in the inegalitarian nature of most households. The power of patriarchy and age in controlling resources, in organizing production, and in appropriating surplus should not be minimized. It is not too uncommon to hear stories of sons who, after years of laboring for their father, find out that he has sold the "family" land rather than pass it along to "his rightful heir." A difficulty, however, with any simple characterization of social relations of inequality is that it tends to reinforce their treatment as homogeneous categories (Moore, 1988). While it is certainly true, for example, that females in general are culturally subordinate to males, it is equally correct that there are important differences in life chances among women. An eighteen-year-old female from a resource poor household, for instance, has far fewer options in terms of wage-labor activities than do those from wealthier households, but both suffer significantly fewer opportunities than do their male counterparts. Or, a young man recently returned from some years in the military, with severance pay in his pocket, will relate differently to the village elders than will one who has stayed behind.

Individuals, as members of households, thus confront a variety of processes that decidedly affect the household's reproduction. Household members must respond to their surroundings by formulating livelihood strategies to meet these pressures, but with strategies conceived on the basis of socially constructed identities. Sometimes strategies are successful, at other times they fail. Even when they are successful, however, new pressures in the form of opportunities and constraints arise as a result of that success. Whatever the outcome, individuals and households are pulled in certain directions, which impacts the (re)production form of the household and the social relations of its members and may, in fact, undermine the household's condition of existence. Changes in the (re)production form of the household, however, may never comprise a conscious strategy. Actual outcomes are rarely, if ever, the product of what people envision since structural forces usually remain outside of an individual's frame of reference.

Household Reconsidered

At its most abstract level, household is a basic unit and primary site of social and biological reproduction. Nevertheless, there are no requisite household forms—the character and composition of households are mutable—and the importance of certain activities varies markedly from region to region and over time. Household, although not a primordial institution, assumes certain primordial functions (e.g., giving birth, preparing food, providing affection) that are fundamental to human social and biological existence (Stauth, 1984:91). These base functions inherent in the household are crystallized and given concrete meaning by the household's relation to the wider society. That is, households are organized and structured by a given context, deriving means to meet subsistence requirements in the broad sense, but in accordance with the logic of that particular context. And, if the ensuing social relations encapsulated within a household entail multiple forms of social organization, various logics come into play. It is for this reason that households can be especially malleable as members are involved in variant economic, political, and cultural practices derived from different organizational forms.

Moreover, tensions resulting from the interplay of lineage/family, privileges/rights, exchange-value/use-value, and accumulation/leveling exert strong cross-cutting pressures at the household level. In this way, households function as a conduit for wider contradictions and tend to be no less susceptible to outside pressures than do other structures. Consequently, households continuously compose, decompose, and recompose. But, households are also enmeshed in extrahousehold domestic networks where, for example, neighboring households share food and labor or watch each other's children in order to free up female members for off-farm work. These relations are important for comprehending the continuity of particular household forms. Where household membership is fluid, the presence of extrahousehold networks provides a degree of stability to people in an otherwise chaotic world.

Household transformation is a dynamic process that does not always lend itself easily to momentary encapsulation. But, by understanding how particular households are contextualized and their social relations activated, we can begin to discern the "behavior" of households at different moments. Among the Shatt, for example, traditional control over the circulation of women, bridewealth, defence, and raiding parties enabled lineage elders, as household heads, to effectively dominate young males and women. That dominance and the presence of nafir prevented the generalized buying and selling of labor within the village. Present economic opportunities outside the village now threaten that dominance, altering the organizational basis of households (and the village in general), as young men increasingly migrate in order to eke out an existence, leaving females, the young, and the aged to sell their labor to wealthier households.

In summary, households reflect contradictions presented by the society, but which are worked out within the household. Within lineages, households are structured around kinship. As such, households tended to be complex and multiple, depending on the power of the senior male. Marriage enables a junior to escape the confines of the elders and begin his own household. Household stability is maintained through elaborate mechanisms of marriage and fostering, as well as through age-grades and nafir. The tributary/slave systems either strengthened or weakened households, depending on the ability of lineage elders to organize defenses and initiate raids. In these instances, various lineages probably splintered into smaller and more isolated groups or else grew more powerful, allowing them to prey on weaker neighbors. And now, the forces of modernization (including the spread of capitalism) instill their own pressures; namely, the need to rationalize production through the sale of products and labor, the privatization of land, the mechanization of agriculture, and so on. In those communities feeling the full impact of modernization, the organizing principles of households changed with the waning of the power of elders. Moreover, integration into the modern world reinforces the trend towards the depersonalization of social relations and further "monetizes" relationships within and between households. By the time of Nadel's study the modernization of households in the Nuba Mountains had begun.

The aim of the following chapters is to explore household livelihood strategies in the three villages with the aim, not of distilling individual motivations, but of drawing people closer to the structural parameters that condition those responses. This will be accomplished through an understanding of variations in livelihood strategies among household (re)production forms within the respective villages. Further, an understanding of the construction of inequality in this region affords greater insight into the contradictory pressures shaping the Nuba Mountains.

Notes

1. Accordingly, "An ideal-type is formed by the one-sided *accentuation* of one or more points of view and by the synthesis of a great many diffuse, discrete, more or less present and occasionally absent *concrete individual* phenomena, which are arranged according to those one-sidedly emphasized viewpoints into a unified *analytical* construct (*Gedankenbild*)" (Weber, 1949:90).
2. Household concerns in terms of substantive rationality rest with the production and consumption of use-values and not specifically with exchange values, the function of the formal rationality.
3. "The concept of 'substantive rationality'...is full of ambiguities. It conveys only one element common to all 'substantive' analyses: namely, that they do not restrict themselves to note the purely formal and (relatively) unambiguous fact that action is based on 'goal-oriented' rational calculation...but apply certain criteria of ultimate ends, whether they be ethical, political, utilitarian, hedonistic, feudal (*ständisch*), egalitarian, or whatever..." Weber, 1978:85).
4. While class and status posit different analytical categories, they nevertheless are empirically similar. For purposes here, we will primarily refer to class in our discussion.

7

Somasem: Alienation on The Home Front

The first thing an outsider notices in Somasem at the beginning of the rainy season is the use of tractors in the fields. The development of the conditions for the modernization of agriculture, however, must be viewed in a wider context. This type of change did not originate within the confines of the village but came from without. Nevertheless, external conditions were only partially successful in restructuring village life; the remainder of the equation resides in the villagers' attempts to adjust to these transformations. Some welcomed the change as something that provided wonderful new opportunities; others viewed them fearfully. Recent changes appear to have divided the village, pitting those favoring production for exchange against those opting for production for use, juniors against elders. Yet, reality is seldom black or white, and many households are seemingly caught in the contradictions wrought by two incompatible social systems.

The use of a tractor is not value neutral; land size must be increased, additional labor obtained and organized, and money accumulated to meet the increased costs of production. Neither is a nafir labor party value neutral; relations of personal obligation must be nurtured, activated, and reciprocated. Consequently, livelihood strategies are difficult to retreat from once set in motion. And, what is increasingly evident in the outcome of livelihood strategies in Somasem is the rationalization of production and the "depersonalization" of political, social, and economic roles. Access to land and labor no longer guarantees that a household will effectively reproduce itself as a social entity over time. A household's livelihood also depends increasingly on the mix of economic activities in which household members engage and on the range of resources its members can marshal.

179

Contemporary Context

In many ways Somasem appears to be a village whose inhabitants seem anxious to leave—if not this day than perhaps another. In the center of the village a cluster of young men seem to be playing endless games of dominos under the shade of a *rakuba*.[1] As the busses and lorries rumble past, heading for distant cities, they wistfully look up and begin talking of better lives in El Obeid, Port Sudan, or Khartoum. They are always making plans for the day of their departure. Stories of those who have "made it" elsewhere punctuate the heavy sighs of boredom. Even the layout of Somasem imparts this image of pervasive discontent, with its division into three separate sections.

Shardi, approximately one hour drive south of Dilling, is split by the tarmac road. It extends westward from the base of a small protective hill, and the physical condition of many constructions attest to the ferocity of the wind-born storms of seasons past, through their various states of disrepair. Shardi also claims the market, which contains three shops, a flour mill, an oil press, two tea stalls, a mosque, and a small shelter to house adult literacy classes.

Situated out of sight of Shardi, some 15 minutes northwest by foot, are the adjoining village sections of Belangadu and Shenku. These two communities are separated from each other by a seasonal khor. Like their neighbors in Shardi, the inhabitants of both Belangadu and Shenku have also sought shelter at the base of hills from the near-constant winds.

No one can say with any confidence the exact date of Somasem's settlement, although most concur that it was around 1920.[2] Prior to the accelerated pace of slave raids during the latter 1800s, however, travellers of the day reported agricultural activity "on the plains some 10 miles north of Jebel Ghulfan" (Sagar, 1922:140). As the site of far farms, Somasem was probably populated at this time, at least through the growing season. With the deployment of Condominium forces to the area in the aftermath of the Mahdi uprising, the Ghulfan once again felt secure and journeyed forth from various outlying mountain strongholds such as Jebel Sigda, Muring, Namma, and Shagra to occupy their main farms and/or to acquire new lands around present-day Somasem. Others followed later, arriving from nearby villages such as Engarko and Dileba, in search of fresh lands. Without question, the "original" settlers claimed the best fields nearest to the village and kept other lands as "family reserve."

Of the sampled households "originally" from Somasem, 60 percent own more than 20 feddans, and 40 percent more than 40. On the other hand, slightly more than 71 percent of households coming later own 20 feddans or less.[3] For the newcomer today, those without roots in Somasem, "it is impossible to acquire land." At best, a local farmer may provide a nonvillager with the use of land for one to three years, after which he is obliged to move on.

The commencement of Islamization in the Ghulfan range can be pinpointed with more precision. As with other communities in the Nuba Mountains, the Ghulfan found themselves overrun by the Mahdist forces, which abducted many villagers as slaves and slave soldiers for its army. Following their release with the Mahdist defeat at the battle of Omdurman in 1898, the former captives made their way back to their home villages. As Baumann (1987:123) notes for the Miri, a large gabila west of Kadugli, for the first time "villagers were exposed, in their daily lives, to a community of Muslim converts among their own kinsmen, clansmen, and neighbors." Likewise, the manner of Islam's introduction among the Ghulfan attests to the speed in its widespread adoption, especially with the social dislocation induced by the terrors of the Mahdist insurgency. Indigenous Ghulfan beliefs among the inhabitants of Somasem, however, have paid a heavy price. Gone are the various priests, village-based sibirs, and codified age-grades. In fact, many of the villagers are embarrassed to discuss these beliefs, feeling that somehow this past marks them as "backwards." The last kujur died in 1966, leaving only the very aged to mourn his passing.

Nevertheless, the adoption of Islam and the Arabic language does not necessarily signify that the Ghulfan desire to be Arabs. Besides, old suspicions and grudges die hard, and the Ghulfan, like other Nuba communities, have a long memory for past injustices. This is evident in their relations with many Arabs, especially the Hamar and Dilling jallaba. Somasem bisects a major north/south route used by Hamar nomads in their seasonal trek to obtain adequate pasture for their livestock. One day a group of nomads stopped in Somasem and asked a few of the men if they might water their sheep and camels at the village Hafir. The men responded that for a certain price they were welcome to quench their animals thirst and hastened to add that the people could drink for free. The Hamar grew agitated, dismissing the villagers' concern that their sole source of water, the Hafir, was already low. As the conversation grew more heated, the women and children of the village quickly and quietly retreated to their houses, while the men slowly moved up to form a line between the Hamar and their fellow villagers. Each man held a spear, axe, or agricultural implement. The Hamar soon moved on. Past experiences with many Arabs have united the villagers in their steadfast refusal to allow any to take up residence in Somasem or to use ancestral lands, proudly claiming that "there are only Nuba here!"

Rancor against Arabs shows in other ways. The villagers take exception to the fact that in Dilling "the Nuba have only small shops, but the Arabs own big shops." And, when the question arose over the loss of livestock, the villagers roundly blamed Arabs for the theft of 7 cows, 48 goats, and 3 camels over the past five years.

Relations with other non-Nuba groups are less forbidding. A "Fellata" named Mohammed arrived in Somasem in the mid 1970s. Obtaining permission from the sheikh and other prominent elders, the man built a store and a living compound for his large family. Nevertheless, the family departed after only a few months because the villagers refrained from patronizing his store, preferring their neighbors' businesses instead. On the other hand, Abdul Gadir, also a "Fellata," fared far better in his encounter with the people of Somasem. His friendly demeanor persuaded the elders to grant him access to unused village lands. After a number of successful agricultural seasons he relocated to Dilling and opened a shop, although he still has economic ties to Somasem, renting out the tractor he now owns. The relationship proved equally profitable for a number of Somasem men as well. In 1976 Abdul Gadir organized 43 other men in Somasem and together they rented 1,000 feddans of land in Habila. The first year the group undertook all of the labor themselves. With the profits from that first year, they hired labor throughout the subsequent years and even leased an additional 500 feddans in 1979. The land was left fallow in 1986 and 1987.

Agents of modernization assume many forms. None have exerted as powerful an impact on contemporary Somasem as did the advent of the tractor in about 1970. According to Khamis Ali, one of the first to employ a tractor in his farming operations, the village labor cooperation system began to deteriorate at this time because "now people are more interested in making money." Another villager responded that nafir is becoming difficult to organize and that "it is expensive." Prior to the introduction of tractors, the use of nafir labor was much more extensive. In the past, farmers would meet informally to schedule nafir parties in order to avoid conflicts in their timing. This practice has since broken down so that, on some days, there might be several nafir parties, thus reducing the size of some of the nafir. Moreover, a type of bidding war has diluted the ethos of nafir, with participants attending those that offer meat (preferably goat) and plentiful marissa over those that do not.[4] But, as explained by Idris, most farmers having the means do not mind, as a "good" nafir accrues status and good will for the host and provides a hedge against future labor shortages.

Tractors also require some degree of economies of scale and, therefore, larger fields to make the use of a tractor profitable.[5] Access to sufficient labor, especially for *jankab* (second weeding) and harvesting, can be problematic, though dependent on an individual's household composition, community standing, and cash on hand. As a result, sections of fields are often left unweeded, which, according to local estimates, reduces the yield by 30 to 50 percent. Yet, tractor use has somehow entered into the local conception of what constitutes a good farmer, regardless of the bottom line. Peer pressure prompted a number of farmers to begin employing tractors. After a lengthy explanation regarding his reason for expanding production, Salaam conceded that he finally began hiring a tractor because "everyone else was using tractors." Another farmer replied: "I saw everyone getting ahead of me, so I decided to do it also." Still another claimed, "A neighbor told me that a tractor is better than a digging stick." One respondent also admitted that his brother pays for a tractor to disc his field because "he does not want to be embarrassed by me." Tractors are never used to plough the jubraka, as "it is small and is no problem," and besides, "the jubraka is women's work."

Agricultural cooperation is not lacking altogether, as evidenced by the group of 44 villagers leasing land in Habila. This undertaking required a large measure of mutual trust. The lease is in the name of five men, who also maintain the records, control the money, and manage the labor. Over the years the group purchased three tractors and disc ploughs as well as a small lorry. When the land was left to fallow, two members bought a couple of the tractors, leaving one tractor and the lorry for the coming season. It has proved to be a profitable undertaking over the years. Aside from the sale of dura, the group rents out the tractors to other area farmers. Nonetheless, not all of the participants will rejoin the group when they start up again, citing old age, lack of money, or general misgivings.

On the whole, civic spirit and village pride in Somasem are largely absent. Of the sampled households not originally from Somasem, nearly 57 percent made the move to be closer to their main farm or to acquire land, while roughly 26 percent came as children accompanying their parents. While this in itself may not be surprising, given the concept of ancestral land and access to it, few respondents in private spoke warmly of Somasem.[6] Some listed the lack of suitable water, a school, and a health clinic as reasons for their dislike of Somasem. Water presents a particularly acute problem.[7] With the exception of the Hafir, the nearest water sources are hand pumps located in Engarko, 1 1/2 hours by foot. This burden adds to the labor load of women. Water delivery lies out of the reach of most, at a cost of 60 piasters per five gallon jerry can and £S7.50 per 44 gallon barrel. The village elders are slow to petition the Water Corporation to construct an appropriate Hafir because, as explained by Abdullai, "the people are afraid that they will have to spend money, and no one wants to spend money on water." Other villagers mention the unfriendliness of their neighbors: "We do not know why, if you go to anyone's house they do not care; they will greet you and then say 'ma'a salaam' (good-bye). They are just like dead people." Another added that the villagers in Engarko and Dileba look contemptuously upon them and consider them lazy and indifferent. Most of the insults within Somasem are reserved for Shardi, with one resident of Belangadu scoffing: "And they think that they are civilized."

The village elders are trying to reach an agreement on reducing brideprice. They understand that it can pose a barrier to marriage for both males and females alike. Currently, the typical brideprice consists of four to five cows and *shayla*—an agreed upon amount of sugar, oil, rice, dates, coffee, onions, lemon juice, sweets, and clothes, especially *tobes* for the women and *jellabiyas* for the men. In addition, the groom must provide a house and furnishings for his new wife and undertake repairs on the house of his future in-laws. A father, if able, usually will help his son(s) with the first wife by providing some cattle and/or land, but the hopeful youth invariably finds that he must migrate to earn sufficient cash for the shayla. Still, vested interests in brideprice make consensus on its reduction difficult; the more prestigious the girl's family, the greater the shayla.

In Somasem, the paternal uncles also contribute cows for their nephew's brideprice since, according to local custom, "when you receive cows from your daughter's brideprice, you give some to your brothers." Abas received four cows from his brothers when their daughters married and used them to wed his uncle's daughter. His uncle, in turn, used the cows to obtain a wife for his son. There are voluntary exceptions, of course, to sharing cattle. Mohammed received a total of seventeen cows when his daughters wed; he gave each of his three brothers two and his sister six so that her sons might marry. When Mohammed's niece wed he wanted none of the cows, as his brother "was poor and should keep all of the cows." Moreover, the villagers believe that the transference of cows binds a husband to his wife. Not surprisingly, in the case of a "justifiable" divorce, the woman's father is obliged to return at least some of the cows, depending on the duration of the marriage. Kurtukella, after divorcing his wife of eleven years, received two of the four cows he paid as brideprice. "I divorced her because she was *haramia* (bad). She would [have sex with] any man she wanted. I did not want to kill anyone, and I did not want to be killed. I had to fight every day, so I sent her back to her father." Another man took all four cows back after a similar problem, but he remained married for only one year.

The role of cattle in brideprice highlights other issues, most notably the values attached to the end-use of material goods. Traditionally, cattle convey a variety of meanings. According to one old man, who had owned more than a hundred cows in the past:

1. "Cows provide the means to marry your sons."
2. "If a man has many cows he can attain high status; people from all around will know him as a 'rich' man."
3. "If a man has many cows people will come to him for advice and favors, such as milk, in time of need."
4. "Cows are necessary to leave your sons so they will not be thought of as 'poor' men."

Nowhere did he include consideration for their exchange value. Many of the young men, on the other hand, see only this aspect. They care neither for a wife nor for a life in the village. Ismail, 17 years of age, argued repeatedly with his father. Two of the cows from the family herd were his. His father considered the cows as potential brideprice; Ismail viewed them as a source of immediate cash to fund his resettlement to Khartoum. His father was adamant, upon which Ismail told his friends: "If he does not give me the cows to sell, I will go to Khartoum anyway, and I never want to see his face or my mother's again." Harsh words anywhere, but especially so in a lineage system. He eventually left, much to his parent's anguish.

Even the authority of the village elders and the sheikh has waned. Clearly, social roles are changing in Somasem. No longer is it sufficient for a male to found his own household to ensure prestige, status, and wealth. The elders' absolute power in their respective lineages remains, but only insofar as the juniors depend on them for land or other resources. Opportunities outside of the purview of the lineage and the importance of money have undermined older social relations. Regardless of the changing socioeconomic environment, however, the position of women evidences little improvement, in part due to the canons of Islam. Similarly, the villagers no longer automatically look upon the sheikh with respect and trepidation. Today the sheikh's role is limited to arbitrating boundary disputes, settling petty civil infractions, and collecting the government animal tax (*Dariba*).[8] Previously, a sheikh had the power to send a person to prison or to fine him, and he had policemen at his disposal. In addition, before 1982 the sheikh received ten percent of the taxes he collected. When asked who the important men of the village are now, the villagers cite those men with large landholdings and profitable business enterprises, regardless of seniority, lineage size, or knowledge of Ghulfan customs.

The following story illustrates the decline of both the authority of the village elders and the sheikh.[9] Juma'a, a married man of about 45, had sexual relations with Halima, the young second wife of Ali, who was 65. When Ali found out he confronted Juma'a, whereupon Juma'a added insult to injury by soundly beating Ali with his axe handle. As an act of contrition, Juma'a paid Ali's doctor bills and then ignored the matter. Ali sought recourse, first through the sheikh and later through the village elders. Eventually they ordered Juma'a to recompense Ali seven cows. Juma'a laughed and refused. Ali was forced to go to Dilling and lodge a formal complaint with the judge, who ordered Juma'a to pay fourteen cows or face a prison sentence. The elders and the sheikh told Juma'a to heed the judge, but to no avail. One dark night, Juma'a went to Halima's sleeping quarters and tried to convince her to go to the judge and tell him that she had not had sex with Juma'a. Ali heard them talking and called out: "Who is there?" Juma'a replied: "*Iblise* (the devil)." Cocking his gun, Ali aimed and shouted: "Let me show you where *Iblise* lives! I will send *Iblise* home!" Juma'a began to cry loudly. Hearing his frightful sobs, the neighbors ran out and protected Juma'a. The next day Juma'a paid the fourteen cows. The point is, neither the elders nor the sheikh could force Juma'a to pay. It was only after Ali threatened his life that he saw the wisdom of their advice.

The practice of *karama* also contributes to the deepening pattern of social stratification. In the past the burial of a family member was followed by death commemorations on the third, seventh, fifteenth, and fortieth day, and on the first anniversary. This sequence is still maintained but is now understood more as familial obligation than as community hospitality to ease bereavement. It is frequently an expensive undertaking for the surviving household members. Howa, for example, slaughtered a goat on each of the appointed days and a cow for the year anniversary of her husband's death. In addition, she exhausted the granary store of dura in the process of commemorating her husband. "If you do not provide a lot of food it is shameful; it means that you did not love the (departed). We have to do it." Most villagers agreed that people spent too much on karama, "but if you do not, you will not be in a good situation." Only Ali said that "for myself, I believe that it is better to keep the money for the children." But then, he is still alive. Needless to say, karama is particularly onerous for those households with minimal stocks and can cause impoverishment, especially when the primary adult male dies. Hasania and her aged mother were forced to borrow £S700 from the shayl. Her brother repaid the loan with a large cow worth £S1,000. Another elderly woman, Kafi, sold her husband's last cow to pay for his karama.

A final point regarding social inequality in Somasem concerns the drought of 1984. Overall, Somasem fared relatively well, although the cost of a sack of dura (approximately 100 pounds) shot up from £S90 to £S150. Needless to say, the coffers of the three village shayl swelled as the unfortunate of the village had little recourse but to turn to them. Moreover, those fortunate enough to have ample grain reserves or cash on hand purchased cattle from the surrounding hard-hit areas, as well as from passing nomads. One sack of dura bought two to three cows. Even Juma'a purchased fifteen cows for £S2,000, where one cow the previous year normally sold for over £S600. The volatile grain market continued through 1985. Immediately prior to and after the commencement of harvesting, a sack of dura sold for £S120 to £S125. By the conclusion of the harvesting season the price had dropped to £S35 per sack. The fortunate few earned windfall profits while, for most, "They cried big tears." Of greater importance, the drought exacerbated social inequality within Somasem and revealed the degree to which lineage bonds had dissolved.

Household Organization

An important characteristic distinguishing household (re)production forms is their mean size (table 7.1).[10] Capitalist entrepreneurs and small-scale capitalists show larger mean household sizes, at 11.5 and 6.9 members respectively. In addition, with more children than the other forms, their mean age is lower. Wage-labor and lineage subsistence households, to the contrary, contain the fewest members, with 2.9 and 3.3 per household, an indication of the lack of adequate family labor for economically productive undertakings, including main farm agriculture and off-farm employment.

Lineage market households, with a mean size of 5.5, member age of 31.4, and household head age of 53.8, are both larger and younger than their nonmarket counterpart. The latter form is an aging household with fewer replacement members. On the surface, the difference between the two lineage forms may appear to be a stage in the household's life cycle in general, but it is, in fact, more a testimony to the incremental rise in the standard of living and of people's expectations of daily necessities, both of which are increasingly at odds with the more self-sufficient mode of existence of the lineage subsistence form. In other words, overall the lineage (re)production forms exhibit economic pressures that are pushing households towards greater market activities. In general, the trend towards increase economic rationalization and all that this entails presents evidence of the decline of the lineage. Those households unable or unwilling to make the transition to regularized commercial production are forced in the other direction, to wage laborers.

The sex of household heads across (re)production forms is an important consideration of the general distribution of power between genders and reflects the available economic opportunities and constraints, espe-

TABLE 7.1
Household Size and Age Structure by (Re)Production Form

All households	CE	SC	LM	LS	WL	Total
% of households	3.3%	65.0%	10.0%	10.0%	11.7%	100.0%
Mean household size	11.5	6.9	5.5	3.3	2.9	6.1
Mean member age	18.9	21.2	25.2	31.4	24.4	22.1
Mean no. <16	8.5	4.5	3.3	1.7	1.7	3.9
Mean age of head	34.0	47.3	43.3	53.8	41.1	45.8
(n=)	(2)	(39)	(6)	(6)	(7)	(60)

cially for those living in households headed by women (table 7.2).[11] Female headed households differ significantly from those headed by males, with the former relatively evenly divided between all but the capitalist entrepreneurial form, in which there are none. Male headed households, on the other hand, are concentrated predominantly within the small-scale capitalist form, reflecting different sorts of pressures as well as a broader range of opportunities. Most households, in line with Ghulfan convention, contain a single head. The two exceptions are joint headed households—one male and the other female.

In the first instance, Habila and his eldest son, Idris, share a large domestic compound with their families. Idris, recently returned from Khartoum, will eventually inherit his father's land, but has claimed and cleared some of his own. Both men stressed the closeness of their relationship as the reason for sharing a household: "Some people don't like to spend and help their children, but my father and I are very close and money has never been a problem." Usually such an arrangement signifies the elder's incontinence in daily affairs. This is not the case, since Habila continues to cultivate his main farm and is capable of providing for his wife and four children by himself. They routinely consult each other on important decisions, and both families, drawing on a common food stock, regularly take their meals together. The second case concerns the three widows of Abu Ali.[12] Together, they inherited six cows and 45 feddans of land, although the women serve essentially as caretakers. The cows are intended to help meet the brideprice for Abu Ali's sons, and the land will eventually be claimed by them. Aside from the obvious economic considerations, the three women enjoy a warm relationship. The main farm is jointly cultivated, and the grain goes into a

TABLE 7.2
Sex of Household Head by (Re)Production Form

	CE	SC	LM	LS	WL	Total	(n)
Male	4.4%	75.5%	6.7%	6.7%	6.7%	100.0%	(46)
Female	.0	28.6	21.4	21.4	28.6	100.0%	(14)
(n=)	(2)	(39)	(6)	(6)	(7)		(60)

common granary. Nonetheless, each woman has her own jubraka and chickens, which are important sources of personal income. They take turns preparing meals, gathering wood, and hauling water for the collective household. Decisions are mutually arrived at, although the rule of seniority still is in force. For example, when they decide to sell a goat, Zirega, the youngest, journeys to Dilling to sell it. Hakuma and Miriam hope that one day soon Zirega will remarry since she had no children with Abu Ali.

In conjunction with the marital status of household heads (table 7.3), a clearer pattern begins to emerge. Female household heads, either widowed or divorced, gain head status by default. Without adequate resources, there is often little compensation in this status. Hakuma, for example, solemnly described how she lost her husband in 1977 to a sudden illness and how her only child, a son, was killed in the civil war raging in the south. Most female heads candidly admitted that, while their husbands were alive, life was much easier. Without an adult male, the primary responsibility for cultivating the main farm shifts entirely to women, in addition to the already taxing domestic operations. Moreover, opportunities for off-farm employment are far less generous for females. Male household heads, on the other hand, are usually married. More importantly, when a spouse dies, proves barren, or divorces, males find remarriage easier and, thus, do not suffer the same fate as women. Seven of the male heads presently married had wives who had died or were childless.[13] Remarriage is not really an option open to women. Only one woman remarried after the death of her spouse, wedding her husband's younger brother according to Ghulfan practice of leviratic marriage, which reintegrates a widow into another male-headed household. Polygamous marriage also presents an active livelihood strategy for a male in his adult life course, extending the household's life cycle. Twelve of the forty-six sampled male heads presently have two wives, and two have three wives. Ironically, the

TABLE 7.3
Marital Status of Household Head by Sex and (Re)Production Form

Male	CE	SC	LM	LS	WL	Total
Married	100%	94.1%	100%	100%	50.0%	91.2%
Single	.0	2.9	.0	.0	.0	2.2
Widower	.0	2.9	.0	.0	25.0	4.4
Divorced	.0	.0	.0	.0	25.0	2.2
Total	100%	100%	100%	100%	100%	100%
(n=)	(2)	(34)	(3)	(3)	(4)	(46)
Mean age head	41.0	48.5	49.7	67.7	40.0	48.8
Female						
Married	NA	20.0	.0	.0	25.0	11.8
Widow	.0	40.0	80.0	100	50.0	64.7
Divorced	.0	40.0	20.0	.0	25.0	23.5
Total	100%	100%	100%	100%	100%	100%
(n=)	(0)	(5)	(5)	(3)	(4)	(17)
Mean age head	NA	38.6	39.4	40.0	42.3	39.9

main reason females outlive their mates is not necessarily due to their longevity, but to the sequence of wives and the difference in marriage ages. Only males in wage-labor forms find remarriage a closed option, due to the inability to meet brideprice.

By far, the dominant types of household residential arrangement in Somasem, with the exception of wage-labor form, is nuclear and complex (table 7.4).[14] Nevertheless, single adults, with or without dependents, constitute 25 percent of the household sample, although most are concentrated in the wage-labor, lineage market, and lineage subsistence forms, accounting roughly for 71, 33, and 50 percent of these three forms respectively. Five households contain a single member (two male and three female) and another ten, single adults with dependents (one male and nine female). In light of the sex, marriage status, and age of household heads, a different picture emerges, revealing distinct dimensions to the economic hardships facing many in the village, especially those with minimal or no kinship bonds within the village.

Historically, the lineage system prescribes specific responsibilities and obligations, which define an individual's role within the community. Specific social mechanisms provide an important security network

TABLE 7.4
Household Residential Type by (Re)Production Form

All households	CE	SC	LM	LS	WL	Total
Single adult	.0	10.3	33.3	33.3	28.6	16.7
Single—w/ dependents	.0	2.5	.0	16.7	42.8	8.3
Nuclear	50.0	66.7	16.6	50.0	14.3	53.3
Complex	50.0	20.5	48.1	.0	14.3	21.7
Total	100%	100%	100%	100%	100%	100%
(n=)	(2)	(39)	(6)	(6)	(7)	(60)

that invariably sees people through often difficult times, such as the loss of a spouse or old age. In the case of a single mother with young children—her brothers and brothers-in-law assume responsibility for the "heavy" agricultural tasks. After her husband's death, Ima Salim moved her family to Somasem to be near her brother. He gave Ima land and each season prepares it for planting and transports grain from the field following the harvest. Similarly, mothers move in with sons to take control of domestic operations. Following the death of his wife, Al-Nour's mother came to help raise his two small children. In the case of the elderly, fostering is a common occurrence, where a grandchild resides with an aged grandparent(s). Three of the elderly women have grandsons living with them, helping with household chores and agricultural operations.

The modernization of village life alters the possibility and quality of these relations. It is not necessarily out of indifference to the plight of kin, but more out of time and labor constraints associated with the modernization (and attendant depersonalization) of the local economy, which undermines the traditional support structure. Of course, neglect is not absent. Hamra Shatir's son, a prominent farmer and a local shop owner, ignores his mother because she does not conform to the Muslim norms of physical shame. The point is, when lineage principles do not predominate, at least at the local level, it is difficult to maintain the full force of kinship relations. Many villagers are increasingly reluctant to assume the additional burden kinship obligations impose, a further indication of the growing rupture in lineage relations in Somasem. Halima and her children arrived from Kurgul after her husband died in 1980 to be nearer to her husband's family. Much to her consternation, they do not provide any assistance: "I don't know why they won't help me; they are of no use. I think they have forgotten me." Halima feels betrayed because she left her husband's land to his brothers and now cannot return. Similarly, Bakhit must labor alone and complains that his brothers would rather give him seed before helping in his fields. Moreover, the absence of younger family members due to out-migration contributes to the neglect of the elderly. Halwa's children, for example, have all left Somasem, five to Khartoum and two to Namma, and now she has no kinship network to help in her old age.

Finally, spatial residency patterns are important outcomes of household livelihood strategies (table 7.5). With the exception of single member households, approximately 28 percent of households have members residing temporarily outside of the primary residence, while another 5 percent of households are composed of multiresidences. Slightly more than 3 percent combine both spatial patterns. Out-migration of members is frequently a crucial element in the reproduction of the household from one cycle to the next by the temporary removal of an unproductive member, especially during the "hungry season," or through remittances sent back by gainfully employed members. On the other hand, the labor of long-term migrants is lost for household agricultural production, and many migrants are either unwilling or unable to send cash. Especially hard hit are the two lineage forms. In this instance, some households find the shayl the only answer to their reproductive requirements. Whatever the outcomes, the differentiation of households in Somasem, as well as of individual members, presupposes particular economic relations that are clarified in household activities.

TABLE 7.5
Household Spatial Residency Patterns by (Re)Production Form

Spatial pattern	CE	SC	LM	LS	WL	Total
Coresidence	50.0%	59.0%	66.7%	66.6%	14.3%	55.0%
Dispersed	50.0	30.8	16.7	16.7	28.6	28.4
Multiresidence	.0	5.1	.0	.0	14.3	5.0
Disp/multiresidence	.0	2.6	16.7	.0	.0	3.3
Single member	.0	2.6	.0	16.7	42.9	8.3
Total	100%	100%	100%	100%	100%	100%
(n=)	(2)	(39)	(6)	(6)	(7)	(60)

Sources of Household Income

Household self-sufficiency in Somasem is more mythic than real. Those celebrating its virtues nostalgically dream of a distant past, to a time before money acquired such important dimensions in the household's life course. No longer is it possible to meet the needs of household members through the inclusive activities of the household as a production unit. Very few individuals, including those in lineage forms, felt that they could manage entirely from the efforts of agricultural pursuits in meeting their perceived needs. Brideprices, metal implements, and culinary needs, like tea and sugar, have long forced household members into market exchanges, whether barter or cash. Moreover, money and the goods it can buy have become the mark of success and evoke the social worth of an individual. As one man remarked, "In Somasem it is important to make money. A man with a lot of money is important. If a man has no money people don't care about him; he is nothing."

The reproduction of households is no longer possible solely through agricultural and animal production. Consequently, the combination of these activities with other economic endeavors is widespread and reveals the complexities of livelihood strategies. The nature and number of income sources expose strong differences between (re)production forms (table 7.6). Capitalist entrepreneurs depend primarily on agricultural sales and household businesses to generate income, while small-scale capitalist and wage-labor households illustrate the multiplicity of activities necessary to secure cash needs. Lineage market households also participate in a wide variety of income-generating activities, but only in activities with flexible time demands and which do not detract from lineage responsibilities. Lineage subsistence households display the fewest off-farm activities. Both lineage forms, however, indicate the importance of remittances in meeting their relatively simple reproduction requirements, with nearly 68 percent of these households receiving them.

The survey data also highlight the contribution of nonagricultural activities to the formation of household incomes by the variety of its sources (table 7.7). Only capitalist entrepreneurs obtain the bulk of their incomes from crop sales, while small-scale capitalists do so from both the sale of crops and of animals. Wage-labor households generate more than two-thirds of their income through employment in off-farm nonagricultural occupations, significantly exceeding all other sources

TABLE 7.6
Source of Income-Generating Activities of Household by (Re)Production Form

Activities	CE	SC	LM	LS	WL	Total
Crop sales	100.0%	79.5%	83.3%	50.0%	28.6%	71.3%
Animal sales	50.0	79.5	50.0	50.0	28.6	57.7
Businesses	100.0	66.7	50.0	16.7	.0	53.3
Ag. labor	.0	2.6	.0	.0	14.3	3.3
DaHwa	.0	28.2	83.3	.0	57.1	33.3
Nonag. labor	.0	17.9	.0	.0	42.9	16.7
Remittances	.0	12.8	66.7	66.7	28.6	25.0
Mean no. sources	2.5	2.9	3.3	1.8	1.9	2.7
(n=)	(2)	(39)	(6)	(6)	(7)	(60)

of income. Income-generating activities not organized and owned by the household are of little importance to lineage forms in meeting reproductive requirements, although nearly 7 percent of the lineage market households have members toiling in daHwa labor. Of greater interest, remittances comprise notable sources of income for both lineage forms, yet neither has household members engaged in off-farm nonagricultural labor. This points to the continued significance of broad lineage relations in securing access to the incomes of juniors.[15] Yet, remittances also show the precariousness of the lineage system. In addition, lineage subsistence households account for more than half of their income through household businesses, relying on a mere 12.6 percent of their income through the sale of crops and animals. Food self-sufficiency remains an important value: "Your own dura always tastes better than dura you buy in the suq. Also, if you have your own dura you can withstand drought or any hard times."

Mean net incomes across (re)production forms disclose substantial social inequality among households. The mean net income (£S2,556) is significantly higher than the median (£S989), evidence of wide variances in the sample. By far, the three nonlineage household forms—those most affected by the rise of a capitalist economy—have higher incomes than the lineage forms. Net incomes of lineage market households is only marginally higher than that of lineage subsistence households, due to greater market participation. Although the former evidences more sources of income, the latter indicates more lucrative household

TABLE 7.7
All Households: Contribution of Sources of Income Activity to
Total Household Incomes by (Re)Production Form

All Households	CE	SC	LM	LS	WL	Total
Income sources						
Crop sales	64.3%	45.2%	36.2%	7.0%	.8%	47.7%
Animal sales	.7	14.5	7.8	5.6	11.0	10.3
Businesses	35.0	31.8	22.3	59.0	.0	31.2
Ag. labor	.0	.8	.0	.0	12.4	1.1
DaHwa	.0	.5	6.7	.0	3.7	.7
Nonag. labor	.0	5.5	.0	.0	67.1	7.0
Remittances	.0	1.7	27.0	28.4	5.0	2.0
Mean net income						
(£S)	20,784	2498	334	298	1510	2556
Median net income						
(£S)	20,784	1377	200	138	906	989
Total	100%	100%	100%	100%	100%	100%
(n=)	(2)	(39)	(6)	(6)	(7)	(60)

businesses. The fact that both incomes are lower than the other three household forms is explained by the fact that the two lineage forms have a greater economic orientation towards self-sufficiency and participate irregularly in market activities. Too, much of the marketing is done on the basis of bartering, something for something as opposed to straight cash transactions.

The analysis of income composition for female headed households emphasizes a different trajectory than does the sample as a whole (table 7.8). Overall, these households enjoy far fewer opportunities and face more constraints. In fact, much of the variation in the sample incomes derives from the substantially lower access of female headed households to resources. DaHwa, or day labor, for example, pays poorly and consequently only women, children, and the aged engage in it. Due in large measure to cultural biases favoring males, farmers choose not to hire them for piece work, preferring adult males, who are paid by the feddan.[16] Thus, men can earn more from agricultural labor in a given day. DaHwa accounts for slightly more than 35 percent of incomes in female headed lineage market households. Furthermore, income from the sale of crops and animals betrays the tenuousness of female headed

TABLE 7.8

Female Headed Households: Proportional Contribution of Sources of Income Activity to Total Household Incomes by (Re)Production Form

Income sources	CE	SC	LM	LS	WL	Total
Crop sales	NA	48.4%	31.8%	30.6%	1.6%	16.9%
Animal sales	NA	7.9	19.5	26.0	.0	4.6
Businesses	NA	28.5	.0	.0	.0	7.3
Ag. labor	NA	.0	.0	.0	.0	.0
DaHwa	NA	12.0	35.7	.0	7.4	9.9
Nonag. labor	NA	3.2	.0	.0	87.1	55.8
Remittances	NA	.0	13.0	43.4	3.9	5.5
Mean net income (£S)	NA	398	147	117	117	507
Median net income (£S)	NA	240	151	94	444	146
Mean income sources	NA	2.3	3.3	2.3	2.0	2.4
Total	100%	100%	100%	100%	100%	100%
(n=)	(0)	(4)	(3)	(3)	(4)	(14)

households in the lineage subsistence form. Unquestionably, these sales cut into the household's consumption stock, which can only be offset by remittances if the household agricultural work force is to be kept intact. Aside from crop and animal sales, lineage subsistence households do not participate in off-farm economic activities. Small-scale capitalists, on the other hand, rely significantly on household businesses, while wage-labor households depend on nonagricultural off-farm employment, indicating their difficulty in sustaining main farm agriculture.

Finally, *zakha*, or the Islamic practice of tithing, contributes significantly to the maintenance of penurious households and provides an indication of the minimum number of marginal households across (re)production forms. Not every household in need of additional food accepts "charity" because of its negative connotations, especially for healthy adult males. Rather than cash contributions to the poor, zakha assumes the form of sacks of dura in Somasem and augments the grain stocks of nearly 17 percent of both lineage forms and 43 percent of wage-labor households. Some 8 percent of the small-scale capitalists also receive zakha. The difficulties encountered by female headed households in meeting at least subsistence requirements is drawn into question: while no small-scale capitalists accepted zakha, one-half of the lineage market, two-thirds of the lineage subsistence, and two-thirds of the wage-labor households did.

Household Reproduction Strategies

It is difficult to pinpoint the precise moment in time when Somasem transformed from a relatively self-sufficient village, firmly organized in the lineage system, to one increasingly integrated within the wider modernizing economy. Young men have long migrated to seek their fortunes, although most migration was seasonal, tied to the rhythms of the agricultural season, with the two main periods coming immediately after the planting of main farms and following their harvests. Not until the 1950s did long-term migrants begin to outnumber more temporary and seasonal varieties, and it appears to have reached significant proportions when the Nuba Mountains became fertile recruiting grounds for the army and police. During this period, the purpose for the majority of migrants began to change from simply acquiring resources to marry and start an independent homestead, and now includes capital to enter commercial agriculture.

Individual motivations are often rather tenuous and subject to frequent revision. Perhaps the seductive face of consumerism smiled upon Somasem with the return of early migrants, creating endless rounds of new needs and desires. Possibly, the rapid spread of the mechanized schemes in Habila and elsewhere stimulated local imaginations to previously undreamt of possibilities. What is certain is that the desire to increase agricultural production has come to dominate the livelihood strategies of most householders in Somasem. Even those households not engaged in commercial agriculture partake of the cash economy in one way or another through the periodic sale of labor, business enterprises, or money remitted from kinsmen. Participation in the consumption of cash commodities is now widespread; coffee and tea provide relaxing libations, clothes must be worn, medicines purchased, dura ground, and karama dispensed for the deceased.

Agricultural Assets

Livestock and land comprise the core of wealth in Somasem for the vast majority of sampled households (table 7.9). Together, they form the basis of livelihood strategies, which, in one way or another, involve food security, cash incomes, brideprices, a hedge against future uncertainties, and a means to provide sons opportunities, either as farmers in their own right or in some other occupation. More durable than other forms of agricultural surplus, livestock frequently represents the difference between success and failure in achieving household reproduction goals. And, unlike cash savings, through careful husbanding these animals are truly interest bearing. Consequently, their loss from disease or theft is hard felt. Without question, cattle afford the greatest store of wealth, followed by goats. Chickens, in many ways, represent the savings accounts of women and the poor, providing more steady sources of income throughout the year. Traditionally, chickens are primarily left to women to dispose of as they choose, but in resource-poor households profits from the sale of poultry inevitably slip from the control of women.

Among small-scale capitalists the sale of a few cows or goats provides funds for farm operations—hiring tractors and paying wages for laborers—and to satisfy consumption requirements. Nearly 39 percent of these households sold cows and a further 50 percent, goats. Lineage forms part with cows only under extreme duress since they are needed for brideprice, as well as for the status they impart for the lineage elders. Hassan believes that his manhood was debased when he lost his cows to the 1984 drought and all of his goats to poachers in 1985. Only one lineage market household sold a cow, because of indebtedness, to a shayl, though a third of each lineage form sells goats. Goats and chickens also incorporate important elements in labor recruitment strategies, essential to the provisions that ensure a well-attended nafir or to attract wage-laborers. Sales of surfeit grain following a successful harvest, in turn, permit farmers to periodically replenish livestock. Only in well-off households do goats and chickens provide a source of protein; rarely are healthy cows slaughtered. Those without animals, such as the majority of wage-labor households, thus find themselves placed at a distinct disadvantage in formulating agricultural production strategies. Without alternative income sources, fewer feddan are cultivated, and then only in relation to available household labor.[17] With the exception of chickens, female headed households own few animals and, consequently, cultivate far fewer feddans.

Access to arable land presently poses little problem, although the newer farmer must be prepared for a long walk. In the main, villagers are limited more by access to satisfactory labor resources than by any-

TABLE 7.9
Household Agricultural Assets: Land, Cows, Goats, and
Chickens by (Re)Production Form

All households	CE	SC	LM	LS	WL	Total
Land						
% who own	100.0%	97.4%	100.0%	66.7%	71.4%	91.7%
Mean feddan	116.0	44.7	16.2	9.4	9.4	38.4
Mean cult.	102.2	18.3	5.4	2.9	1.6	17.3
Cows						
% who own	100.0	66.7	50.0	33.3	14.3	56.7
Mean no. own	15.0	15.2	8.0	2.0	2.0	3.3
Goats						
% who own	100.0	79.5	100.0	66.7	18.6	75.0
Mean no. own	17.5	17.0	7.5	7.3	5.0	14.4
Chickens						
% who own	100.0	92.3	100.0	82.3	42.9	86.7
Mean no. own	19.0	10.7	10.2	5.0	3.3	9.5
Total	100%	100%	100%	100%	100%	100%
(n=)	(2)	(39)	(6)	(6)	(7)	(60)
Female headed households						
Land						
% who own	0.0	100.0	100.0	66.7	50.0	78.6
Mean own	—	7.3	15.4	11.2	9.2	10.6
Mean cultivate	—	5.7	2.7	2.5	1.8	2.8
Cows						
% who own	NA	0.0	33.0	33.3	25.0	21.4
Mean no. own	—	—	10.0	3.0	2.0	5.0
Goats						
% who own	NA	50.0	0.0	0.0	25.0	64.3
Mean no. own	—	6.3	—	—	4.7	5.5
Chickens						
% who own	NA	75.0	100.0	100.0	50.0	78.6
Mean no. own	—	5.3	10.3	4.7	6.5	6.7
Total	100%	100%	100%	100%	100%	100%
(n=)	(0)	(4)	(3)	(3)	(4)	(14)

thing else. Nonetheless, the villagers realize that one day a shortage of land will arise and, therefore, strong social pressures exist against its sale. Even then, there are exceptions. Izrak, preferring marissa and gambling to farming, sold his land. Other than express their total contempt for him, however, the villagers did not ostracize Izrak, citing the facts that his grandfather had been the sheikh, the land was very far from Somasem, and that it was at least sold to neighboring Namma Nuba.

None of the sampled farmers initially accumulated sufficient income directly from agriculture to further the development of productive agriculture. The means to employ tractors and to hire wage-labor in the early 1970s derived principally from the sale of cattle, often acquired through previous off-farm employment. Of the 25 sampled households heads originally from Somasem, 13 had engaged in wage-labor outside of Somasem when they were younger.[18] There were exceptions, of course. According to Abas Jalil, "Many of the rich farmers here made money from their father's cows. They sold them and went into agriculture, using tractors and hired labor." By the size of his herd at one time, Allah Jabo was an extremely influential elder, with over 100 cows and 45 goats. He was able to give each of his six sons 4 cows with which to marry, and when Allah Jabo grew old, he divided the remainder among them. Hussain promptly sold his share and was one of the first to dramatically expand agricultural production in 1970; he now cultivates 131 feddans. He later opened a store, where he is also ensconced as a shayl. Khamis, on the other hand, worked in Khartoum from 1964 to 1968 as a policeman. Upon his return to Somasem he purchased 10 cows. Three years later Khamis sold 7 and now cultivates 100 feddans. With his earnings he, too, opened a shop and began speculating in dura and simsim. Today, both Hussain and Khamis are the two wealthiest men in Somasem.

Although cows are still important for expanding agriculture, cash savings is now the dominant trend among Somasem's migrants. Omar worked for nine years as a policeman and, in 1985, ended his service, with £S3,328 in severance pay. He immediately hired labor to assist him in clearing his field and made arrangements with a local tractor owner to plow it. Only after he had completed this business did Omar contemplate buying cows. He plans on enlarging the area under cultivation each year, as finances allow. Similarly, Abdul Karim spent twenty-eight years in the army and returned with £S16,000 in savings and severance pay for farming expenses. In addition to hiring labor for his fields, Abdul Karim also purchased a lorry for business purposes.

Most stories, however, are not as spectacular. The typical early migrant contented himself with acquiring a few cows, such as Abdul Gadir, who managed to obtain three small cows before homesickness drove him back to his family. And besides, he merely wanted to marry. Most migrants did not consider mechanizing land preparation and regularizing commercial agriculture until the late 1970s, when household reproduction became increasingly difficult without it due to the flow of commodities into the area and the loss of active laborers through out-migration. The point is, however, lacking cows or cash a farmer cannot mechanize land preparation and employ wage-labor without at least having access to other marketable resources. Osman, for example, was forced to sell his two rifles and a tape recorder in 1984 in order to expand agricultural production and meet growing household demands. Those bereft of resources must shape alternate household livelihood.

Not every migrant, however, succumbed to pressures to significantly capitalize agricultural production. The two lineage household forms, though certainly changed, provide socioeconomic parameters that are not always easy to break. Omar worked as a railroad policeman in Khartoum for five years in the early 1960s. As soon as he earned enough money to procure five cows, Omar returned to Somasem and married with two of his cows and two of his father's. Giving in to the cajoling of his father and uncles, he retained three cows for the time his sons would marry. Omar never really considered the possibility of commercial agriculture and remains satisfied with working his small landholdings. To be sure, lineage forms are diminished, as indicated by the age of households in the lineage subsistence form and the increasing shift towards cash incomes of lineage market households. On the other hand, young adults frequently find themselves emersed in economic activities that offer greater opportunities; albeit, opportunities that strike at the heart of lineage relations.

The advantage of off-farm employment for the original inhabitants is obvious in the number of feddans cultivated and owned when they are compared to the twelve original households, whose heads did not migrate. On the average, past migrants currently cultivate 32.5 feddans and own an additional 28.9, as compared to 16.9 and 34.4 feddans cultivated and owned by those choosing not to migrate. The latter group, composed mostly of lineage forms, owns more cows however, a further indication of the importance of older values and their resistance to commercial agricultural production. As summarized by Jabouna Omar, a lineage market householder, "it is all right to own a shop or work in Khartoum, but is better to be a farmer, to take care of your family and help your neighbors."

Interestingly, the mean number of cows owned by original migrating villagers is 5.3, but 10.0 for migrants from the lineage market form, evidence of the difference in livelihood strategies and the relative importance of cows. In addition, those who did not migrate, primarily lineage members, currently own more cows, at 12.2, than those who did. Late-comers to Somasem evidence little difference in whether or not they had migrated when younger. They cultivate less feddan and own fewer cows. Their dilemma lies in land and labor access, length of residence in Somasem, kinship connections, and stage in the household's life cycle. On the average, late-comers are at either extreme of the life cycle and, consequently, are either older or younger than the original inhabitants, especially in male headed households. There is little significance in mean household size, although original migrating heads have slightly larger households.

Agricultural Labor

In conjunction with household landholdings, access to labor further distinguishes household livelihood strategies by (re)production forms. Throughout the history of the Ghulfan, lands were cultivated primarily by nafir labor—planting, weeding, harvesting, threshing, and, when required, the clearing of new fields. Nafir also extended to the construction of houses, which need to be replaced every seven to ten years on the average. The great stress placed on ties of obligation and cooperation bound the community, each household to the other, on the basis of kinship, seniority, and fellowship. In short, nafir functioned to define the community and assured a well-ordered subsistence agriculture. Withholding participation went against postulated norms and lay outside the Ghulfan conception of a sensible or rational person. Refusal to help thus constituted denial of core values integral to the logic of the lineage system and abrogated one's position within it. Now, however, as a result of pressures exerted by the wider economy, coupled with out-migration, commercial activities have led to larger field sizes, which rapidly undermined nafir, replacing it with wage-labor. In fact, some farmers eschew the use of nafir altogether, denigrating it as inefficient, the tool of the poor and "backwards."

Although nafir constituted the primary labor force for agricultural activities, household labor provided a means to complete unfinished tasks, especially when particularly wet seasons produced excessive weed growth. No household in the past entered an agricultural season with the intention of relying singularly on the labor of its members. The responsibilities and obligations enacted by nafir thus conditioned the household labor process. Even the elderly, who at the end of their life cycle cultivated just a jubraka, counted on nafir as well as on the labor of younger lineage members. The present trend towards dependence on family labor divulges the difficulty in organizing nafir and the impecunious state of many households, which prevents the hiring of labor.

Wage-labor in the fields gained momentum during the 1960s with the stress exerted on the agricultural economy by the outflow of young men, though contract labor initially prevailed as a casual undertaking to supplement the loss of migrating active adults. In the main, the villagers responded to the loss of young kinsmen through expanding the recruitment basis of nafir beyond the conventional mechanisms of consanguinity. Bound by the language of lineage, one still spoke of the necessity of helping a brother or sister, an uncle or aunt, regardless of actual lines of descent. If anything, reciprocity and mutual dependence intensified within the village. Even more striking, the absence of young active adults pushed women on to the main farms and ruptured the gender division of labor that restricted females to the jubraka and males to the main farm or *zera*. Furthermore, the continuance of out-migration has left many females as de facto household heads; unfortunately, this also has diminished a man's responsibilities to provide for women.[19] The loss of young males, however, probably affects poorer lineage household forms to a greater degree by undermining the ethos of nafir. Nevertheless, young men will continue to seek their fortunes outside of the village because, as one man said: "People think that if a man does not make money it is because he is lazy or stupid; it is his own problem." The decline of lineage cohesion thus rapidly opened the door for the reorganization of agriculture and domestic life, though certainly in line with male interests.

Important distinctions differentiate nafir from wage labor. The hallmark of nafir revolves around reciprocal obligations, such that every villager is expected to help any other in a nafir party and, conversely, everybody is expected to assist them. What must be borne in mind, however, is that the consumption of comestibles does not equate with the purchase of labor and, thus, a sponsor cannot dictate the pace of work of a nafir party. There are certain standards but, paradoxically, the participants rather than the host will usually chide individuals not fulfilling their obligations. Wage-labor, on the other hand, involves an entirely different set of social relations. The selling of one's labor for field work presumes, at best, marginal access to resources that compels an individual to work for cash or some other form of remuneration. Consequently, those controlling resources employ those who do not, dictating the nature and tempo of work. As a specific transaction, the relation ceases with the expiration of the contract. Of greater relevance, the hiring of wage-labor excludes the broader obligations and responsibilities imposed by the lineage system and permits rational calculation of costs and benefits. The duration of nafir transactions, on the other hand, take years before labor exchanges balance out and, even then, require the attainment of elder status. Therefore, those elders unable or unwilling to use nafir now lost years of invested labor.

To describe the demise of nafir solely in economic terms provides only a partial understanding, for in reality its demise affected the entire edifice of the lineage in Somasem. Nafir, aside from its practical necessity in an agriculture marked by low technology, evokes the social nature of the work group as well as of the wider community. After a particularly enjoyable nafir, for example, a host may spontaneously slaughter a goat or a chicken, and the participants will eat and drink into the evening, accompanied by humorous stories and favored songs. More importantly, the intense feelings of fellowship aroused by such displays accentuate group cohesion by mitigating lines of individual difference. These exuberant demonstrations of fellowship do not make sound economic sense in terms of capitalism, and today seldom punctuate the conclusion of a nafir party.[20] Most older farmers reminisced sadly about the loss of nafir, acknowledged that they missed these occasions of merriment, and were quick to point accusatory fingers at commercial farmers and shop keepers, citing their greed for wealth and urban demeanor as the cause for its decline.

Only one of the two capitalist entrepreneurs currently uses nafir. Khamis still hosts a nafir for weeding, not out of nostalgia, but as a conscious strategy intended to maintain secure links to a potential labor source and to retain the good will of his neighbors. In the latter case, nafir also functions as a type of zakha, since he could easily employ wage laborers instead. Khamis regularly attends one nafir per season in order to satisfy the local perception of reciprocity. Hussain, to the contrary, disdains the formalities involved in nafir and prefers to rely on wage-labor for all agricultural activities. Any weeding left undone is then finished by the women of the household. Only 14 percent of wage-labor households utilize nafir, although some 60 percent indicated a preference for it. Incidences of nafir use among these households is low primarily because insufficient stocks would force wage-labor households to purchase comestibles in the market, and off-farm employment restricts members' time. Those hosting a nafir serve marissa but are unable to provide meat. Slightly more than 32 percent, however, attend other people's nafir parties on an average of eight times per season. The higher rate of participation, in part, is one element in these household's consumption strategies during the "hungry period" preceding the harvest of early maturing dura. A household finding it difficult to make ends meet would rather accept prepared food than a sack of grain.

Nearly 60 percent of small-scale capitalist households sponsor at least one nafir during the agricultural season, while all households in the lineage forms do so. A common reason offered by the former for the abandonment of nafir is their adherence to the Muslim taboo on the consumption of alcohol. In all fairness, the strong association between nafir and marissa turns a number of farmers away from calling a nafir work party. It is not the fact that an individual may choose not to drink marissa, but that those who do are viewed with shame and scorn. Younger people not exposed to the time when everyone freely partook of marissa find abstinence much easier and tend to be more critical of its usage. On the other hand, every inhabitant of Somasem accepts Islam, yet not everyone strictly adheres to its prescripts. The public consumption of marissa is frowned upon in Somasem, yet when an individual drinks it as part of a nafir party, they do so as a farmer, which, in effect, provides special dispensation.[21] Most hosts also offer *medida*, a nonalcoholic drink made from dura, as a substitute for marissa. Some villagers, critical of what they consider the equivalent of moral turpitude, privately contend that it is not so much a sign of piety, but a means to cease sponsoring a nafir and participating in other people's work parties. In all probability, dislike of marissa merely reinforces the tendency towards wage-labor. Such changes are not readily perceptible in the short-term; rather, they have been gradual processes.

On first impression, there appears to be little dissimilarity in the use of nafir between small-scale capitalist and lineage forms. Closer examination, nevertheless, shows entirely different strategies in the numbers of nafir parties held and in the rates of reciprocity. Small-scale capitalist households sponsored an average of 1.4 nafir work parties per season, while lineage market households hosted 2, and lineage subsistence households, 3. Fragmentation of the cooperative nature of nafir is confirmed in the former's lower rates of reciprocation. Even though approximately 21 individuals attend the nafirs of small-scale capitalists, reciprocation consists of the participation of 1, and occasionally 2, household members nine times throughout the growing season. Interestingly, 13 percent of small-scale capitalists, those with larger land holdings, do not reciprocate at all. The lure in attracting participants to a nafir hosted by small-scale capitalist households is not, perforce, shared labor obligations, but the dietary supplement. Some 91 percent provide meat, although 40 percent do not include marissa.

Lineage market households, to the contrary, reciprocate a mean 25 times, sending 2 household members, which roughly approximates the number of individuals attending their cooperative labor parties. Marissa is offered by 67 percent of these households, and 83 percent provide chicken or meat available in the market. Lineage subsistence households reciprocate an average 12 times per season, with 2 household members in attendance. Rates of labor exchange are similar, but because of the smaller size of land cultivated, fewer people are required in nafir work parties. Furthermore, these household forms generally have less surfeit grain with which to attract larger nafir parties.

Comparison of the utilization of wage-labor indicates more clearly the principles upon which agricultural production is organized by the respective forms. Capitalist entrepreneurial households contract a mean of 18 men, who are paid by the feddan, and 12 laborers, paid at a daHwa rate. In addition, threshing is accomplished by machine and 2 laborers. Overall, small-scale capitalist households employ a mean of 4 men for piece work and 5 daHwa laborers for weeding and, sometimes, harvesting. Households cultivating more than 15 feddan seasonally hire a mean of 7 piece workers and 2 daHwa laborers, while those cultivating less retain a mean of 1 and 2 respectively. Moreover, those with larger cultivations also employ mechanical threshers.

The majority of capitalist entrepreneurial and small-scale capitalist households believe that hired labor is superior to nafir. The primary criticisms leveled against cooperative labor concern its expense, inefficiency, and lack of control when compared to wage-labor. In the opinion of Krutukella, a small-scale capitalist: "I don't like nafir; it is expensive. They eat and drink too much and do very little work. If a person prepares for a nafir and it rains, they will eat but not work." Clearly, in these terms capitalist entrepreneurial and small-scale capitalist households calculate the costs of both wage-labor and nafir on the basis of profit and loss.[22] Slightly more than 33 percent of small-scale capitalist households, however, prefer nafir, but the structural organization of this (re)production form impedes its use; household consumption needs must be met, children educated, and agricultural production costs paid. Most of these farmers turn to nafir in order to break a labor bottleneck during times of wage-labor scarcities and shortages in family labor. Nafir labor thus affords capitalist entrepreneurial and small-scale capitalist households an ancillary source of labor, critical for such labor intensive activities as weeding and harvesting. Nonetheless, household labor is critical in agricultural activities, especially for small-scale capitalist households cultivating less than 15 feddans. As Khalil responded, when asked about family labor: "If your sons and daughters don't work, why have them? If they didn't work, I would throw them from the house."

Wage-labor households do not hire labor, although 42 percent indicated that they would if resources permitted. Lacking sufficient resources, these households must rely on their own labor to meet agricultural demands, regardless of labor preference. Small plot sizes work against the use of either hired labor or nafir. At best, these households can only satisfy a scant two-thirds of their yearly food requirements from their own fields, which precludes surfeit necessary for securing outside labor, notwithstanding the source.

Lineage market households find themselves turning to daHwa and to family labor in order to supplement cooperative labor exchanges because of increasing difficulties encountered in organizing nafir, competition with other nafir, which raises its "cost," and the enlargement of field sizes. Nonetheless, the use of daHwa is intermittent and is restricted to weeding. Lineage subsistence households do not employ wage labor; working within a cooperative group is far too important. What nafir does not finish is completed by the household. Regardless of the form, most lineage householders agreed that nafir provided the best source of labor because "it is good to work with your neighbors," because of the ability to "complete a large number of feddan in a given day," and because "the nature of reciprocity brings a measure of labor security to the household."

Concomitant with out-migration, the use of tractors for field preparation and planting activities in the 1970s permanently exposed the fragility of nafir labor within Somasem and within the lineage in general. The expansion of field sizes simply precludes the capabilities of nafir and requires careful manipulation of all sources of labor, especially the labor of all capable household members. Household relations for those unable to hire labor, and due to the decline of nafir, changed with the increase in reliance on family labor. It has become commonplace for marginal households to pull children from school, especially females, and bring them into the fields at an increasingly younger age. Adult females also found that their work load now regularly includes laboring on the main farm, aside from the traditional domestic operations in which they daily engage.

Whatever the motives prior to 1984, the drought created cheap labor supplies, both within and outside of Somasem. When people first began hiring wage-labor, no one thought of employing his neighbor or kinsman. Besides, working in another's field for cash compromised a farmer's standing in the village as self-reliant and independent. Consequently, farmers preferred to hire outsiders. Now, capitalist entrepreneurial and small-scale capitalist farmers draw no distinction, since they are concerned more with its cost and less with its source, and even employ lineage members. Many of the same people continue to labor in other farmers' fields, the difference being that it is no longer a nafir party but a work group. Households in need of money frequently find few alternatives to offering the labor of its members to their neighbors and kinsmen. In addition, for households in debt to the shayl, repayment demands more than the swallowing of pride.

Yet, change in the labor force speaks of other transformations. To suggest that the desuetude of traditional labor patterns is solely responsible for the reorganization of households and its activities misses other important concerns. One obvious mistake conflates result with cause by locating the problem in the failure of community or the perceived cultural deprivations of other ethnic groups. In the words of Al-Bai:

> People helped each other more in the past and wanted everyone to do well. Now people are jealous of each other, each wants to be rich. During the time of my grandfather, a good person was one who had many cows and a lot of sorghum, and would unselfishly help anyone. Thirty years ago if a person had nothing to eat, the one who had the cows would give one or two so the hungry person would have milk. Those with sorghum would give that. After the problem was over the cows were returned. Now the feeling of community spirit is dead. The Arabs and jallaba teach people to be unkind, to think only of yourself.

In short, change in access to labor, and life in general, is nothing less than the manifestations of forces and contradictions generated by the transformation process itself.

Overall, female headed households experience greater problems in securing labor outside of the household. As a result, they are unable to cultivate the same amount of land as do their male counterparts. Even though females can now acquire rights to main farms, they soon discover themselves at a distinct disadvantage in recruiting labor. In the main, female headed households contain fewer members and, simultaneously, have less access to both wage-labor and nafir. Although a female farmer may have cash, many male laborers are reluctant to work for a woman if other employment opportunities exist, preferring to take orders from a man. And, with regards to nafir, cooperation among women is traditionally restricted to the jubraka. Women do participate in nafir parties, although they accompany husbands, who are responding to other males. In conjunction with the chronic shortage of nafir labor within Somasem, women enjoy far fewer historical links to cooperative labor, from the breadth of activities to the depth of relations of obligation.

Business Enterprise Activities

In Somasem, ensuring a household's livelihood requires the careful allocation of the labor of its members in a series of productive activities. As noted, agriculture comprises an important, though not exclusive, undertaking. In a normal year, a central goal revolves around meeting household food needs and then producing a surplus to acquire other items of use. To have no dura imparts a severe loss of respect. In some ways, however, agricultural production is antipathetic to the rapid escalation in consumption and production standards. Yet, for all but the largest cultivators, agricultural surplus is too variable to provide the sole source of subsistence. And, for the largest cultivators, agricultural surfeit provides the means to branch out into other lucrative ventures. Achieving household reproduction thus compels the inclusion of specifically nonagricultural productive activities into livelihood strategies. This, in itself, is not new; after all, at a minimum, metal tools must occasionally be replaced, clothes purchased, rituals observed, and so on. What is different is the intensity and scope of these endeavors. Furthermore, interviews revealed stark differences between household forms in perceived production and consumption necessities, from field preparation to diet.

In the face of modernizing pressures, the ability to protect oneself from indebtedness and hunger currently requires multiple economic strategies. Without access to nonagricultural sources of income, a household's only recourse during times of production shortfalls is increasingly the shayl, which brings loss of others' respect and, more significantly, diminishes independence. Once trapped, extrication from the debt cycle proves illusive for most. As explained by one such borrower, "What you pay today makes you poor tomorrow." Beyond some minimum of subsistence, to be a salaried worker, to work for others, lessens a man's self-esteem, especially if it involves being ordered around in another's field. Therefore, it is better to own a business, to obtain cash through one's personal efforts. Interestingly, this concept of respect and pride does not extend to women, who find few off-farm business opportunities.

Table 7.10 shows the percent of households owning a business enterprise and the mean number owned for all households. Interestingly, wage-labor households operate no businesses. Of course, time frequently conflicts with opportunity, especially for those whose cash needs are immediate and pressing. Wage-labor households must struggle daily to satisfy subsistence needs in the absolute sense. As one wage-laborer grumbled: "The pay (to wage laborers) is very little; you cannot live on it. How can you live on a few pounds a year?" In this framework, reliance on wage employment, in addition to meager household cultivation, precludes the cash savings and extra time necessary to initiate a business. In the past, men collected gum arabic or engaged in artisan

TABLE 7.10
Percent of Households Owning Business Enterprises by (Re)Production Form

All households	CE	SC	LM	LS	WL	Total
% who own	100.0%	66.7%	50.0%	16.7%	0.0	53.3%
Mean no. owned	3.5	1.3	1.0	2.0	—	1.4
(n=)	(2)	(39)	(6)	(6)	(7)	(60)

production during the dry season. These, nonetheless, require the expenditure of time, especially gum collection since the acacia trees are found in the sands far to the north of Somasem. In addition, demand for artisinal crafts is low[23] and must now compete with less expensive goods available in the Dilling suq.

A wide variety of business enterprises contribute to the formation of incomes for over half of the sampled households, with the exception of wage-labor households. Because access to resources differs, it is not surprising that the types of enterprise differ as well. Table 7.11 illustrates that capitalist entrepreneurs and, particularly, small-scale capitalists engage in a diverse range of business activities. Most of these enterprises stand out due to their higher capital requirements, which serves as an entry barrier. They also generate higher incomes. The small-scale capitalist's initial investment capital usually came from past employment in the army. Currently, three household heads stationed for a number of years in Khartoum, for example, rent their former residences in the capital, while another invested his military savings in a lorry before returning to Somasem.

Low capital enterprises such as a tea stall, marissa brewing, gum collection, wood and thatch cutting, and artisinal handicrafts yield meager incomes and, consequently, are dominated by small-scale capitalists cultivating less than 15 feddan. Females monopolize tea stands, marissa brewing, and *zir* (clay pot) manufacturing, which are specifically female endeavors. Males control the remaining activities and usually undertake them during the dry season, after the completion of agricultural tasks. What is striking about low capital activities, with the exception of gum collection, is the types of goods that are now routinely marketed. Farmers whose wives refuse to brew marissa for a nafir must purchase it, while single males seek fellowship at tea stalls. That there is a market for wood and thatch for the construction of domestic compounds and

TABLE 7.11
Types of Enterprises Owned by Household Members by (Re)Production Form

Type of enterprise	CE	SC	LM	LS	Total
General store	25.0%	5.9%	.0%	.0%	8.5%
Tractor rental	25.0	.0	.0	.0	4.3
Agricultural broker	12.5	5.8	.0	.0	6.4
Real-estate rental	.0	8.8	.0	.0	6.4
Lorry transport	.0	2.9	.0	.0	2.1
Shayl	12.5	.0	.0	.0	2.1
Oil press	.0	2.9	.0	.0	2.1
Agricultural scheme	25.0	23.5	.0	.0	21.3
Tea stall	.0	2.9	33.3	.0	4.3
Gum collection	.0	23.5	66.7	.0	21.3
Cut wood/thatch	.0	8.7	.0	.0	6.3
Artisan/craft production	.0	11.6	.0	100.0	12.6
Brew marissa	.0	2.9	.0	.0	2.1
Total	100%	100%	100%	100%	100%
(Total n of enterprises)	(8)	(34)	(3)	(2)	(47)

wooden handles for agricultural implements further attests to the break-down of nafir, as well as to the demands placed on people's time. Not too long ago, no one would have thought of buying what he could have accomplished himself or what he could have done with fellow villagers and a pot of marissa. To pay another would have meant that a man had no kinsmen or friends, no standing in the community. Today, only those in the lineage forms look down on such ventures. Similarly, handicrafts were made to order rather than explicitly produced for a faceless market and were paid for in kind or cash. The reorganization of space and time in Somasem is expressed daily in the lives of individuals and in the quality of everyday relations.

Lineage market households exhibit far fewer business enterprises. Gum collection, a long-standing means to acquire cash income, is an arduous task that requires the tapper to be absent for up to three months. Nonetheless, lineage market households continue to collect gum since it can command a good price in the market and does not detract from the household's agricultural labor force. In fact, gum collection enables these households to pay for tractor rental and daHwa labor. One household operated a tea stall alongside the tarmac road. Howa, the sixteen-year-old daughter of Suliman, recently bore a child out of wedlock and began selling tea and coffee to provide for her infant son. Nevertheless, when needed she still labors in her father's fields. Lineage subsistence households continue to produce their traditional handicrafts, bartering with those who need and appreciate their skills.

Few business opportunities exist for females in Somasem. As a result of gender barriers, especially in the broadened domestic labor requirements, women usually are forced to work daHwa in order to obtain cash incomes. Women used to dominate the collection of wood but were squeezed out when men took up this activity, primarily because of the distances one must now travel in search of wood, and the higher price wood now fetches in the market. Only one female, Umkom, operated outside of the traditional female domain, brokering okra. Of course, this niche did not directly compete with village males and thus posed no threat.

The story of Umkom, a small-scale capitalist, deserves further elaboration since she is atypical of most villagers. A 50-year-old divorcee, Umkom currently lives with her five children and a "servant."[24] Her philosophy of life is straightforward: "If you are poor, you sleep on the floor. After that you try to buy an *angerib* (bed). It's like land; you try to increase the size (under cultivation) and improve it. You must be able to control your budget, to save money and improve your life."[25] Perhaps the lack of help from other relatives following her divorce turned her away from lineage responsibilities, or the fact that her former husband offers no assistance: "He doesn't care about this family." Umkom began hiring a tractor in 1983 and only hires wage-labor if the work proved too much for the household (two sons and three daughters) to complete. She earns cash by purchasing okra from neighboring women at one pound per *malwa* (4.125 liters) and sells them for five pounds in Dilling. Umkom is equally shrewd in selling surplus grains, patiently watching the market for the optimum price. She is resigned to profit as the "way of the world." According to Umkom, "Profit is okay for the one who makes it, but bad for the one who has to buy from that person."

Off-Farm Employment

Somasem's encounter and subsequent integration into the wider society affects households in various ways. It affects households differentially to the degree that their reproduction depends on cash incomes; hence, their access to resources determines, in large measure, livelihood strategies. The household labor process is not always sufficient to provide the minimum of food and cash either for daily or for generational reproduction. As noted, inconsistencies in agricultural yields require alternative means to ensure at least basic subsistence. Unfortunately, not all households are able to overcome this difficulty through self-employment, or the market is such that there is low demand among the local clientele.[26] These households would not survive on a daily basis without some sort of outside involvement, nor would young men be able to marry and begin their own families. Thus, the increased reliance on the sale of labor further distinguishes the (re)production forms. Moreover, when the marginal productivity of labor has reached the point of diminishing returns within the household unit, individuals less critical to the household labor process seek outside employment. On the other hand, not every individual aspires to an agricultural life, and off-farm opportunities offer a way out of this existence.

Of the sampled households, nearly 37 percent of small-scale capitalist households have at least one member engaged in off-farm employment, while 100 percent of lineage market and wage-labor households do. No member from the capitalist entrepreneurial or lineage subsistence forms labors in activities not directly controlled by the household, though for different reasons. The pursuit of off-farm employment, however, is not without its consequences and often creates a tension between the logic of household reproduction and the mechanisms of the larger economy within which households are located. In other words, outside involvement frequently places members in distinctly different economic circumstances, which can frequently redefine household relations. The need to engage in outside employment creates the basis for independent income-streams and probably contributes to a weakened commitment to the household as a shared unit of reproduction. An independent source of income also functions to erode patriarchal authority by lessening a junior's dependence on his elders.

Table 7.12 shows the disparities in the distribution of wage-labor activities by sex for household members working off the farm. Most males still refrain from laboring in other villager's fields, yet seemingly experience no conflict in sending female household members for daHwa work. The only source of cash from off-farm employment for lineage

TABLE 7.12
Distribution of Off-Farm Employment by Sex and (Re)Production Form

Male	SC	LM	WL	Total
Skilled employment				
Teacher	7.7%	.0%	.0%	5.6%
Civil servant	7.7	.0	20.0	11.1
Electrician	.0	.0	20.0	5.6
Semiskilled employment				
Flour mill attendant	7.7	.0	.0	5.6
Store clerk	15.4	.0	.0	11.1
Prayer caller	7.7	.0	.0	5.6
Manage ag. scheme	.0	.0	20.0	5.6
Unskilled employment				
Tend livestock	.0	.0	20.0	5.6
Manual laborer	15.4	.0	.0	11.1
DaHwa laborer	38.5	.0	20.0	33.3
Total	100%	.0%	100%	100%
(n=)	(13)	(0)	(5)	(18)
Female				
Skilled employment				
Teacher	9.1	.0	.0	5.6
Semiskilled employment				
Store clerk	4.5	.0	.0	2.8
Unskilled employment				
DaHwa laborer	86.4	100	100	91.7
Total	100%	100%	100%	100%
(n=)	(22)	(9)	(5)	(36)

market households, for example, is females engaged in daHwa labor. Even more striking, daHwa is one of the few avenues of employment available to females within the village. When we consider female headed households, this fact becomes clearer. Of the sampled women working off the farm in this category, 84, 100, and 72 percent of females in small-scale capitalist, lineage market, and wage-labor households respectively work daHwa. Males, on the other hand, evidence a greater range of occupational pursuits. Certainly, male mobility comprises an important factor in securing gainful employment since Somasem, like most villages, offers a limited number of opportunities. With the exception of Khadija, a school teacher in nearby Dilling, all of sampled females work in the village. Khadija regularly remits her earnings to her father (a small-scale capitalist). Only two women worked in occupations other than daHwa labor in Somasem—one as an adult literacy teacher and the other as a clerk in a general store, though she was the owner's niece. Nearly 38 percent of males, to the contrary, migrate, usually to Khartoum, El-Obeid, Dilling, and Kadugli.

Migration Activities

As indicated, cash needs coupled with meager employment potentials in the Somasem vicinity forces young men to migrate elsewhere. Some may never return, forsaking agriculture for urban opportunities. Others do return, marry and begin their own families. Still others return already married and claim lands of their own. Women, on the other hand, either join newly married husbands or leave temporarily to visit family members. Only one female respondent temporarily migrated for employment purposes and then only as far as Dilling. What is of concern here, however, are those whose migration is temporary; that is, migrants who remain household members. Not surprisingly, given greater male mobility and the money demands of marriage and agriculture, men evidence a higher incidence of temporary out-migration, with nearly 20 percent of male household members leaving Somasem. In distinction to males, only 13 percent of females migrate for short periods of time. No male members of lineage subsistence household migrate, nor do females

TABLE 7.13
Patterns of Temporary Migration by (Re)Production Form

	CE	SC	LM	LS	WL	Total
Households						
% w/migrants	50.0%	30.8%	33.3%	.0%	57.1%	41.7%
Mean number	1.0	2.0	1.3	0	2.3	1.7
% of household members by sex						
Male	8.3%	20.3%	25.0%	.0%	30.0%	19.5%
Female	9.1	16.4	.0	.0	9.1	13.1

from either lineage form. Table 7.13 displays the percentage of households with incidences of temporary migration and the mean number of
migrants, as well as the percentage of household members by sex who
temporarily migrate.

Equally revealing are the primary objectives underlying migration
episodes (table 7.14). What is immediately apparent is the fact that, overall, only some 27 percent of males migrate for other than economic
purposes, while 92 percent of females do. Young men labor at a wide
variety of jobs, although manual labor is more common, with 21 percent of males engaged in this activity. Older men, accounting for 59
percent of employed male temporary migrants, collect gum arabic. Aside
from attending a secondary school, 52 percent of female migrants temporarily leave Somasem to visit relatives or accompanying other household members. Overall, females tend to remain in Somasem until they
are married, when they join their husband's household.

Although male migration certainly contributes to the decline of nafir
and increased rates of separation of men from their families,[27] distance does not necessarily dissolve household bonds. Cash remittances
as well as food and clothing from working migrants continue to be an
important source of household sustenance, with temporary migrants
sending an average of £S284 a year, and food and clothing an average
of 1.5 times during the year.[28] As long as lineage obligations are met,
husbands sustain ties to families, and single males retain their claims
on ancestral lands. In general, all but the wealthiest households feel
the pressures of a cash economy and are more prone to migrate as the
result of lack of opportunities. At the other end, wealthy households
are able to fall back on their own resources, so that sons and daughters
migrate primarily in search of education or to access other sources of
economic mobility.

When compared to males permanently leaving the household, 73
percent initially migrated to gain employment, with 3 men traveling as
far as Iraq and Saudi Arabia. Permanent migrants, those severing household ties, also work in various jobs, although 37 percent are manual
laborers and 21 percent are in the army or police. Only 17 percent of
permanent male migrants remained in Somasem, having married and
begun their own households. Of the permanent female migrants, 90 percent severed household ties only after marriage, while the remaining 10
percent joined the household of another relative.

TABLE 7.14
Primary Reason for Temporary Migration by Sex and (Re)Production Form

	CE	SC	LM	WL	Total
Male					
Employment	.0%	19.2%	.0%	00%	23.5%
Seek employment	.0	7.7	.0	.0	5.9
Tend livestock	.0	15.4	25.0	.0	14.7
Collect gum	.0	30.8	50.0	.0	29.4
Attend school	100.0	15.4	25.0	.0	17.6
Visiting	.0	11.5	.0	.0	8.8
Total	100%	100%	100%	100%	100%
(n=)	(1)	(26)	(4)	(3)	(34)
Female					
Employment	.0	4.3	.0	.0	4.0
Attend property	.0	4.3	.0	.0	4.0
Attend school	100.0	34.8	.0	100.0	40.0
Visiting	.0	30.4	.0	.0	28.0
Accompany others	.0	21.7	.0	.0	24.0
Total	100%	100%	.0%	100%	100%
(n=)	(1)	(23)	(0)	(1)	(25)

Notes

1. A *rakuba* is thatching raised on poles to provide shade and is left open to any comforting breeze.
2. As noted in chapter 2, the tumultuous Mahdist period created a disjuncture among many groups in the
Nuba Mountains.
3. The relationship between amount of land owned and time of arrival of late-comers yielded a
correlation coefficient of .428 and is significant at the .01 level.
4. One day, for example, four nafir parties were held for weeding. After visiting each, I noticed a strong correlation between the amount of provisions and the size of the nafir.
5. In Somasem the field sizes are given in *mukhamas*, which is larger than the feddan, at 1.6 feddan. The relationship between a household's amount of land under cultivation and net income produces a correlation coefficient of .8108 and is significant at the .001 level. When controlled for by tractor usage, the correlation coefficient is .8256, significant at the .001 level.
6. Control of lands by the village, and the near absence of a land market, limits intrarural mobility in general, as access to land is based on village membership.

7. In all fairness, there are technical difficulties involved since Somasem rests on a thick rock layer (conversation with director of UNICEF water operations in Kadugli, 1987). Nevertheless, the Hafir is contaminated by runoff carrying human and animal excrement.

8. This is £S1.75 per cow, £S3.00 per camel, £S.5 per goat or sheep, and £S1.00 per donkey. Needless to say, the sheikh underreports their number to the government's tax collector.

9. This incident occurred three months after I first arrived in Somasem. With each visit I quickly caught up on each new twist. In fact, I made one last visit to Somasem before leaving the Nuba Mountains to learn of the conclusion.

10. CE refers to capitalist entrepreneurial households, SC to small-scale capitalist households, LM to lineage market households, LS to lineage subsistence households, and WL to wage-labor households. Throughout the following chapters, these notations are used in the tables for matters of convenience; they are specified within the text, however.

11. With respect to household size and age structure, female headed households differ little from table 7.1. Although the mean age of members and household heads is younger, much of the difference is attributable to earlier age of marriage of women and the fact that the female heads are primarily divorced or widowed.

Characteristics of female headed households:

% of households that	CE	SC	LM	LS	WL	Total
are female headed	.0%	28.6%	21.4%	21.4%	28.6%	100.0%
Mean household size	—	4.3	6.0	3.3	3.0	4.1
Mean member age	—	20.2	21.8	24.4	21.7	21.8
Mean number age <16	—	2.0	3.3	1.7	1.5	2.1
Mean age of head	—	40.8	39.4	40.0	42.3	40.6
(n=)	(0)	(4)	(3)	(3)	(4)	(14)

12. The three women spent heavily on karama for their deceased husband, including 2 cows, 7 sacks of dura, 3 goats, 4 pounds of sugar, 5 pounds of tea and 3 of coffee, 15 pounds of rice, 50 pounds of onions, and 2_ gallons of oil. They admitted that this represented much of what their husband had left them outside of land.

13. Two wives had been unable to bear children, and a third died in childbirth. Given the practice of female circumcision prevalent among the Ghulfan, this is not unusual.

14. Female headed households: marital status

	CE	SC	LM	LS	WL	Total
Single adult	—	25.0%	.0%	33.3%	25.0%	21.4%
Single—w/dep.	—	75.0	66.7	66.7	50.0	64.4
Nuclear	—	.0	.0	.0	25.0	7.1
Complex	—	.0	33.3	.0	.0	7.1
Total	100%	100%	100%	100%	100%	100%
(n=)	(0)	(4)	(3)	(3)	(4)	(14)

15. Seventy percent of the remittances received by lineage subsistence households come from former household members, while lineage market households obtain 60 percent from former household members and 10 percent from other relatives.

16. Every farmer I talked with insisted that men can do more agricultural work in one day than can a female. In all probability, proof of this resides more in gender bias. With regards to weeding, for example, physical differences should not prevent women from working as quickly and efficiently as men, as is the case in India.

17. The correlation coefficients for amount of land cultivated and the numbers of cows, goats, and chickens owned proved significant, at the .001 level.

18. One capitalist entrepreneurial, ten small-scale capitalist, and two lineage market household heads.

19. Men held an important stake in the breaking down of land restrictions since fathers, brothers, and husbands were obliged to provide for their daughters, sisters, and wives.

20. During my stays in Somasem only one such festive occasion transpired, with the slaughter of a goat leading to laughter and songs long into the night. Young people, on the other hand, periodically gathered around a cassette in the evening to listen and dance to music popularized in Khartoum. If anything, this activity further distanced the young from the elders.

21. When I first asked about marissa, I was told that it was *haram* and that no one drank it. I was somewhat surprised, then, when I went to a nafir and saw bountiful supplies of marissa. Yet it is not that the people were hypocritical, but that marissa is such an integral part of nafir.

22. Interviews with small-scale capitalists revealed a consistent concern with production costs and a frustration over the fact that nafir labor could not be controlled to the degree that hired labor can.

23. Handicrafts include saddles, mortars for pounding grain, bed frames, gates, stools, rope, and *zirs* (large clay pots for holding water).

24. The status of Mohammed was not clear. Originally from Chad, he has been with Umkom's household for twelve years and does all of the heavy work and many of the domestic chores, such as carrying water and cooking. He is paid very little for his contributions.

25. Umkom also had a wonderful sense of humor. One day her daughter returned from the store with coffee beans. There was a small hole in the wrapping through which beans had fallen. When Umkom noticed, she told her daughter: "Go back and pick them up, we aren't planting coffee this year."

26. In fact, in 1985 Juma'a was forced to close his general store due to lack of business.

27. Roughly 43 percent of male migrants are married and another 11 percent are sons and brothers of the household head.

28. Migrants from small-scale capitalist households remit an average of £S460 per year, £S240 from wage-labor households, but only £S20 from lineage market households, reflecting the type of employment. Most migrants from the latter form are cow herders, guards, or construction laborers, all earning meager salaries.

8

Shair Tomat: Yeoman Farmers
in the Nuba Mountains

Success is measured in different ways; for some it is determined by an
individual's proficiency in amassing material wealth, and for others it is
by the ability to fulfill social responsibilities. To be successful in Shair
Tomat requires both, but the pursuit of riches should never come at the
expense of another person, especially a relative. Unlike Somasem, success is not solely an individual affair but imparts an obligation to other
household members, to the wider lineage, and then to the village as a
whole. In short, success translates more as a collective endowment than
as an individual attribute. The household centeredness of the production
and consumption unit both facilitates and ensures this. To be sure, issues
of patriarchy, age, and gender structure household relations and, thus,
define the scope of opportunities open to the respective members. Nevertheless, within these parameters members work to promote their respective pursuits, ever mindful that an individual's good fortune is conditioned
by the household's providence and the well-being of the village.

Within Shair Tomat, food self-sufficiency dominates all other livelihood considerations. When this condition is met, growing cotton, off-
farm employment, and household businesses take on a different character.
These activities provide an abundance, something apart from self-
sufficiency. Thus agricultural endeavors lie first and foremost at the center
of household livelihood strategies. Yet, despite the importance of agriculture, most villagers acknowledge that the reproduction of the household requires a careful mix of other economic activities, but only as
long as they do not interfere with the household unit's basic sustenance
and needs. Consequently, livelihood strategies are formulated around
the household's agriculture schedule and rely on the invocation of patri-

archy, the position of women, and the general ideology of kinship in their implementation.

Contemporary Context

Shair Tomat, with approximately 380 people, isn't a particularly populous village but seems typical to others found throughout the Nuba Mountains. The houses are characteristically round, constructed of mud, with thatched conical roofs.[1] The living compounds are scattered across the top of a large rolling knoll and extend down the gentle slopes to its base and beyond. The original families occupy the uppermost area, in part for the panoramic view of the plains and the distant jebels beyond, and also because it is commonly assumed that there are fewer mosquitos here during the rainy season. In a small clearing atop the knoll stands a large shade tree, which is a favorite place for the elders to congregate in the evening to discuss matters of the day. The young boys patiently serve the elders, shuttling back and forth from the living compounds to bring a glass of cool water or hot tea. The faces of the boys reflect the gravity of the on-going conversations, with their somber looks for serious news or mirthful grins for humorous stories.

The manner of Shair Tomat's settlement goes to the core of Sudanese history. With the consolidation of Condominium rule in the Nuba Mountains during the 1920s and 1930s, British policy was carried out with the twin missions of regularizing the production of agricultural commodities, most notably cotton, and collecting taxes. After years of internecine warfare throughout the jebels, this proved no easy feat. The objectives of pacification involved relocating various Nuba communities to the plains, demobilizing the Arabs, and minimizing contact between the two "tribes" (see Stevenson, 1984). The establishment of Shair Tomat grew directly out of those efforts. The initial Hawazma (*dar Jama'a*) settlers arrived in the area in 1933, forcibly moved by the British from Daloka in the Shatt range. They were given specific instructions to take up farming and to desist from future raids on their Nuba neighbors. In many respects, then, the Hawazma of Shair Tomat were "created" in the pastoral image of the English yeoman farmers.

The extended family of Al-Haj Abdullah was the first to be relocated by the British from Daloka to Shair Tomat. The move, however, was not a matter of choice. The mid-nineteenth century witnessed the rise of the

Mahdi movement and the siege of El Obeid. At this time many Hawazma fled southward to the Nuba Mountains in order to escape the chaos engulfing Northern Kordofan. Al-Haj's family eventually made their way to Daloka along with other Hawazma. Having lost their livestock, and not being sedentary agriculturists, the Hawazma took up slave raiding and, eventually, cattle rustling in the outlying areas adjacent to their new home. Al-Haj's grandfather, and later his father, organized the incursions with military precision. The captured Nuba slaves were sold in towns such as El Obeid and Al Nahud, or to passing Hamar Arabs. The cattle were disposed of locally. Needless to say, these activities proved intolerable to the British, and it was decided that they would make better farmers, but not in their old hunting grounds. Nevertheless, not all of the Hawazma were forced from Daloka, and today Al-Haj still has a few relatives residing there.

One day Kafi, a Miri Nuba from Seraf Al Dai, came to visit the wife of Moustafa Abdullah, the granddaughter of one of the wives of Al-Haj's deceased uncle. His story illustrates the rather curious and complex ties that bind people in Shair Tomat. Kafi's grandfather, as a small child in Miri, was kidnapped by Arabs and sold in Northern Kordofan. Tio managed to escape after three months and find his way home. Unfortunately, he was kidnapped again, but his luck held firm. On the way north he managed to kill a guard and flee to Seraf Al Dai, where he was given shelter (or held) by an old man in return for helping the old man in his fields. When Tio became older, his benefactor adopted him and gave him land, as he would to a son. Eventually Tio's father learned of his son's whereabouts and travelled to Seraf Al Dai to ask Tio to come home. Tio explained to his father that his life was good in Seraf Al Dai and that he was happy. Tio's father was pleased with his son's good fortune and sent two of his daughters to live with Tio. One day a sister was kidnapped by Al-Haj's grandfather (old habits die hard) and was married to the brother of Al-Haj's father. That woman's granddaughter, the one Kafi came to visit that day, is married to Moustafa. Moustafa is the son of Al-Haj, making Moustafa's wife's grandmother his paternal great-aunt.

Other people settled in Shair Tomat in the intervening years. Like Somasem, the availability of unclaimed fertile lands provided the main attraction. The newcomers found it necessary to adopt the Hawazma customs practiced by Al-Haj's family, especially Islam, in order to re-

main in Shair Tomat. The family of Yagoub Omar, for example, journeyed from Northern Darfur by way of Zolatair. Unlike the Hawazma
of Daloka, the *Bergu* had a history of farming and nafir labor parties.
Nonetheless, the drinking of marissa stopped in Shair Tomat, as Al Haj's
father was a devout Muslim, who did not tolerate its use even in the
fields. El Baroud Kuku's family, the second largest in Shair Tomat after
Al-Haj's, originally hailed from the Miri range, although their far farm
was in the vicinity of present-day Shair Tomat. As peace slowly came to
the area, the Kuku family edged ever closer to their primary lands, first
settling in Seraf Al Dai, then Tesse, and finally in Shair Tomat. Like
Yagoub Omar, El Baroud and his brother readily reply that they are
Hawazma.[2] With the exception of one Keiga Nuba family, all of the
inhabitants of Shair Tomat today claim to be Hawazma, having fully
adopted the customs.

Family ties run deep in Shair Tomat. Perhaps it is the Hawazma customs coupled with the manner of the village's settlement that make kinship bonds so strong. At any rate, these ties mitigate against the full
rationalization of agriculture, the "rational" pursuit of profit, and the
full subsumption of labor to the demands of capital. According to the
village elders, a successful farmer, first and foremost, is one who is able
to feed his family and meet their needs. Any money left over should be
utilized to purchase animals, an important "store of wealth" against future uncertainties. "If you are very rich," added one elder, named Al
Yas, "you must be *harami*, not taking care of the family." Individuals
are also obligated to assist members of their extended family or lineage,
not necessarily on a day to day basis, but always with life's larger problems and uncertainties. Mahdi, for example, helped feed his brothers'
families during the drought of 1984 with his ample grain reserves. El
Baroud and Ismail unquestioningly undertake each other's field chores
when one is too ill to work. Moreover, El Baroud's son tends both his
father's and uncle's cattle since Ismail also operates the tahona (flour
mill) in nearby Seraf Al Dai, although cattle sales are kept separate. It is
difficult to imagine anyone in Shair Tomat refusing a legitimate request
from a relative. As summarized by Issah, "If you cannot depend on your
family, who can you depend on?"—to which the elder Adam added,
"No one will care for you like family."

The people of Shair Tomat exhibit a strong attachment to the land; it
is the source of everything that is good in the village. Not only does

land provide the means necessary to live and prosper in the village, it is at the heart of local values, which place great importance on being independent. To perform manual labor for cash, especially on another's field, is to ignore one's own farm and family, and is considered the closest thing to being a slave. Finally, land is what ultimately holds the family together and, in part, defines household relations. Farmers rely principally on family or household labor in their agricultural operations. According to the household division of labor, male members are entrusted with cultivating the main farm and females the family jubraka. Both may, however, work on either, depending on the labor requirements of a given day, although women will never work the main farm if nonlineage males are present, since female exclusion prohibits this interaction.[3] Older children toil alongside their parents until they marry and begin families of their own, helping out wherever they are needed. What the family is unable to accomplish in the main field is completed by wage-labor and/or nafir, depending on the availability of each, as well as on household finances. Optimally, most farmers plant their fields with the intention of doing all of the work with family labor and resort to outside labor as the last recourse.

The importance of family labor cannot be overstated, in part because of the difficulties involved in obtaining nonhousehold labor. The overall scarcity of wage-labor reflects the competing employment opportunities in Kadugli, Khartoum, and elsewhere, placing its use out of the range of many household budgets for all but the most labor-intensive tasks, such as weeding and picking cotton. Even then it can be difficult to locate and frequently must be enticed through the provision of a mid-morning meal, replete with meat of some kind. This can significantly add to the already expensive cost of wage-labor.

The practice of nafir in Shair Tomat suffers a similar fate, especially in the absence of a strong tradition of nafir throughout the village as a whole. In the face of limited consanguine relations, no other mechanisms of recruitment exist to buttress nafir relations of obligation. Accordingly, attending four other nafir parties is considered a reasonable number by many farmers. As a result, the average nafir size is much smaller in Shair Tomat than in either Somasem or Shatt Damam, even given the smaller population of Shair Tomat.[4] Moreover, nafir parties in the past were scheduled in consultation with relatives and neighbors to limit the number of nafir in a given day. Now nafir parties contend for village labor by providing meat such as beef, goat, or chicken, which can make a nafir gathering a rather expensive undertaking. Many villagers prefer wage-labor to nafir since they believe that it can accomplish more work in a day than can the latter. In line with Hawazma customs, nafir activities are organized by gender, and the sexes are kept separate. Further, in accordance with the tenets of Islam, no marissa is served.

Bounded by Saraf Al Dai to the west, Tesse to the north, Al Kamboi to the east, and Shimal Morte to the south, there are not a lot of unclaimed land reserves available to the inhabitants of Shair Tomat. A unique inheritance system has emerged that effectively copes with the relative shortage of land in conjunction with maintaining the viability of the size of holdings. Land inheritance is adelphic, according to Hawazma customs—land is always inherited by males—but with an added twist. In order to inherit land a male must marry his first cousin from within the village, preferably his father's brother's daughter (patrilateral cross-cousin marriage). This also empowers a male to claim and clear available unused village lands. If a young male does not have at least one wife according to the dictates of custom or indicates no desire to farm, he, like his sisters, can inherit anything but land.[5] This practice preserves the integrity of family fields and, of equal importance, village lands. Strong informal sanctions exist to preserve this convention. In the words of Daoud:

> The old people see who married within the family and divide their land among them. Those who did not can only get land temporarily, maybe for two or three years. If people break this custom, people will come and tell you. You must make things right or you will be isolated and forced to go. Otherwise no one will have enough land or outsiders will get it.

It is the function of the sheikh to oversee the village lands, especially important for those lands left idle by temporary migrants.

Furthermore, village lands are not rented out for a period of more than two years. The elders have strong opinions on this matter. According to Ibrahim:

> If your sons leave the village for a while and you rent your land, they will not return because you have no land to give them. It can be a big problem for those who return and find no land to farm. Renting land is bad for the family.

If, at the end of two years, the lessee wants to own the land or shows a reluctance to vacate it, the elders go to the police and force his eviction.

As a result of past difficulties, most villagers in Shair Tomat are leery of renting lands to outsiders. The one exception to this occurred in 1970, when the elders quarreled incessantly over what to do with excess uncleared village lands after the government made moves to confiscate it. Some wanted to rent the lands to a jallaba; others did not. In the end the elders contacted Ismail Mousa, a jallaba of acquaintance from Kadugli (he was originally from El Nahud), who cleared and farmed 1,250 feddans until 1972. Ismail gave the villagers some dura so that they would feel good about him. After Ismail departed, the land was left fallow for two years, after which the villagers attempted to reclear the land by hand. This task proved too difficult an undertaking. Hashim Abdullah then suggested that the village apply to the Nuba Mountains Agricultural Production Corporation (NMAPC) for inclusion in their cotton schemes. In this way, the matter of the excess land was finally resolved, when the NMAPC consolidated the village landholdings and redivided it into dura and cotton fields; the land was subsequently reparceled out among the villagers.

The NMAPC ploughs the cotton fields and, for a fee, the dura fields, although some farmers rent private tractors for the latter activity, due to the logistical problems inherent in the NMAPC operation.[6] Most farmers are dissatisfied with cotton now, citing its low price and the insufficiency of rain. In fact, Al Nour fully expects cotton to fail every fourth year. As a result, many neglect their cotton fields and concentrate on the other crops. No one is forced to grow cotton and can exchange their cotton field for lands solely within the dura section. Still, few opt for this, as farmers have become accustomed to the NMAPC ploughing their fields, and at a much lower cost than the jallaba charges for his tractor.

Life is far from idyllic and self-contained for the people of Shair Tomat. There is a small community-owned shop, but it is open intermittently at best. All other services must be attained at Seraf Al Dai, approximately a one-hour walk. The marketing of crops poses an additional burden, as the village is some thirty minutes walk from the tarmac road. Those without a donkey or the cash to rent a lorry or a donkey must haul the crops to the road, which places limits on the amount farmers can sell at any one time. The jallabas who venture to Shair Tomat in order to purchase crops directly from farmers are a poor alternative since they offer prices substantially lower than the suq in Kadugli. Furthermore, the rise in brideprice over the years continues to force young men to migrate and decreases the supply of family labor. Currently, a typical brideprice consists of between £S300 to £S500 in addition to clothes, one sack each of sugar, onions, charcoal, and wheat flour, two sacks of dura, two jerry cans of oil, one carton each of sweets and washing soap, one gallon of kerosene, five pounds of tea and ten of coffee, and twelve bottles of perfume. The groom must also provide a house for his wife. As in Somasem, a community consensus has proved illusive in reducing the brideprice, although cattle are no longer required.

Finally, karama can deplete a household's resources, placing marginal households at risk. And, since husbands and fathers customarily command more respect than do wives and mothers, more is spent on their karama. Fahtma, for example, sold her deceased husband's last two cows in order to commemorate him. Social convention cannot easily be disregarded, and family pride requires obeisance such that older lineage members will quietly urge a reluctant widow or son to spend. But, as explained by Hamid, "If a person spends a lot of money on karama then Allah will bless you." Batul, on the other hand, chided Hamid, replying that "the dead don't work!"

In spite of these problems, Shair Tomat is a tightly knit community. Neighboring men often carry their dinners to a convenient location to dine in the company of their friends, while women and children similarly eat together with their neighbors. Relatives also routinely take their meals jointly, with the women alternating the cooking. This sense of the collective well-being extends to other areas as well. There is no shayl in Shair Tomat, primarily because the villagers refuse to grant them a foothold. The importance of this is not lost on the villagers. Outside of the household, and even the village, one must avoid being in debt in order to remain independent. Consequently, the economic hardships affecting households in Somasem loses its harshness of impact in Shair Tomat. Essaug, for example, advanced the £S800 needed to cover the village sugar ration and, at times, will lend his neighbors money for unforeseen expenses. Loans are always repaid, but when people have the money and at no interest. Overall, the degree of social differentiation through indebtedness is limited in Shair Tomat in comparison with the other two villages of Somasem and Shatt Damam.

Unlike Somasem, the village of Shair Tomat withstood the more deleterious effects of the drought of 1984. Although social stratification exists, it was not exacerbated through the institution of the shayl, the depletion of granaries, or the loss of livestock. To be sure, many people suffered, but not to the extent of other villages, such as Shatt Damam. In part, kinsmen with a surfeit of grain opened their stocks to needy relatives, and better-off households did not abandon the practice of zakha. Moreover, Shair Tomat was able to access international food relief agencies through influential former village inhabitants in Kadugli; of course, the fact that the village is Hawazma was not lost on the northern Sudanese administrators in Kadugli.

Household Organization

On the whole, the village of Shair Tomat is relatively prosperous by Nuba Mountain standards. No one goes hungry, nor are villagers, with very few exceptions, reduced to selling their labor to their neighbors. In fact, rarely are household members compelled to abandon the village during the hungry season in order to leave more food for those remaining. People do leave, but for different reasons. The degree of social inequality found in Somasem and in Shatt Damam is strikingly absent in Shair Tomat. Few households are considered poor by Nuba Mountain standards, yet fewer still enjoy an abundance of wealth. Most households remain small-scale enterprises, with some 68 percent engaged in small-scale capitalism and another 13 percent in lineage market transactions. This not only reflects present realities of multiple economic strategies but the level of market integration; i.e., the transformation of the lineage. Within this context, the regularized production for the market and/or sale of labor are increasingly a precondition of household reproduction. Young people are especially prone to the demands of the market and a cash economy, particularly in their efforts to marry or to meet household consumption requirements. Consequently, the lineage forms are both aging households and small. What allowed lineage forms to remain viable in the recent past, ironically has led to their demise; namely, the system of land inheritance, education of male children, and subsequent off-farm employment of sons. Table 8.1 summarizes household size and age structure by (re)production form.

The sex of household heads is indicative of the intensity of Islamic patriarchy, the strength of female subservience to males, and the general lack of female empowerment (table 8.2). Female headed households, absent in the capitalist entrepreneurial and lineage market forms, are struc-

TABLE 8.1
Household Size and Age Structure by (Re)Production Form

All households	CE	SC	LM	LS	WL	Total
% of households	3.3%	66.7%	13.3%	6.7%	10.0%	100.0%
Mean household size	8.0	7.1	4.3	3.0	6.3	6.4
Mean member age	9.8	22.1	33.1	24.5	16.1	22.4
Mean no. age <16	5.0	3.2	1.3	1.5	4.0	2.9
Mean age of head	52.0	51.5	60.8	52.5	41.3	51.8
(n=)	(1)	(20)	(4)	(2)	(3)	(30)

turally similar to their male counterparts in small-scale capitalist and lineage subsistence forms. This, however, is no consolation for the women themselves of Shair Tomat, but reflects the severe state of inequality between men and women in general. Contrasts between male and female headed households are more revealing among wage-labor households. Of the three wage-labor households, one is made up of a single aged female with no dependents, placing the entire burden of the household workload on her, while those headed by males contain dependents with whom the work load may be shared, if not now, then in the near future. Nevertheless, statistical differences across household forms do foreshadow the overall lack of opportunities available to females in the higher rate of male headed households in small-scale capitalist, the lower rate in wage-labor, and the absence in lineage subsistence households.[7]

Consideration of the marital status of household heads further contrasts men and women (table 8.3). Female heads are disproportionately widowed or divorced; none are married, and all obviously gain head status by default. Even then, women do not completely gain independence of action when elder male lineage members reside in the village. Male elders of the same lineage customarily consult each other in reaching important decisions regarding such issues as out-migration and

TABLE 8.2
Sex of Household Head by (Re)Production Form

	CE	SC	LM	LS	WL	Total	(n)
Male	4.3%	69.6%	17.4%	NA	8.7%	100.0%	(23)
Female	NA	62.5	NA	25.0	12.5	100.0%	(8)

TABLE 8.3
Marital Status of Household Head, by Sex and (Re)Production Form

Male	CE	SC	LM	LS	WL	Total
Married	100%	93.8%	100%	NA	100.0%	95.7%
Widower	.0	6.3	.0	NA	.0	4.3
Total	100%	100%	100%	100%	100%	100%
(n=)	(2)	(34)	(3)	(0)	(4)	(46)
Mean age head	52.0	52.4	60.8	NA	37.0	52.5
Female						
Widow	NA	80.0	NA	100	100.0	87.5
Divorced	NA	20.0	NA	.0	.0	12.5
Total	100%	100%	100%	100%	100%	100%
(n=)	(0)	(5)	(0)	(2)	(1)	(8)
Mean age head	NA	48.4	NA	52.5	50.0	49.6

household businesses, with the senior male (*rab al-usra,* or family head) exercising greater authority. Despite being a household head, women do not become part of this inner circle of kinsmen and still find that they must present their opinions through a male relative. Moreover, the brother-in-law of a widow, for example, serves as the caretaker of the deceased husband's assets. Fahtma's brother-in-law kept a firm hand on the household's purse strings, allowing Fahtma sole discretion only in sales that did not involve his dead brother's estate. Most of the female heads resent this exclusion but adhere to it since they depend on the help of male relatives to preform the heavy main-farm tasks. Despite objective limitations over the assistance male relatives are able to extend, the alternative to no aid can be frightening and ensures female compliance to the commands of male relatives.

Remarriage for women is rare, even leviratic marriage in the case of widowhood. Males, on the other hand, find no social obstacle to remarrying. Three currently married male heads had out lived at least one wife. Another four of the twenty-three sampled male heads presently had two wives. As in Somasem, polygamous marriage provides a distinctive livelihood strategy, either to extend the household's life cycle or to increase the number of children of the same age group through the immediate addition of fertile women. In accordance with the system of land distribution, the first wife of male residents is always a first cousin from Shair Tomat, while the second or third are usually Nuba women from surrounding villages.

All of the households in Shair Tomat contain a single head, with the exception of one headed by two widowed females who jointly pool their resources on the basis of friendship and need. Although Miriam's brother was the husband of Katchi, their household arrangement was not forged through kinship bonds. According to Miriam, "We had been friends for a long time, so when our husbands died we decided to make a single household. This way, life is a little easier for both of us." The single female household also merits special consideration. Ammu was never able to bear children. Nonetheless, she and her husband raised three of his nephews, who have since migrated from Shair Tomat. Her brother-in-law took her husband's land upon his death and now she cultivates only a jubraka, a gift from her late brother. Having no males to assist her, Ammu relies on cash remittances from her nephews.

Without question, the dominant type of residential arrangement is nuclear, followed by complex. Single adults, either alone or with dependents, comprise only slightly more than 13 per cent of all household types (table 8.4). Three households contain a single adult with dependents, two in the small-scale capitalist and one in the lineage subsistence household forms, and one household holds a single adult in the wage-labor form.

TABLE 8.4
Household Residential Type by (Re)Production Form

All households	CE	SC	LM	LS	WL	Total
Single adult	.0%	.0%	.0%	.0%	33.3%	3.3%
Single—w/deps.	.0	10.0	.0	50.0	.0	10.0
Nuclear	100.0	50.0	100.0	.0	66.7	60.0
Complex	.0	35.0	.0	50.0	.0	26.7
Total	100%	100%	100%	100%	100%	100%
(n=)	(1)	(20)	(4)	(2)	(3)	(30)
Female headed households						
Single adult	—	.0	—	.0	100.0	14.3
Single—w/dep.	—	25.0	—	50.0	.0	28.6
Complex	—	75.0	—	50.0	.0	57.1
Total	100%	100%	100%	100%	100%	100%
(n=)	(0)	(4)	(0)	(2)	(1)	(7)

TABLE 8.5
Household Spatial Residency Patterns by (Re)Production Form

Spatial pattern	CE	SC	LM	LS	WL	Total
Coresidence	.0%	60.0%	50.0%	100.0%	.0%	53.3%
Dispersed	100.0	30.0	50.0	.0	33.3	33.3
Multiresidence	.0	5.0	.0	.0	33.3	6.7
Disp/multiresidence	.0	5.0	.0	.0	.0	3.3
Single member	.0	.0	.0	.0	33.3	3.3
Total	100%	100%	100%	100%	100%	100%
(n=)	(1)	(20)	(4)	(2)	(3)	(30)

Female headed households are primarily single adults with dependents or are complex in organization. Complex households demonstrate the necessity of drawing in other active adults in order to meet household labor requirements, including labor for domestic activities.

Spatial residency patterns reveal the paucity of economic opportunity within Shair Tomat (table 8.5). Although some 53 percent of households are coresidences, one-third have members living outside of the primary residence at some time throughout the year. Another 10 percent are multiresidential or dispersed/multiresidential. Out-migration represents an important element of livelihood strategies, through various forms of remittances. In addition, migration enables young men the occasion to accumulate resources necessary for marriage and for beginning an independent household of their own. Incidences of off-farm employment, however, draw individuals into variant class relations that can place younger members at odds with the desires of elders. All of the single member households are found in the wage-labor form and underscores the role of kinsmen in helping some households resist the pull into relying solely on the sale of household labor in reproducing the household.

Sources of Household Income

When asked to characterize the village ideal for securing the household's livelihood, Mahdi doffed his *tagia*[8] and rubbed his head slowly as he mulled over his response. Finally Mahdi answered: "To be a farmer, to work on your own land. Other work is okay, but you aren't independent." Nevertheless, the people of Shair Tomat realize that agriculture is a deferred investment whose return must literally mature in the field. Moreover, food is not always available when needed, nor is there always a marketable surplus to satisfy cash needs. In short, other economic pursuits provide greater economic flexibility and ensure income on a regular basis. Yet, in Shair Tomat few employment opportunities exist outside of agricultural labor, a fact that forces young males to look elsewhere. In addition, the dependence on multiple sources of income has consequences on social inequality, which frequently introduces strong contradictions in traditional household relations.

Certainly new needs have been created in the last two decades. Nonetheless, villagers maintain hard distinctions between necessities, luxuries, and vices. Necessities are culturally and historically molded and embrace anything that includes simple reproduction in its most basic sense. The notion of necessity, therefore, fluctuates over time and for most has now come to include the education of sons, tractor rental through the NMAPC, and the occasional hiring of agricultural labor to break labor bottlenecks. These new needs require a cash income, invariably with some sort of certainty. Luxuries represent an abundance, something extra, and permit a household to move beyond necessary subsistence, such as educating daughters, hiring additional labor to replace labor lost to out-migration, and purchasing better furniture, a radio, or a bicycle. Vices are to be avoided at all costs since they are the antithesis of "proper" behavior and undermine the well-being of the household. Vices, mainly integral to the prescriptions of Islam, include alcohol, tobacco, and gambling, as well as any necessity or luxury carried to the extreme (for some the education of daughters).

As table 8.6 indicates, household reproduction encompasses a wide range of economic activities for all but the two lineage forms. The type and quantity of income sources outlines stark differences between nonlineage and lineage households. Previously, cotton, cattle, and goats comprised the essential sources of cash income for all households. But, in the past cash needs were certainly more minimal. Today agriculture is unable to generate sufficient income for most households. And besides, cotton no longer is a reliable income strategy due to the paucity of rainfall in recent years and mismanagement within the NMAPC. Furthermore, farmers part with their animals only to meet pressing needs, mainly agricultural expenses, karama, or crop failure.[9] The sale of surplus dura and sesame still is not intended to meet all cash expectations.

TABLE 8.6

Source of Income-Generating Activities of Households by (Re)Production Form

Activity	CE	SC	LM	LS	WL	Total
Crop sales	100.0%	95.0%	75.0%	50.0%	.0%	80.0%
Animal sales	100.0	70.0	100.0	100.0	33.3	73.3
Businesses	100.0	40.0	.0	.0	33.3	33.3
Ag. labor	.0	35.0	.0	.0	.0	33.4
Nonag. labor	100.0	35.0	.0	.0	67.7	33.3
Remittances	.0	35.0	50.0	.0	33.3	33.3
Mean no. sources	4.0	3.2	2.3	1.5	1.7	2.8
(n=)	(1)	(20)	(4)	(2)	(3)	(30)

Of the sampled households, only capitalist entrepreneurs and small-scale capitalists sell more than 10 percent of these crops and, then, primarily because they cultivate more land. Wage-labor households, on the other hand, do not sell any crop since they refrain from planting cotton and plant grain solely with household needs in mind, while a mere 33.3 percent of these households evidence animal sales to make up for shortfalls in food production.

Small-scale capitalist households alone depend to some degree on agricultural labor for cash, reflecting their greater need for immediate sources of cash. Household businesses and off-farm employment also comprise important sources of cash, principally for capitalist entrepreneurial and wage-labor households, although 35 percent of small-scale capitalist households have members employed off the farm. In striking contrast, both lineage forms depend entirely on agriculture surfeit and/ or livestock sales, with the exception of two lineage market households receiving cash remittances. Roughly a third of small-scale capitalist and wage-labor households are also the beneficiaries of cash remittances. Yet, remittances also reveal the extent of cash shortfalls affecting small-scale household-based producers; off-farm employment out of the village is assuming greater importance to household reproduction.

Further analysis of income composition discloses the contribution of nonagricultural activities in those households most integrated into the market economy (table 8.7). Capitalist entrepreneurial, small-scale capitalist, and wage-labor households generate the bulk of their incomes through some combination of off-farm nonagricultural employment and

TABLE 8.7
Proportional Contribution of Source to Household
Income by (Re)Production Forms

All households	CE	SC	LM	LS	WL	Total
Income Source						
Crop sales	14.0%	27.5%	38.2%	26.4%	.0%	20.9%
Animal sales	18.3	15.1	44.4	73.6	1.8	14.4
Businesses	49.9	7.5	.0	.0	19.6	14.5
Ag. labor	.0	3.2	.0	.0	.0	2.0
Nonag. labor	17.8	40.3	.0	.0	77.2	43.1
Remittances	.0	6.4	17.4	.0	1.4	5.1
Mean net income						
(£S)	5,554	1,476	427	146	3,037	1,540
Median net income						
(£S)	5,54	887	355	146	167	759
Total	100%	100%	100%	100%	100%	100%
(n=)	(1)	(20)	(4)	(2)	(3)	(30)

household-owned businesses. Off-farm employment accounts for approximately 77 percent of the income of wage-labor, 40 percent of small-scale capitalist, and 18 percent of capitalist entrepreneurial households. Household-owned businesses contribute only slightly more to incomes than do remittances for small-scale capitalist households, but nearly half for capitalist entrepreneurial households, and 20 percent for wage-labor households. Both lineage forms continue to rely on crop and animal sales to meet household needs and are differentiated from each other by quantity sold and quality of market interactions. Lineage subsistence households have very limited market transactions and tend to barter directly for what they need rather than sell for cash. Interestingly, some 17 percent of lineage market households meet their cash needs through remittances, although no household member is engaged in off-farm employment. This points to the continued importance of wider lineage relations in gaining access to the cash incomes of junior lineage members.

Examination of mean net incomes by (re)production forms reveals a stark division between nonlineage and lineage based households, especially in the greater orientation of the lineage forms towards household self-sufficiency and their minimal integration into the market. The difference between the mean net income (£S1,540) and the median net income (£S759) in Shair Tomat is not as wide as in Somasem and suggests that social inequality within the village is not as advanced or as pronounced. Nevertheless, the large discrepancy between the two measures in the wage-labor form records wide differences in types of employment opportunities. Of greater significance, the trend towards increased income needs implies possible grounds for future inequality, since the need for cash is largely realized through off-farm employment (43.1 percent of all households engage in this activity).

Female headed households evidence a different outlook than does the sample as a whole (table 8.8). In general, female headed households must depend significantly on adult male household members or on other male relatives. Katchi's son-in-law, for example, makes the arrangements with the NMAPC for cotton seed and ploughing. Moreover, adult males are important in recruiting both nafir and wage labor. As a result of social and cultural constraints, small-scale capitalist households generate 12 percent of their incomes from agricultural labor, and only 8.6 percent from crop and animal sales. Lineage subsistence households depend entirely on agricultural activities. The two households in this form maintain strong ties to neighboring Nuba villages, placing claims on the lineage obligations and responsibilities of their kinsmen. Ammu, a single female wage-labor householder, is no longer able to work and receives all of her income through the largess of her nephews.

Finally, zakha represents an important means of redistribution within Shair Tomat and provides a crude indicator of economic stratification, especially evident during the "hungry season." Roughly 23 percent of all households receive grain in this manner. Nonetheless, not every household in need of additional grain accepts zakha, since it connotes a lack of independence and calls into question the farming abilities of a household. Only after the death of a main provider, or in the aftermath of a severe catastrophe such as the drought of 1984, do households readily accept zakha. Lineage subsistence and wage-labor households are the most dependent on zakha, with 50 and 33 percent of these households respectively receiving one sack of dura. Some 20 percent of small-scale capitalist and 25 percent of lineage market households are the beneficiaries of zakha, but accept only half a sack. Not surprisingly, slightly more than 57 percent of female headed households receive an average of three sacks of dura, a further indication of their precarious economic position.

TABLE 8.8
Female-Headed Households: Proportional Contribution of
Source to Household Income by (Re)Production Form

Female headed	CE	SC	LM	LS	WL	Total
Income Source						
Crop sales	NA	4.6%	NA	26.4%	.0%	5.5%
Animal sales	NA	4.0	NA	73.6	.0	7.0
Businesses	NA	0.8	NA	.0	.0	O.7
Ag. labor	NA	12.1	NA	.0	.0	11.4
Nonag. labor	NA	70.4	NA	.0	.0	65.7
Remittances	NA	8.1	NA	.0	100.0	9.7
Mean net income						
(£S)	NA	1,526	NA	146	150	935
Median net income						
(£S)	NA	804	NA	146	150	193
Mean income sources	NA	4.0	NA	1.5	1.0	2.9
Total	100%	100%	100%	100%	100%	100%
(n=)	(0)	(4)	(0)	(2)	(1)	(7)

Household Reproduction Strategies

In the main, change is an incremental process occurring over time. It is difficult for a social scientist to isolate with any certainty its exact dynamics. In Shair Tomat, the task is made easier by the manner of its settlement. By creating ready-made farmers in the perceived image of the English yeoman, Condominium administrators at once undermined broadscale lineage relations; that is, they rewrote social relations away from lineage obligations. The Al-Haj family certainly was no stranger to market transactions, although they had been on the fringe through the sale of slaves and cattle. And, not having a tradition of nafir at once reinforced the organization of agricultural production through the household and then forced households into the wage-labor market in their efforts to expand agricultural production. Even the late-comers to Shair Tomat, who brought a tradition of nafir, found their own use of this form of labor attenuated.

So too with individual motivations—why this strategy and not some other? Hence, we are not overly concerned with singular variations, but more with the wider structural constraints and opportunities. And, depending upon the household's (re)production form, households devise particular types of strategies. Once strategies are pursued, it is difficult to retreat and embark in different directions. More importantly, a particular behavior develops in consonance with specific social relations, behavior which also imparts a particular way of looking at the world and one's position in it. One of the outcomes of this is the fact that households, through the actions of its members, are structured by multiple economic circumstances that tend to place a member's notion of household responsibilities at odds with other members. In other words, traditional ideas of seniority and gender are no longer sufficient in themselves to ensure compliance to prescribed norms.

Agricultural Assets

Unquestionably, land and livestock form the basis of household livelihood strategies in Shair Tomat. To be a full member of the community requires land ownership, whatever the extent of its cultivation. Without land, an adult male never gains a voice in village affairs, and women whose husbands do not have land never fully acquire standing among their peers. Each of the sampled households owns land (table 8.9).[10] Land cultivation, however, is not sufficient, by itself, to ensure a household's basic reproduction, even self-sufficiency in food. Livestock, especially cattle and goats, provides an important source of savings, which a household may draw on to supplement the household diet, attract both nafir and wage labor, satisfy social and religious obligations, or sell in the market to meet expenses incurred throughout the course of the year. Only one household keeps sheep; most do not because of unfavorable foraging conditions. Chickens, as in Somasem, comprise the primary store of wealth for women and poorer households. In the main, women sell chickens to augment domestic budgets and to purchase luxuries such as clothes, scents, kerosene, and rice.

Overall, less than half of the sampled households own cattle. In part, this is due to the original inhabitants' relocation to Shair Tomat with little else but their immediate personal possessions. Condominium forces confiscated most of their cattle since ownership proved questionable, or else took them in fines for civil infractions, leaving the founding families with only a few goats. It is probably for this reason that agreement among the elders could be reached over removing cattle from the stan-

TABLE 8.9
Household Agricultural Assets: Land, Cows, Goats,
And Chickens by (Re)Production Form

All households	CE	SC	LM	LS	WL	Total
Land						
% who own	100.0%	100.0%	100.0%	100.0%	100.0%	100.0%
Mean feddan own	21.5	27.5	29.1	8.8	14.2	24.9
Mean cultivate	17.5	16.1	10.3	3.6	2.7	13.2
Cows						
% who own	100.0	35.0	75.0	50.0	33.3	43.3
Mean no. own	7.0	8.7	17.0	2.0	2.0	9.5
Goats						
% who own	100.0	90.0	75.0	100.0	100.0	90.0
Mean no. own	25.0	9.4	14.3	9.0	8.3	10.4
Chickens						
% who own	100.0	100.0	75.0	100.0	100.0	96.7
Mean no. own	7.0	11.3	6.0	9.5	12.0	10.6
Total	100%	100%	100%	100%	100%	100%
(n=)	(1)	(20)	(4)	(2)	(3)	(30)
Female headed households						
Land						
% who own	NA	100.0	NA	100.0	100.0	100.0
Mean own	—	22.4	—	8.8	.6	15.4
Mean cultivate	—	10.5	—	3.6	.0	7.0
Cows						
% who own	NA	0.0	NA	50.0	0.0	14.3
Mean no. own	—	—	—	1.0	—	.3
Goats						
% who own	NA	100.0	NA	100.0	100.0	100.0
Mean no. own	—	2.3	—	9.0	1.0	4.0
Chickens						
% who own	NA	100.0	NA	100.0	100.0	100.0
Mean no. own	—	8.0	—	9.5	6.0	8.1
Total	100%	100%	100%	100%	100%	100%
(n=)	(0)	(4)	(0)	(2)	(1)	(7)

dard brideprice. The original inhabitants own an average of 2.3 cows, while those settling later own 6.2. Lineage market households possess the largest herds, regardless of time of arrival, with an average of 17 cows. A third of these houses sell approximately one cow per year, invariably to meet agricultural costs or karama, while nearly 43 percent of small-scale capitalist households market one or two cows during the year for similar reasons. The lone capitalist entrepreneurial household sold two cows for £S1,870 in order to pay for relocation costs from Shatt Safiya. Al-Nour and Batul no longer felt safe due to the rapid deterioration in Shatt-Arab relations. In addition, they needed to replace some of the 22 goats stolen from them in Shatt Safiya.

Some 90 percent of the sampled households own goats, although 25 percent of lineage market households do not, preferring cattle instead. Similarly, nearly 97 percent of households keep chickens. By far, goats account for most livestock sales, with 74.1 percent of households selling an average of two goats. Only 13.8 percent of households market chickens, maintaining them instead for a dietary supplement. Thus, most households in Shair Tomat enjoy a relative bounty of animals, including female headed households, with the exception of cattle.

Land scarcity presently poses no problem in Shair Tomat, mainly because the size of landholdings remains moderate. Agricultural expansion remains more constrained by the paucity of available labor than by accessible land. Currently, the villagers cultivate 53 percent of claimed land. Female headed households evidence a more difficult time and farm only 45 percent of feddans owned by those households. Most farmers, nonetheless, remain content with the arrangement worked out with the Nuba Mountain Agricultural Production Corporation, in part because tractor and seed expenses do not need to be paid until after the harvest is complete, when farmers have cash on hand. Consequently, households are not compelled to market livestock for this part of household operations. Few farmers expressed a desire to significantly expand the scope of their agricultural undertakings, citing the general paucity of labor. If anything, farmers would prefer to raise production through intensification practices such as fertilizer and pesticide applications. In fact, 50 percent of small-scale capitalist and lineage market households use fertilizer and DDT in their operations, while the lone capitalist entrepreneur and 75 percent of the small-scale capitalist and lineage market households use treated seeds.

Overall, 53 percent of households receive technical assistance from the Nuba Mountain Agricultural Production Corporation and another 20 percent from the Agricultural Extension office in Kadugli or from the Western Sudan Agricultural Research Project.[11] Participation in these programs is not equal. Aside from the capitalist entrepreneur, 90 percent of small-scale capitalist and 75 percent of lineage market households receive technical assistance. Neither the lineage subsistence nor the wage-labor forms are contacted, nor do these households employ extra inputs in their operations. Most of the farmers not benefiting from technical services would like to improve their agricultural situation and are aware of the advantages of inputs like treated seeds but cannot afford them. Some of these farmers have appealed to agencies, but as one farmer bitterly complained: "[The government] only helps rich farmers; they don't care for the poor ones like me."

Unlike Somasem, little significant difference exists in the size of landholdings between the original inhabitants and those coming later, although farmers' proximity to their landholdings depends on time of arrival.[12] The original settlers own an average of 26.7 feddan, while latecomers possess 23.4 feddan. The key distinction between the two groups lies in their general economic organization and cultural background. The first group predominates within the three capitalist (re)production forms and the latter in the two lineage forms. Again, the manner in which the groups came to Shair Tomat explains this phenomenon to a large degree. Latecomers did not undergo the same socioeconomic rupture that the founding families experienced and, thus, were able to accommodate pressures to rationalize production and also to minimize their sales of household labor. Moreover, both lineage forms have maintained closer ties to their former villages, giving them greater access to other resources, especially important during times of economic hardship.

Interestingly, no advantage seems to have been gained from previous instances of off-farm employment by household heads. Approximately 44 percent of the sampled household heads from among the original inhabitants had migrated for employment purposes, while some 55 percent of household heads settling later had done so for similar reasons. In general, migrants from all of the (re)production forms secured employment as soldiers, policemen, construction laborers, or agricultural laborers. Past off-farm employment appears to have been exclusively for marriage purposes, household formation, and the procurement of cattle

rather than for agricultural expansion, however. The present arrangement with the Nuba Mountain Agricultural Production Corporation miti-
gates attempts to increase areas under cultivation, as the agency will
only plough dura/sesame fields in relatively close proximity to cotton
fields. Moreover, private tractors for hire usually arrive late since they
begin on lands near Kadugli and work towards Shair Tomat. And, with
the exception of cotton, planting must still be accomplished by hand.
Difficulties encountered in securing wage-labor further exacerbates the
dilemmas posed by attempts to expand agricultural production. As a
result, most households have come to rely on nonagricultural activities
to ensure a cash income.

Agricultural Labor

By far, access to labor presents pressing problems for farmers in Shair
Tomat, especially in light of the restricted notion of nafir. The history of
the village reveals a household agricultural production strategy of labor
made possible by patriarchy and the general ideology of kinship. From
its initial settlement, labor marshalled through the family has undertaken the majority of work in the fields. No child, male or female, would
refuse to work in their father's fields (or in their mother's jubraka).[13] To
go against a father's will denies the sanctity of the family and abrogates
one's position in it. Nor would an adult's siblings fail to respond to a
nafir call without good cause. The emphasis placed on family ties, both
nuclear and extended, thus reaffirms mutual obligations and responsibilities, although gender and age distinctions evoke different ranges of
roles. Thus, elders enjoy a wider latitude in their ability to solicit labor.
    With few exceptions, the male head of household is historically the
ultimate authority. Al-Haj Abdullah's father and grandfather before him,
for example, ruled the family with an iron hand. Not only did they control the destinies of their sons and the women of the household but, as
senior lineage males, unmarried brothers would defer to their judgment
before making important decisions. Even today, a son must solicit permission from his father to leave Shair Tomat in order to pursue higher
education or to seek his fortune. Consent is granted only if his labor is
not essential to the farm operations. On balance, relations between fathers and older sons exhibits certain strains since it is in the interest of
the former to hold junior members in the household as long as possible,

while sons desire to leave in order to gain control over their own labor and its products. Daughters, on the other hand, provide both domestic and agricultural labor until their marriage is arranged at around 14 to 16 years of age, and they remain largely uneducated since little benefit is seen in their education. Temporary out-migration by unmarried females, except to visit relatives, is not an option, as it is for males. Consequently, sons can hope to eventually cease working for their elders through beginning families of their own, but daughters simply go from one set of inequitable power relations to another.

Interestingly, labor demands in Shair Tomat have yet to break gender distinctions in agriculture. In other words, a household will cultivate fewer feddans in order to maintain the separation of the sexes in the fields. Indeed, the increase of male out-migration has failed to diminish this aspect of Hawazma culture, even among labor deficient households. Thus, gender discrimination can prove more onerous for female headed households than for those headed by males. Females are automatically denied direct access to nonkin male labor and, consequently, are unable to cultivate as many feddans. This tendency is reinforced by the inheritance system, which effectively bars women from outright land ownership. Widowed or divorced female household heads, therefore, find that rules of patriarchy make their reliance on nonhousehold male relatives indissoluble. Without adult male relatives within the village, a widow such as Ammu is quickly reduced to reliance on zakha and other forms of charity.

On the other hand, the absolute authority of family elders is now diminishing vis-à-vis sons. When Al-Haj's third son, Moustafa, informed his father that he wanted to leave the village in order to further his studies and become an accountant, Al-Haj immediately dismissed his request. Moustafa, however, was persistent and, at times, the arguments grew heated. Eventually Al-Mahdi, the eldest son, interceded and an agreement was reached by which Moustafa would be allowed to pursue his ambitions in return for his continued work in the fields for a period of two seasons. Al-Mahdi, with an eye towards the future, realized that the family would benefit from economic contacts outside of Shair Tomat. Today, Moustafa is a government accountant and has managed to purchase a lorry. Moustafa, however, did not permanently leave the household until he was 22 years old and continues to assist his father when possible. Since Moustafa now helps his brothers by transporting their grain to market, Al-Haj has all but forgotten the original conflict with his son. Still, a son (or any other family member) will never publicly defy his father.

Not all family or kinship ties are economically important nor fundamentally of a value-producing or consuming nature. Nonetheless, households as economic units are dependent upon and reproduced through kinship ties, while production relations are generally intertwined with domestic relationships and conditioned by sex and age. Hence, family bonds appear as moral equivalents that can be manipulated according to household needs, especially in satisfying agricultural sustenance. Viewed from within this parameter, domestic activities begin and end with the family for most households. In terms of household agriculture, the majority of households prefer family labor (50 percent), followed by wage-labor (26.7 percent) and nafir (23.3 percent). Nearly 80 percent of respondents favoring household labor list pride in the family's ability to farm and its superior quality of work. Other considerations include difficulties in organizing nafir or in securing wage-labor.

Nafir similarly operates on kinship principles and is solely intended to break labor bottlenecks, especially acute during weeding and harvesting. No farmer would think of sponsoring a nafir party for work normally undertaken by household labor unless circumstances presented unforeseen hardships such as illness or some other sudden change in the family situation. In principle, a man organizes a nafir party from among his kinsmen for work on the main farm. The timing of a nafir reflects the individual's position within the extended family or lineage. Al-Baroud, for example, as the eldest married Kuku male holds his nafir before his younger married brothers. Likewise, Al-Mahdi's nafir is called first among the Abdullah family members. Not all communal labor, however, comes under the rubric of nafir. Lineage members frequently extend assistance to those members unable to sponsor a formal nafir. Al-Haj's relatives regularly help him in his fields even though they realize that he is too old to reciprocate in kind and that they are responsible for bringing their own food to the fields.

Nearly 78 percent of sampled households sponsored an average of one nafir party throughout the agricultural season. The lone capitalist entrepreneur held an average of 1.5 nafirs, small-scale capitalist and lineage market households, one each, lineage subsistence households, two, and wage-labor households, none. A third of the wage-labor households indicated that they had sponsored nafir parties in the past but were no longer able to due to a lack of food reserves, death of a husband, absence of adult male relatives in the village, or the small size of the area under cultivation. The remaining wage-labor households had never done so. Similarly, 15 percent of the small-scale capitalist households had never sponsored a nafir, citing its inefficiency and expense. Goat meat or chicken is served in 40 percent of nafir parties, while only 13 percent of households indicated that they never included meat. Over half of both lineage forms do not provide meat, a further reflection of their economically precarious position within the village. Nevertheless, the shortage of meat does not deter kinsmen from answering a nafir call. Today, since a number of household heads do not have many male relatives resident in the village, any man may respond without invitation. But, when two or more nafir parties are scheduled on the same day, nonrelatives go to the one supplying meat.

Those households preferring nafir labor, most notably the lineage forms, cite its low cost and efficiency as primary reasons for its use. Strikingly absent are any references to feelings of good will emanating from communal labor. Small-scale capitalists, on the other hand, note the difficulty in locating wage-laborers before commenting on the cost or efficiency of nafir labor. Only a couple of the aged Nuba residents who are no longer economically active reminisced about the lack of a "real" nafir and the positive feelings gained from working with one's fellow villagers.

Although nafir parties are technically organized along lineage lines, as noted, the least advantaged in the village nowadays also attend. Yet, the presence of nonrelatives does not invoke mutual obligation and reciprocity. In this manner an unequal transfer of labor occurs between households. This permanent imbalance in labor exchanges between households is at the heart of contemporary social inequality in Shair Tomat. In short, the lack of reciprocity within the system of nafir recruitment can quickly undermine the basis of household equality, interdependence, and subsistence. A number of households indicated that they frequently attend more nafir parties than the number of people participating in theirs, if they hold a nafir at all. Although wage-labor households do not sponsor nafir parties, an average of 1.5 members participate in approximately 6.5 nafir parties during the agricultural season. Both lineage forms evidence a similar disparity, though to a lesser degree. As a result, disadvantaged households neglect their own fields during critical periods in order to provide nafir labor for better-off households in return for food during the "hungry period."[14] In this way more food becomes available to household members, but at the cost of a households's own agricultural needs. Wealthier households, on the other hand, are able to attract additional labor for the price of a couple of chickens or a kilogram of goat meat.

Nafir also provides an important source of labor for building houses. Slightly more than 63 percent of sampled households sponsored a nafir for such activities, although the capitalist entrepreneur preferred to employ wage-labor for this task, and two-thirds of wage-labor households do not sponsor a house-building nafir. The remaining households not utilizing nafir generally rely on more informal labor arrangements to raise the roof, a task that takes but three or four hours. Such arrangements, sporadically requested during an individual's lifetime, do not require food, nor is an obligation to return the work incurred. Free time, rather than blood lines, determine who will help among one's neighbors, friends, and kin. Many of the workers will bring food of their own to share among their fellow laborers. Informal work parties serve to reaffirm feelings of community, especially if two men have experienced recent disagreements. Helping a neighbor build a house provides an acceptable means to ameliorate tensions.

Women, too, arrange nafir parties among their female relatives and friends, primarily for work on the jubraka. Labor exchanges provide an important supplement, since women must also undertake a broad range of domestic activities. Like nafir parties held by their male counterparts, food is served to participants, although not meat, since this would be considered a luxury. A single female head of household generally relinquishes control of the agricultural labor process to the eldest adult son, or even nephew or cousin, who will call his kinsmen to the main farm nafir. The women of the household will prepare and transport the food; assistance in the fields depends on whether or not nonrelative males are present. Without the active aid of adult male relatives, single females are unable to sponsor a nafir party for the main farm. In contrast to males, a woman must present her individual needs to the man's consideration before he will assist her in calling a nafir party. The amount of aid offered by a nonhousehold male relative is restricted by his own sense of responsibility. Consequently, widowed and divorced females are totally dependent upon male relatives for the construction or repair of houses, since they are unable to call a nafir composed of men. Informal exchanges of labor are more common, where two or three women will assist a neighboring woman in need, or simply work together just to enjoy each other's company.

Increased incidences of out-migration of young men during the last decade have tended to undermine the family work unit. In the past, the absence of young men could easily be made up by sponsoring a nafir party; this is no longer possible given the small population of Shair Tomat. The loss of villagers due to out-migration in conjunction with mechanized cotton production necessitates the employment of wage-labor, particularly for labor deficient households. Of course, some households simply cultivate fewer feddan in response to decreases in household labor, but for those households whose production process is firmly rationalized, wage-labor proves essential to agricultural operations.

With the exception of the capitalist entrepreneur, employment of wage-labor, like nafir, is intended to augment household labor during peak periods of the agricultural season. The capitalist entrepreneur contracts an average of nine workers, who perform the bulk of agricultural labor, a pattern in effect for the last fourteen years. Overall, 63.3 percent of households hire agricultural labor, primarily for weeding and the harvesting of cotton. Lineage subsistence households have never used wage-labor in their fields, preferring to accomplish agricultural tasks with household labor and, then, with nafir. Of those households contracting labor, small-scale capitalists (75 percent) and lineage market households (70 percent) employ an average of six and five agricultural workers annually and began the practice with the arrival of the Nuba Mountain Agricultural Production Corporation tractors ten years ago. Wage labor households (33.3 percent) hire an average of two men for weeding, a recent occurrence started in the past two years. Only the capitalist entrepreneur employs a thresher. Not surprisingly, two-thirds of the agricultural workers hail from distant villages, with the remaining residing in Shair Tomat or nearby. Of those households preferring wage labor, 75 percent stress the fact that it is easiest to control, 12.5 percent claim that wage-laborers work hard, and 12.5 percent argue that it is less expensive than nafir.

Remarkably, the local laborers employed by farmers are women. In spite of the prejudice against village women moving about freely in public, the need for labor seemingly blunts this area of concern. The economic rationale for employing women should be self-evident; male agricultural laborers are scarce, and females can be paid less per feddan. The more relevant question is why farmers hire women, when to do so goes against local Hawazma conventions. The female field workers come from small-scale capitalist households—one female and two male headed. Within each, adult females outnumber adult males. Coupled with the already precarious economies of these households and the absence of other alternatives to cash incomes, household heads see little choice to making household women labor in their neighbors' fields. Furthermore, the use of female labor occurs because it is largely unseen. That is, distant relatives employ them as a last resort, and they labor in the fields by themselves and not alongside men.

Labor is also employed by households with large cattle herds. The capitalist entrepreneur, three small-scale capitalists, and one lineage market household regularly employ Shatt herdboys to tend their cattle. Rarely are they given cash for their services. Typically, payment consists of a small cow per year. This arrangement is fairly common throughout the Nuba Mountains and represents the traditional means used by young men to obtain cattle for brideprices.

As mentioned, female headed households find it difficult to directly employ agricultural laborers. Overall, only 37.5 percent of these households employ wage-labor, although 50 percent of the female heads indicated that their husbands had regularly done so. In the main, female headed households must limit cultivation to what family members are able to accomplish in a given season. As a result, female headed households are more dependent upon zakha and other forms of village largess.

Business Enterprise Activities

The village of Shair Tomat, compared to either Somasem or Shatt Damam, appears to be insular and seemingly unaffected by events occurring elsewhere in the Nuba Mountains. But, to argue the case of relative isolation because the village lies at the fringe of change does not mean that it is independent of the influence of wider pressures of modernization. To the contrary, the mere presence of the Nuba Mountain Agricultural Production Corporation contradicts any claim to village autarky. And, although farming remains the principle activity of most households, increasingly the monetization of the rural economy coupled with growing expectations and needs compels a number of households to seek alternatives to agriculture. Satisfying household reproduction thus requires the inclusion of specifically nonagricultural economic activities into livelihood strategies. Still, household independence and agricultural self-sufficiency provide the backdrop for village life in Shair Tomat. To be dependent on others for labor or dura dishonors the household.[15] Similarly, the sale of labor to a fellow villager compromises a household's image of self-reliance and calls into question an individual's standing within the community. Household-owned businesses comprise one such endeavor that does not necessarily undermine the notion of pride and respect.

Table 8.10 indicates the percent of households owning a business enterprise as well as the mean number owned. Of immediate interest is the fact that only those households firmly within the ambit of the capitalist economy operate some type of business. Moreover, revenues from businesses contribute just 14.5 percent to total household incomes, although nearly 50 percent to the capitalist entrepreneurial household. Lineage forms, although smaller in size and slightly older than the capitalist forms, devote household energies to agricultural and livestock production. The production strategies of these households more closely approximate the Chaynovian life cycle, with agricultural activities expanding and contracting according to household requirements. Too, cash needs are significantly less, especially for lineage subsistence households. As Zayda, a widow in the lineage subsistence form, commented: "My husband was a strong farmer; he could do everything himself. When the children were here, they helped in every way. Now, I have enough and my children still help. I need very little." With regards to lineage market households, only one child attends school, and the use of wage-labor remains intermittent, as it is dependent upon the cotton crop. According to Hamad: "If the cotton doesn't fail and is good, I will hire labor. If the cotton is poor but too much for the family, I will use nafir."

The cash sphere of Shair Tomat's economy remains limited, primarily by the prevalence of and desire for domestic self-sufficiency. To be sure, most households have some cash savings, but locally there are remarkably few money transactions between households. Cash usually changes hands between individual households and government agencies, such as the Nuba Mountain Agricultural Production Corporation.

TABLE 8.10
Percent of Households Owning Business Enterprises by (Re)Production Form

All households	CE	SC	LM	LS	WL	Total
% who own	100.0%	40.0%	0.0%	0.0%	33.3%	33.3%
Mean no. owned	3.5	1.5	—	—	1.5	1.6
(n=)	(1)	(20)	(4)	(2)	(3)	(30)

Rarely do households produce anything that other households are unable or unwilling to make themselves. Consequently, few business opportunities exist within the confines of Shair Tomat. Only two of the businesses serve the villagers; the provision of sesame oil and various goods in the general store.[16] Four of the remaining enterprises are located in Kadugli and Shatt Safiya, while eight traders ply their merchandise in the surrounding villages.

As table 8.11 shows, the capitalist forms engage in a narrow range of business activities. The enterprises owned by the capitalist entrepreneur and wage-labor households stand out in sharp contrast to those of the small-scale capitalists. Aside from brokering in agricultural commodities, the enterprises of the former necessitate significantly greater inputs of capital, which effectively place these activities out of reach of small-scale capitalists. Moustafa (wage-labor) acquired a lorry through capital accumulated from his accountancy position with the government. Batul (capitalist entrepreneur), on the other hand, first began purchasing grain from her neighbors in Shatt Safiya in 1966 with the help of her husband, Al-Nour, who worked as a guard. Later, she started selling cloth, dye, and matches. Batul's activities proved profitable and, by 1972, she and Al-Nour opened a general store in Shatt Safiya, selling a wide range of goods, including tea, coffee, and sugar as well as purchasing small amounts of grain offered by the Shatt.[17] With the profits generated by the store, they had a house constructed in Kadugli and, subsequently, rented it out.

The majority of small-scale capitalists, to the contrary, engage in the low-capital enterprises of wood and thatch cutting. More importantly, these activities do not diminish the household's agricultural labor force, as they are undertaken during the dry season. Lacking a market in Shair Tomat, the wood and thatch is sold in nearby villages such as Seraf Al-Dai and in Kadugli. Businesses dominated by small-scale capitalists

TABLE 8.11
Type of Enterprise Owned by (Re)Production Form

Type of enterprise	CE	SC	WL	Total
General store	33.3%	10.0%	.0%	14.3%
Agricultural broker	33.3	.0	.0	7.1
Real-estate rent	33.3	.0	.0	7.1
Lorry transport	.0	.0	100.0	7.1
Sesame oil	.0	10.0	.0	7.1
Cut wood/thatch	.0	80.0	.0	57.2
Total	100%	100%	100%	100%
(Total n of enterprises)	(3)	(10)	(1)	(14)

generate very little profit but afford an important source of cash income, principally for paying hired labor.

Given the nature of gender relations in Shair Tomat, it is not surprising that few occasions exist for females to possess their own businesses.[18] If anything, most women, like the village men, consider such activities to be male interests. Socially ascribed gender divisions are too deeply imprinted in community values, which restrict female mobility and public visibility. Only two females operate business enterprises; both are from depressed small-scale capitalist households. Miriam started cutting thatch as a business enterprise following the death of her husband. Katchi's brother sells the thatch for her in Kadugli, and the proceeds are used to hire field laborers. Amal, a sixteen-year-old neighbor of Miriam's, first began accompanying Miriam when she was fourteen and now markets her own thatch to supplement the household budget. If anything, the cases of Miriam and Amal point to the economic difficulties beginning to beset more marginal households. Women, nonetheless, do contribute to the economic well-being of the household, though on an irregular basis, by selling surfeit okra, groundnuts, and corn to merchants in Seraf Al-Dai. Profits are used to procure household necessities or luxuries, such as kerosene, coffee, or meat.

Off-Farm Employment

The full-scale integration of Shair Tomat into the wider market economy has taken a number of forms and affects households differentially. As noted, few alternatives exist to generate additional income through business enterprises. Yet, household-based agriculture is no longer able to satisfy the reproductive requirements of most households. As a result, households look to other economic activities. Off-farm employment provides cash incomes to some 67 percent of sampled households. Very few householders from the three capitalist forms feel that they could manage solely on what they are able to produce on the land. Some type of regular income is felt to be needed by all but the lineage forms, who believe that they can ill afford to till another's field or labor for another person when their own farms require attention and, consequently, they do not turn to off-farm employment. Thus, the strong reliance of the majority of households on the sale of labor serves to further differentiate capitalist from lineage (re)production forms.

Off-farm employment for males is hardly new. Young men labored off the farm in the past to obtain cash in order to marry and begin their own homesteads. What differs is the fact that one-third of those working off of the farm are females. Although their labor is minimal and predominantly restricted to the fieldwork, not too long ago this would have been unspeakable. Off-farm employment by females suggests a strong indication of the need for cash among small-scale capitalist households. Although only women from four households pursue this type of activity, in all probability the inclusion of females into the labor force will spread in Shair Tomat, as it did in both Somasem and Shatt Damam. Moreover, control over the incomes generated by females introduces new stresses within the household. Aside from wanting more say in the disposition of their earnings, a number of the young female workers mentioned that they believe women should have equal access to education. As with females, a number of males working outside of the house are disgruntled with their current status. At a certain point, the labor of children produces more than the cost of their maintenance. But, in line with lineage mandates, elders want to retain control over children for longer periods of time. This is evident, in part, in the later age of marriage for many females and males. In general, the opening up of greater economic opportunities underscores tensions inherent in most household relations and loosens commitments to family cooperation.

Table 8.12 displays the distribution of wage-labor activities by sex of household member. A single member of the capitalist entrepreneurial form works as a guard, but by choice rather than necessity. Al-Nour

TABLE 8.12
Distribution of Off-Farm Employment by Sex and (Re)Production Form

Male	CE	SC	WL	Total
Skilled employment				
Civil servant	.0%	7.7%	50.0%	12.5%
Semiskilled employment				
Military	.0	7.7	.0	6.3
Store clerk	.0	7.7	.0	6.3
Flour mill attendant	.0	7.7	.0	6.3
Driver	.0	.0	50.0	6.3
Unskilled employment				
Tend livestock	.0	7.7	.0	6.3
Manual laborer	.0	15.4	.0	12.6
Agricultural laborer	.0	46.2	.0	37.5
Guard/watchman	100.0	.0	.0	6.3
Total	100%	.0%	100%	100%
(n=)	(1)	(13)	(2)	(16)
Female				
Semiskilled employment				
Nursing aid	.0	12.5	.0	12.5
Unskilled employment				
Agricultural laborer	.0	87.5	.0	87.5
Total	100%	100%	100%	100%
(n=)	(0)	(8)	(0)	(8)

dislikes farming as much as he fears his wife and thus prefers to work as a guard in Kadugli; she resides in Shair Tomat. Small-scale capitalist households evidence a wide range of off-farm employment activities; albeit, most prefer agricultural or manual labor, in part due to its flexibility, which enables them to work around the labor needs associated with household production. Two members from the wage-labor form enjoy high-salaried positions; Moustafa is a government accountant and Khalif is a driver in Saudi Arabia. In terms of gender, without doubt male mobility provides greater opportunities in pursuing employment.

Given the demands of the household agricultural schedule, slightly more than 58 percent of off-farm workers engage in activities that do not conflict with the household's need for family labor. On the other hand, the pursuit of off-farm employment frequently leads household members out of Shair Tomat, with 56 percent migrating to such areas as Kadugli, El-Obeid, Khartoum, and Saudi Arabia. Not every male is content with the meager wages paid in the surrounding areas or aspires to a life of farming. Migration provides a way out. Only one female worked outside of the village, in Juba, where she lived with her brother's family. Nevertheless, the effect of out-migration spreads throughout the entire household.

Migration Activities

Out-migration is a relatively common occurrence in Shair Tomat today, given the paucity of economic opportunities in the area. After all, young men must acquire money for brideprices and the ensuing demands of household operations that marriage brings. Not all return, however. New networks are established, lifestyles formed, and livelihoods earned. Some 87 percent of males permanently residing outside of the household live elsewhere, with 52 percent in Kadugli and Khartoum alone. Some may eventually come back, but the inheritance laws governing the distribution of land make this unlikely. Of the five surviving sons of Al Haj, Mahdi and Hassan live in Shair Tomat, two make their residence in Kadugli, and Moustafa has primary residences in both Shair Tomat and Kadugli. Table 8.13 shows the percentage of households with incidences of temporary migration and the mean number of migrants, as well as the percentage of household members by sex who temporarily migrate. Overall, 67.7 percent of households have at least one member temporarily residing outside of the village. The difference between male and female rates of migration reveals the lack of mobility of women; 31 percent of male household members migrate, while only 8.7 percent of women migrate.

Equally interesting are the primary reasons cited for episodes of migration (table 8.14). The majority of males migrate for economic reasons or to pursue higher education. Noneconomic objectives overwhelmingly underlie incidences of female migration. Men work at a variety of jobs, although 31 percent labor in the fields of Habila or in the construction industry. Of the males who permanently leave the household, 83 percent initially left for economic reasons, with 43 percent finding employment in the army and police. Fewer now follow that path. In

TABLE 8.13
Patterns of Temporary Migration by (Re)Production Form

Households	CE	SC	LM	LS	WL	Total
% w/migs.	100.0%	75.0%	50.3%	.0%	67.7%	67.7%
Mean number	3.0	1.5	1.0	0	.7	1.3
% of household members by sex						
Male	50.0%	32.4%	30.8%	.0%	12.5%	31.0%
Female	.0	9.9	.0	.0	9.1	8.7

TABLE 8.14
Primary Reason for Temporary Migration by Sex and (Re)Production Form

	CE	SC	LM	WL	Total
Male					
Employment	33.3%	34.8%	.0%	100%	32.3%
Tend livestock	.0	4.3	75.0	.0	12.9
Attend school	66.7	39.1	25.0	.0	38.7
Visiting	.0	4.3	.0	.0	3.2
Accompany others	.0	17.4	.0	.0	12.9
Total	100%	100%	100%	100%	100%
(n=)	(3)	(23)	(4)	(1)	(31)
Female					
Employment	.0	14.3	.0	.0	12.5
Attend school	.0	14.3	.0	100.0	25.0
Visiting	.0	71.4	.0	.0	62.5
Total	100%	100%	.0%	100%	100%
(n=)	(0)	(7)	(0)	(1)	(8)

general, females remain in Shair Tomat until they marry and join their husband's household. Cash remittances from working migrants provide an important supplement to the household budget. Temporary migrants remit an average of £S212 per year.[19] No members from lineage subsistence households migrate.

In many respects, the village of Shair Tomat is rather atypical to many of those in the Nuba Mountains. Unquestionably, the manner of its founding has as much to do with this as does the culture of its first settlers. Still, the ideology of lineage and patriarchy run deep, providing a basis for linking a household to the world outside. Increasingly, this link will probably become more one-sided, channeling the flow of resources (human and material) from the village outward. One indication of this trend is the paucity of savings reinvested within the village. Nevertheless, the villagers of Shair Tomat appear to be coping rather well with the forces of modernization that are actively transforming their area of the Nuba Mountains.

Notes

1. These structures, called *goteas*, are the most prevalent type of houses in the Nuba Mountains. Square houses are more recent and are influenced by urban Arab culture.
2. When I first began interviewing Ismail and Baroud, I was surprised when they replied that they were Hawazma, since they looked like Miri people. It was through these two men that I began to appreciate the fluidity of so-called tribal distinctions.
3. Roughly 63 percent of the sampled adult male farmers reported that they worked in the main farm and jubraka, while nearly 73 percent of adult females did both.
4. When I told farmers in Shatt Damam about the number of nafir people attended in Shair Tomat, they laughed and said: "That is because they are not Nuba; they don't know nafir."
5. In practice, females generally inherit little, if anything. It is assumed that their husbands have sufficient means to take care of them and that their husbands will inherit from their fathers.
6. Unlike Somasem, the correlation coefficient for household income and area under cultivation is not significant when controlled for by tractor use.
7. Female headed households

	SC	LS	WL	Total
% of households	57.1%	28.6%	14.3%	100.0%
Mean household size	7.0	3.0	1.0	5.0
Mean member age	20.3	24.5	50.0	21.9
Mean number age <16	3.0	1.5	NA	2.1
Mean age of head	48.4	52.5	50.0	49.6
(n=)	(4)	(2)	(1)	(7)

8. A *tagia* is a "skullcap" worn by male Muslims.
9. In the past two seasons, 40 percent of farmers noted at least one partial crop failure, usually of cotton, although 17 percent indicated the partial failure of the dura crop.
10. In fact, every household in Shair Tomat owns land, regardless of whether the members work elsewhere or not.
11. Most of the assistance from WSARP comes in demonstration plots and herds on the WSARP grounds. WSARP transports the farmers to its locations.
12. Of the sampled households, 53 percent were original settlers of Shair Tomat, and 43 percent arrived later.

13. In general, males do not have to work in the jubraka, and young females will work in their father's field only if unrelated men are not present.

14. Essentially, nafir in these instances is little more than a food for work arrangement and assumes a form of wage-labor.

15. Of course, exceptions are made for female headed households, who,through no fault of their own, must rely on others to some degree for the reproduction of the household.

16. The general store is a community enterprise, although Hassan is allowed to sell other commodities in exchange for operating the store.

17. Batul and Al-Nour still own the store but returned to Shair Tomat in 1987, when Arab-Nuba relations soured. They continue to operate the store but are trying to sell it to a local Fellata.

18. Batul represents a "deviant" case. Clearly, she is more enterprising in economic affairs than is Al-Nour, although he is technically the "boss." Most of the village men are aware of the arrangement and quietly laugh at Al-Nour for his perceived lack of "manliness."

19. Migrants from small-scale capitalist households remit an average of £S308 per year, £S200 from lineage market households, and £S150 from wage-labor households.

9

Shatt Damam: Living on the Edge

The air is cool in the shade beneath the rakuba, where the elders discuss the affairs of Shatt Damam. The flow of conversation rises and falls with the heat of the moment, punctuated by heavy sighs, rich with frustration and despair. The elders are all too aware that life for the Shatt is rapidly changing and that its direction is largely outside of their control. Obedience of juniors and women is not assured as it was in the old days, and the elders struggle to find new ways to maintain the authority of their roles. Accounts of two villages forming a large-scale nafir now begin with the words "in the past." Sitting in silence, the men pass the gourd filled with marissa, finally laughing as one begins to tell a humorous story.

Shatt Damam is an historical precipitate, to be comprehended both as it is now and in terms of the conditions in which the village was created. Presently, pressures exerted by modernization, realized primarily through state functionaries, Islamic development agencies, and private merchants, preclude visions to the past. Increasingly, successful livelihood strategies must now include activities that involve cash remuneration, from the selling and buying of labor to "making business." And, for those unable to compete on new terms, the ever-present shayl is quick to lend money, but at the cost of household integrity. More importantly, the price of success frequently requires turning one's back on kinsmen and friends. If nothing else, people do not always have the time to devote to sustaining lineage and village relations. In short, the monetization and the depersonalization of social relations has drawn forth a new day that clearly requires innovative strategies. Thus, the crisis of the lineage in Shatt Damam occurs against the backdrop of new structural realities that take old relations and invest them with new meaning.

Contemporary Context

Nestled within a series of jebels, approximately 15 kilometers south-east of Kadugli, lies the picturesque village of Shatt Damam. The construction of many of the houses attests to the rugged topography of the mountainsides, with walls fashioned from rock and earth. The living compounds are widely scattered on the tops and slopes of the surrounding jebels. Many of the jubraka are neatly enclosed by *shok* (thorny brush) fences to keep out the occasional foraging pig or goat. Women sing bawdy grindstone songs as they pound dura in rhythmic unison; men sit drinking marissa, enthralled by a comic anecdote from a migrant newly returned from Khartoum; small boys practice the latest wrestling moves on each other; and young girls make a game of rounding up crying babies. All in all, Shatt Damam appears to be a very pleasant village. Closer inspection, however, reveals a different story. Times are increasingly difficult. Aside from inadequate rains in recent years, the paucity of available farm lands, the prolonged absence of adult males, and a mounting indebtedness to the local merchant are frequently heard laments.

Shatt Damam is a rather large village and is subdivided into the settlement clusters of Kadamiro, Gurdum, Zarick, and Dong. These communities are not physically distinct, and the divisions are more a matter of logistical convenience than anything else. Kadamiro is the largest and contains the village suq, with an elementary school, dispensary, tahona, and six shops. The omda, or village head, who presides over the divisional sheikhs, resides here.[1] The omda, as well as the sheikhs, are men of property and influence within the community; hence, their words carry more authority than the mere trappings of their offices convey. The local merchants also play a significant role in village affairs; albeit, less overt. But, theirs is certainly more pernicious to the well-being of the local community and, hence, to the lineage itself. Too, they are patient men, content in the knowledge that as the economic situation in Shatt Damam continues to deteriorate, the villagers will have to come to them for assistance.

The Shatt people are one of the more distinct Nuba groups in the region, despite sharing a number of characteristics with other gabila, such as age-grades, ritual practices, and cicatrization. Little is known of their origin or precisely how long they have resided in their present area. The Shatt are allegedly a branch of the Daju who migrated some

600 miles from Darfur, and they still share linguistic commonalities with the Daju. When asked the time period of Shatt Damam's founding, most villagers reply: "Before the Mahdi."

The outward appearance of the Shatt is perhaps their most unique trait. The women braid their hair down the back of their heads and coat it with animal fat, giving the braid the look of a flat paddle. Young men wear brightly colored trunks and frequently color their upper torsos and heads. Finally, the Shatt still maintain their matrilineal system of inheritance, despite governmental pressures to adopt the patrilinear practices of the dominant Northern-Sudanese Arab culture. Nevertheless, Shatt Damam is changing, due to the scarcity of available lands for agricultural expansion and the resulting need to migrate, as well as the practices of local and area merchants.

Unlike the Ghulfan of Somasem, the Shatt have managed to resist most facets of the process of "Arabicization." In fact, relations between the Shatt and Arabs remain hostile to violent, and few Shatt willingly trust their Arab neighbors. Although the Shatt suffered during the slave raids associated with both the Turkiyya and the Mahdiyya, the western and northern jebels of the province withstood the worst effects, especially during the latter period, which witnessed the destruction of whole villages and the forced removal of their inhabitants to Omdurman. In this respect, the internal social relations of the Shatt probably did not undergo the same fragmentation as did the Ghulfan and other gabila, nor did they endure as lasting a blow to their self-esteem and gabila identity. Nevertheless, even today the Shatt are particularly leery of outsiders, particularly of non-Nuba. At the nearby village of Kalulu, for instance, children flee and women retreat into their houses with the approach of a khawaja. In addition, Condominium policy of "tribal separation" conceivably allowed the Shatt time to reconsolidate by minimizing contact with Sudanese Arab culture and northern jallaba.

The Shatt are generally looked down upon by other Nuba communities,[2] Fellata, and Arabs, who consider them "peculiar" and "backwards." This tends to reinforce the Shatt feeling of togetherness vis-á-vis the outside world. With the exception of a few Fellata merchant families in Kadamiro, all of the inhabitants of the larger village are Shatt.[3] The relationship between the villagers and their non-Shatt neighbors within and, particularly, with those outside the village fluctuates between commercial necessity and outright animosity.[4] The Shatt are equally suspicious of the government, and many view the elementary school, dispensary, and tahona as simply another means to convert the villagers to Islam and undermine Shatt culture. It is not the belief in Allah, the One God as revealed by the Prophet Mohammed, that the Shatt object to, but Islamic interdictions against nudity, abstinence from drinking marissa, and avoidance of eating pork. All three practices are still relatively common in Shatt culture. These prohibitions thus seem to the typical Shatt as a direct assault on their communal consciousness—the very essence of what it is to be a Shatt.

Admittedly an extreme example, the following incident characterizes the underlying nature of the Shatt relation with outsiders (especially non-Nuba). Late in 1987, the senior Fellata merchant responsible for distributing the government allocation of sugar unilaterally decided that it might be a good idea to introduce a new method of rationing the sugar. He took the sugar to Kadugli and sold it in the suq. Not surprisingly, the people of Shatt Damam were very angry over this, and several decided to take their grievance directly to the merchant's house. The merchant refused to discuss the matter with them; it was dark, so they burned his house down. The merchant, to say the least, was impressed with the magnitude of the anger and promptly fled with his family. The Arabs in the area, finding the merchant missing, decided that the Shatt had killed him. Seeking revenge they turned up in force one day and proceeded to burn as many Shatt houses and as much of the dura crop as possible. In the process, they managed to kill five Shatt (four men and a woman). The merchant showed up a few days later, unscathed. In an attempt to calm the situation, the government called for a conference between the warring factions, to which the Shatt elders promptly replied: "We will talk to the Arabs when the dead Shatt begin talking again." The Shatt needed only to recall the government's most recent attempt at reconciliation at the neighboring village of Shatt Safiya (see chapter 5, Institutions and Services).

The indigenous religion of the Shatt still exerts a powerful influence in village life as evidenced by the continued importance of the *kujurs*, rainpriests, and healers. The traditional occasions of celebrating and feasting, such as *Sibir al Diboia* and *Sibir al Boksa*, are eagerly anticipated by young and old villagers alike. Not only are festivities joyous events, these occasions reaffirm what it means to be Shatt. Although the intensity of belief may have waned in recent years, Shatt ceremonies and rituals still provide a bulwark against external forces and bind the community together. During *Sibir al Diboia*, for example, the *kujor* and select elders retire to the dark and ominous oracle hut where the *kujor* falls into a trance and reveals the cause of past calamities, foretells the outcome of impending plans, or confers advice on current domestic and village problems. Shatt religion thus not only imparts a sense of community, it offers a unique way of looking at the world and the Shatt place within it. The importance of the Shatt religion is especially evident during the more important *sibir* when the population of the village swells from the influx of returned migrants.

Music and song similarly provide important forms of expression for the Shatt. Of course, most villagers are familiar with the genre of songs of the northern Arab-Sudanese tradition, but still, local songs remain the favored. Dances held under the moonlight also offer a chief form of entertainment, especially for young people, and are notable occasions for flirtation, courtship, and sexual innuendo. Two popular styles of dance are promenade and foot stomping, although the former is preferred by teens as it permits a certain degree of physical touching absent in the other. Throughout the night songs fill the air, old village favorites as well as songs of the moment. The latter also provide an important means of social control and a check on deviant behavior. The following story illustrates this point. An elderly man had been sexually harassing young girls. When scolded by some of the villagers he simply pretended ignorance and ignored their protestations. One night during a moonlight dance the women prepared a song in his "honor." The song explicitly suggested that the man found it necessary to bother young women because he was afflicted with a very small penis. That night the man left Shatt Damam and did not return for six months. He never bothered women again.

The long-standing connection between ritual and social behavior is also readily observable in agriculture. Many farmers continue to heed the providential wisdom of the *kujur* and rainpriest in signalling the propitious time for planting or harvesting. In the collective mind set of the Shatt, any violation of this natural order through irreverence or impiety can easily summon catastrophe on the whole village, not just the offending individual. Consequently, any breach in spiritual decorum is dealt with according to the perceived severity of the infraction. Unquestionably the most grievous transgression that a Shatt can commit is stopping the nourishing rains and it invites grave consequences that can lead to the burning of the guilty party's house and the beating of the culprit (usually to death). In 1978, for example, the rains began and then abruptly ceased. The farmer suspected by the rainpriest of violating a natural observance had his house razed with him in it. Miraculously the farmer managed to escape to Khartoum where, according to local legend, he stopped the rains again.

The healer is also an important figure who rids the afflicted of bad spirits or evil curses by dashing the patient with special water, administering herbal concoctions, or applying hot spear tips to the inner elbow or lower neck, depending on the particular symptoms. There are no direct payments for "services rendered," but few would care to incur the ill will of the healer by appearing unappreciative. Consequently, gifts or labor services are "freely" imparted. Healers also have a practicing knowledge of herbal medicines. One time when an individual received a bad sting at the base of his thumb from a rather large scorpion, the healer went into the bush and returned with a handful of leaves. He quickly ground them, added water, and prepared a paste. Moments after covering the wound with the salve, both the pain and the swelling subsided, much to the relief of the victim.

The structuring of an individual's life course though codified age-grades (*bobongabani* or "friends from the same age period") is undoubtedly one of the more important aspects around which Shatt society is organized. Age-grades underpin the Shatt division of labor by distinguishing categories of activities by age classification and gender. The first two grades extend from birth to approximately 14 years of age and correspond to infant and child. Little is expected of boys and girls throughout this period although during childhood boys tend goats while girls watch younger siblings and assist in light domestic chores. The next age grade, youth or young adult, ranges roughly from 15 to 25 years of age and formally ends with marriage, marking the commencement of adulthood.

When a male child makes the transition to youth, they are sent to the "bush" with elders from the village. It is at this time that young males learn what it fully means to be a Shatt man. As part of this training, the youths are trained in the art of wrestling. Throughout this time period, the young men live collectively at the village *zariba* (cattle camp) where they tend the cattle and continue wrestling, frequently competing against other communities. The winner of these occasions

not only increases the stature of his lineage, but adds to his own standing within the community as well. It is often at this time that a young
man will work as herdsman for others such as the *Baggara* Arabs. The
herder is traditionally paid one cow per season which will go towards
the eventual brideprice he must pay. Nowadays, the youth of Shatt
Damam increasingly prefer migrating to towns in order to seek their
fortunes. Young men between the ages of 20 and 25 also provide for
village security by protecting the main farms, retrieving stolen cows,
and (though less common now) poaching cows not owned by Shatt.
Females, following menarche, are considered young women and are
trained in the domestic tasks that will see them through life. The status
of elder for males and married woman for females is achieved upon
marriage. The last age grade, senior elder and senior women, begins
around the age of 45.

The intrinsic and powerful bond linking age-mates endures throughout an individual's life. Though not imparting the same status of kinship, age-mate (*wopisko*) indicates ties far stronger than mere friendship
implies.[5] Age-mates apprehend and learn life's lessons together and it
is through these common experiences that hard-felt bonds are forged.
Further, the mutual obligations and responsibilities instilled in each
person of a similar age-grade forms a social core around which labor
is organized.

Fellowship, in all of its forms, is inimitably a condition of mutual
survival and requires the careful nurturing of all three types of attach-
ments; kinship, age-mate, and friendship. Agriculture for both the household and village instills mutual dependence and is primarily realized
through nafir labor. So too is the construction of a house, as well as any
other labor intensive activity. Farming, especially given the basic level
of technology in Shatt Damam, is not an individual affair but a cooperative undertaking requiring numerous hands. Thus the successful art of
living depends on an individual's ability to assemble the assistance of
others. Aside from enabling the completion of specific tasks, nafir vali-
dates feelings of reciprocity and good will within the village and reaffirms an individual's dependence on one's kin, age-mates, friends, and,
even neighbors. The spirit of cooperation also extends to informal work
parties such that men invariably cut gaish or shok and make charcoal in
the company of one another, while women routinely collect wood, grind
dura, and fetch water together. These activities could quite easily be

accomplished alone, but seldom if ever are for the very reason that to do so would signify to others some illness or deep inner malaise.

The Shatt practice of matrilineal inheritance reflects the orientation of kin-based social relations. In general, males inherit land and cattle from their mother's brothers, a pattern termed avuncular inheritance. On the other hand, "if your mother has no brothers, usually the oldest son will ask the *sheikh* for some land. He will give some land to his younger brothers, or they can ask the *sheikh* themselves." Females frequently inherit land from their mothers. Disputes over land inheritance are increasingly common in Shatt Damam primarily due to the paucity of available lands. Increasingly, young males are turning to the court system for adjudication instead of the local elders, particularly in cases where a son wants to retain his father's land as the court system does not recognize the Shatt system of matrilineal inheritance. In this case, the court inevitably rules in favor of the father's son. Kuku's father upon his death, for example, left his main farm to his sister's son. It happened that his farm was more fertile than the land inherited by Kuku from his maternal uncle. Kuku, bypassing the sheikh and village elders brought the matter directly to the local magistrate in Kadugli who promptly awarded the lands to Kuku in accordance with *shari'a* or Islamic legal tradition. These types of disputations have tended to erode the Shatt inheritance system and increased village tensions.

The relationship between a boy and his maternal uncles is customarily quite strong: "You can take anything from your [maternal uncle], even a watch if you need it. But you never take anything from your father unless he wants to give it to you." When faced with a problem, young men will seek the council of their mother's brothers over that of their father's family. Of greater consequence, males are obligated to attend to their maternal uncles' fields and care for their animals as well. They may help their fathers if they choose to do so, but are under no compulsion. When a young man approaches the age of marriage, he will request the assistance of his maternal uncles who will perform the delicate marriage negotiations and assist their nephews in the payment of brideprice. Generally a lad's father does not pay anything unless he wants to and "usually he does not want to help because he has to help his sisters' sons."

The standard brideprice consists of three to five cows, three to six goats, two to three pigs, one gun, six spears, and two jerry cans of oil. In recent years money has assumed a more prominent role, with "requested" amounts ranging between £S 50 to £S 200. In addition, the groom is obliged to perform brideservice, working on his future father-in-law's field for a period up to four years. The young man undertakes this with the aid of his similarly betrothed age mates. This practice has decreased in recent years as a result of the high rates of out-migration by young men and has been replaced with the inclusion of money assuming a larger portion of the brideprice. The preferred form of marriage among the Shatt is between matrilateral cross-cousins, whereas unions between parallel cousins is considered incestuous. Marriage between non-kin is also common. Arab patterns of marriage (as in Shair Tomat), however, are increasing in Shatt Damam and this is an indication of the strength of conviction by recent converts, as well as of recent inroads of Arabicization.

Presently, older forms of social organization and exchange centrally associated with the lineage remain—brideprice, bride service, and labor obligations of juniors to elders, women to men, and villagers to priests—though certainly they are attenuated. What has changed significantly within the lineage is their context brought about by the overall growth of the cash economy. Changes have been induced by the monetization of brideprice and, more revealing, as a result of the process of out-migration itself. In the past, out-migration consisted of a young man leaving on a one-time basis to amass the resources necessary for marriage. Migrants worked primarily as herders or as wage laborers in the large mechanized schemes, usually in Habila or Gezira, and returned after a year or so. Now, most leave for other types of work in the cities and for much longer periods of time. More revealing about the changes within the lineage system is that brideprice is no longer the sole motivation; young men simply leave to seek what they consider to be a better opportunities outside of the village.

Most migrants today believe that they have little choice but to depart Shatt Damam and seek their fortunes elsewhere because of the small size of most farms and the severe limitations on acquiring new lands. Ironically, out-migration helps ease land pressures since men working outside of Shatt Damam for an extended period of time typically lend or lease their lands to those who stay behind. Leasing generally constitutes payment of a fixed amount of dura to the migrant's family. Even those with no lands of their own to leave behind are at least not adding to the number of people requesting village land. On the other hand, not only does migration pose a drain on household labor and add to the already heavy work load of females, but it also requires access to additional labor at peak agricultural periods. The demand for labor has led to the necessity of meat to attract a nafir and, in some cases, to offer cash loans that will never be repaid, in addition to pushing some farmers to hire wage-labor. The prolonged absence of young males also contributes to the break down of age grades as juniors do not all undergo the same ritual inclusion into the village. Consequently, the door is opened wide to outside modernizing pressures.

A telling instance of recent changes in Shatt Damam is found in the role of village merchants. The merchants purchase the small volumes offered periodically by villagers at low prices and resell them in Kadugli at a much higher price. In 1986, for example, a sack of simsim costing a merchant £S 90 in Shatt Damam sold for £S 120 in Kadugli, and an £S 80 sack of *waka* (dried okra) sold for £S 110. In the words of one local merchant, "Owning a store is good business because you can make a big profit, they [the villagers] have no one else they can sell to." Ostensibly, the villagers could travel to Kadugli where they would find more favorable prices, but the long walk coupled with the small quantities offered precludes this in most instances. The largest merchant (whose primary residence is in Kadugli) combines this activity with transport services.

The relative closeness of Shatt Damam to Kadugli also allows local merchants to pursue other profitable business ventures. Two merchant brothers in Shatt Damam own several sewing machines and employ local labor (men) to sew clothes for sale in the Kadugli market. Of course, the work is organized so as not to interfere with agricultural activities but given the small field sizes of many of the villagers and the indebtedness of some, obtaining labor is never a problem. And besides, many young males see this type of work as a valuable experience that can lead to good jobs in either El Obeid or Khartoum.

In addition to these economic enterprises, money lending provides a profitable activity for the merchants since many households chronically run short of dura, sugar, and oil, especially during the "hungry period" preceding the first harvest in the jubraka. Again, given the relatively small field sizes of many villagers, some households find that they must mortgage their crops before they are harvested. The beneficiary of this misfortune is the shayl who provides short-term credit at a price far below the market price of either dura or simsim at the time of harvest. Or, in lieu of repayment in crop, the shayl will take repayment in labor services, the burden of actual repayment invariably falling on the shoulders of women.

A final word must be mentioned on the form of governance in Shatt Damam. Before the system of sheikhs, a council of village elders managed village affairs. The council of elders selected the "chief" (or master of the path) on the basis of a combination of traits, including fierceness in battle, number of cattle owned, prowess as a wrestler, and, sometimes, on his ability to poach cattle from non-Shatt gabila. Many of these men later assumed the roles of sheikh and omda, bridging both lineage and capitalist modes of production, and profited simultaneously from both sets of social relations. By assuming both roles, past power could be effectively turned into present wealth, an increasing necessity for elders, given the uncertain economic environment of Shatt Damam. Most of the village inhabitants have not been as fortunate and their life chances have diminished, as is evident in the steady increase in the rates of migrating children, indebtedness, and sale of household labor (particularly to fellow villagers).

Household Organization

Paradoxically, unlike the villages of Somasem and Shair Tomat, Shatt Damam exists on the margins of modernization; it is neither here nor there. An important characteristic differentiating Shatt Damam from the other two villages is the number of households based in the lineage (re)production forms; 65 percent of the sampled households (table 9.1). Furthermore, no household is dependent exclusively for its reproduction through the sale of labor. Hence, there are no wage-labor households. The strength of lineage relations serves as a bulwark against rationalization and the cash economy through the provisioning of critical organizing principles, particularly in agricultural production. Nevertheless, the number of small-scale capitalist households provides evidence that modernization, in many ways, is inevitable, mainly visible in the growing market relations and long-term out-migration. With the exception of the capitalist entrepreneurial households, the other forms are structurally similar, suggestive of the fine line separating the domestic sphere from the cash sector. The capitalist entrepreneurial households are comprised of more recent arrivals, non-Shatt Fellata merchants, who tend to have older household heads and larger families.

TABLE 9.1
Household Size and Age Structure by (Re)Production Form

All households	CE	SC	LM	LS	WLP	Total
% of households	3.3%	31.7%	35.0%	30.0%	.0%	100.0%
Mean household size	14.0	7.4	7.7	5.6	NA	7.2
Mean member age	19.2	17.3	19.3	20.5	NA	18.9
Mean n. age <16	8.9	7.1	8.3	7.9	NA	7.8
Mean age of head	42.5	37.1	35.9	36.6	NA	36.6
(n=)	(2)	(19)	(21)	(18)	(0)	(60)

The sex of household heads across the various household forms provides insights into the general distribution of power between genders. Except for the capitalist entrepreneurial households, table 9.2 reveals greater empowerment of women compared to the other two villages. This is not surprising since the Shatt practice matrilinear descent. Slightly more than 29 percent of household heads are females, though with the majority in lineage subsistence households, followed by lineage market and small-scale capitalist households. Households exclusively headed by females comprise 17 percent of the total sample and differ only slightly from their male counterparts, albeit without a current mate female headed households tend to be smaller in size.[6] In general, statistical differences do not of themselves signify inordinately greater hardships for female headed households than for male. In part, the matrilinear system of kinship which facilitates life-long relations between brothers and sisters, coupled with female access to land, cross-cuts the more negative effects of patriarchy.

Of equal importance, some 18 percent of the sampled households are jointly headed. This type of household more closely resembles those headed by males.[7] Nine are made up of husbands and wives, one by a father and son, and one by three brothers. Joint head arrangements more clearly reflect the lineage system at the household level; ten of the eleven are in the lineage forms. In the case of females, husbands may desire sole authority but women are also notable actors in their own right, including at the household level, and enjoy greater economic opportunities than their female counterparts in either Somasem or Shair Tomat. Access to arable land, in particular, not only enables women the occasion to produce grain for household needs, but with control over any

TABLE 9.2
Sex of Household Head by (Re)Production Form

Sex	CE	SC	LM	LS	WLP	Total	(n)
Male	3.9%	31.4%	35.3%	29.4%	NA	100.0%	(51)
Female	.0	14.3	28.6	57.1	NA	100.0%	(21)
(n=)	(2)	(19)	(24)	(27)	(0)	(72)	

surfeit, it provides a cash income which she can use at her own discretion.[8] In other words, males do not exercise automatic control over women's incomes simply by virtue of being a man. The style of headship in this case is less teamwork and more accurately approximates independent consultation.

In addition, consideration of the marital status of household heads (table 9.3) offers a better understanding of female opportunities in Shatt Damam. Not every female gains headship status by virtue of divorce or death of spouse; 57.1 percent of female heads are married. Nevertheless, nearly 43 percent of females heads are, for whatever reason, unmarried as opposed to male heads who are predominantly married. Despite the strength of brother-sister bonds, female-headed households face additional burdens. Brothers do routinely offer their sisters assistance in the field, but without adult children at home female-headed households cultivate fewer feddan, primarily because they are also responsible for domestic chores. Females still lack the latitude in remarriage enjoyed by males. In the case of divorce or the death of a wife, male reliance on females for domestic activities compels a man to quickly remarry; no man dies a widower.

Polygamous marriage perhaps best reflects the dominant ideology of patriarchy. Accordingly, the possibility of multiple marriages open solely to men affords both a livelihood strategy as well as a sign of affluence. Twelve men presently have two wives and one has three. Not only does this expand the household labor pool, but multiple wives symbolizes a man's wealth and standing within the community, principally in the lineage forms. There are no household heads who have never been married since marriage is a requirement of household formation.

Households are fluid by definition, a point made amply evident in Shatt Damam. Overall, nearly 47 percent of households are complex. As table 9.4 shows, members of these households consist of a wide assortment of

TABLE 9.3
Marital Status of Household Head by Sex and (Re)Production Form

Male	CE	SC	LM	LS	Total
married	100%	100%	94.5%	100%	98.0%
divorced	.0	.0	5.6	.0	2.0
Total	100%	100%	100%	100%	100%
(n=)	(2)	(16)	(18)	(15)	(51)
Mean age head	42.5	37.1	35.9	36.6	36.6
Female					
married	NA	.0	50.0	75.0	57.1
widow	NA	66.7	.0	8.3	14.3
divorced	NA	33.3	50.0	16.7	28.6
Total	NA	100%	100%	100%	100%
(n=)	(0)	(3)	(6)	(12)	(21)
Mean age head	NA	40.7	40.3	34.7	38.6

kinship and generational arrangements, including elderly parents, siblings, in-laws, cousins, and grandchildren. Not only does this represent a household labor strategy, but complex households verify the importance of lineage bonds in defining social security. Specifically, where kinship networks tend to be exclusive in the other two villages, they are more inclusive within Shatt Damam. To deny a member of one's lineage food and shelter is tantamount to denying the sanctity of lineage obligations and responsibilities. Shawaish, for instance, took in his paternal cousin's wife, children and mother when his cousin was forced to flee to Khartoum after a severe altercation in the village. It was never a question of room or sufficient comestibles, Shawaish merely did what any other Shatt would have done without calculation or consideration. Moreover, the fluidity of composition acts to offset the loss of household members through the increased out-migration of the young. Female and joint-headed households reflect similar considerations. Some 40 percent of female and 46 percent of joint-headed households are complex types.

Finally, spatial residency patterns provide important insights into household livelihood strategies (table 9.5). Although some 43 percent of households are coresidential, slightly more than 53 percent have at least one member residing temporarily outside of the household, indicating the high degree of spatial mobility in Shatt Damam. Out-migration

TABLE 9.4
Household Residential Type by (Re)Production Form

All households	CE	SC	LM	LS	Total
Single—w/dependents	.0%	21.1%	4.8%	16.7%	13.4%
Nuclear	.0	26.3	42.9	55.6	40.0
Complex	100.0	52.6	52.4	27.8	46.7
Total	100%	100%	100%	100%	100%
(n=)	(2)	(19)	(21)	(18)	(60)

embodies an important livelihood strategy; both during the dry season to reduce demand on the household granary, and for the money and goods remitted by migrants. Furthermore, young men must still accumulate cash and goods for brideprice and to provision a home for his wife. Another 3 percent comprising the capitalist entrepreneurial households possess two primary residences in addition to having members reside temporarily outside of the house. The heads of these households own houses in Kadugli where they have substantial business interests. Most of their family members currently live outside of Shatt Damam due to the deterioration of security in the Nuba Mountains.

Sources of Household Income

Tio Kapi has worked in Kadugli for the past three years as a bakery employee. He lives in the hills nearby with his wife, her young sister, and their two small children. Tio's wife supplements his meager pay with food grown in the small jubraka surrounding the modest house. They both miss Shatt Damam but know that for now they must continue to save money for the day Tio can acquire a field of his own. Tio's (maternal) uncles are still active farmers and he has no access to land. In addition, one of his uncle's sons has already advanced a claim to the land despite customary Shatt law. Nevertheless, he visits the village frequently during the growing season to help in his uncles' nafirs. After all, lineage obligations run deep and Tio continues to hope that one day he too will have land in Shatt Damam. The case of Tio is not unusual; it reflects the growing hardships and uncertainties confronting households in Shatt Damam. Tio's family is merely a consequence of contradictory pressures affecting the village as a whole.

TABLE 9.5
Household Spatial Residency Patterns by (Re)Production Form

Spatial pattern	CE	SC	LM	LS	Total
coresidence	.0%	47.4%	28.6%	61.1%	43.4%
dispersed	.0	52.6	71.4	38.9	53.3
disp/multiresidence	100.0	.0	.0	.0	3.3
Total	100%	100%	100%	100%	100%
(n=)	(2)	(19)	(21)	(18)	(60)

To farm a good sized land holding and maintain a herd of cattle and goats, and perhaps a few pigs in Shatt Damam requires a large family and retaining grown children in the village, as well as maintaining relations of reciprocity and good will inherent in calling a nafir party. Economic success was also guaranteed as long as the authority of elders over their lineage and village affairs went unchallenged and, of course, ample land reserves existed. Today, this is no longer assured. The encroachment of the slave/tributary systems and later the spread of a specifically capitalist economy, as noted, both created new economic opportunities and introduced new constraints. Concomitant with a general increase in customary consumption standards, pressures increasingly necessitate market strategies requiring the sale of goods and/or services, both of which strike directly at the heart of the lineage system and consequently the household. Particularly deleterious to the household and village in this respect has been the out-migration of young people, especially of young males.

Paradoxically, what initially permitted elders greater status and wealth is ultimately causing their undoing. With the monetization of brideprice, elders strongly encourage juniors to migrate for employment purposes. But while this may have allowed elders to amass a greater array of wealth, it has come at the cost of labor and thus of nafir. The rapid rise in the out-migration of young men in recent years erodes the core of the lineage economy; namely through the increased reliance on wage-labor and the rise of the shayl in meeting household reproduction requirements. Certainly many elders are better able to employ laborers and/or intensify the use of household labor (particularly women), but not all can or want to. Furthermore, those elders without the necessary means frequently find it necessary to turn to the village shayl in order to make up for shortfalls in production due to the lack of labor within the village.

In addition, population pressures on available land coupled with the assault on matrilinear inheritance customs by Islamic patrimony, have further undermined Shatt lineage principles. Hence, access to wives, land, and labor are becoming problematical within traditional lineage norms of behavior. And of course, new consumption needs have emerged that have expanded the realm of necessity, needs which in the main can only be satisfied in the market. Of course, this does not mean that self-sufficiency is no longer deemed important, it simply signifies that traditional ways of ordering economic and social life are increasingly at odds with present realities and circumstances.

Given present conditions within Shatt Damam today, household livelihood strategies now embrace a multiplicity of income generating activities pursued by household members, including the sale of household labor and the marketing of goods (table 9.6). Crop and animal sales continue to provide important sources of cash incomes for most households. The same is true of off-farm employment, except that it is no longer dominated by young men working to acquire brideprices. The survey data also emphasize key distinctions between small-scale capitalists and the two lineage household (re)production forms. Some 42 percent of small-scale capitalist households own businesses compared to only 9.5 percent of lineage market households. Both of these forms exhibit similar rates of participation in agricultural and non-agricultural off-farm employment, although daHwa labor provides incomes for almost 62 percent of the lineage market households and only 37 percent for small-scale capitalist households. No member of the capitalist entrepreneurial households engage in wage-labor. Lineage subsistence households rely almost exclusively on cash earnings from daHwa labor and only marginally on nonagricultural employment, primarily because daHwa employment is flexible and employs more redundant household labor.

Of greater interest, remittances comprise important sources of cash for both of the two lineage forms, particularly the subsistence oriented households, indicating the significance of lineage relations in securing access to the incomes of migrating members, present and past. More importantly, remittances also reveal the precariousness of a household in meeting its consumption requirements and can signify the difference between subsistence goals and the local shayl. Only 5.9 percent of small-scale capitalist households receive remittances.

TABLE 9.6
Source of Income-Generating Activities of Households by (Re)Production Form

Activities	CE	SC	LM	LS	Total
Crop sales	100.0%	84.2%	81.0%	83.3%	83.3%
Animal sales	50.0	42.1	52.4	38.9	45.0
Businesses	100.0	42.1	9.5	.0	20.0
Ag. labor	.0	10.5	14.3	.0	8.3
DaHwa	.0	36.8	61.9	38.9	45.0
Nonag. labor	.0	36.8	33.3	5.6	25.0
Remittances	.0	5.3	19.0	33.3	18.3
Mean no. sources	2.5	2.7	3.0	2.3	2.7
(n=)	(2)	(19)	(21)	(18)	(60)

The composition of household incomes further distinguishes the capitalist from the lineage (re)production forms (table 9.7). Household-owned businesses generate the bulk of incomes for the two capitalist entrepreneurial households and contribute to nearly 27 percent of the incomes of small-scale capitalist households. On the other hand, off-farm nonagricultural employment comprises the most important component of household income for small-scale capitalists (45.9 percent), but at the expense of household labor since most members find employment outside of South Kordofan. Capitalist entrepreneurs sell an average of 36 percent of their dura and all of their simsim, yet crop sales contribute a scant 2.4 percent of the total income of these households. Crop sales, however, account for 17.4 percent of the total incomes of small-scale capitalists who market 16 and 43 percent of their dura and simsim crops respectively.

The two lineage (re)production forms exhibit different economic considerations. In general, these forms remain dependent upon agriculture and livestock for income generation, although rarely are healthy cattle sold.[9] Lineage market households sell an average of 16 percent of their dura and 25 percent of their simsim crops, while lineage subsistence households part with only 10 percent of their dura and 15 percent of their simsim. In general, lineage subsistence householders exchange grain for other goods at the local shop or use it to repay the shayl in-kind. Off-farm non-agricultural employment makes up 38 percent of the total income of lineage market households, but only 13.8 percent of the lineage

TABLE 9.7
All Households: Proportional Contribution of Various Sources of
Income Activity to Total Household Incomes by (Re)Production Form

All Households	CE	SC	LM	LS	Total
Income sources					
Crop sales	2.4%	17.4%	20.2%	59.5%	10.8%
Animal sales	1.2	8.3	28.6	13.2	7.7
Businesses	96.4	26.5	3.2	.0	59.8
Ag. labor	.0	1.1	4.3	.0	1.0
DaHwa	.0	.7	2.6	4.1	0.7
Nonag. labor	.0	45.9	38.0	13.8	19.3
Remittances	.0	0.1	3.1	9.4	0.7
Mean net income					
(£S)	21,388	1204	587	124	1337
Median net income					
(£S)	21,388	1018	318	111	315
Total	100%	100%	100%	100%	100%
(n=)	(2)	(19)	(21)	(18)	(60)

subsistence households. Labor lost through out-migration in both of the lineage forms is minimal since most incidences of migration occur to nearby areas such as Kadugli and Dilling.

Analysis of mean and median net household incomes across forms of (re)production discloses the extent of inequality within the village. The large disparity between the two measures (±£S 1022) reveals the wide range in household incomes and the potential for future economic stratification. Without additional lands for expansion, concomitant with an increase in market activities, the trend in off-farm employment can be expected to continue. Although the two lineage forms demonstrate greater orientation towards household self-sufficiency, on average the variability in household income suggests wider economic pressures necessitating alternative sources of household sustenance; that is, the effects of modernization sundering traditional lineage relations. Furthermore, the disparity between mean income of capitalist entrepreneurial households and the other household forms reveals the market power of merchants in the market, as well as their potential influence on the reproduction of the other households in general.

TABLE 9.8

Female Headed Households: Proportional Contribution of Sources of Income Activity to Total Household Income by (Re)Production Form

Income sources	CE	SC	LM	LS	Total
Crop sales	NA	17.6%	21.4%	72.5%	19.8%
Animal sales	NA	.0	.0	.0	.0
Businesses	NA	11.3	.0	.0	7.6
Ag. labor	NA	.0	.0	.0	.0
DaHwa	NA	.0	11.0	27.5	3.9
Nonag. labor	NA	71.1	67.6	.0	68.7
Remittances	NA	.0	.0	.0	.0
Mean net income (£S)	NA	796	296	32	364
Median net income (£S)	NA	162	132	19	101
Mean income sources	NA	1.7	2.5	1.0	1.8
Total	100%	100%	100%	100%	100%
(n=)	(0)	(3)	(4)	(3)	(10)

The survey data also discloses a different outlook for female headed households, despite the wider range of economic opportunities open to women in general, and is particularly evident in lineage subsistence households (table 9.8). Not only are the incomes of female headed households disproportionately less than the total sample, but they enjoy fewer mean sources of income. A primary impediment confronting females is restricted access to land and livestock. Females traditionally inherit their mothers' "near" farms which are significantly smaller than the main ("far") farms inherited by males.[10] Moreover, cattle belong exclusively to males, although females may own goats and pigs. Female headed small-scale capitalist households rely significantly on off-farm nonagricultural labor (71.1 percent) and to a lessor degree on household-owned businesses (11.3 percent). The female headed lineage forms, on the other hand, depend on daHwa labor to help meet cash incomes. Moreover, the lack of remittances reveals the absence of the elder/junior relation in these households, as well as the diminishment of the brother-sister bond when the brother leaves the village.

Finally, zakha (or its Shatt counterpart of communal obligations to the less fortunate in times of crisis) suggests the number of households expe-

riencing economic hardships. With the exception of the capitalist entrepreneurial households, 15 percent of sampled households supplement
domestic grain supplies with an average of 1.6 sacks of dura. Overall, the
majority of recipients of zakha are small-scale capitalist households followed by lineage market households. What this suggests is the economic
instability associated with volatility of the market and the lack of an effective cushion to buttress these households. Interestingly, only two female headed households benefit from this type of assistance; females
generally rely instead on the support of their brothers within the village.

Household Reproduction Strategies

A common complaint heard in Shatt Damam nowadays is that people
must work longer hours in their fields but for a smaller harvest. Consequently, with the narrowing resource base for agricultural production in
Shatt Damam, alternative economic activities have become a necessity
for most households in securing their reproduction. Though outward
changes are often not as visible as in the other two villages, what is
evident is the beginning change from domestic subsistence to cash sales.
True, nafir labor parties continue to work the majority of fields and much
of the dura is still turned into marissa. Equally true, however, is the
sight of daHwa laborers composed of women, children, and the elderly
laboriously weeding; the multiplicity of small transactions at the general store; and the lorries carrying passengers and goods to and from
Kadugli. Nevertheless, the initial link connecting the subsistence sphere
with the cash sector came not from the market per se, but in the increased rationalization of the production process itself. Transformations
in household livelihood strategies thus reflect the realities of the day
and the altered context for organizing production in Shatt Damam.

Agricultural Assets

Access to land constitutes a core value in Shatt Damam. Without
land of his own a man never really becomes a full member of the community, nor can a women completely gain security from want. Moreover, food self-sufficiency is an intended goal of every Shatt household.
To be dependent on the grain grown by another is a sign of weakness, of
being a poor provider. In the past, acquisition of land was often contin-

gent on the death of a maternal uncle, although an aged uncle might provide a nephew with land when he was no longer economically active. Traditionally, males acquire land around the time of their marriage so that the two are intimately connected. Marriage and land thus demarcate elders from juniors. Females, on the other hand, are often bequeathed small plots by their mothers and sisters, or, less frequently, maternal aunts after a young women marries.

Table 9.9 indicates the high degree of land pressure currently in Shatt Damam; nearly 29 percent of households do not own a main farm. Three of the men are farming lands borrowed from their fathers and one from a friend. Although each claimed that he would eventually inherit land from his maternal uncle, two privately indicated that they would seek to retain their fathers' lands through arbitration in Kadugli. In addition, the negligible difference between the number of feddans owned and cultivated discloses the absolute shortage of arable lands available to the community. One of the consequences of this is the over-exploitation of the land which explains, in part, declining yields. A further consequence of the land scarcity is that more and more of the village youth, males and females, are migrating for longer periods of time. Of greater significance, the crisis in land adds to the erosion of the lineage system. Without the promise of land, young men are less willing to obey the dictates of village elders.

Livestock also comprises an important element of agricultural strategies, particularly cattle and goats. Unquestionably, the Shatt prefer to keep cattle. Overall, 48 percent of households maintain cattle with an average herd size of 10, ranging from 3 to 98. Not only are cattle a currency of brideprice, but they comprise a large measure of an individual's prestige within the community. The largest herd of cattle, for example, belongs to one of the more influential sheikhs of Shatt Damam. A customary means for young males to acquire cattle entails working as herd boys for other Nuba gabila or Baggara Arabs. As a boy Kuku Anduma received 3 cattle in this manner and now owns 34. Inheritance is equally common. Tio Gadam received 18 cattle when his maternal uncles passed away. Rarely do Shatt sell cattle. Likewise, loss of cattle through theft is hard felt. In the previous year eight cattle were stolen, ostensibly by Arabs if public opinion is to be believed. Only Said Mohammed, a wealthy merchant, keeps cattle purely for income purposes. He owns 35 cattle which he routinely markets in Kadugli.

TABLE 9.9
Household Agricultural Assets: Land, Cows, Goats,
Chickens, Sheep, and Pigs by (Re)Production Form

All households	CE	SC	LM	LS	Total
Land					
% who own	100.0%	94.7%	85.7%	100.0%	71.4%
Mean feddan own	13.0	6.6	8.2	4.9	6.8
Mean cultivate	29.0	6.5	4.8	4.1	5.6
Cows					
% who own	50.0	47.4	47.6	50.0	48.3
Mean no. own	35.0	19.3	5.6	3.0	10.1
Goats					
% who own	50.0	68.4	71.4	44.4	61.7
Mean no. own	18.0	6.2	7.0	3.4	6.2
Chickens					
% who own	50.0	89.5	90.5	67.8	85.0
Mean no. own	15.0	7.2	6.5	5.0	6.5
Sheep					
who own	100.0	26.3	9.5	5.6	16.7
Mean no. own	17.5	6.4	6.0	2.0	8.1
Pigs					
% who own	.0	9.8	18.4	22.9	17.0
Mean no. own	NA	3.0	3.5	2.7	3.2
Total	100%	100%	100%	100%	100%
(n=)	(2)	(19)	(21)	(18)	(60)
Female headed households					
Land					
% who own	NA	100.0	100.0	100.0	100.0
Mean own	—	6.3	3.8	3.5	4.5
Mean cultivate	—	5.5	3.5	2.5	3.9
Goats					
% who own	NA	33.3	50.0	0.0	30.0
Mean no. own	—	2.0	4.0	—	3.3
Chickens					
% who own	NA	100.0	75.0	33.3	70.0
Mean no. own	—	3.7	4.3	5.0	4.1
Pigs					
% who own	NA	0.0	25.0	0.0	10.0
Mean no. own	—	NA	2.0	NA	2.0
Total	100%	100%	100%	100%	100%
(n=)	(0)	(3)	(4)	(3)	(10)

Goats, held by 62 percent of households, are primarily kept for slaughter to mark village celebrations and provide meat for nafir parties. Pigs, though declining in popularity, are ritual animals and are slaughtered to mark important Shatt rituals or to signify solemn occasions such as the death of an elder, the birth of a male child, or the return of a family member after a prolonged absence. Currently, just 17 percent of households continue to raise pigs. Sheep, a relatively recent addition, provide ready sources of cash to nearly 17 percent of households and are usually marketed in Kadugli prior to Islamic holy days. Aside from the capitalist entrepreneurial households, livestock sales are primarily undertaken by small-scale capitalist households and, to a lessor extent, lineage market households. Receipts from cash sales enable households to purchase needed goods and hire labor. Chickens are commonly kept (85 percent of households) and are the domain of females, to be sold or eaten at their discretion. Ownership of land and livestock (excluding cattle) are only slightly lower for female headed households. Over all, animal protein does not comprise a large portion of the diet of most Shatt households in spite of the relative abundance of farm animals.

Interestingly, except for the few Fellata families, 87 percent of the sampled household heads cite Shatt Damam as their home village. The remainder are Shatt from nearby villages such as Shatt Safiya who either relocated to be with relatives, accompanied parents while young, or joined spouses. And although 53 percent of household heads had migrated for employment purposes in the past, earlier instances of migration appear to have been exclusively for the purpose of marriage and household formation. Consequently, no advantage seems to have been gained in ownership of agricultural assets either by time of arrival or through previous off-farm employment of household heads.

An important characteristic in lineage relations in Shatt Damam is communal proprietorship of land. In other words, traditionally land is not alienable and cannot be bought or sold. Recent years, however, have witnessed the development of a land market, albeit minor. The two capitalist entrepreneurs—both Fellatas—as outsiders, rent village lands through the omda who shares some of the rent-in-kind with the sheikhsuu of Kadimiro, although he reserves the greatest share for himself. Other examples include the case of Tutu Kuku who sold 12 feddan for 10 cows, and Kuku El Madir who purchased three feddan for £S 700. Such occurrences indicate the potential for the creation of a land market and

thus the further transformation of the village. Nonetheless, the encirclement of Shatt Damam by surrounding villages as well as Kadugli to the
north, provide the basis for a different valuation of land, predicated not
on lineage rights but on capitalist principles of supply and demand. Such
a situation bodes poorly for those not connected to the powerful elders
and the result may well be to further stimulate off-farm employment
and out-migration.

Agricultural Labor

The consequences of social transformation at the village level are
often subtle and complex. Although the market provides the backdrop
for change, pressures internal to the village are equally important for
comprehending the emergence of different livelihood strategies. The
traditional organization of agricultural production remained relatively
unaffected as long as land and labor had relatively "low opportunity
costs." The increased scarcity of land and out-migration of the youth,
however, introduced changes in production relations. Now, lineage
obligations and responsibilities have become diluted and their functions altered. To be sure, at least on the surface, agriculture in Shatt
Damam is still predominantly structured by lineage principles, but it
is precariously poised between personal obligation and impersonal
need. According to the Shatt, nafir has provided the primary source of
labor for as long as anyone can recall. Nafir is equally important in
most other labor-intensive activities, especially in house construction.
Yet many of the elderly inhabitants proclaim that it is not quite the
same as in the past, citing that farmers do not sponsor as many nafirs
nowadays, that cash or snuff is sometimes used to attract more participants, and that the villagers do not heed the call to labor as readily.
Certainly too, the basis of nafir recruitment has widened along with
the concurrent decline in reciprocity.

As in Somasem, nafir helped to define the community and enabled
the functioning of a well-ordered subsistence economy. The importance
centered on lineage bonds of obligation and responsibility which bound
each adult individual to the community, though in accordance to rules
governing lineage, seniority, and gender. No rational adult would have
entertained the notion of refusing a legitimate call to participate in a
nafir. To do so would have invited grave consequences, from social iso-

lation to public scorn. Older inhabitants were mildly baffled when such a question was posed to them, at first replying that they had never considered such a proposition. Even younger people were somewhat surprised, although their range of acceptable refusals was much broader. Interestingly, reasons listed by young men revolve around individual rather than community concerns and include job commitments, work in household fields, and anticipated absence from the village. In other words, the obligations and responsibilities enacted by nafir have ceased to condition the village and household labor process in the same way.

Traditionally, a nafir party is composed of lineage members and age-mates. In essence, the system of nafir in Shatt Damam operates along the same principles as those in Somasem, with slight variations due to the differences in their lineage relations. Similarly, the timing of a nafir is in accordance with seniority and status. More importantly, each household entered the agricultural season with the intention of undertaking the majority of laborious activities through nafir labor. Of course, household labor was necessary, but only for the chores not accomplished by nafir (or brideservice). On the surface, little seems to have changed. With the exception of the two capitalist households, only one of the sampled households no longer sponsors a main farm nafir during the agricultural season due to the prolonged absence of its adult male members from the village. Closer inspection, however, reveals that on average, households currently sponsor approximately two nafirs per season, primarily for the first weeding and harvest. Not surprisingly, wealthier households are in a better position and sponsor more nafirs parties than poorer households.

Although nafir is still relatively easy to organize, nowadays its basis of organization reflects the growing difficulties in recruiting sufficient numbers. Now, not only do lineage members and age-mates attend, invitations extend to friends and neighbors even though they are not connected to the sponsor through lineage ties or of the same age-grade classification. In addition, members of marginal households also freely participate, but without any expectations of returned future labor. Hence, wealthier farmers can expect to receive more labor than the household will expend in reciprocation. Every household in Shatt Damam sponsoring a nafir reciprocates an average of 16 times with two members in attendance. Rates of reciprocation, however, clearly differentiate small-scale capitalist from the two lineage forms. Lineage market and lineage subsistence households contribute a mean of 49 and 43 labor days respectively to other farmer's nafir parties, while small-scale capitalist households contribute only 27. Furthermore, whereas every sponsor serves participants marissa, only 44.6 percent routinely provide meat and 25.4 percent never do. As elsewhere, meat provides an important draw. The current trend in nafir usage thus discloses an important basis for social inequality and economic stratification.

Change in the mechanisms of labor recruitment is a powerful source of tension in the community and imparts profound implications for household reproduction. In the past most farmers would have spoken of the influential elders with awe, increasingly it is with contempt or jealousy. For those households able to attract large nafirs, hire labor, or make do with household labor, the erosion of nafir bears fewer negative consequences. On the other hand, households unable to attract a reasonable nafir and with few adult household members frequently experience shortfalls in production and find that they must resort to off-farm employment, increase the number of days spent in other farmers nafir parties, or visit the shayl. While any of these strategies may provide temporary relief, a negative multiplier effect is set into motion; less time spent in the household's fields, smaller harvest, fewer resources to attract nafir, and so on.

As mentioned, the increased out-flow of village residents from Shatt Damam has contributed significantly to the breakdown of traditional labor arrangements; not only nafir but brideservice as well. For example, 21 percent of sampled households were beneficiaries of brideservice labor in the past. According to elderly informants, as recently as thirty years ago most betrothed young men met this marriage condition. The monetization of brideprice, however, also led to the monetization of brideservice and further contributed to the migration of young men. Of course, those receiving money in lieu of labor can always hire any additional labor that the households might need but at the cost of another cornerstone of the lineage system. But again, it is clearly the marginal households, those who can ill afford to hire labor, who bear the brunt of another diminished source of communal labor.

In this framework, reliance on hiring laborers need not immediately signal the disintegration of traditional labor supplies. Rather, wage-labor often provides additional hands during peak periods of the agricultural season. Analysis of the survey data, however, point to the differential usage of wage-labor among the respective household forms. The two capitalist entrepreneurs employ an average of six laborers to undertake all of the field activities while 57 percent of small-scale capitalists hire an average of 3.5 workers by the piece for such activities as field clearing, weeding, and harvesting. Because small-scale capitalist households have less cash resources, it is not surprising that an average of 26.8 daHwa laborers were also employed over the course of the agricultural season, since they are comparatively less costly. Only 28.6 percent of lineage market households employ an average of one worker at the piece rate and 11.5 percent at the daHwa rate; lineage subsistence households do not employ wage laborers. Nearly 75 percent of those hired are fellow villagers, particularly for daHwa work. The main reason give by those preferring wage labor is the ability to control the work pace with the exception of lineage market households who note the difficulty in organizing nafir as their primary reason for turning to wage labor.

Female headed households evidence a slightly different pattern in labor recruitment. Nafir labor still provides the dominant source for all but the lineage subsistence households who rely instead on the beneficence of brothers. Nonetheless, female sponsored nafir parties tend to be half as large (six to eight participants) as those held by their male counterparts, and despite the fact that on average female households contribute 40 labor days to the nafir parties held by other farmers. Only small-scale capitalist households employ an average of two wage laborers for their fields, though no daHwa laborers.

Business Enterprise Activities

As in most villages throughout the Nuba Mountains, the successful reproduction of households in Shatt Damam requires careful consideration of needs and resources. Access to the resources alone, however, is not always sufficient to reproduce a household over time.[11] This depends on a variety of factors which can forestall even the most basic reproduction of a household; composition may change unexpectedly, meager grain stores may frustrate the sponsoring of a nafir, insufficient cash reserves may prevent the hiring of labor, or rains may be sporadic. Any of these can represent the difference between meeting household subsistence requirements and its disintegration through out-migration or chronic indebtedness to the shayl.

The type of business household members engage in is based not only on the complex interaction between the household's composition and resource base but on the geographical location of the village, as well as its relationship with the wider encompassing society. Proximity to Kadugli and the limited monetization of the village economy opens up distinct business possibilities. Yet ownership of a business does not automatically infer capitalist status on a household. The operation of a business may only be intermittent at best and provide the means necessary for a household to hire additional labor, sponsor a nafir, or procurement of food during the 'hungry season' prior to the ripening of grain in the jubraka. In addition, household-owned businesses (like off-farm employment) may also lend flexibility to a household in the marketing of its crops or livestock, lowering its dependence on the local jellaba and village shayl.

Table 9.10 provides information on the percent of households owning businesses and the mean number households owned. Although 20 percent of sampled households have businesses, their importance varies significantly by (re)production form. Both of the capitalist entrepreneurs derive some 96 percent of their incomes from a variety of enterprises, while household businesses contribute nearly 26 percent to incomes of slightly more than 42 percent of small-scale capitalist households. Businesses enterprises are less important for lineage market households with just 9.5 percent operating an enterprise, and comprise only 3.2 percent of the incomes of these households. Lineage subsistence households own no businesses.

Significant differences exist in the numbers and types of business activities pursued by households (table 9.11). The business ventures engaged in by capitalist entrepreneurs stand out in stark contrast to those owned by other two (re)production forms. All of the enterprises owned by the capitalist entrepreneurs require substantial inputs of capital which

TABLE 9.10
Percent of Households Owning Business Enterprises, by (Re)Production Form

All households	CE	SC	LM	LS	Total
% who own	100.0%	42.1%	9.5%	.0%	20.0%
Mean no. owned	3.5	1.4	1.0	—	1.7
(n=)	(2)	(19)	(21)	(18)	(60)

places these types of businesses out of the reach of the other households. Said Mohammed, for example, owns a general store, a lorry, and
a flour mill. In addition, he is a shayl-cum-grain broker. Most of the
money lending activities occur in the form of small grain advances.
Ironically, many of the more marginal households are forced to sell grain
to Mohammed only to have to borrow some at a future date; repayment
is not in equivalent amounts. Abdullah Said also owns a general store
but he also rents sewing machines to the village tailor and markets the
finished products in Kadugli's large suq. Like his brother Said, he too is
a shayl. Another business activity, though requiring more moderate outlays of capital is tailoring. Kuku Hamdan and Kuku Jama'a, both small-
scale capitalists, rent pedal operated sewing machines and sew garments
by order. They remarked that the income is lower than in Kadugli but
that tailoring does not interfere with their farming activities.

Small-scale capitalist and lineage market households operate a wide
variety of low capital input enterprises such as thatch cutting, charcoal
making, and constructing bed frames. Most of these activities are undertaken during the dry season and therefore do not detract from household
member's agricultural tasks or nafir obligations. Only Tia Moju operates
his business year round, baking bread for the few wealthy households in
Shatt Damam. He places the loaves on a large round metal tray and covers
them with a an shallow round cylindrical wash basin.[12] He then covers the
top of the basin with hot coals to complete his make-shift oven. On average, low capital pursuits generate little income but the benefits to the
household's economic security should not be minimized.

Businesses activities pursued by females illustrates the restrictive and
more precarious position in which women find themselves in petty trade.
A noted feature of these businesses is that they fall within the female
domain and thus do not conflict with male operated enterprises. Koshi
brews marissa, primarily for young unmarried or to farmers needing additional marissa for their nafir. Three young women from a female headed
household reside in Kadugli during the dry season where they pump and
transport water for sale to private residences. The work is hard. Throughout the day the women fill and carry five gallon jerry cans; profits are
small. Women also contribute to household security through irregular sales
of surplus vegetables and chickens, particularly in the large suq in Kadugli.
Although the money belongs solely to women, invariably all members of
the household benefit from the necessities it purchases.

TABLE 9.11
Type of Enterprise Owned by (Re)Production Form

Type of enterprise	CE	SC	LM	Total
general store	28.6%	.0%	.0%	10.0%
agricultural broker/shayl	28.6	.0	.0	10.0
flour mill	14.3	.0	.0	5.0
lorry transport	14.3	.0	.0	5.0
rent sewing machines	14.3	.0	.0	5.0
tailor	.0	18.2	.0	10.0
bakery	.0	9.1	.0	5.0
make beds	.0	18.2	.0	10.0
cut thatch	.0	9.1	.0	5.0
brew marissa	.0	9.1	.0	5.0
make charcoal	.0	9.1	.0	5.0
carry water	.0	18.2	100.0	20.0
sell salt/onions	.0	9.1	.0	5.0
Total	100%	100%	100%	100%
(Total n of enterprises)	(7)	(11)	(2)	(20)

Off-Farm Employment

Every household within Shatt Damam cultivates a main farm as well as a jubraka, ostensibly to satisfy the household's basic food requirements. This is true even for the capitalist entrepreneurial households who otherwise are in a position to purchase all of their household necessities from the market. Hence, a household's access to sufficient land, by definition, determines its ability to meet the requirements of its basic reproduction over time. Given both the relative and absolute shortage of land confronting the villagers, not every household attains this goal. Strategies to offset this dilemma can assume any number of forms: lowering consumption levels—but this leads to a decline in nutritional levels and caloric intake and reduces the capacity of members to labor in the fields; abandoning or reducing the size and number of household nafirs—but this adds to the labor load of household members; and, curtailing the sharing marissa with age-mates—but at the cost of losing social prestige.[13] On the other hand, as noted, household members acquire cash incomes through business activities. Of greater importance for household livelihood strategies in Shatt Damam is off-farm employment which is undertaken by 70 percent of all households.

The integration of Shatt Damam within the wider Sudanese political economy presents certain structural imperatives for household reproduction. The types of employment Shatt routinely engage in reveals nothing if not the manner of that integration. In general, occasions for off-farm employment favor unskilled laborers, in part due to the paucity of employment opportunities within the village, but also because the low level of education prevents most Shatt from gaining access to other occupations requiring a higher degree of skill. Here too we must recall that outside of this localized region, the Shatt are considered "different" or "strange." Public discrimination therefore effectively restricts the Shatt to low-paying manual-labor positions. It is not surprising then that only four males have semi-skilled employment, all within the village of Shatt Damam. Furthermore, women face an additional barrier to securing employment, even as servants in Kadugli; many have a limited grasp of the Arabic language. Occupations for slightly more than 20 percent of the male household members is unknown, only that they are in Khartoum. In all probability, if working, they are intermittent day laborers on construction sites.

Closer examination of off-farm employment among households suggests the difficulties most households have in meeting their basic consumption requirements through household-based endeavors (table 9.12). Some 74 percent of small-scale capitalist, 86 percent of lineage market, and 56 percent of lineage subsistence households have at least one member engaged in employment off the farm (no member of capitalist entrepreneurial households works). The high incidence of daHwa labor further reveals the extent of economic stress besetting a number of households. Not surprising, with the absence of other opportunities, females dominate daHwa labor. As with the other types of unskilled employment, daHwa, in particular, does not allow for capital accumulation. At best, off-farm employment merely forestalls the immediate disintegration of the household since nearly 63 percent of males must leave the village to gain employment.

Migration Activities

An elder's ability to control juniors and females depends largely on access to and size of landholdings, by far the most important resources.

TABLE 9.12
Distribution of Off-Farm Employment, by Sex and (Re)Production Form

Male	SC	LM	LS	Total
Semiskilled employment				
store clerk	.0	4.0	.0	1.7
flour mill attendant	5.0	.0	.0	1.7
medical technician	5.0	.0	.0	1.7
tailor	5.0	.0	.0	1.7
Unskilled employment				
tend livestock	.0	12.0	7.1	6.8
manual laborer	42.0	48.4	42.8	45.8
agricultural laborer	5.0	8.2	.0	5.1
daHwa	20.0	16.0	7.1	15.3
don't know	15.0	12.0	42.8	20.3
Total	100%	.0%	100%	100%
(n=)	(20)	(25)	(14)	(59)
Female				
Unskilled employment				
daHwa	92.3	100.0	100.0	97.8
manual laborer	7.7	.0	.0	2.2
Total	100%	100%	100%	100%
(n=)	(13)	(23)	(9)	(45)

Not only do landholdings directly influence the household size and organizational structure, but the possibility for economic success and material well being. Other factors, to be sure, come into play; adherence to the gender and generational division of labor, brideprice/brideservice and the circulation of women, and local concepts of appropriate patterns of consumption. Yet without the promise of land, little incentive exists to retain young men, let alone ensure their obedience. Coupled with limited local economic opportunities, 27.6 percent of male household members migrate (table 9.13). In fact, almost 62 percent of households have at least one member temporarily migrating. Rates of return, however, do not bode well for the household anticipating a reunion; 87.5 percent of former household members reside outside of Shatt Damam with 47 percent of the migrants living in Khartoum.[14]

Temporary out-migration, as in other Nuba communities, is not new. As elsewhere, Shatt left in the past to amass the necessities of brideprice,

TABLE 9.13
Patterns of Temporary Migration by (Re)Production Form

	CE	SC	LM	LS	Total
Households					
% w/migrants	100.0%	57.9%	81.0%	38.9%	61.7%
mean number	10.5	1.5	1.5	1.4	2.0
% of household members by sex					
Male	70.6%	21.4%	29.6%	18.9%	27.6%
Female	50.0	2.9	1.2	.0	3.8

TABLE 9.14
Primary Reason for Temporary Migration by Sex and (Re)Production Form

	CE	SC	LM	LS	Total
Male					
employment	.0%	86.7%	83.4%	80.0%	67.2%
seek employment	.0	.0	4.2	10.0	3.3
tend livestock	.0	.0	8.3	10.0	4.9
attend school	50.0	6.7	.0	.0	11.7
visiting	.0	.0	4.2	.0	1.6
fear for security	50.0	.0	.0	.0	9.8
village conflict	.0	6.7	.0	.0	1.6
Total	100%	100%	100%	100%	100%
(n=)	(12)	(15)	(24)	(10)	(61)
Female					
visiting	.0	100.0	100.0	.0	37.5
fear for security	100.0	.0	.0	.0	62.5
Total	100%	100%	.0%	100%	100%
(n=)	(5)	(2)	(1)	(0)	(8)

either through herding cattle or working as a common laborers in the city. Reasons behind migration have altered only slightly (table 9.14). Two exceptions include migration for security and higher education. Both capitalist entrepreneurial household heads sent all of their family members to Kadugli during the high point of military activity against the Sudanese People's Liberation Army in South Kordofan. Other children were already residing in Kadugli where they attend secondary school. Over 75 percent of male migrants continue to leave the village for economic reasons, with 44 percent going only as far as Kadugli and another 29 percent as far as Khartoum and Gezira. In general, females tend to remain in Shatt Damam. So too with former female members who married; 87.5 percent still reside in Shatt Damam.

Remittances of cash, food, and clothing by temporary migrants augment the incomes of 18.3 percent of households with over 29 percent of male migrants sending an average of £S 57, and food and clothing an average of one time per annum.[15] The small amounts of remittances underscores the types of employment Shatt obtain and not necessarily a lack of lineage obligation and household concern. Nearly 21 percent of permanent male migrants also send money, food, and clothing, though less regularly, and the amounts are negligible (an average of £S 7 per annum). Nevertheless, out-migration of young males for longer and longer periods can be expected to further undermine the lineage system, both with the loss of labor and the break in the traditional means of marriage as more young men marry while migrating without the intercession of their elders.

Of the three villages, Shatt Damam perhaps best exemplifies the impacts of modernization on premodern societies, especially in its more subtle forms. Outward appearances may suggest little if any change from the past, yet closer inspection reveals a different story. Further, what is happening within the village is rarely a long-term conscious strategy on the part of villagers; they simply react to present circumstances and try to cope in the ways known and open to them. Yet these strategies are slowly and silently dismantling the lineage system and eroding the basis of the moral economy.

Notes

1. For these reasons and for sampling purposes, Kadamiro was selected for this study. It should be emphasized that in all other aspects these communities are similar.
2. The "Arabized" Nuba such as the Miri and Kadugli, for example, laugh derisively at the Shatt. Consequently, a number of people would scratch their heads in wonderment that I was undertaking fieldwork in Shatt Damam instead of a more "civilized" village. One Miri man I was talking to in Kadugli found it hard to believe that the Shatt practiced matrilinear inheritance and thought it a rather peculiar custom.
3. One Shatt man's wife in Kadamiro was a Dinka from the southern area of South Kordofan.

4. When I first arrived in Shatt Damam, some of the Shatt took me on a tour of the village. They never introduced me to the merchants. Later when I asked them why one man replied: "Because they are not Shatt, they are just here."
5. The strength of these bonds cannot be overstated. In fact, one of the difficulties in pinpointing the Shatt household is the common practice of sharing meals and living quarters, especially with one's age-mate. As this is a relatively common occurrence, however, the numbers even out leaving the household relatively intact.
6. With respect to household size and age structure, female headed households differ little from table 7.1. Differences are attributable to earlier age of marriage of women and the fact that the female heads are primarily divorced or widowed.

Female headed households	SC	LM	LS	Total
% female headed	30.0%	40.0%	30.0%	100.0%
Mean household size	4.7	6.5	3.7	5.1
Mean member age	19.8	21.2	15.3	19.5
Mean number age <16	9.3	7.5	4.7	7.3
mean age of head	40.7	40.3	34.7	38.6
(n=)	(3)	(4)	(3)	(10)

7. Size and Age Structure of Jointly Headed Households by (Re)production Form

Joint headed households	SC	LM	LS	Total
% joint headed	9.1%	27.3%	63.6%	100.0%
Mean household size	10.1	8.0	6.3	7.1
Mean member age	15.8	17.0	19.3	18.2
Mean number age <16	7.5	7.4	7.7	7.6
mean age of head	39.0	30.0	33.0	32.8
(n=)	(1)	(3)	(7)	(11)

8. Men can, however, gain access to the dura of wives through "legitimate" requests for marissa.
9. Cattle sales throughout Shatt Damam are negligible due to their store of value, symbolic prestige, and use in brideprice. Goats overwhelmingly make up livestock sales.
10. Traditionally, females cultivated "near" farms; lands close to the protective hills of the village. Males, to the contrary, worked the "far" farms, located on the fertile plains at a distance from the village. Land inheritance patterns thus favors males.
11. For some households, the size of landholding is such that successful reproduction strictly through agricultural activities requires optimal conditions.
12. The wash basins are made by cutting the ends from 55 gallon drums and are generally used for scrubbing cloths.
13. In this case, reduction in the intake of food is not distributed evenly within the household; females tend to suffer disproportionately.
14. The number of former residents living in Khartoum provides an important network for new arrivals and in fact helps determine choice of destination.
15. Temporary migrants from small-scale capitalist households remit an average of £S 25 per year, £S 98 for lineage market households, and £S 34 for lineage subsistence households.

10

Conclusion

In conclusion, I return to the theoretical and substantive issues with which I began this book and offer some final reflections upon them in light of the analysis of the formation of households and livelihood strategies in the three Nuba Mountain villages of Somasem, Shair Tomat, and Shatt Damam. It is clear that the issues raised by this research experience do not begin and end in the Nuba Mountains. It is not possible to abstract a single household or even village from its context without recourse to the encompassing imperatives of global forces of change. This statement is not meant as an interdiction against more bounded micro-level studies; certainly these have merit. Nevertheless, the breadth of modernization now extends beyond mere geographical, political, and regional boundaries, while still providing the backdrop against which social life unfolds. At the same time, the development process has been and continues to be unevenly experienced, guided as much by local particularities of traditional organization, economy, and rural life. The historical transformation of the Nuba Mountains and other regions also point to the need for a more sophisticated treatment of what is popularly termed development; one that permanently eschews notions of progress, unilinearity, and homogeneity, yet one that can accomodate ideas of modernization and globalism. The methodological challenge, however, is to effectively combine theory with empirical circumstance, and structure with agency.

Overview

The realization that the Nuba Mountains is a complex society structured by multiple modes of social organization reveals the need for more focused consideration on what is broadly termed development; specifically, we are lacking in our comprehension of the dynamics and mechanisms associated with the interrelation between premodern and modern societies. And, when the structural parameters to human behavior are multiple, there is considerable latitude, and empirical variations abound in the way practices are actually constituted. The continuous capacity of transformation is thus both simultaneously internal and external to a given society.

In order to transcend earlier lines of reasoning, equating modernization with convergence, we chose to reinterpret modernization—specifically over how and to what degree the Nuba Mountains has been integrated into the wider Sudanese society and the world beyond—in such a way that neither outcome nor form is inevitable; development, after all, has proven to be an uneven and unpredictable process in the Nuba Mountains, as elsewhere. How this issue is resolved has great import for our understanding of household livelihood strategies and, ultimately, of the multiform dimensions of rural transformation. There is no reason for a process that was slow and extremely complex in Europe to be swift and decisive in the Nuba Mountains.

An additional line of inquiry also concerned variations in smallholders or the peasantry and, specifically, comprehending small-scale producers through considerations of patterns of social differentiation, market integration, and overall extent of modernization. And, for us, the household provides a convenient unit of analysis with which to scrutinize this process and its effects on the everyday lives of people. This directly addresses the extent and meaning of modernity. What must be recalled is that the production and sale of goods was hardly new to the Nuba Mountains and was under way long before Condominium rule. What differs now is the intensity and extent of transactions—the widening and deepening of calculable actions. Previously, the production and purchase of goods and services was largely intermittent, undertaken essentially in the forms of tribute and exchange of use-values. The local economy in which these activities took place allowed for the reproduction of what was primarily internal to a village. Although the current process of market rationalization is turning production towards exchange-value, the formal separation of business enterprise from domestic unit is far from clear. As Netting (1993:226) recognizes in his own study, smallholders are remarkably resilient and have survived "even in developed capitalist economies such as those of Germany and Japan." Nevertheless, not all smallholders are the same; i.e., they do not all share the same conditions of existence.

In the end, dialogue is important and illustrates the complexities of the issue. It is only through a vigorous exchange of ideas that we begin to grasp the nature and meaning of change, as well as what makes change possible in the first place. I chose to explore this issue through the study of households and the livelihood strategies that households formulate to ensure their reproduction, at least in the short-run. And, rather than posit a homogeneous undifferentiated peasantry, households were differentiated on the basis of capitalist and lineage principles of organization. The conceptualization offered here, in these concluding pages, thus begins in the broad sweep of historical forces and ends with a consideration of the impacts of modernity on the everyday lives of the people of the Nuba Mountains. Further, a comparative perspective, drawing important inferences at the community level, allows for a more refined understanding of households and livelihood strategies relative to their local contexts, and permits greater appreciation of how the respective villages are incorporated into the wider society. But, first, some summarizing statements are in order.

Household is the unit of analysis. As an organizing concept, household represents a universal presence that facilitates comparative inquiry. It is operationally defined as a group of individuals (rarely one) who identify with a specific domicile and whose livelihood efforts, in the broad sense, are focused towards "mutual" survival. Household, thus, is a way by which individuals are effectively grouped and, for the researcher, it is an especially important one in areas where small-scale agricultural production predominates. This requires an understanding of the internal characteristics of households with the resources and activities of its members, bearing in mind that households are ultimately irresoluble apart from the larger social formation. In this way, household serves to connect the individual to the wider environment, relating human agency with structure.

A recurring theme in the livelihood strategies is that they are not so much the intended outcome of conscious, purposive decision making, but more the "art of muddling through." Individual behavior per se, in and of itself, reveals little of consequence for social analysis; rather, the concern is with social relationships set against the backdrop of structure and process. It was argued that structural parameters condition livelihood strategies so that decisions are often arrived at by patterned human behavior, or in response to sudden changes in the actor's environment. And, for present purposes, I am convinced that an important line of inquiry relates to how individuals, as members of households, respond to the new opportunities and constraints presented by modernity and capitalism. Either way, actors seldom, if ever, have complete information, and the benefit of hindsight is often lost. The analysis of livelihood strategies, then, is undertaken with an aim to understanding the conditions underlying the formation of those strategies.

While we could have stratified the households solely according to scale indicators, such as age(s) of household head, income, size, and landholdings, this tends to homogenize or, even worse, to dismiss the relevance of the wider socioeconomic environment and the impress of history. To this end, households are differentiated according to (re)production forms: (1) capitalist entrepreneurial households with substantial nonagricultural business interests; (2) small-scale capitalist households which are *not* able to withdraw from the market in times of adversity; (3) lineage market households able to withdraw from and enter the market at will; (4) lineage subsistence households with minimal "market" relations; and (5) wage-labor households with supplemental agricultural production. This classification permits a more sophisticated treatment of the peasantry and rural transformation.

Comparative Perspectives

Nuba Mountains society has been increasingly integrated into the modern world over the past several decades. Here, as noted, modernization refers to the capacity for social transformation in terms of structural differentiation and the formal rationality of social organization and behavior. This process intensified during Condominium rule and, especially, since the creation of an independent Sudanese state. At first, the spread of cotton production was particularly important in extending a specifically capitalist market throughout the region. The cyclical nature of the world cotton market, coupled with marginal growing conditions, however, failed to fully reshape households and to routinize production for the market throughout the region. Today, the introduction of new technologies, most notably the tractor, have served to further intensify market-oriented production and to reorient the reproductive cycles of households from internal needs of subsistence to external requirements of profit.

Technology alone, however, cannot account for every change in the patterning of household activities. Certainly, other factors of equal importance include the monetization of obligations of juniors to elders, the spread of consumer goods, the increased value of education, and the expansion of nonagricultural employment opportunities. Needless to say, these processes have exerted a profound effect on how households look and what household members do. At the village level, those without the ability to expand agricultural production are invariably faced with the choice of either realizing other sources of cash incomes, especially through activities requiring out-migration, or lagging behind the culturally and socially acceptable consumption standards. Most households opt for the former, except those nearing a terminal or re-generating point in their "normal" life cycle. And, even then, most of these households are able to secure necessary goods from former household members through the obligations of lineage or through the Islamic institution of zakha (tithe giving).

The intensification of market activities does not immediately create a modern society, nor does it always lead to inequality within the villages—and when it does, it is not necessarily experienced in the same way or with similar consequences. Variations within and between categories of households abound. In this respect I have not constructed ideal-types that require no further explanation. In the Nuba Mountain case, the resiliency of some lineages cannot be underestimated. And, since the development process is invariably uneven, we should not expect homogeneous results. Further, we must anticipate differential effects, for there are significant social and economic variabilities within lineages. In short, there is no absolute logic of development, no "iron law" providing for neat unilinear outcomes; modernization can and does assume multiple paths.

Human responses to complex issues are seldom, if ever, crafted in isolation from life experiences. Most householders confront the sociocultural terrain from different perspectives and formulate livelihood strategies accordingly, on the basis of past decisions, present needs, and future expectations. These decisions, needs, and expectations are usually in line with the individual actor's perception of the "world" and his or her position in it. Moreover, past knowledge comes to people as tradition, which serves as a type of cognitive map used to interpret everyday occurrences and to guide daily activities. This can help to explain why some people find comfort in tradition; not every event must be processed and analyzed anew.[1] This in no way detracts from the merit of a householder's response; it simply reaffirms the fact that actors operate with a limited knowledge of structural parameters at any given point in space and time—an individual's world is indeed small.

Community

Unquestionably, the historical manner of integration of the three villages into the modern world varied. As a result, the distribution of life chances among the three villages reveals significant differences in opportunities and constraints. In the past, Condominium policies regarding the Nuba Mountains discriminated against the jallaba (Arab merchants) and attempted to isolate and "protect" the Nuba from Arabization. Clearly, these policies were untenable. On the other hand, Nuba contacts with Arabs predated Condominium rule, and many converted to Islam of their own accord. Now, migrants become exposed to Northern Sudanese lifestyles in urban centers, such as El Obeid and Khartoum, and bring new tastes, ideas, and perceptions back to the villages. Still, the heavy hand of government continues to alienate the Nuba, especially the Islamic relief agency *(Dawa al-Islamia)*, which implements the tacit state policy of religious proselytization in return for needed services.

In practice, the forces of modernization restructuring the Nuba Mountains are felt by every villager—young and old, male and female, Nuba and non-Nuba. The effects of these forces are real and observable in the daily routines of a village. Each villager, by virtue of this continuous process, recognizes malleabilities in parameters to behavior and, in the chapters directly concerned with the villages, I have pointed to some of the dimensions along which differentiation tends to run. Moreover, each village views its collective destiny differently—Somasem with indifference, Shair Tomat with hope, and Shatt Damam with rancor. The following presents a brief synopsis of the three villages.

Somasem. The Ghulfan Nuba of Somasem benefited from their early conversion to Islam, an abundance of arable lands, and a proximity to state-sponsored mechanized farming schemes such as Habila. Consequently, tractorization proceeded rather quickly, financed by some households converting cattle into cash and by some households acquiring money from returned migrants. The sociocultural and economic dislocation wrought by the Mahdist period opened up the area to "new ways of doing things," while the availability of tractors in the vicinity provided the means. Not everyone benefited from these changes; consequently, many households have been impoverished and their members compelled to sell their labor-power. Social differentiation and inequality are readily apparent in Somasem.

Shair Tomat. The Hawazma Arabs of Shair Tomat, on the other hand, were forced to adopt a sedentary agricultural life as a substitute for their earlier habit of raiding neighboring Nuba villages. Given the absolute paucity of arable lands for expansion and the fierce independence of the Hawazma, most households strive to balance agricultural needs with off-farm employment. The villagers, however, have accepted some forms of mechanization that have been made available by the Nuba Mountain Agricultural Production Corporation, though they still cultivate their new lands primarily with household labor. Certainly, too, the fact that they are Arabs provides them with some employment opportunities not open to non-Arabs. A strong sense of community well-being permeates Shair Tomat and has helped stem the more onerous effects of social differentiation and inequality.

Shatt Damam. Shatt Damam, to the contrary, has met with a remarkably dissimilar fate than have the other two villages. Aside from complications in consolidating landholdings, it is difficult for a Shatt to rent a tractor from a jallaba. And besides, it would mean abrogating the conventional notion of nafir and the subjective benefits of working together. On the other hand, the government is reticent to assist the Shatt precisely because they are not Arab or at least Arabized Nuba. Lastly, although land scarcity and monetization of brideprice and brideservice has long forced out-migration of the Shatt, as "Africanized" Nuba, alternatives to agricultural production are significantly limited. Apart from the "Fellata" merchants, the pace of social differentiation has been relatively slow, and inequality remains minor.

Household (Re)production Forms

The three villages of Somasem, Shair Tomat, and Shatt Damam were differentiated by a typology employing categories based on the household's (re)productive form. The following overviews these forms.

Capitalist Entrepreneurial Households. Capitalist entrepreneurial households generate their incomes in trade and transport, urban property, and moneylending. Most importantly, they function as brokers, monopolizing the flow of commodities into and from other households, relying on the age-old merchant credo of "buying cheap and selling dear." Differences in this (re)production form among the villages mainly have to do with availability of land resources, the structure of agriculture, and the character of the regional markets. Capitalist entrepreneurial households in Somasem, for instance, have rather extensive landholdings, are able to make better use of agricultural technologies, and employ wage-labor. Capitalist entrepreneurial households in Shair Tomat, on the other hand, operate at a more marginal level with respect to agricultural production. In Shatt Damam the capitalist entrepreneurial households—all outsiders—have virtually no landholdings and are not involved in agricultural production.

Small-Scale Capitalist Households. Small-scale capitalist households differ form capitalist entrepreneurial households in the scale of their economic operations. They also have invested in improved factors of production and are able to compete rather successfully with farms operated by capitalist entrepreneurs. Nonetheless, in this context the small-scale capitalist is not fully rationalized in the same sense because of their continued reliance on family labor in agricultural and nonagricultural activities. This allows for a degree of flexibility not open to capitalist entrepreneurs since small-scale capitalist households can intermittently leave the market. Yet, unlike lineage market households, total withdrawal is an illusion and not a realistic option. Flexibility also results largely from the diverse mixture of economic enterprises such that at least one guarantees a household's subsistence. Nonetheless, the distinction between capitalist entrepreneur and small-scale capitalist is not always clear, since it is more a matter of degree than of kind.

As with capitalist households, variations between small-scale capitalists among the three villages concern the diversity of economic opportunities. Overall, the expansion and/or intensification of agricultural production is constrained by a rigid land market and a constricted labor market. Consequently, small-scale capitalist households require a variety of business activities and off-farm employment in order to remain viable. Reliance on household instead of on wage-labor ironically limits their ability to accumulate and further erodes the communal labor system of nafir. Moreover, time spent in nonagricultural pursuits generally requires redundant household labor, however defined, in order to offset lost opportunity costs. More often than not, those left to labor in the fields, especially females, frequently find that their work hours increase.

Wage-Labor. The wage-labor households, like the capitalist entrepreneurial form, are distinguished by the separation of production from consumption within the household. Few households in the village willingly withdraw from agriculture of their own accord, although some do after members of the household secure relatively high-paying jobs. Not surprisingly, then, most wage-labor households are squeezed out of agriculture for a variety of reasons, including insufficient household labor, lack of agricultural surfeit for nafir, and pressing cash needs, such as repaying the shayl. Whatever the circumstances, once agriculture is abandoned it is difficult, if not impossible, to reenter without the money to obtain land and hire labor, for wage-labor erodes one's position within the village and, hence, one's ability to organize nafir. Further, wage-labor pursuits detract from household-owned and -operated businesses; wages are generally too low to afford any significant accumulation, and the time demands are too consuming to allow for other activities.

Lineage Market Households. Both lineage (re)production forms differ substantively from those created via capitalist economic activities. Only within Shatt Damam are lineage forms dominant, and the lineage in general continues to provide important bases for social organization, though certainly different than in past times. In part, this is due to the Shatt people's commitment to their ideological and economic life. Lineage forms within Somasem and Shair Tomat are certainly more marginal and exist in large measure by the conscious maintenance of lineage ties to kinsmen residing within the villages, as well as those in other nearby villages. In the case of Somasem, lineage members also live in close physical proximity, removed from the dominant commercial center of Shardi. In the face of current changes induced by civil war in the Sudan, the long-term outlook for these forms is not good.

Lineage market households, as noted earlier, are similar to small-scale capitalist households, with the essential exception that they are able to withdraw from the market, even permanently. The greater proportion of these household forms in relation to their subsistence, nevertheless, provides evidence of the growing importance of commercial activities in everyday life, at least cyclically. Essentially, the breakdown in the lineage households, in general, occurs with the intensification of market activities and the loss of young men through out-migration. At a certain juncture, withdrawal from the market is no longer possible. With the erosion of the lineage market form, the viability of lineage subsistence households is also at risk, particularly with the demise of kin-based and communally organized labor and resource sharing.

Lineage Subsistence Households. Lineage subsistence households are relatively self-sufficient and rarely engage in market activities, and then only in terms of trade and barter—money merely assumes another item for barter. Members of these households did not historically specialize in the production of certain goods for trade and so devote the majority of their labors to meeting household needs. The success of the reproduction of this form is most intimately subject to the requirements of a reciprocally-based communal labor system, most notably nafir. With the exception of Shatt Damam, the lineage subsistence form is comprised of aging households, which indicates the depth of the erosion of the lineage system and the reorientation in the livelihood strategies of younger householders.

Social Differentiation

Class/status, gender, generation, ethnicity, and religion affect the viability of households and directly determine the economic opportunities open to household members. At the historical level we find that the complexities of people's lives often places them in a variety of social relations of inequality, even within the same household. Households are not egalitarian institutions, nor are they tranquil islands in the press of change; they are real sites for the struggle over resources. For example, it is one thing for a junior to labor for his father (elder) within a lineage complex, but it is quite another thing when that same junior also works for wages off of the farm, or when he himself makes saddles to be sold in the local market. When other household members are also engaged in multiple social relations, the potential for internal household conflict increases. Some tensions strengthen the household; others lead to its disintegration.

Overall, relations engendered within the tributary system are passing out of existence. In the main, these types of relations, when they were the norm, depended upon the relative isolation of village communities and the sanctity of local religions. The expansion of the capitalist economy and the advance of Islam are eroding older lineages. Lineage relations nonetheless continue to provide important bases for social organization, though in different ways than in the past. Elders continue to demand benefits from juniors and women through such mechanisms as brideprice, nafir labor, remittances, and domestic/agricultural activities. Present patterns of change associated with modernization, however, are intensifying, as evidenced by the employment of fellow villagers, government-sponsored agricultural schemes, out-migration, local markets, and the shayl.

Concluding Comments

It is often difficult to distinguish social cause from social effect or, for that matter, to argue convincingly about the social antecedents of contemporary conditions. For this reason three villages were studied in an effort to understand, at least in these particular instances, the diversity of the Nuba Mountains. Here I present some conclusions regarding salient trends in household formation and the livelihood strategies designed to ensure their survival.

The paucity of lands, either for the entry into or the expansion of agriculture, is exacerbating tensions within the village community. Within areas where commercial agriculture and market penetration is greatest, those households that did not or that are unable to expand agricultural production find that they must increasingly seek and devote more time to generating livelihoods off the farm. Individuals unable to acquire land invariably migrate. This strikes at the core of older lineage relations and undermines at least the pretence that a junior will eventually become an elder. It also calls into question the social valuation of wealth, once exclusively assigned to agricultural products and cattle. Consequently, the orientation of agricultural production is increasingly for sale purposes and less for domestic consumption. So, too, with cattle, which are becoming capital investments ("chattel") rather than a symbol of status and a means to assure that sons are married well. In effect, the privatization and commercialization of production occurs at the expense of lineage relations.

The erosion of communal labor systems from a variety of directions contributes to the undermining of the older lineage system and reorients agricultural production towards the household rather than the community. In short, households are approaching the "classic" smallholder fusion of enterprise and household. The use of nafir labor is rapidly deteriorating as external pressures are felt in the villages, particularly in the face of out-migration. The initial monetization of brideprice provided new sources of wealth accumulation for village elders, but it also compelled young men to migrate. This trend continues, along with the expansion of a cash-based economy, although now more villagers migrate, thus reducing the sources of potential nafir in the local setting. Increasingly, households are forced to seek wage-labor and the cash necessary for its deployment. All of these activities bring market forces deeper into the village.

The sustainability of many communities is questionable, as evidenced by the deterioration of older patterns of inter- and intra-household cooperation and mutual assistance, in part due to the increased commercialization of the local economy. In such circumstances, communities are unable to withstand widespread calamities, placing more people at risk during periods of misfortune, such as the drought of 1984. Personal ties of obligation engendered within lineage relations no longer operate to spread hardships throughout the community during particularly onerous times.

The rigidity of land markets also pushes households increasingly into nonagricultural commodity production and wage-labor sales in an effort to meet their reproduction requirements. Households with small parcels of land are also looking towards other income-generating activities. It is not unusual to see household members engaged in a variety of income-generating activities in order to ensure at least a minimum household subsistence. Of course, the availability of a variety of economic opportunities is what gives smallholders their resilience, such that the notion of the "disappearing middle" is not much of a concern.

New patterns of gender inequality have worsened opportunities for women relative to those for men, however. Female heads of households, as with females in general, face a different set of constraints than do their male counterparts, due in part to the erosion of kinship relations such as brother-sister bonds, the inability to meet agricultural labor needs, and the greatly limited off-farm employment opportunities. Further, the out-migration of men contributes to the already heavy work load of women. Females in Muslim households face further constraints, though the intensity of seclusion is tempered by the wealth of the household

and its reliance on their labor in the fields. In this respect, female seclusion assumes the form of a status symbol, a measure of a man's wealth.

With the passing of lineage society, households are increasingly structured by nonlineage relations. Relations of seniority still persist but are
increasingly restricted to individual households rather than to trans-
household lineage relations. In the communal sense, access to the labor
of the young is thus becoming more problematic. Children still help
out,but assistence is directed primarily to their immediate households
and then, frequently, with off-farm sources of income rather than with
contributions of labor to household needs. This is particularly the case
of members of the capitalist entrepreneurial and small-scale capitalist
households. Those households with greater access to production factors, such as land and labor, are able to secure reasonably well-paying
employment for their children, primarily as civil servants/military personnel, merchants, or teachers.

These conclusions make no attempt to argue an irreversible household or village trajectory resembling a predetermined outcome of desti-
tution for the many and the "good life" for the few. On the other hand,
the conditions in which household livelihood strategies are forged are
not voluntaristic in the sense that people have unlimited choices. The
trends I have outlined demonstrate clear forces that channel these transformations, but a given village does not one day simply resolve to become modern and replace older lineage relations. The observed trends
created by individuals—deciding to sell agricultural surfeit to purchase
better farming implements, migrating to Habila to earn brideprice, or
deciding to employ hired labor for their agricultural enterprises because
it is easier to control than the local nafir—usually have not been dramatic. Change is generally incremental and, thus, the impact of decisions is often slow to unfold. Exactly how developmental processes will
eventually restructure the social organization of rural villages in the Nuba
Mountains region remains to be seen.

Epilogue

Recent events—particularly the escalation and brutality of the civil
war—have pushed the Nuba to reevaluate their relation to the Sudanese
nation-state. The category of nation-state itself implies an inherent complexity that tends to magnify Nuba disenchantment with a centralized

Sudan run by Arabs from the north. The history of violent incursions into the Nuba Mountains seems endless; people are still being torn from their villages and must seek sanctuary deeper into the hills. The Beshir/ Tourabi regime in Khartoum has unquestionably intensified the civil war in the Nuba Mountains area of Kordofan. Recent occurrences in the Nuba Mountains continue to bear this out. According to world news sources and human rights organizations, those unlucky in finding sanctuary are being transported northward and placed into forced labor. A front page article in the *New York Times* (16 September 1992) reported that "50,000 Nuba have been relocated in the last two months from their homeland in southern Kordofan Province to camps in the northern part of the province." The British- and U.S.-based Africa Watch (9/8/92) further reported that "men are taken to labor camps in large commercial farms and the women and children to work as domestic servants in northern Arab households." Other reports such as *Amnesty International* cite the existence of "killing fields"—massive graves filled with Nuba bodies. And now the military has been given orders "to shoot on sight" in an effort to ethnically cleanse the region (*Sudan Democratic Gazette*, November 1994). It is these latest atrocities, in addition to past enmity, that one finds particularly distressful.

Given present conditions in the Nuba Mountains, it is increasingly difficult to find much to be optimistic about in this region today. The continued conflict is destroying the economy, is ripping apart the socio-cultural fabric, and, more importantly, has cost the lives of thousands of Nuba. This civil war is different from its predecessor, for it is clearly the riverain "Arabs" against the rest of the population and is fueled by the currents of Islamic fundamentalism currently sweeping across North Africa. Now, the Muslim fundamentalist dominated government in Khartoum is actively trying to Arabize the non-Muslim Nuba. Sadly, the prognosis for their survival is not favorable, and it appears that the last vestiges of the Nuba Mountains' lineage past will finally be swept away, swiftly and decisively, in the blink of an eye.

Note

1. Tradition is not stagnant nor constant, but always changes. The traditions of one generation may or may not be those of the preceding one. This in no way invalidates tradition, setting it at opposite ends of a "development" pole; it merely underscores the fact that references change with current realities.

Appendix

Source of Household Labor for Main Farm Cropping Activities by Village. Percent of feddans cultivated and sacks of sorghum/millet threshed by type of labor.

Activity	Shair Tomat			Somasem			Shatt Dammam		
	FL	WL	NL	FL	WL	NL	FL	WL	NL
Clear	**91.1**	7.4	1.5	69.9	**29.3**	0.8	62.2	20.9	**16.9**
Plow/plant	**65.7**	34.3	0.0	8.6	**90.7**	0.7	78.8	12.9	**8.3**
1st weed	**67.2**	14.6	18.2	71.7	2.4	25.9	42.5	22.1	**35.4**
2nd weed	**82.4**	12.0	5.5	36.9	**53.6**	9.5	83.9	10.6	5.5
Harvest	**82.1**	12.6	5.3	65.7	**61.0**	3.3	51.6	14.1	**34.3**
Thresh	**67.1**	28.8	4.1	22.2	**74.2**	3.6	62.6	19.0	**18.4**
		MMFS=10.75		MMFS=17.98		MMFS=5.67			

FL=family labor   WL=wage-labor   NL=nafir labor   MMFS=mean main farm size

Bibliography

Affan, K. 1984. *Towards an Appraisal of the Tractorisation Experience in Rainlands of Sudan.* Development Studies and Research Centre: Monograph series no. 19. Faculty of Economic and Social Studies, University of Khartoum.

Ahmed, A. 1976. *Aspects of Pastoral Nomadism in Sudan.* Khartoum: Economic and Social Research Council.

Aijmer, G. n.d. "Some Reflexions on the Notion of 'Household.'" Unpublished manuscript.

Ali, G. 1980. "Industry and Peripheral Capitalism in the Sudan." Unpublished Ph.D. dissertation. Los Angeles: University of California.

Amin, S. 1976. *Unequal Exchange: An Essay on the Social Formations of Peripheral Capitalism.* New York: Monthly Review Press.

Badigian, D., and Harlan J. 1983. *Economic Botany.* Nuba Agriculture and Ethnobotany: 37(4), pp. 384–95.

Barnett, T. 1977. *The Gezira Scheme: The Illusion of Development.* London: Frank Cass.

Barry, S. 1984. *Households, Decision Making, and Rural Development: Do We Need to Know More?* Development Discussion Paper, no. 167. Harvard Institute for International Development, Harvard University.

Bauer, P.T. 1984. *Reality and Rhetoric: Studies in the Economics of Development.* Cambridge: Harvard University Press.

Baumann, G. 1987. *National Integration and Local Integrity.* London: Clarendon Press.

Bell, G.W. 1938. Nuba Agricultural Methods and Beliefs, Sudan Notes and Records; XXI, pp. 237–49.

Benton, T. 1984. *The Rise and Fall of Structural Marxism: Althusser and His Influence.* London: MacMillan.

Beshir, M.O. 1970. *The Southern Sudan: Background to Conflict.* London: Hurst.

Bjorkelo, A. 1989. *Prelude to the Mahdiyya: Peasant and Traders in the Shendi Region, 1821–1885.* Cambridge: Cambridge University Press.

Bolton, A.R.C. 1948. "Land Tenure in Agricultural Land Use in the Sudan," in *Agriculture in the Sudan.* Edited by J.D. Tothill. London: Oxford University Press.

Bouquest, M., and de Haan, H. 1987. "Kinship as an Analytical Category in Rural Sociology: An Introduction." *Sociologia Ruralis*, XXVII (4), pp. 243–62.

Bruce, J. 1873. *Travels in Abyssinia and Nubia*. Edinburgh: Black.

Burckhardt, J.L. 1822. *Travels in Nubia*. London: John Murray.

Campbell, J. 1988. *The Power of Myth*. New York: Doubleday.

Chayanov, A.V. 1986. *The Theory of Peasant Economy*. Translated and edited by D. Thorner, R.E.F. Smith, and B. Kerblay. Madison: University of Wisconsin Press.

Collins, C. 1976. *Colonialism and Class Struggle in Sudan*. Middle East Research and Information Project; no.46, pp. 3–20.

Cooper, F. 1981. "Peasants, Capitalists, and Historians." *Journal of Southern African Studies*; 7 (2), pp. 284–314.

Corkhill, N. 1939. The Kambala and Other Seasonal Festivals of the Kadugli and Miri Nuba. Sudan Notes and Records; XXII, pp. 205–19.

Daly, M.W. 1986. *Empire on the Nile: The Anglo-Egyptian Sudan, 1898–1934*. Cambridge: Cambridge University Press.

Davidson, A. 1991. "Rethinking Household Livelihood Strategies," in *Research in Rural Sociology and Development: Household Survival Strategies*, Volume 5, pp. 11–28. Edited by D. Clay and H. Schwarzweller. Greenwich, Conn.: JAI Press.

———. 1989. "Mode of Production: Impasse or Passe?" *Journal of Contemporary Asia*; 19 (3), pp. 243–78.

Davidson, A., and Schwarzweller, H. 1995. "Marginality and Uneven Development: The Decline of Dairying in Michigan's North Country." *Sociologia Ruralis*; XXXV(1), pp. 40–66.

Deere, C. 1990. *Household and Class Relations: Peasants and Landlords in Northern Peru*. Berkeley: University of California Press.

de Jonge, K. 1985. "Demographic Developments and Class Contradictions in a 'Domestic' Community: The Nyakyusa (Tanzania) Before Colonial Conquest, in *Old Modes of Production and Capitalist Encroachment: Anthropological Explorations in Africa*, pp. 39–70. Edited by W. Binsbergen and P. Geschiere. London: KPI.

Democratic Republic of the Sudan, Department of Statistics. *1983 Census*. Population Studies Centre, University of Gezira, Faculty of Economics and Rural Development. Gezira, Sudan; Project doc. no. 1.

Duffield, M. 1981. *Maiurno: Capitalism and Rural Life in Sudan*. London: Ithaca Press.

Dunn, S.C. 1921. Native Gold Washings in the Nuba Mountains Province. Sudan Notes and Records; IV, pp. 139–45.

El-Din, A.S. 1983. "A Survey of the Sudanese Economy," in *Socio-Economic Change in the Sudan.* Edited by M.H. Awad. Graduate College Publications, Selected Essays: Monograph 6, University of Khartoum, pp. 11–38.

Elles, R.J. 1935. The Kingdom of Tegali. Sudan Notes and Records, XVIII, pp. 1–35.

Ewald, J. 1991. *Soldiers, Traders, and Slaves.* Madison: University of Wisconsin Press.

———. 1982. *Leadership and Social Change on an Islamic Frontier: The Kingdom of Taqali, 1700–1900.* Ph.D. dissertation, Department of History, University of Wisconsin.

Fadlalla, B. 1986. "Financing Regionalization in the Sudan: Centre-Region Fiscal and Financial Relations," in *Perspectives on Development in the Sudan,* pp. 187–238. Edited by P. Van der Wel and A.G.M. Ahmed. The Hague:Institute of Social Studies and Development Studies and Research Centre.

Fernandez-Kelly, M. 1982. *For We Are Sold, I and My People: Women and Industry in Mexico's Frontier.* Albany: State University Press of New York.

Fife, C. 1927. *Savage Life in Black Sudan.* Philadelphia: Lippincott.

Fortes, M. 1958. Introduction to *The Development Cycle in Domestic Groups,* by J. Goody. Cambridge: Cambridge University Press.

Friedmann, H. 1986a. "Postscript: Small Commodity Production." *Journal of Canadian Labour Studies,* 19 (1), pp. 117–26.

———. 1986b. "Family Enterprises in Agriculture: Structural Limits and Political Possibilities," in *Agriculture: People and Politics,* pp. 41–60.Edited by G. Cox, P. Lowe, and M. Winter. London: Allen and Unwin.

———. 1980. "Household Production and the Natural Economy: Concepts for the Analysis of Agrarian Formations." *Journal of Peasant Studies*; 7 (2), pp. 158–84.

———. 1978. "World Market, State, and Family Farm: Social Bases of Household Production in the Era of Wage Labor." *Studies in Comparative History*; 20 (4), pp. 545–86.

Geschiere, P., and Raatgever, R. 1985. Introduction to *Old Modes of Production and Capitalist Encroachment: Anthropological Explorations in Africa,* pp. 1–36. Edited by W. Binsbergen and P. Geschiere. London: KPI.

Government of Sudan. 1979. *Draft Report on the Hydrometeorology of South Kordofan Province.* Khartoum, Sudan.

Guyer, J. 1984. "Intra-Household Processes and Farming Systems Research: Perspectives from Anthropology," in *Understanding Africa's Rural Households and Farming Systems.* Edited by J. Moock. Boulder: Westview Press.

———. 1981. "Household and Community in African Studies." *African Studies Review*; XXIV (2/3), pp. 92–104.

Hadari, A. 1974. "Some Socio-economic Aspects of Farming in the Nuba Mountains." *East African Journal of Rural Development*; 17 (3), pp. 157-76.

Hareven, T. 1987. "The Family at the Crossroads." *Journal of Family Studies*; 1:IX-XXIII.

Hassan, Y. 1967. *The Arabs and the Sudan: From the Seventh to the Early Sixteenth Century*. Edinburgh: Edinburgh University Press.

Hawkesworth, D. 1932. The Nuba Proper of Southern Kordofan. Sudan Notes and Records; 15 (2), pp. 159-99.

Henderson, K. 1987. *Set Under Authority*. Somerset: Castle Cary Press.

———. 1946. *Survey of the Anglo-Egyptian Sudan, 1898-1944*. Toronto: Longmans.

Hill, R. 1959. *Egypt in the Sudan, 1820-1881*. London: Oxford University Press.

Hodgkin, T. 1971. "Mahdism, Messianism and Marxism in the African Setting," in *Sudan in Africa*. Edited by Y.F. Hasan. Khartoum: Khartoum University Press.

Holroyd, A. 1837. "Notes on a Journey to Kordofan in 1836-7." *The Journal of the Royal Geographical Society*; 9, pp. 163-91.

Holt, P. 1958/63. *A Modern History of the Sudan*. London: Weidenfeld.

Holt, P. and M. Daly. 1988. *A History of the Sudan*. London: Longman.

Ibrahim, A. 1985. *The Dilemma of British Rule in the Nuba Mountains, 1898-1947*. Graduate College Publication, no.15. Khartoum: University of Khartoum.

Iten, Oswald 1979. *Economic Pressures on Traditional Society*. Bern: Peter Lang.

IBRD. 1982. *Investing for Economic Stabilization and Structural Change*. Washington, D.C.: International Bank for Rural Development.

ILO. 1976. *Growth, Employment, and Equity: A Comprehensive Strategy for the Sudan*. Geneva: International Labour Organization.

Jackson, H. 1953/55. *Behind the Modern Sudan*. London: MacMillan and Co.

Jewsiewick, B. 1981. "Lineage Mode of Production: Social Inequalities in Equatorial Africa," in *Modes of Production in Africa*, pp. 93-114. Edited by D. Crummey and C.C. Stewart. Beverly Hills: Sage.

Kapteijns, L. 1984. "The Organization of Exchange in Precolonial Western Sudan," in *Trade and Traders in the Sudan*, pp. 49-80. Edited by L. Manger. Bergen: University of Bergen.

Kapteijns, L., and Spaulding, J. 1988. "Pre-Colonial Trade Between States in the Eastern Sudan c. 1700-1900," in *Economy and Class in Sudan*, pp. 60-89. Edited by N. O'Neill and J. O'Brien. Aldershot: Avebury.

Keith, N. W., and Keith, N. Z. 1988. *New Perspectives on the Social Class and Socioeconomic Development on the Periphery*. New York: Greenwood Press.

Kelly, R. 1993. *Constructing Inequality*. Ann Arbor: University of Michigan Press.

Khalafalla, E. 1982. *The Mechanisms of Proletarianisation in the Sudan.* Development Studies and Research Centre, Discussion Paper, no. 6. Faculty of Economic and Social Studies. Sudan: University of Khartoum.

Kopytoff, I., and Miers, S., eds. 1977. *Slavery in Africa: Historical and Anthropological Perspectives.* Madison: University of Wisconsin Press.

Kursany, I. 1983. "Peasants of the Nuba Mountains Region." *Review of African Political Economics*; 26 (special issue).

Laslett, P. 1972. Introduction to *Household and Family in Past Time,* pp. 1–90. Edited by P. Laslett. Cambridge: Cambridge University Press.

Lloyd, W. 1910. "Notes on Kordofan Province." *Geographical Journal*; XXXV.

Long, N. 1984. *Family and Work in Rural Societies.* London: Tavistock.

Lovejoy, P. 1983. *Transformations in Slavery: A History of Slavery in Africa.* Cambridge: Cambridge University Press.

Lyson, T., and Falk, William, eds. 1993. *Forgotten Places: Uneven Development in Rural America.* Lawrence, Kansas: University of Kansas Press.

McIntyre, R. 1992. "Theories of Uneven Development and Social Change." *Rethinking Marxism*; 5 (3), pp. 75–105.

McLoughlan, P. 1962. "Economic Development and the Heritage of Slavery in the Sudan Republic." *Africa*; 32, pp. 355–91.

MacMichael, H. 1967. *The Tribes of Northern and Central Kordofan.* London: Frank Cass.

McMichael, P., and Buttel, F. 1990. "New Directions in the Political Economy of Agriculture." *Sociological Perspective;* 33 (1), pp. 89–109.

Mefeji, J. 1971. "The Ideology of Tribalism." *Journal of Modern Africa Studies*; 9 (2), pp. 253–61.

Mahmoud, F. 1984. *The Sudanese Bourgeoisie: Vanguard of Development?* London: Zed Books.

Mandel, E. 1968. *Marxist Economic Theory.* New York: Monthly Review Press.

Mann, A. 1954. *Where God Laughed: The Sudan To-day.* London: Museum Press.

March, G. 1948. "Kordofan Province," in *Agriculture in the Sudan.* Edited by J.D. Tothill. London: Oxford University Press.

Martini, Fr. G. 1961. An Impression of the Nuba and Their Country in 1875. Sudan Notes and Records; XLII, pp. 122–26.

Marsden, T. 1991. "Theoretical Issues in the Continuity of Petty Commodity Production," in *Rural Enterprise,* pp. 12–33. Edited by S. Whatmore et al. London: David Fulton Publishers.

Marsden, T., Lowe, P., and Whatmore, S., eds. 1990. *Rural Restructuring: Global Processes and Their Responses.* London: David Fulton Publishers.

Meillassoux, C. 1991. *The Anthropology of Slavery: The Womb of Iron and Gold* [Anthropologie de L'esclavage le ventre de fer et d'argent, 1986]. Chicago: University of Chicago Press.

————. 1983. "The Economic Bases of Demographic Reproduction: From the Domestic Mode of Production to Wage-Earning." *Journal of Peasant Studies*; 1 (1), pp. 50-61.

————. 1973. "The Social Organization of the Peasantry." *Journal of Peasant Studies*; 1 (1), pp. 129-57.

Mire, L. 1985. "Al-Zubayr Pasha and the Zariba Based Slave Trade in Bahr al-Ghazal 1855-1879," in *Slaves and Slavery in Muslim Africa*, vol. II. Edited by J.R. Willis. The Servile Estate, London: Frank Cass.

Mohammed, G. 1982. "An Analysis of Smallholder Rainfed Crop Production Systems: A Case Study of the Nuba Mountains." Unpublished Ph.D. dissertation, Michigan State University, East Lansing.

————. 1986. "Traditional Smallholder Rainfed Crop Production: A Characteristic Farm in the Nuba Mountains," in *The Agricultural Sector of the Sudan*, pp. 115-44. A.B. Edited by Zahlan and W.Y. Magar. London: Ithaca Press.

Moore, H. 1988. *Feminism and Anthropology*. Minneapolis: University of Minnesota Press.

Moore, W. 1979. *World Modernization: The Limits of Convergence*. London: Elsevier.

Nadel, S. 1947. *The Nuba: An Anthropological Study of the Hill Tribes in Kordofan*. London: Oxford University Press.

————. 1941. A Shaman Cult in the Nuba Mountains. Sudan Notes and Records; XXIV, pp. 85-112.

Nakash, Y. 1988. "Reflections of a Subsistence Economy: Production and Trade the Mahdist Sudan 1881-1898," in *Essays on the Economic History of the Middle East*, pp. 51-67. Edited by E. Kedourie and S. Haim. London: Frank Cass.

Nasr, A. 1971. British Policy Towards Islam in the Nuba Mountains, 1920-1940. Sudan Notes and Records; LII, pp.23-32.

Netting, McC., Wilk, R., and Arnould, E. 1984. Introduction to *Households: Comparative and Historical Studies of the Domestic Group*, pp. xiii-xxxviii. Edited by Netting et al. Berkeley: University of California Press.

Netting, McC. 1993. *Smallholders, Households*. Stanford: Stanford University Press.

Niblock, T. 1987. *Class and Power in Sudan*. Albany: State University of New York Press.

Nour, M., Hadafi, A., and McLean, M. 1987. *Rapid Drought Assessment Survey of Kordofan Region*. Interim Report, Ministry of Agriculture, Khartoum, Sudan.

O'Brien, J. 1983. "The Formation of the Agricultural Labour Force in Sudan." *Review of African Political Economy*; 26, pp. 15-34.

————. 1980. "Agricultural Labor and Development in Sudan." Unpublished Ph.D. dissertation, University of Connecticut, Storrs.

―――. 1978. "How Traditional Is Traditional Agriculture?" *Sudan Journal of Economic and Social Studies*; 2 (2), pp. 1-10.

Oesterdiekhoff, P., and Wohlmuth, K. 1953. *The Development Perspectives of the Democratic Republic of Sudan*. London: Weltforum.

O'Fahey, R. 1985. "Slavery and Society in Dar Fur," in *Slaves and Slavery in Muslim Africa*, vol. II. Edited by J.R. Willis. The Servile Estate, London: Frank Cass.

―――. 1973. Kordofan in the Eighteenth Century. Sudan Notes and Records; LIV, pp. 34-42.

O'Fahey, R., and Spaulding, J. 1974. *Kingdoms of the Sudan*. London: Methuen.

Pallme, I. 1844. *Travels in Kordofan*. (English translation). London: J. Madden and Co.

Parsons, T. 1943. "The Kinship System of the Contemporary United States." *American Anthropologist*; 45, pp. 22-38.

Perelman, M. 1983. *Classical Political Economy: Primitive Accumulation and the Social Division of Labor*. London: Rowman and Allanfield.

Petherick, J. 1869. *Travels in Central Africa*. London: Tinsley Brothers.

―――. 1861. *Egypt, the Soudan and Central Africa*. London: William Blackwood.

Popkin, S. 1979. *The Rational Peasant*. Berkeley: University of California Press.

Post, K. 1978. *Rise Ye Starvelings: The Jamaican Labour Rebellion of 1938 and its Aftermath*. The Hague: Natinus Nijhoff.

Roberts, B. 1990. "Peasants and Proletarians." *Annual Review of Sociology*; 16, pp. 353-77.

Roden, D. 1972. Down-Migration in the Moro Hills of Southern Kordofan. Sudan Notes and Records; LIII, pp. 79-99.

Roseberry, W. 1978. "Peasants as Proletarians." *Critique of Anthropology*; 11, pp. 3-18.

Roxborough, I. 1979. *Theories of Underdevelopment*. London: Macmillan.

―――. 1988. "Modernization Theory Revisited." *Society for Comparative Study of Society and History*; 88, pp. 753-61.

Saeed, A. 1988. "Merchant Capital, the State and Peasant Capital in Southern Kordofan," in *Economy and Class in Sudan*, pp. 186-212. Edited by N. O'Neill and J. O'Brien. Aldershot: Avebury.

Sagar, J. 1922. Notes on the History, Religion, and Customs of the Nuba. Sudan Notes and Records; V, pp. 137-56.

Sahlins, M. 1972. *Stone Age Economics*. New York: Aldine Publishing Press.

Sanderson, L. 1963. "Educational Development and Administrative Control in the Nuba Mountains Region of the Sudan." *Journal of African History*; IV (2), pp. 233-47.

Schmink, M. 1984. "Household Economic Strategies." *Latin American Research Review*; 3, pp. 87-101.

Scott, J. 1976. *The Moral Economy of the Peasant*. New Haven: Yale University Press.

Segalen, M. 1984. "Nuclear Is Not Independent," in *Households: Comparative and Historical Studies of the Domestic Group*, pp. 163–186. Edited by McC. Netting, R.R. Wilk, and E.J. Arnould. Berkeley: University of California Press.

Seligman, C., and Seligman, B. 1932. *Pagan Tribes of the Nilotic Sudan*. London: George Routledge and Sons.

Shepard, A. 1983. "Capitalist Agriculture in the Sudan." *Development and Change*; 14 (3), pp. 297–321.

Smith, G. 1985. "Reflections on the Social Relations of Simple Commodity Production." *Journal of Peasant Studies*; 13 (1), pp. 99–107.

Sorokin, P. 1947. *Society, Culture, and Personality*. New York: Harper and Row.

Spaulding, J. 1988. "The Business of Slavery in the Central Anglo-Egyptian Sudan, 1910–1930." *African Economic History*; 17, pp. 23–41.

———. 1987. "A Premise for Precolonial Nuba History." *History in Africa*; 14, pp. 369–74.

———. 1985a. *The Heroic Age in Sinnar*. Monograph, no. 15. African Studies Center, Michigan State University, East Lansing.

———. 1985b. Personal communication to myself.

———. 1984. "The Management of Exchange in Sinnar, c.1700," in *Trade and Traders in the Sudan*. Edited by L. Manger. Bergen. University of Bergen.

———. 1982. "Slavery, Land Tenure and Social Class in the Northern Turkish Sudan." *The International Journal of African Historical Studies*; 15 (1), pp. 1–20.

———. 1979. "Farmers, Herdsmen, and the State in Rainland Sinnar." *Journal of African History*; 20 (3), pp. 329–47.

Spiegel, A. 1986. "The Fluidity of Household Composition." *African Studies*; 45 (1).

Stevens, E. 1912. *My Sudan Year*. London: Mills and Burns.

Stevenson, R. 1984. *The Nuba People of Kordofan Province*. Graduate College Publications, Monograph 7, University of Khartoum, Sudan.

———. 1963. Some Aspects of the Spread of Islam in the Nuba Mountains. Sudan Notes and Records; XLIV, pp.9–20.

———. 1940. The Nyamang of the Nuba Mountains of Kordofan. Sudan Notes and Records; XXIII, pp. 75–98.

Strachan, R. 1951. "With the Nuba Hillmen of Kordofan." *The National Geographic Magazine*; XCIX, no. 1., pp. 249–78.

Thompson, E. 1966. *The Making of the English Working Class*. New York: Vintage Books.

Tilly, C. 1987. "Family History, Social History, and Social Change." *Journal of Family History*; 12 (1-3), pp. 320-30.

———. 1984. *Big Structures, Large Processes, Huge Comparisons*. New York: Russell Sage Foundation.

Tilly, L. 1975. "Individual Lives and Family Strategies in the French Proletariat." *Journal of Family History*; 4 (2), pp. 137-52.

Tilly, L. and J. Scott. 1978. *Women, Work and Family*. New York: Holt, Rinehart and Winston.

Todd, E. 1985. *The Explanation of Ideology: Family Structures and Social Systems*. New York: Basil Blackwell.

Tothill, J. 1948. *Agriculture in the Sudan*. London: Oxford University Press.

Trouillot, M-R. 1988. *Peasants and Capital*. Baltimore: Johns Hopkins University.

Tully, D. 1988. *Culture and Context in Sudan: The Process of Market Incorporation in Sudan*. Albany: State University Press of New York.

Vandergeest, P. 1988. "Commercialization and Commoditization: A Dialogue Between Perspectives." *Sociologia Ruralis*; XXVIII (1), pp. 7-29.

Vandergeest, P., and Buttel, F. 1988. "Marx, Weber, and Development Sociology." *World Development*; 10, pp. 683-95.

Warburg, G. 1981. "Ideological and Practical Considerations Regarding Slavery in the Mahdist State and the Anglo-Egyptian Sudan: 1881-1918," in *The Ideology of Slavery in Africa*. Edited by P. Lovejoy. Beverly Hills: Sage.

Weber, M. 1978. *Economy and Society*. Berkeley: University of California Press.

———. 1949. *The Methodology of the Social Sciences*. New York: The Free Press.

Whatmore, S. 1991. "Life Cycle or Patriarch? Gender Divisions in Family Farming." *Journal of Rural Studies*; 7 (1/2), pp. 71-6.

Whatmore, S., Lowe, P., and Marsden, T., eds. 1991. *Rural Enterprise: Shifting Perspectives on Small-Scale Production*. London: David Fulton Press.

Whatmore, S. et. al. 1987. "Towards A Typology of Farm Businesses in Contemporary British Agriculture." *Sociologia Ruralis*; xxvii (1), pp. 21-37.

Wilk, R., and Netting, McC. 1984. "Households: Changing Forms and Functions," in *Households: Comparative and Historical Studies of the Domestic Group*, pp. 1-28. Edited by McC. Netting, R.R. Wilk, and E.J. Arnould. Berkeley: University of California Press.

Wingate, F. 1968. *Mahdism and the Egyptian Sudan*. London: Frank Cass.

Wolf, D. 1991. "Does Father Know Best? A Feminist Critique of Household Strategy Research," in *Research in Rural Sociology and Development: Household Survival Strategies*, vol. 5, pp. 12-28. Edited by D. Clay and H. Schwarzweller. Greenwich, Conn.: JAI Press.

Wood, R. 1971. *Agricultural Systems in the Nuba Mountains, Sudan*. Ph.D. dissertation, University of California, Los Angeles.

World Bank. 1984. *World Development Report*. Washington, D.C.

Index